FLORIDA STUDIES
IN THE HELPING PROFESSIONS
by Arthur W. Combs

*with Daniel W. Soper, C. Thomas Gooding,
John A. Benton, Jr., John Frederick Dickman,
and Richard H. Usher*

UNIVERSITY OF FLORIDA PRESS / GAINESVILLE, 1969

COPYRIGHT © 1969 BY THE BOARD OF
COMMISSIONERS OF STATE INSTITUTIONS
OF FLORIDA
SECOND PRINTING, 1970
THIRD PRINTING, 1971

LIBRARY OF CONGRESS
CATALOG CARD No. 71-625778
ISBN 0-8130-0271-0

PRINTED BY STORTER PRINTING COMPANY
GAINESVILLE, FLORIDA

CONTRIBUTORS

ARTHUR W. COMBS. University of Florida, Gainesville

DANIEL W. SOPER. Southern Illinois University, Edwardsville

C. THOMAS GOODING. State University of New York, Oswego

JOHN A. BENTON, JR. Episcopal Counseling Center, Tampa, Florida

JOHN FREDERICK DICKMAN. St. Andrews Church, Tampa, Florida

RICHARD H. USHER. Colorado State College, Greeley

PREFACE

Over the past ten years at the University of Florida we have been engaged in a series of explorations of the helping relationship. These studies have attempted to discover the principles governing the nature and effective practice of helping relationships.

From a theoretical orientation the search has led through a series of seminars to a conception of the helping relationship based upon humanistic, perceptual approaches to psychological thought. Experimentally, we have sought to test a program of hypotheses in a series of research studies with teachers, students, nurses, counselors, college professors, and Episcopal priests. Some of these studies have been published in professional journals, and some exist at this point only as unpublished doctoral dissertations. Many requests have been received for reports of these studies which until now have existed in so many diverse places that access for interested readers was most difficult. Accordingly, in this monograph we have tried to bring them all together with a delineation of some of the thinking which preceded the studies, accompanied the researches in progress, or which came about as a consequence of our findings. In addition to convenience for interested students, this monograph may serve another function. It represents an illustration of how knowledge grows and develops on a college campus as a consequence of the interaction of teachers and students in the dialogue provided by continuous discussion and the trial and error brought about by participation in careful research.

Many people have been involved in these explorations: faculty members, seminar discussants, graduate students, school administrators and, of course, the subjects of our researches—teachers, students, counselors, nurses, and Episcopal priests. Although Professor Arthur W. Combs, senior author of this monograph, served as the catalytic agent for these studies and the permanent thread which bound them together over the ten-year period, the studies reported here are truly the result of a major cooperative effort. The theory and concepts we arrived at in these explorations are a product of continuous dialogue. They are the result of the pulling and hauling and searching contributions of a very large number of people whose individual efforts can no longer be discriminated from the whole fabric. To emphasize that fact we have abandoned the usual "objective" format of research reporting in the discussion sections of this monograph in favor of the collective "we."

The material included herein is presented in three parts. Part One deals with the background of our studies and the evolution of the thought that established our hypotheses. Part Two presents in capsule form each of the researches completed to date. Part Three includes a further look at the helping relationship from the vantage point of our completed studies.

AWC

February 12, 1969

CONTENTS

Part One

The Evolution of Hypotheses

1. THE BACKGROUND

One of the interesting developments of the past fifty years has been the emergence of a whole series of helping professions in addition to the very old ones such as medicine, teaching, and the clergy. This new group of professions is especially concerned with assisting people in one way or another to cope with the increasing complexities of life and to achieve a greater measure of personal fulfillment. Included among these are social workers, counselors, human relations experts, social action workers, school psychologists, school social workers, visiting teachers, public health nurses, psychiatrists, psychiatric nurses, rehabilitation counselors, play therapists and, most recently, a whole constellation of professions concerned with helping people in groups such as basic encounter groups, sensitivity training groups, and T-groups. Each of these professions has emerged in response to a fairly specific and practical human need. Once come into being they continued to develop in their early days quite pragmatically in response to the problems of their special area and developed a methodology and philosophy out of the experiences of their practitioners. In this fashion the helping professions have become established, each with its own philosophy, techniques, possibilities, limitations, and training procedures becoming more and more clearly differentiated with time and more or less lustily defended by its adherents.

More recently a number of voices have been raised suggesting that these professions are not nearly so clearly differentiated from each other as they appear at first glance. Like other observers elsewhere, the editor of this monograph gradually came to this realization as the result of his study and experience in teaching, in counseling, and in the practice of psychotherapy in collaboration with psychiatrists, nurses, and social workers. It seemed reasonable that since all these professions are forms of applied psychology, though they may vary in practical expression, the principles governing their operation must find common roots in the fundamental discipline of the science of behavior. The fundamental question of the helping professions is, after all, human behavior and misbehavior, and that is the basic problem of psychology.

Contributing further to the belief in the common character of the helping professions was the editor's involvement in the development of perceptual or phenomenological psychology. This is a frame of reference which attempts to understand behavior from the point of view of the behaver himself rather than the external observer.[1] Perceptual psychology takes a humanistic view of man and so lends itself especially well to the understanding of the problems of behavior as the practitioner confronts them. It has even sometimes been described as a "practitioner's psychology." Examined from this standpoint the principles and practices of the various helping professions look remarkably similar. Accordingly, we embarked upon a series of studies of the helping professions designed to tease out their fundamental structure and the determinants of effective practice.[2]

The original impetus for our experiments came about as a consequence of two research studies and a learned paper which so corroborated the general feeling kindled by our studies in perceptual psychology as to set our series of studies in motion.

The first of the researches was a paper by Dr. Fred Fiedler.[3] Dr. Fiedler was interested in finding out what beginning and expert psychotherapists believed was the nature of an ideal therapeutic relationship. To examine this question he had beginners and experts from a number of different schools of thought about psychotherapy complete a Q-sort about the nature of the therapeutic relationship. Two of his findings were especially significant in stimulating our studies.

1. Expert psychotherapists, no matter what school of thought

1. Combs, A. W., & Snygg, D. *Individual behavior: A perceptual approach to behavior.* Boston: Harper and Brothers, 1959.
2. Although this monograph deals primarily with a series of research studies on the helping professions, readers interested in exploring the theoretical bases of these professions more deeply may find some of the following papers of special interest from a theoretical orientation: Combs, A. W. *The professional education of teachers: A perceptual view of teacher preparation.* Boston: Allyn and Bacon, 1965. Combs, A. W. The personal approach to good teaching. *Educational Leadership,* 1964, 21, 369-378. Combs, A. W. Phenomenological concepts in non-directive therapy. *Journal of Consulting Psychology,* 1948, 12, 197-208. Combs, A. W. A phenomenological approach to adjustment theory. *Journal of Abnormal and Social Psychology,* 1949, 44, 29-35. Combs, A. W., & Soper, D. W. The self, its derivative terms and research. *Journal of Individual Psychology,* 1957, 13, 134-145. Combs, A. W., Courson, C. C., & Soper, D. W. The measurement of self concept and self report. *Educational and Psychological Measurement,* 1963, 23(3), 439-500.
3. Fiedler, F. E. The concept of an ideal therapeutic relationship. *Journal of Consulting Psychology,* 1950, 14, 239-245.

they began from, were more alike in their conception of the nature of a good therapeutic relationship than were beginners and experts from the *same* school of thought. This would seem to suggest that there is a "good" therapeutic relationship toward which good practitioners drift no matter what their beginning frame of reference. It would seem to imply the existence of a fundamental approach to helping people. As Fiedler put it, "The therapeutic relationship may be but a variation of good interpersonal relationships in general."

2. A second finding of Fiedler's was that the man in the street could describe a good helping relationship about as well as the experts. This rather astounding finding would seem to suggest that, not only is there a "good" helping relationship, but almost any of us can recognize it when it exists.

Fiedler's study thus seemed to corroborate the general hunch we had developed that helping professions were basically highly similar. The impression was further confirmed by a study by Heine.[4] Heine carried out an experiment much like Fiedler's and concluded from his results that there probably is *a* psychotherapy and that all existing psychotherapies are more or less approximations of that fundamental relationship. This again seemed to suggest a common character to the helping professions and further encouraged the development of the studies herein.

The second major stimulus to the researches reported here was provided by a most provocative paper by Carl Rogers on "The Characterisics of a Helping Relationship."[5] In this paper Dr. Rogers reviews a number of studies bearing upon the nature of helping relationships and comes to the following conclusion: "It seems clear that relationships which are helpful have different characteristics from relationships which are unhelpful. These differential characteristics have to do primarily with the attitudes of the helping person on the one hand, and with the perception of the relationship by the 'helpee' on the other." The corroboration of our hunches afforded by Fiedler, Heine, and Rogers launched us on a series of studies designed to explore these matters further.

4. Heine, R. W. A comparison of patients' reports on psychotherapeutic experience with psychoanalytic, non-directive, and Adlerian therapists. Unpublished doctoral dissertation, University of Chicago, 1950.
5. Rogers, C. R. The characteristics of a helping relationship. *Personnel and Guidance Journal*, 1958, 37(1), 6-16.

Are Good Teachers Like Good Therapists?

The first study in our series[6] sought to discover whether good teachers were similar to good psychotherapists. To examine this question the Q-sort used by Fiedler for his examination of psychotherapists was adapted for use with teachers by simply changing the word *therapist* to *teacher* and the word *client* to *student* in each item of the Q-sort. The following illustrate a few of these items as they appeared in Fiedler's Q-sort and in ours.

The Eight Most Ideal and Least Ideal Items as Sorted by Our Teachers and by Fiedler's Therapists

8 *Most Ideal Items*

RANK	OUR TEACHERS	FIEDLER'S THERAPISTS
1.	The teacher directs and guides the student.	The therapist is able to participate completely in the patient's communication.
2.	The teacher sees the student as co-worker on a common problem.	The therapist's comments are always right in line with what the patient is trying to convey.
3.	The teacher greatly encourages and reassures the student.	The therapist is well able to understand the patient's feelings.
4.	The teacher really tries to understand student's feelings.	The therapist really tries to understand the patient's feelings.
5.	The teacher usually maintains rapport with the student.	The therapist always follows the patient's line of thought.
6.	The teacher is well able to understand student's feelings.	The therapist's tone of voice conveys the complete ability to share the patient's feelings.
7.	The teacher is sympathetic with the student.	The therapist sees the patient as a co-worker on a common problem.
8.	The teacher gives and takes in the situations.	The therapist treats the patient as an equal.

6. Soper, D. W., & Combs, A. W. The helping relationship as seen by teachers and therapists. *Journal of Consulting Psychology*, 1962, 26, 288.

8 *Least Ideal Items*

75. The teacher is hostile toward the student.

The therapist shows no comprehension of the feelings the patient is trying to communicate.

74. The teacher is rejecting to the student.

The therapist acts in a very superior manner toward the patient.

73. The teacher's own needs completely interfere with understanding of student.

The therapist is very unpleasant to the patient.

72. The teacher is very unpleasant to the student.

The therapist is punitive.

71. The teacher feels disgusted by the student.

The therapist is hostile toward the patient.

70. The teacher is seductive toward the student.

The therapist feels disgusted by the patient.

69. The teacher is punitive.

The therapist's own needs completely interfere with his understanding of the patient.

68. The teacher cannot maintain rapport with student.

The therapist cannot maintain rapport with the patient.

For a sample of good teachers the faculty of the P. K. Yonge Laboratory School at the University of Florida was used. While this faculty would surely not claim to be composed 100 per cent of superb teachers, the staff is unusually carefully selected and would certainly represent a better than average sample of Florida teachers. Each member of this faculty completed the Fiedler Q-sort as modified to apply to teachers. When the Q-sorts of these teachers were compared with the Q-sorts of Fiedler's "good" psychotherapists, they proved to be highly similar. The correlation between the teachers' Q-sort and Fiedler's therapists was .809. These results seemed clearly to support our belief in the common basic character of helping professions.

The results of this study were met with great enthusiasm by Combs and Soper. They were delighted to find their hypothesis confirmed. In fact, the results seemed so clear that the experimenters were led to believe they had stumbled upon an effective device which might be used as a measure of good teaching. Accord-

7

ingly, they set about a second study to determine whether this Q-sort would clearly distinguish between "good" and "poor" teachers.

Is Good Teaching a Function of Knowledge About the Helping Relationship?

To explore the question of whether good teaching is a function of knowledge about the helping relationship, a sample of "good" teachers and "poor" teachers who would be willing to cooperate by completing our modification of the Fiedler Q-sort was needed.[7] To obtain these two samples, freshmen and sophomore students at the University of Florida, enrolled in a beginning course in the College of Education, were asked as part of a class assignment to tell us of the very best teacher they had ever had and the very worst teacher they had ever had. These teachers were then contacted by mail and asked if they would be willing to participate in our study on effective teaching. The teachers, of course, did not know how they had been selected for this rare privilege beyond a card sent to them which read as follows: "We are engaged in a study of effective teaching. You have been nominated by one of your former students as a person who once had a profound effect upon him. . . ." The card then went on to request their cooperation. Those who expressed a willingness to help were sent the modified Q-sort.

The results of this experiment were like a dash of cold water on the expectations of the experimenters. Instead of demonstrating its value as a device for distinguishing between good and poor teachers, the modified Q-sort showed absolutely no difference between the good and poor teachers. Good and poor teachers *both* seem to know what a good helping relationship *ought* to be like even though they may not be putting this knowledge into effect.

The Inadequacy of Methods as a Criterion of Effectiveness

The authors of the two studies reported above were already familiar with the fact that good and poor practitioners cannot be discriminated on the basis of the methods they use. A National

7. Combs, A. W., & Soper, D. W. The helping relationship as described by "good" and "poor" teachers. *Journal of Teacher Education*, 1963, 14, 64-67.

Education Association review of all the research available on good and poor teaching was unable to isolate any method of teaching which could be clearly shown to be associated with either good or poor teaching. This review covered hundreds of studies and the failure of the authors to find definitive "good" or "right" methods of teaching is most significant.[8] A review of research in the other helping professions seems to corroborate the point in those professions as well.

If the results of these studies are to be believed, the key to the nature of effective helping relationships is not to be found in what the helper knows or in the methods he uses. This was a stopper. It was apparent we were groping down the wrong alleys for the answers to our questions. To this point we had been looking at the problem of the helping professions from an objective frame of reference in the manner traditional to external approaches in psychological investigation. We decided to see what would happen if, instead, we approached the problem from a phenomenological orientation, analyzing it perceptually.

8. Ellena, W. J., Stevenson, M., & Webb, H. V. *Who's a good teacher?* Washington, D.C.: American Association of School Administrators, N.E.A., 1961.

2. THE SELF AS INSTRUMENT
CONCEPT OF PROFESSIONAL
WORK

To explore the nature of the helping relationship from a perceptual orientation, a series of seminars open to faculty members and graduate students was instituted in the College of Education at the University of Florida in 1959. These seminars were addressed to the problem of defining the nature and characteristics of the helping professions. They began with a review of the existing literature, searching out all that could be found on the question. This information was subjected to examination and interpretation from a phenomenological or perceptual point of view through a process of continuous dialogue among the seminar participants. As a consequence of this procedure the thinking of the participants gradually changed and we came to see the helping professions in a somewhat different fashion.

Looking at the various helping professions, including teaching, counseling, social work, pastoral care, nursing, and psychotherapy in particular, it soon became apparent to us that the common characteristic of all of these was instantaneous response. That is to say, all of the helping professions seem to be differentiated from more mechanical operations in the immediacy of response required of the helper. For example, in teaching, when the child says something to his teacher, his teacher must respond instantaneously. The same thing is true in the interrelationships of the social worker and his client, the pastor and the parishioner, the nurse and her patient, or the counselor and his client. All of these professions are dependent upon immediate response. Professional helpers must be thinking, problem-solving people; the primary tool with which they work is themselves.

We came to describe this understanding of the nature of the helping professions as the "self as instrument" concept. The term was first introduced to our thinking by Dr. Daniel Soper, but we later found that it had long been used in the social work profession. By the "self as instrument" concept we meant that the outstanding fact about the helping professions was the use of the helper's self in the process. Effective operation in the helping professions, whether we are talking about social work, counseling, teaching, or nursing, is a question of the use of the helper's self, the peculiar way in which he is able to combine his knowledge and understanding with his own unique ways of putting it into operation in such a fashion as to be helpful to others. We gave this understanding a formal statement as follows: "Effective helping relationships will be a function of the effective use of the helper's self in bringing about fulfillment of his own and society's purposes."

The self as instrument concept helps to explain why the attempt to distinguish the helping professions on the basis of knowledge or methods falters. If effective operation in the helping professions is a personal matter of the effective use of a self, then the search for a common knowledge or a common method is doomed before it begins. Since the self of each individual is unique, the search for a common uniqueness is, by definition, a built-in invalidation.

Further reasons why an examination of methods proved so disappointing a key to the helping professions became apparent to us as we applied the principles of perceptual psychology to the problem. In perceptual terms, behavior is always a function of perception. That is, how a person behaves at any moment will always be a function of the nature and condition of his perceptual field at the moment of his behavior. In everyday terms, "people behave according to how things seem to them." In this light, behavior is no more than a symptom, an expression of the dynamics of causation which lie in the perceptual field of the behaver. A given perception may produce many different behaviors. A feeling of thirst, for example, may produce innumerable varieties of drinking behavior. Conversely, the same behavior of taking a mouthful of water could conceivably be produced from many different perceptions, one of which might be thirst. With this understanding, it seems clear that the attempt to describe the helping professions on the basis of common behaviors can at best provide us with little more than a fairly low statistical relationship.

At this point we are confronted with a difficult question. If effective helping calls for instantaneous response which fits the peculiar needs of the person to be helped and if it depends upon the effective operation of the unique self of the helper, how can we hope to be sure the instantaneous use of the unique self will be good for the client? Helping, after all, must be a predictable pro-

11

cess, one in which we can be sure the results will be positive. In answering this question we found it helpful to draw an analogy with a giant computer. The modern computer is a magnificent machine capable of taking in great quantities of data from outside itself and combining this information with that stored in its "memory bank" to give an almost instantaneous "best answer" for the complex of data with which it deals. Like a human being it provides appropriate responses to mountains of data. Now, what kind of answers the computer provides out of the data available to it is dependent upon the formula in the machine, the program. Similarly, for human beings the peculiar responses occurring as a consequence of the circumstances in which people find themselves are also a product of the formula in the person. But the formula in the human case is not a mathematical equation. It consists of the individual's perceptions, especially those we call values, beliefs, and purposes.

Carl Rogers in his article on the nature of the helping relationship observed that it didn't seem to make much difference how the helper behaved if his "intent" (purpose) was to be helpful. We are all familiar from personal experience with how our behavior is an expression of our beliefs. Indeed, this intimate effect of belief on behavior is so strong it betrays us even when we consciously try to hide it. As the old Indian said, "What you do speaks so loudly I cannot hear what you say!" Our friends are aware of this and they say of us, "Well! He would!" Beliefs have a controlling, directing effect. They determine the choices of behavior we make from moment to moment. In the light of this close relationship between behavior and belief, it occurred to us that a study of the beliefs of helpers might provide a more profitable approach to understanding the helping relationships than had heretofore been possible when the problem was approached from the question of knowledge or methods. Before exploring this question further, let us stop for a moment to review some theoretical principles underlying this position.

In perceptual psychology the causes of behavior are ascribed to perception, more precisely, to the perceptual field of the behaver at the instant of action. At any moment a person's behavior, then, is a consequence of all the perceptions available to him just as, in the computer, answers are products of the data fed in or already there. In the computer the organizers of data are the formulae or programs placed in the machine. In people the organizers of perception are themselves perceptions having special relevance for the individual. Existing perceptions have a selecting, determining effect on further perceptions.

In perceptual terms behavior is understood as a consequence of two kinds of perceptions: the perceptions one has about the world and those he has about himself. However, not all perceptions existing for an individual are of equal value to him at any particular time. Some perceptions come to have much greater importance and relevance for the individual as a consequence of his experience. Among the most important of these, of course, are the perceptions a person has about himself, the self concept. Everyone has many different kinds of beliefs about himself which he has acquired in the course of his experience over the years. Some of these will be quite superficial on the periphery of the perceptual field. Others will be quite central to the person's experience, seeming to him to be at the very heart of his being. In a sense, it is the more central character of a perception that changes it from a mere observation into the powerful force we recognize in a belief. Thus, a perception like "I walked to school this morning" is little more than a fact, while an observation like "I am a male" is a matter of much relevance and importance. It is a belief which affects almost everything the person does. Most of an individual's perceptions begin on the periphery of his experience as observations, facts, or knowledge. This is why mere knowledge is not enough to produce a change in behavior. It is only as knowledge is experienced with deeper and deeper meaning so that it takes on the quality of belief (becomes central to experience) that it is likely to produce much change in behavior.

Once established, perceptions having the quality of belief tend to determine further perceptions. This is especially true of the beliefs we hold about ourselves which psychologists have come to describe as the self concept. Other organizers of behavior are perceptions of considerable relevance and meaning which we call beliefs, values, or attitudes. Even ideas about factual matters are unlikely to affect behavior except in the degree to which they develop the quality of belief.

Whatever their origin, beliefs, once established, tend to have an organizing effect upon further perception and so upon the behavior exhibited by an individual. This selective effect on perception gives

13

stability and predictability to behavior. It is these beliefs, these highly meaningful perceptions, then, that we concluded we needed to explore in search of the dynamic bases of the helping relationships. It was to this question our seminar next addressed itself.

HELPING RELATIONSHIPS AS A FUNCTION OF BELIEFS

A special seminar of faculty and graduate students tackled the task of formulating a series of hypotheses for the exploration of helping relationships from a perceptual orientation. The hypotheses isolated by this seminar were reported as: Sample Hypotheses for Exploring the Perceptual Organization of "Helpers" and "Non-Helpers."[1]

As a consequence of our discussions of the helping relationship in phenomenological or perceptual terms, it seemed to us that effective helpers could be described in terms of their perceptions in five major areas: (1) the general frame of reference or point of view from which the helper approached his problem; (2) the ways in which the helper perceived other people; (3) the ways in which the helper perceived himself; (4) the ways in which the helper perceived the task with which he was confronted; and (5) the ways in which the helper perceived appropriate methods for carrying out his purposes. Under each of these headings we listed a series of probable continua with respect to the ways in which the helper saw events under that heading. For example, under the heading "Seeing other people and their behavior," it seemed to us helpers would more often perceive those they worked with as "capable" rather than "incapable," as "trustworthy" rather than as "untrustworthy," and so on down the list.

The Basic Assumption.—The seminar members believe that persons who have learned to use themselves as effective instruments in the production of helping relationships can be distinguished from those who are ineffective on the basis of their characteristic perceptual organizations. More specifically, "helpers" can be distinguished from "non-helpers" with regard to their characteristic ways of perceiving:

1. Adapted from Combs, A. W. A perceptual view of "helpers." *Personality Theory and Counseling Practice, Papers of First Annual Conference on Personality Theory and Counseling Practice.* Gainesville, Florida: University of Florida Press, 1961.

A. Generally—Frames of Reference
B. People and Their Behavior
C. The Helper's Self
D. The Helping Task and Its Problems
E. Appropriate Methods for Helping

Under each of the above headings, the seminar formulated a series of perceptual continua that seemed fruitful for investigation. In each instance the perceptual organization presumed to be characteristic of the helper is stated first.

A. *General Frame of Reference*
Internal—External
Growth orientation—Fencing in or controlling
Perceptual meanings—Facts, events
People—Things
Hopeful—Despairing
Causation oriented—Mechanics oriented

B. *Seeing People and Their Behavior*
As capable—Incapable
As trustworthy—Untrustworthy
As helpful—Hindering
As unthreatening—Threatening
As respectable—No account
As worthy—Unworthy

C. *The Helper's Self*
Sees Self as:
Identified with people—Apart from people
Enough—Not enough
Trustworthy—Not trustworthy
Liked—Not liked
Wanted—Not wanted
Accepted—Not accepted
Feels certain, sure—Doubt

C. (*continued*)
Feels aware—Unaware
Self revealing—Self concealing

D. *The Helping Task and Its Problems*
Purpose is helping—Dominating
Purpose is larger—Narcissistic
Purpose is altruistic—Narrower
Purpose is understanding—Condemning
Purpose is accepting—Rejecting
Purpose is valuing integrity—Violating integrity
Approach to problems is:
Positive—Negative
Open to experience—Closed to experience
Process oriented—Ends oriented

E. *Appropriate Methods for Helping*
Sees helping methods superior to manipulating methods
Sees cooperation superior to competition

15

E. (continued)
  Sees acceptance superior to appeasing
  Sees acceptance superior to rejecting (attacking)
  Sees permissive methods superior to authoritarian
  Sees open communication superior to closed communication

Sees giving methods superior to withholding
Sees vital methods superior to lifeless
R e l a x e d—Compulsion to change others
Awareness of complexity—Oversimplification
Tolerant of ambiguity—Intolerant

Since the original publication of these hypotheses and as a result of our experiences in working with them in practical settings, we have become aware that some do not really represent perceptions. Rather, in stating some of these hypotheses, our seminar quite unconsciously slipped back into more familiar behavioral rather than perceptual descriptions. For example, items in Section B (Seeing People and Their Behavior) are stated in perceptual terms, how the helper sees others. Some of the items in Sections A and D, however, are more behavioral than perceptual. An internal frame of reference, for example, is a way of behaving, not a perception in itself. Similarly, approaches to problems in Section D are ways of acting rather than ways of perceiving. In designing some of our later research studies, some of these errors in conceptualization were corrected before being put to test.

MEASUREMENT PROBLEMS IN RESEARCH

Our original thinking in this exploration had been: "If we can discover valid differences in characteristic ways of perceiving of good and poor helpers, this information should be useful as guidelines for the development of the kinds of programs needed to produce effective helpers." Thus, we were immediately faced with several knotty problems: (1) how to distinguish between good and poor practitioners, and (2) how to measure the perceptions of these persons once they had been isolated.

Distinguishing "Good" and "Poor" Practitioners

Since all reviews of research to date had demonstrated that effective practice could not be distinguished from ineffective practice by objective means (either knowledge or behavior), we were faced with the problem of how to achieve samples of "good" and "poor" helpers for our researches. Clearly, existing means could not be used to provide us criteria. After much discussion we came to the following conclusion: "The task we confront is one of finding valid criteria in the current absence of such distinguishers. We are pioneering. Our problem is similar to that faced by Binet with early intelligence tests when he used teachers' judgments to select more intelligent and less intelligent children, then constructed his tests to differentiate between them. We will, therefore, attempt to differentiate effective from ineffective practitioners on the basis of the best judgments possible obtained from persons in positions to know. In each instance we will accept only those with a minimum of two independent judgments, made by qualified persons, which corroborate each other. Wherever possible we will seek corroboration from more than the minimum sources." In the researches reported later in this monograph it can be observed that these criteria led to a number of ways of obtaining judgments from diverse sources.

THE MEASUREMENT OF PERCEPTION

Since perceptions lie inside people, they are not available for direct manipulation or measurement. It is necessary, therefore, to approach the matter through some form of inference made from a sample of observable behavior. Many writers have maintained that the self concept could be directly measured by more or less sophisticated techniques of asking subjects to report the nature of their self perceptions. This is a straightforward, "logical" approach to the problems of perception measurement of internal phenomena. However, on theoretical grounds, there is serious reason to doubt the adequacy of self reports as accurate measures of perception and self concept. Accordingly, we carried out several theoretical and research investigations to explore whether the relationship between self perceptions and self report was sufficiently close to warrant experimental use. As a result of our theoretical analysis we came to the conclusion that the self report (a behavior) and the self concept (perceptions) cannot be accepted as valid measures of the same phenomena.[2]

2. Combs, A. W., & Soper, D. W. The self, its derivative terms and research. *Journal of Individual Psychology*, 1957, 12, 134-145. Soper, D. W., & Combs, A. W. Planning future research in education. *Educational Leader-*

To test these conclusions empirically several studies were carried out by Combs, Courson, and Soper[3] and by Parker.[4] These clearly confirmed the lack of trustworthy relationships between self report and self concept. With regret, therefore, we abandoned self report forms of measurement and sought to approach the problem of measuring perception by inferential means. This calls for the use of observers specially trained in the making of perceptual inferences from various kinds of behavior samples as illustrated in the research projects reported in the remainder of the monograph.

Having established the hypotheses needing exploration our next step was to find ways of testing them experimentally. The first research was carried out by Combs and Soper with counselors-in-training at the University of Florida. The results were so exciting that we decided to follow it with a much larger study of "good" and "poor" teachers. After months of planning with the cooperation of public schools, a research proposal was finally submitted to the United States Office of Education. The project was "disapproved" by the Cooperative Research Branch with what must surely be one of the more remarkable rejections of all time. We quote: "It certainly is important to have a better understanding of effective teachers. However, the type of study proposed here would be at best useless, and at worst most dangerous to all concerned." We, therefore, decided to reduce the size of our effort and carry out our researches without outside funding. The research reports which follow represent attempts to test some of our fundamental hypotheses on various groups of "helping" persons and were carried out in each instance by the authors indicated with little or no outside support.

---

ship, 1957, 5, 315-318. Combs, A. W. New horizons in field research: The self concept. *Educational Leadership*, 1958, 15, 315-319. Combs, A. W. The self in chaos. Review of R. C. Wylie, *The Self Concept*. University of Nebraska Press, 1962, *Contemporary Psychology*, 1962, 7, 53-54.

3. Combs, A. W., Courson, C. C., & Soper, D. W. The measurement of self concept and self report. *Educational and Psychological Measurement*, 1963, 23(3), 439-500. Courson, C. The use of inference as a research tool. *Educational and Psychological Measurement*, 1965, 25, 1029-1038.

4. Parker, J. The relationship of self report to inferred self concept in sixth grade children. Unpublished doctoral dissertation, University of Florida, 1964. Parker, J. The relationship of self report to inferred self concept. *Educational and Psychological Measurement*, 1966, 26, 691-700.

Part Two
Research Reports

3. THE PERCEPTUAL
ORGANIZATION OF EFFECTIVE
COUNSELORS

by Arthur W. Combs and
Daniel W. Soper

The forty-one hypotheses formulated in 1959 by the seminar of faculty and graduate students were not subjected to experimental study until the fall of 1961. At that time the present study[1] was initiated as the first in a series designed to test the validity of the hypotheses with different branches of the helping professions.

THE ANALYSIS OF PERCEPTUAL ORGANIZATION

During the academic year 1961-62, the University of Florida operated a year-long Guidance Institute. Thirty-one counselors-in-training, nominated by their local school systems and accepted after a screening program by the Department of Personnel Services for this special program, composed the student body. None of the students had done extensive graduate work in the field of guidance and counseling. During their first semester at the university, twenty-nine of these counselors-in-training were enrolled in a graduate course in Personality Dynamics taught by Dr. Arthur Combs. This was not a special class for counselors, but a regular graduate course open to any graduate student in the college, and the guidance group was scattered among the one hundred and ten students enrolled. Four times during the semester each student was required to hand in a description of a "Human Relations Incident" in which he had been involved, including a critique covering: (1) what he thought about it at the time, (2) what seemed to him to be the crux of the problem, and (3) what he now felt he might better have done about it. The protocols produced by the twenty-nine

1. This chapter is adapted from an article of the same title originally published in the *Journal of Counseling Psychology*, Vol. 10, pages 222-227, 1963. Portions reprinted here by permission of the Journal of Counseling Psychology, Inc., published by the American Psychological Association, Inc., at Mt. Royal and Guilford Avenues, Baltimore, Maryland, 21202. This research was awarded a Certificate of Commendation by the American Personnel and Guidance Association in 1962.

counselors-in-training were separated from those of the rest of the class and subjected to a perceptual analysis for the purposes of this research.

Since the forty-one hypotheses proposed by the seminar described in Chapter 2 were much too lengthy for our purposes, we scored the human relations incidents for only twelve perceptual variables defined as follows:

A. With respect to their general perceptual orientations, good counselors will be more likely to perceive:

1. From an internal rather than from an external frame of reference. The protocol writer's general frame of reference can be described as internal rather than external, that is to say, he seems sensitive to and concerned with how things look to others with whom he interacts, and he uses this as bases for his own behavior. He is concerned with perceptions of others as well as their overt behavior.

2. In terms of people rather than things. Central to the thinking of the subject is a concern with people and their reactions rather than with things and events.

B. With respect to their perceptions of other people, good counselors will perceive others as:

1. Able, rather than unable. The subject perceives others as having the capacities to deal with their problems. He has faith that they can find adequate solutions as opposed to doubting the capacity of people to handle themselves and their lives.

2. Dependable rather than undependable. The subject regards others as being essentially dependable rather than undependable. He shows confidence in the stability and reliability of others and does not need to be suspicious of them.

3. Friendly rather than unfriendly. The subject sees others as being friendly and enhancing. He does not regard them as threatening to himself but, instead, sees them as essentially well-intentioned rather than evil-intentioned.

4. Worthy rather than unworthy. The subject tends to see other people as being of worth rather than unworthy. He sees them as possessing a dignity and integrity which must be respected and maintained rather than as unimportant people, whose integrity may be violated.

C. With respect to their perceptions of self, good counselors will perceive themselves as:

1. Identified with people rather than apart from people. The subject tends to see himself as a part of all mankind; he

sees himself as identified with people rather than as withdrawn, removed, apart, or alienated from others.

2. Enough rather than wanting. The subject generally sees himself as enough; as having what is needed to deal with his problems. He does not see himself as lacking or unable to cope with problems.

3. Self revealing rather than self concealing. The subject is self revealing rather than self concealing; that is, he appears to be willing to disclose himself. He can treat his feelings and shortcomings as important and significant rather than hiding them or covering them up. He seems willing to be himself.

D. With respect to purposes, good counselors will perceive their purposes as:

1. Freeing rather than controlling. The subject's purpose is essentially freeing and facilitating rather than controlling, dominating, coercing, or manipulating.

2. Altruistically rather than narcissistically. The subject appears to be motivated by feelings of altruism rather than narcissism. He is concerned about others, not merely about self.

3. Concerned with larger rather than smaller meanings. The subject tends to view events in a broad rather than narrow perspective. He is concerned with larger connotations of events, with larger, more extensive implications than the immediate and specific. He is not exclusively concerned with details but can perceive beyond the immediate to future and larger meanings.

Using these definitions a score sheet was made on which each of the above perceptual categories could be scored on a seven point scale. Blind analyses of the protocols were then made in the following manner. The four "Human Relations Incidents" written by each of the counselors-in-training were kept in a folder identified only by a number. These folders were checked out, one at a time, by each of our four research assistants. The protocols were carefully read with an eye to the kinds of perceptions held by the writer in describing the human relations incident. Research analysts asked themselves, "How must this person have perceived to have written of this incident this way?" Raters were not permitted to read more than two cases at a sitting in order to avoid halo effect and were not permitted to discuss their findings with each other until all research team members had completed the analysis of a given case.

We were fortunate in having available for our perceptual analysis an experienced team of four graduate research assistants who had no connection with the guidance institute and who had been making perceptual inferences for six months as part of another research on the perceptions of children.[2] The competence and reliability of these people in making such analyses had been demonstrated statistically in the factor analyses of our previous study. To confirm their reliability in the present experiment, however, we subjected them to a retraining period for this study and did not use them for making perceptual inferences until we were satisfied they were making common judgments. The per cent of agreement of our four raters with themselves and with each other on a sampling of ten cases is indicated in Table 1.

TABLE 1. PER CENT OF SCORING AGREEMENT
AMONG RATERS ON TEN SAMPLE CASES

Raters	A	B	C	D
A	89.4			
B	87.0	90.5		
C	84.7	83.8	91.0	
D	88.1	88.8	82.3	88.7

The perceptual inferences obtained in the above manner were recorded on a seven point scale for each item on the score sheet. The sum of the four ratings assigned to each item was used as the final score for each counselor-trainee on that particular item. When all the perceptual scores had been recorded, the counselors-in-training were placed in rank order with respect to each of the perceptual items under investigation and with respect to the total score for all items summed. These rank orders were then correlated with effectiveness ratings made by the faculty.

THE COUNSELOR EFFECTIVENESS RATINGS

The University of Florida 1961 Guidance Institute participated in a national program of research which required extensive testing of students and a number of ratings by the faculty at various points

2. Combs, A. W., & Soper, D. W. *The relationship of child perceptions to achievement and behavior in the early school years.* Cooperative Research Project No. 814, University of Florida, Gainesville, Florida, 1963.

throughout the year. The faculty evaluations needed for this research were requested along with those called for by the national program during the last week of the institute. Without fanfare the faculty was simply asked to evaluate the students in the institute in this additional way during a time set aside in the last faculty meeting of the year. Only the department chairman had been told the precise nature of the experiment we were conducting.

The group making the evaluations included the professors who had been responsible for training and supervising students in the strictly counseling aspects of the program. It also included those professors and graduate assistants who had served as supervisors in the practicum phases of training. All but two of the sixteen members of the staff were present. A series of twenty-nine cards, each bearing the name of one of the counselors-in-training, was scattered on a table before the group. They were then asked to come to a consensus as to the proper order in which the trainees should be placed in respect to their promise as counselors. More specifically, the faculty was told, "Let us suppose you are in a position to hire a number of counselors. Put these Institute counselors in the order in which you would hire them for your staff." In a case conference procedure the faculty then arranged the twenty-nine counselor-trainees in order from best to poorest counselor. In this fashion we acquired a rank order of probable effectiveness of our counselors-in-training. Rank order correlations were then computed between each perceptual variable and the counselor effectiveness rankings provided from the staff judgment. These correlation coefficients are reported in Table 2.

It is apparent from an examination of Table 2 that all of our predictions are supported. All but two of the correlations are significant beyond the .01 level. Apparently it is possible to distinguish good counselors from poor ones on the basis of their perceptual organization. With more refined techniques of perceptual analysis and counselor ratings the correlations achieved here would probably be higher still.

Since the faculty in this institute have all been more or less affected by client-centered approaches to counseling, the question might be raised whether similar correlations would be found for a group of counselors whose effectiveness had been rated by experts from a different school of thought. That question, of course, can only be answered by further research. We venture the prediction, however, that similar results would occur for there is evidence in the work of Fiedler[3] and Heine[4] that expert counselors, even those from quite different schools of thought, nevertheless show high degrees of agreement as to what constitutes a good counseling relationship.

The definition of "good" and "poor" workers is of great importance to all the helping professions including counseling, social work, medicine, law, teaching, or the clergy. It is equally important in such relationships as those between foreman and worker, supervisor and staff, parent and child, or the myriad interrelationships of administrators and their staffs. Almost without exception,

TABLE 2. RANK ORDER CORRELATIONS BETWEEN STAFF JUDGMENTS OF
COUNSELOR EFFECTIVENESS AND PERCEPTUAL INFERENCES
FOR TWENTY-NINE COUNSELORS-IN-TRAINING

Perceptual inference	Rank order correlation	Significance level
Internal—External frame of reference	.496	.01
People—Things orientation	.514	.01
Sees people as able—unable	.589	.01
Sees people as dependable—undependable	.489	.01
Sees people as friendly—unfriendly	.555	.01
Sees people as worthy—unworthy	.607	.01
Sees self as identified—unidentified	.556	.01
Sees self as enough—not enough	.394	.05
Sees self as revealing—not revealing	.447	.02
Sees purpose as freeing—controlling	.638	.01
Sees purpose altruistically—narcissistically	.641	.01
Sees purpose in larger—smaller meanings	.475	.01
Total categories	.580	.01

the attempt to distinguish between effective and ineffective persons in such relationships on the basis of their overt behavior has proven most disappointing.

In the light of the almost universal failure to find objective behavioral criteria which differentiate "good" and "poor" professional workers, correlations of the magnitude obtained in this study

3. Fiedler, F. E. The concept of an ideal therapeutic relationship. *Journal of Consulting Psychology*, 1950, 14, 239-245.
4. Heine, R. W. A comparison of patients' reports on psychotherapeutic experience with psychoanalytic, non-directive, and Adlerian therapists. Unpublished doctoral dissertation, University of Chicago, 1950.

assume a very great significance. They seem to suggest new directions for research on this important problem that may eventually provide us with more satisfactory answers than we have had heretofore. These findings suggest that what we have failed to define objectively we may be able to distinguish perceptually.

4. THE PERCEPTUAL
ORGANIZATION OF
EFFECTIVE TEACHERS
by C. Thomas Gooding

The results of the study of counselors reported in Chapter 3 proved so exciting we turned next to apply these techniques to the problem of effective and ineffective teachers. This study was therefore designed to determine whether certain perceptual organizations, as inferred from observations and interviews of selected teacher subjects, are clearly characteristic of effective teachers.[1]

THE PERCEPTUAL CHARACTERISTICS

Twenty perceptual hypotheses were investigated in this study; twelve were identical with those in our research on counselors (Chapter 3), and eight additional dimensions were selected from those originally proposed by the Helping Relationship Seminar (Chapter 2). They were as follows:

A. Perceptions of people and their behavior
   1. Able—Unable
   2. Friendly—Unfriendly
   3. Worthy—Unworthy
   4. Internally motivated—Externally motivated
   5. Dependable—Undependable
   6. Helpful—Hindering
B. Perceptions of self
   7. With people—Apart from people
   8. Able—Unable
   9. Dependable—Undependable
   10. Worthy—Unworthy
   11. Wanted—Unwanted
C. Perception of the teaching task

---

1. Gooding, C. T. An observational analysis of the perceptual organization of effective teachers. Unpublished doctoral dissertation, University of Florida, 1964.

12. Freeing—Controlling
13. Larger—Smaller
14. Revealing—Concealing
15. Involved—Uninvolved
16. Encouraging process—Achieving goals
D. General frame of reference
17. Internal—External
18. People—Things
19. Perceptual meanings—Facts and events
20. Immediate causation—Historical

THE SELECTION OF EFFECTIVE AND INEFFECTIVE TEACHERS

A group of teachers clearly identified as effective and a group of teachers equally well identified as ineffective were required for this research. The two groups were identified as follows: The principal and curriculum coordinator from each of the elementary schools in the project were called to a meeting at which they were instructed to list independently the names of the very best and very worst teachers in their buildings. In order for a subject to be selected for participation in the research both the teacher's principal and curriculum coordinator had to arrive at independent, identical classification of the prospective subject as among "the very best or poorest in your school." The agreement on nominations between principals and curriculum coordinators was 52.5 per cent.

In an effort to control certain variables not related to the purpose of the study, no men were used in the sample. Groups were also compared on the basis of age, years' experience in the county system, total years of teaching experience, National Teacher Examination (NTE) scores, and academic training. Tests of significance of differences between means of the two groups on age, experience in the county, total experience, and NTE scores revealed no statistically significant differences between means on any of these criteria. All teachers in both groups held at least a bachelor's degree. Five members of the effective group and one member of the ineffective group held master's degrees.

Initial letters were sent to seventy-seven prospective subjects requesting their participation in "a study of effective teaching." Affirmative replies were received from thirty-three subjects. One teacher in the effective group dropped out due to illness, leaving

29

a final sample of nineteen teachers classed as effective and thirteen classed as ineffective.

It is interesting to note that there was a considerable difference in the rate of agreement to participate between teachers judged effective and those judged ineffective. The rate of acceptance for the effective group was 51.3 per cent whereas the rate of acceptance for the ineffective group was 38.2 per cent. It would, of course, be desirable to have unanimous acceptance in both groups. However, in practical research conditions the investigator is seldom able to achieve the exact sample which would be theoretically most desirable. In fact, when the difficulty of getting permission of an entire county school system to conduct research in such a sensitive area is considered, the degree of cooperation received seems excellent indeed. Experimenters cannot force prospective subjects to participate in a study of this nature and still remain on firm ground in terms of the ethics of research. However, the two groups were clearly different in respect to being judged effective and ineffective. Factors affecting the degree of response from the two groups, while intriguing, do not destroy this basic difference.

COLLECTING THE PERCEPTUAL DATA

Four carefully selected observers were given special training, over a one-month period, in making perceptual inferences from observations of teacher behavior in the classroom and from interviews with teachers. This training enabled them to arrive at highly reliable inferences regarding the perceptual organizations of subjects on the series of twenty hypotheses. Table 3 summarizes reliability data after training.

During the course of the research additional weekly calculations of the reliability of ratings were made. At the close of the data collection phase the overall reliability remained quite constant at 80.5 per cent. A summary of individual and overall rater reliability will be found in Table 4. An inspection of this table reveals that, while overall reliability was quite high, the reliability level for the interviews dipped to the minimum 75 per cent level stated as acceptable at the beginning of the research. This appears to indicate that further refinement of self as instrument inferential methodology should be continued to increase reliability and validity.

TABLE 3. PERCENTAGE OF AGREEMENT[a] OF OBSERVERS WITH
EACH OTHER ON TEN PRACTICE CASES AFTER A
ONE-MONTH PERIOD OF TRAINING

Observer	Inferences from observations (per cent)	Inferences from interviews (per cent)	Overall reliability (per cent)
1	82.5	75.0	78.8
2	80.7	80.0	80.8
3	81.6	76.3	78.8
4	78.0	81.3	81.3
All observers	80.7	78.2	79.2

a. Percentage of agreement is a ratio arrived at by computing the inference scores on which an observer agrees with the other three observers and dividing by the number of possible agreements.

Trained observers visited each of the teachers for three observation sessions and one interview. Neither they nor the teachers had any knowledge of how the teachers were classified. Each observer made his ratings independently although they visited teachers in teams of two. Ratings were made on a perception score sheet which included each of the twenty perceptual variables. On this instrument each of the twenty hypotheses was described as a seven point scale. For example, in the case of the first hypothesis "does the teacher see others as able or unable?" the observer made an inference on the basis of his observations, then rated the teacher from highly able (1) to highly unable (7).

To reduce halo effect the score sheet was divided into two forms, X and Y. One of these was filled out after observation number 2 and the other after observation number 3.

TABLE 4. SUMMARY OF OBSERVER RELIABILITY BASED ON
PERCENTAGE OF AGREEMENT OF
OBSERVER INFERENCES

Observer	Inferences from observations (per cent)	Inferences from interviews (per cent)	Overall reliability (per cent)
1	80.6	72.5	78.4
2	81.1	71.7	78.3
3	84.1	76.7	82.2
4	85.0	78.3	83.3
All observers	82.7	74.8	80.5

RESULTS

The ratings of the teachers' perceptual organizations as inferred from the observations and from the interview sessions were subjected to discriminant function analysis. The data from the inferences on observation yielded results which were significant at better than the .01 level of confidence (see Table 5). The data from inferences on interviews did not yield significant results. However, the interview data revealed trends which were in the same direction as the observation inferences.

TABLE 5. DISCRIMINANT ANALYSIS RESULTS

Inferences	Sample size	Mean Z	Variance Z	Standard deviation Z	F $f_2=20,f_1=11$	Significance level
From interviews						
Effective group	19	.01343	.01005	.10024	1.41	Not significant
Ineffective group	13	—.01973	.01256	.11208		
From observations						
Effective group	19	.42339	.03732	.19310	4.43	.01
Ineffective group	13	—.61959	.03093	.17588		

CONCLUSIONS AND IMPLICATIONS OF THE STUDY

Conclusion 1.—Apparently in teaching as in counseling there is a strong relationship between the perceptual organization of the person and his effectiveness as a professional worker.

Conclusion 2.—A statistically significant difference was demonstrated to exist between groups of effective and ineffective teachers on the basis of perceptual organization as inferred from observation of the teachers' classroom behavior.

The effective group of teachers was characterized by perceptual organizations as follows:

A. The general frame of reference of effective teachers tends to be one which emphasizes:

1. An internal rather than an external frame of reference.

2. Concern with people rather than things.

3. Concern with perceptual meanings rather than facts and events.

4. An immediate rather than a historical view of causes of behavior.

B. Effective teachers tend to perceive other people and their behavior as:
1. Able rather than unable.
2. Friendly rather than unfriendly.
3. Worthy rather than unworthy.
4. Internally rather than externally motivated.
5. Dependable rather than undependable.
6. Helpful rather than hindering.

C. Effective teachers tend to perceive themselves as:
1. With people rather than apart from people.
2. Able rather than unable.
3. Dependable rather than undependable.
4. Worthy rather than unworthy.
5. Wanted rather than unwanted.

D. Effective teachers tend to perceive the teaching task as:
1. Freeing rather than controlling.
2. Larger rather than smaller.
3. Revealing rather than concealing.
4. Involved rather than uninvolved.
5. Encouraging process rather than achieving goals.

Conclusion 3.—Inferences concerning perceptual organization based upon observation of teachers may be made with a high degree of interobserver reliability. This inferential technique may be used with added confidence in further studies of this type.

The results of this study have revealed that effective and ineffective teachers have characteristically different perceptual organizations in terms of the perceptual hypotheses which were tested. In view of the general failure of objective approaches to the question of good and poor teaching, these findings must have great significance. They point the way to what seems likely to be a most fruitful new approach to the study of professional effectiveness and suggest new goals for teacher education programs.

The Teachers' General Frame of Reference

The effective teachers in this study were characterized by a greater degree of sensitivity to the feelings of students. They were more concerned with seeing the child's point of view and were more concerned with people and their reactions than with material

33

things. Further, the effective teachers had more concern for perceptual meanings than had their less effective colleagues.

These differences in perceptual organization suggest that teacher education will need to place greater emphasis on developing sensitivity in student teachers. To do this, teachers' colleges will need to place greater emphasis on perceptual factors during the teacher's training and to include a perceptual emphasis in the psychology taught to teachers in training. They also suggest a different emphasis in observation programs. Traditionally such programs stress objectivity of observation. If developing greater sensitivity on the part of beginning teachers is accepted as a goal of teacher education, however, then observation training will need to emphasize the development of greater sensitivity to the feelings of students and to their perceptions of school experiences rather than factual reporting.

Sensitivity denotes a deeper understanding of how things are perceived by those with whom one works. It does not seem likely that the usual courses in child development, child psychology, etc., can provide the kind of sensitivity characteristic of the good teachers in this research. More than subject matter and methods is required. This calls for greatly increased opportunities to enter into more personal, meaningful relationships with other students, faculty, and the children with whom teacher candidates plan to work.

The Teachers' Perceptions of Self

The effective teachers tended to see themselves as more identified with others, as having the capacity to meet the problems of life successfully, as being someone who is dependable, as having dignity and integrity, and as being likable and attractive.

People learn about themselves from their experience, particularly with the significant persons in their lives. The kinds of self perceptions characteristic of good teachers in this research, then, suggest new criteria for teacher selection and new goals for curricula. Teacher candidates, beginning early in their professional development, must be dealt with in their training as persons of dignity, integrity, and worth. They must be provided with success experiences which will aid them in developing positive attitudes toward themselves.

The Teachers' Perceptions of Others

The effective group of teachers tended to see others more as having the capacity of dealing successfully with their problems, as being friendly, and well-intentioned, and as having dignity and integrity. They also tended· to see other people as creative and dynamic, as dependable and trustworthy, and as sources of fulfillment and enhancement rather than as threatening or sources of frustration and discouragement.

If such characteristic ways of perceiving others are important to teaching effectiveness, then teacher training institutions will need to foster the growth of these attitudes in prospective teachers. The atmosphere needed to facilitate the development of the perceptual organization stated above must be one in which the student teacher himself feels accepted, wanted, valued.

To produce the kinds of perceptions of others characteristic of good teachers in this research calls for rich opportunities for student teachers to interact with students in warm, friendly, cooperative kinds of atmospheres. It requires, also, acquaintance with current scientific findings, opportunities to work closely with others, and exposure to diverse and varying points of view. Teachers need to see others as aids rather than as threats to self. This is difficult if not impossible for those who have inaccurate, distorted perceptions about the nature of people.

The Teachers' Perceptions of the Teaching Task

This research found that the effective group of teachers tended to see the purpose of the teaching task as one of freeing and assisting rather than as controlling or coercing. In addition, the effective group members were more disclosing of their true selves, and they exhibited evidence of greater commitment or involvement in the teaching process. Likewise, they were more concerned with facilitating the process of learning and discovery than the achievement of specific, rigid goals.

The findings concerning the perceptions of the effective group in terms of the purpose of the teaching task provide many implications for teacher training. The effective group members, for example, were characteristically more process oriented than subject matter or ends oriented. This supports the view that we need to foster the development of teachers who see the role of subject matter not exclusively as content to be mastered but as an aid to facilitating growth and discovery. The results seem also to suggest the need for flexibility in approaches to subject matter. Teaching methods do not facilitate optimum growth if they impose a rigid, stereotyped, lockstep progression through a maze of experiences which are meaningful to the teacher but not necessarily to the student. We need to move in the direction of producing teachers who are flexible in terms of methods and approaches to subject matter, who have an abiding concern for fostering the development of search and discovery, who do not insist upon rigid application of predetermined procedures and goals, and who encourage the student to contribute to the interaction. This calls for teacher education programs which do not insist upon particular methods but encourage students to find their own best ways to approach the teaching task with maximal openness. It is difficult to see how this can be accomplished unless the experiences of teacher candidates in the course of their training are such as to lead them to these ways of perceiving. Hence, teacher education programs themselves should encompass wide varieties of approaches.

It is probably easier to teach a student professional worker the steps of a method of teaching or to help him gain an adequate command of a given body of subject matter than to facilitate the development of new and more positive ways of seeing one's self and one's students. However, if this research and other studies which have pointed in this same direction are accurate, teacher education institutions will need to consider the question of the attitudes and perceptions of teachers as significant aspects for the development of effective teachers.

5. PERCEPTUAL
CHARACTERISTICS
OF EPISCOPAL PASTORS
by John A. Benton, Jr.

This research was designed to determine whether two groups of Episcopal priests rated effective or ineffective pastors by their bishops in respect to their counseling could be discriminated from one another on the basis of their perceptual organization.[1] Since the author is himself an Episcopal priest, his major concern was to obtain information concerning the counseling activities of pastors which might be of value in curriculum improvement of theological schools. A theoretical base, outlined in the first chapters of this book, had already been laid down in what has been called the phenomenological orientation for dealing with the problem of the helping professions.

Of the perceptual characteristics formulated in the original seminar,[2] five characteristics, called in this research "dimensions," were selected for study as they applied to clergy and their pastoral counseling. These were: (1) the pastor sees himself in the relationship as identified with people or apart from people; (2) the pastor sees other persons as able or as unable; (3) the pastor perceives other persons primarily as persons or objects; (4) the pastor perceives his role as being involved or not involved with other people; and (5) the pastor sees his task as freeing or controlling. One dimension dealt primarily with how the priest sees himself. Two dimensions dealt with his perception of the parishioner, or other person, in the pastoral relationship, and two dimensions dealt more directly with the pastor's perception of the nature of the pastoral relationship. These dimensions were defined in terms of a continuum as follows.

1. Benton, J. A. Perceptual characteristics of Episcopal pastors. Unpublished doctoral dissertation, University of Florida, 1964.
2. Combs, A. W. A perceptual view of the nature of helpers in personality theory and counseling practice. *Papers of First Annual Conference on Personality Theory and Counseling Practice.* Gainesville, Florida: University of Florida Press, 1961.

Dimension One.—The pastor sees himself, in the pastoral relationship, as more *identified with people* than *apart from people*. The pastor perceives himself to be of a piece of all mankind, to be subject to all of the temptations, troubles, and joys of other human beings; to share a common life and destiny with the parishioner. Contrariwise, the pastor perceives himself as separate from, and unrelated to, the life of people and their problems; as a person alienated from his fellow human beings. His values are unrelated to the welfare of people.

Dimension Two.—The pastor sees the other person in the pastoral relationship as more *able* than *unable*. The pastor perceives the other person as having the capacity to deal with his problems and believes that he can find adequate solutions to his problems. Contrariwise, the pastor doubts the capacity of the other person to handle himself or his life.

Dimension Three.—The pastor sees other people more as *persons* than as *objects*. The pastor relates to the other person as if he were a unique, living, human being possessing uniquely human capacities and meaningful experiences; a being having feelings that are of importance; an individual striving toward goals; a being in process of becoming; dynamic and creative. The pastor perceives the parishioner as, in the words of Buber, a "thou" and not an "it." Contrariwise, the pastor perceives the parishioner more as an object; as an "it" with few feelings or whose feelings are of little meaning or account; as a "problem" or "case"; as simply the personification of his difficulty, e.g., an alcoholic, a gossip, a juvenile delinquent, a sinner, a nagging wife, an adulterer; as a "good" or "bad" statistic in the church records; as one properly and beneficially moved about according to a plan not of the individual's own choosing; as essentially reactive and passive.

Dimension Four.—The pastor sees his role as being more *involved* than *not involved* (with other persons). The pastor perceives that his real personal characteristics and feelings may rightly enter into his relationships in an interactive process. He feels committed to the helping process. He perceives that he may be genuinely warm, interested, and concerned with the other person and that he must enter into the other person's world of feelings and experiences. Contrariwise, the pastor sees his task as a "professional" one characterized by impersonal, distant, and detached attitudes. He feels the ideal pastoral relationship is a formal one in which the pastor should strive for personal anonymity. He may, on the other hand, perceive that an inactive, inert, unconcerned role is appropriate to him.

Dimension Five.—The pastor sees his task more as *freeing* than as *controlling.* The pastor perceives the purpose of his pastoral task is to facilitate growth and to help the person become aware of the number of choices available to him; to create, during the relationship, an atmosphere that enables the parishioner to feel free from threat and external evaluation, to be more open to his experience. Contrariwise, the pastor perceives the purpose of his pastoral task to be the manipulation of the parishioner's perceptions, goals, feelings, and ideas in accordance with a plan judged best by the pastor; the creation, within the parishioner, of feelings of dependency upon the pastor; the assumption of responsibility for the behavior of the other person; the inhibition of feelings of the other person; the evaluation of the other person.

SELECTION OF THE SAMPLE

The sample was drawn from priests who were engaged in work as rectors, curates, or vicars in the diocese under study and who (1) were for four years prior to November, 1963, so engaged in work in the diocese, (2) were members of one of the two groups chosen effective or ineffective by two of the three bishops of the diocese, and (3) consented to participate in the study.

There are in the diocese under study three bishops exercising jurisdiction—a diocesan or chief bishop, and two suffragans or assistant bishops. The panel of bishops was chosen as raters not only because all three men have been in the diocese for over twenty years and know both priests and laity well, but also because, by the nature of their responsibilities, they frequently must make such evaluations in the placement of their clergy.

Each bishop was requested to select from the list of 146 eligible priests 20 whom he considered effective pastors and 20 whom he considered ineffective. Each bishop was told he might use any criteria he chose, but he was requested not to discuss his ratings with either of the other two bishops until after the lists were submitted. All lists were addressed to a confidential secretary who coded them for the research. For a name to be included in the sample, two bishops out of three had to agree on the rating of a priest as effective or ineffective. Thirty-two priests met all criteria, seventeen effective and fifteen ineffective.

THE PERCEPTUAL DATA

Three projective instruments were used in the collection of data: (1) a pastoral problem response blank, (2) a picture story, and (3) three pastoral incidents.

The Pastoral Problem Response Blank.—This consisted of ten problems set forth in direct discourse following a brief introduction of each person and situation. These cases were from the experience of either the researcher or of clergy with whom he was familiar. The ten conversations were read by the researcher in a role-playing type presentation.

Following is an example of one of the ten cases used in this instrument.

> *Problem 1.* The speaker in this instance is a leading layman in your parish and his wife is president of one of the women's guilds. You have seen him lately when you thought that he'd had too much to drink, and gossip has it that he has been a little too friendly with his secretary. He seems to be a good father to his three children. The time is during your regular afternoon office hours and the place is in your office of the church.
>
> *Man:* Well, you see, Father, it's not that I want a divorce because I don't. I don't believe in divorce and I know what the church's teaching is. Maybe it isn't all her fault, but, my God, that woman is hard to live with! I never get a moment's peace around the house because she's always after me, hounding me, just boring in on me.

Standardized instructions for responding to this instrument were read by the researcher and then each of the ten problems was read with a pause following each for the pastor's response. The response was electronically recorded and later transferred to a typescript coded to conceal identity of subjects. This typescript formed the protocol from which judges later made ratings on the perceptual dimensions.

Picture Story Card.—In order to provide a greater latitude in the selection of a problem with which the pastor was compelled to deal, a picture about which the pastor was to compose a story was

40

used. This story was to set forth, within the context of the picture, a personal problem involving one or both of the persons in the picture. The pastor was asked to relate in his story how he would minister to these people.

Card 13 MF of Murray's TAT was chosen. This picture shows a young man standing with downcast head buried in his arms while behind him is the figure of a woman lying in bed. The primary concern was with the pastor's response as to how he would minister to the people involved in the problem as he saw it rather than the problem itself. Each subject was asked to imagine that he had been called to minister to these people in the situation as he saw it in the picture. He was to have one minute in which to compose a story involving the subjects, himself, and the situation, answering these questions: Who are these people? What has happened? Where are they? What is the trouble? Who called you and why? What are you going to do to minister to these people in the situation as you see it? Each was told that the nature of the problem was not the main interest in the research but the manner in which the pastor planned to minister to these people. The card was presented for a fully timed sixty seconds but was not removed from sight while each subject's response was recorded electronically. Later, the response was transcribed and scored in the same fashion as the responses to the Pastoral Problem Response Blank.

Pastoral Incidents.—In order to permit subjects the widest latitude of expression, the third instrument was a series of three incidents freely chosen from the pastoral experience of each priest in which he felt he had done an effective job as a pastor. This approach permitted each pastor to include material which he felt exemplified his best efforts as a pastor. Each subject was asked to think back over his pastoral ministry to three cases where he felt that he had done a particularly effective job as a pastor. He was further requested to try to recall from each of these cases an incident which revealed how he functioned as the pastor. He was told that a bit of conversation from the person and the pastor would be particularly helpful, if it could be recalled at this late date. The point was emphasized that these responses were to be incidents from cases and not the complete case history with preliminary information, total care, and ultimate outcome of the case. Responses to this part of the research were also tape recorded.

In addition to the responses garnered by the three instruments

41

already indicated, the researcher asked each priest for personal information such as age, number of children, the kind and size of congregation in which he now served, his educational background, etc. It was found that there were few differences in the two groups on any of these items with three exceptions. Almost all of the effective pastors were rectors of parishes, that is, held a position which is commonly felt to be more desirable and responsible than the positions in which the majority of the ineffective pastors were found. While the mean and median ages of the effective group were lower than the ineffective group, the effective pastors had been in the priesthood an average of about two years longer than those pastors in the ineffective group.

The ten responses to the Pastoral Problem Response Blank, the Picture Story, and the three Pastoral Incidents from each subject were stapled together to form a single protocol from which global ratings of the five perceptual dimensions were made. These thirty-two protocols were rated by three judges, two of whom were on the faculty of the Department of Personnel Services, College of Education, University of Florida, whereas the third was an advanced doctoral student in the field of Psychological Foundations of Education at the University of Florida. All three of the judges had had considerable experience in making the kind of inferences necessary for making the required ratings.

Judges were asked to rate each dimension on a nine point scale with the high end representing the positive extreme and the low end indicating a relative lack of the perceptual characteristics in the pastor whose protocol was being rated. Each protocol was to receive a global rating on each dimension, that is, the responses of each subject to all three instruments were to be taken into consideration in making the rating on any one dimension.

Each judge read the set of protocols five different times, once for each dimension but in a different order each time. These precautions were taken in order to avoid the possibility of a scoring "set" on the part of the judges. As a further safeguard against judge response set, each judge was instructed to read and rate not more than four protocols per hour, nor more than one dimension per day. Each judge was asked to make global ratings. No instructions were given as to what each judge was to take into consideration in making his ratings, but he was told to use whatever data in the protocol seemed to him significant. After all the rating sheets were scored, these scores were then divided into the two groups by code number, previously rated by the bishops as effective and ineffective.

THE HYPOTHESES

This study was designed to test the validity of five hypotheses. Specifically, it was predicted that a group of pastors rated effective by their bishops would: (1) see themselves, in their relationships, as more identified with people, (2) in their relationships see other people as more able, (3) relate to other people more as persons, (4) see their role more as being involved with people, and (5) see the purpose of their pastoral task more as freeing, than would the group of pastors rated ineffective.

THE RESULTS

To test each of the hypotheses the null hypothesis for each one was formulated and the median test applied to test the difference in medians for each of the five hypotheses. Obtained chi squares were compared with a table of chi square of various levels of probability at one degree of freedom for a one-tailed test. Results of this significance analysis are given in Table 6.

From this table it can be seen that three dimensions, namely, Identified with People, Seeing Others as Able, and Seeing the Purpose of the Pastoral Task More as Freeing, discriminated effective from ineffective pastors beyond the .005 level of confidence. The other two perceptual dimensions, Relating to People More as Persons, and Seeing Role More as Involved with People, discriminated the two groups of pastors at the .05 level of confidence. Because of the reliabilities of the ratings of the three judges, it was believed that the acceptance of the hypotheses at the .05 level of confidence was justified.

In order to determine the reliability of the three judges' ratings, a split-half technique was utilized. This choice was made because both between and within judge reliabilities could be determined in one operation. A Pearson coefficient of correlation of .94 was calculated between the two halves of the 480 scores. The Spearman-Brown prophecy formula was used to produce an estimated correlation coefficient of .97 for the entire group of ratings by the judges.

CONCLUSIONS

On the basis of the results of the study, the following conclusions seemed to be warranted concerning effective and ineffective Episcopal pastors.

1. Priests who perceive that they are persons just as everyone else, sharing a common life and destiny with other people, are more effective pastors than priests whose values are unrelated to people and who perceive themselves to be isolated, or insulated, from the rest of humanity.

TABLE 6. MEDIAN SCORES AND OBTAINED CHI SQUARES BY DIMENSION
FOR TWO GROUPS OF EFFECTIVE AND INEFFECTIVE PASTORS

| Hypothesis | Median score total sample n=32 | No. at or above sample median | | Chi square |
		Ef. n=17	Inef. n=15	
Pastor sees himself as more identified with people (Dimension One)	4.3	13	3	8.03[a]
Pastor sees others as more able (Dimension Two)	4.3	13	3	8.03[a]
Pastor relates to people more as persons (Dimension Three)	4.7	10	3	3.50[b]
Pastor sees role as more involved with people (Dimension Four)	4.7	10	3	3.50[b]
Pastor sees purpose of pastoral task more as freeing (Dimension Five)	5.3	11	1	9.11[a]

a. Significant beyond .005 level, one-tailed test.
b. Significant beyond .05 level, one-tailed test.

2. Priests who perceive other people as human beings capable not only of seeing the right thing for them to do, but also doing it, are more effective pastors than priests who see others as lacking the ability to find adequate solutions to their problems and, therefore, must have answers supplied for them.

3. Priests who relate to their counselees as dynamic, creative human beings striving to live in the best way they know how and whose feelings are of value, significance, and importance to everyone, are more effective pastors than priests who relate to their counselees as if they were reactive and passive beings whose

feelings were not as important as the facts which can be fitted into a diagnostic pattern to form a basis for the priest to give directions.

4. Priests who permit their own feelings to enter into a pastoral relationship, who perceive the possibilities of personal growth existing in all interpersonal relationships, who seek to understand their counselees' feelings, are more effective pastors than priests who will not permit themselves to get involved personally with others, but strive for impersonal, unemotional, detached relationships with their counselees.

5. Priests who perceive their pastoral counseling task to be primarily a freeing of their counselees from the threat of external judgment, including the priest's, the church's, or God's, are more effective pastors than priests who seek to control the behavior and/or feelings of their counselees and who feel it their duty to pronounce judgment upon counselees. Effective pastoral counselors also perceive their task to be freeing of their counselees to discover and be aware of the various solutions to their problems and to choose the solution the counselee thinks the best for himself in his situation.

Some Implications

The findings of this research seem to support several further observations. Contemporary psychologists who have been saying that the perceptual organization of a person provides a fruitful, meaningful, and helpful area of study in order to understand the dynamics of human behavior, specifically helpful behavior, may derive aid and comfort from the results of this investigation into the field of pastoral counseling. The protocols utilized in the research are rich in varieties of behavior manifested by the several pastors, but the perceptions behind the behavioral masks remained consistently stable and describable in the terminology of the dimensions selected for study.

A more general concern of this study was the possible value that the findings might have for seminary education. Without doubt there is need of adequate training of clergy to do pastoral counseling because priests will be faced with a welter of their parishioners' personal problems. The effective pastor cannot be described simply in terms either of what he does or what he knows. Often the effective pastors in this study did little that was very different from what the ineffective pastors did. Few, if any, of the effective

45

pastors seemed to manifest any special ability at diagnosing the emotional problems of their parishioners.

The criteria used by the bishops in making their evaluations of the counseling effectiveness of these priests were not attributes which were specifically related to a polished or particular counseling technique. The three bishops were in general agreed that the pastors' attitudes toward people were of prime importance. That is to say, the bishops valued such qualities as warmth, genuine interest in people, and priests' acceptance of others. They also emphasized whether priests were nonjudgmental in their approach to people and were nonrigid in the sense that there were no absolute answers to problems apart from particular situations and the priest did not possess all the answers to life's problems. They were also concerned with the priests' permissiveness, their willingness to listen to others, a reticence at the imposition of the pastor's will upon decisions, their feelings of security, and their capacity to love.

For theological schools, therefore, to concentrate on the teaching of a technique of counseling to seminarians would seem to be less than beneficial to their students and future counselees of their priests. Seminary faculty who are highly trained in a particular counseling orientation would seem not to be necessary. What would seem to be pointed up by this research is a greater concentration on the creation of a climate for emotional as well as intellectual growth of the seminarian as of greater importance and value. Whether a man is an effective pastor seems to be far more dependent upon how he perceives than upon what he specifically knows or does.

It would seem that seminaries would do well to provide opportunities for seminarians to experience relationships which are nonjudgmental, freeing, and deeply personal as a facilitation to becoming the kind of person who later seems to be an effective pastor. It would seem also that the future pastor should become increasingly familiar with himself, with the structure of his own perceptual world.

The concentration of many contemporary theological educational programs upon clinical training centering in a study of the psychiatric diagnosis and treatment of the mentally ill may be quite unhelpful to the seminarian. Such a program may tend to focus again upon the learning of an extensive body of specialized knowledge somewhat alien to the traditional role of the priest as a helping person. Such clinical training in mental hospitals and exclusively by psychiatrists may tend to convince the seminarian that the only way people can be helped is through psychotherapy. It may also becloud the outlook of the seminarian so that he will see all personal problems as psychopathological. The present findings would seem to indicate that the effective pastor is the one who perceives in a certain way rather than the one who possesses a corpus of professional knowledge, psychiatric or theological.

This is not to deny the value to the pastor of knowledge which will enable him to recognize the pathological nature of certain behaviors in his counselees and make the proper referral to a psychiatrist. But sometimes the net effect of specialized knowledge has been to alienate the possessor from the remaining population. The good pastor, however, is actively involved and identified with his counselees, not for the purpose of directing or controlling them in the right way, but in order that the pastor may help each to be free to grow and develop in his own unique way.

6. PERCEPTUAL ORGANIZATION
OF PERSON-ORIENTED
AND TASK-ORIENTED
STUDENT NURSES

by *John Frederick Dickman*

The[1] American Nurses' Foundation states that nurses must accept the responsibility of meeting psychological needs of the patient since these needs are a major influence in effective treatment.[2] Assuming that the nurse who cares for the patient as a living, feeling person is more effective than the nurse who primarily conceives of the patient as a physiological organism on which to perform prescribed tasks, how may nursing schools select and train student nurses capable of relating helpfully with patients? Data on whether unique personality features characterize the person-centered nurse would help to answer this question. This research was an attempt to throw some light on the matter by examining some personality dimensions of individuals making up two groups of student nurses: a group judged predominantly person-oriented, and a group judged predominantly task-oriented in their professional work.

Generally speaking, research into the relations of various types of personality characteristics with success in nursing has produced equivocal results. Some researches report small positive correlations, but the preponderance of studies have shown no significant relationships.[3] In view of this failure to relate nursing success to particular aptitudes, intelligence levels, or personality traits, the

1. Dickman, J. F. The perceptual organization of person-oriented versus task-oriented student nurses. Unpublished doctoral dissertation, University of Florida, 1967.

2. Whiting, J. S., et al. *The nurse-patient relationship and the healing process.* A Progress Report to the American Nurses' Foundation, June, 1955, to December, 1957. 1958, Pittsburgh, Pennsylvania, Veterans Administration Hospital.

3. Hill, Taylor, & Stacy. Is there a correlation between attrition in nursing schools and the job turnover in professional nursing. *Nursing Outlook,* September, 1964, 11, 666-669. Lentz, E. M., & Michaels, R. G. Personality contrasts among medical and surgical nurses. *Nursing Research,* 1965, 14(1), 43-48.

present research sought to determine whether perceptual characteristics would be more successful.

The decision to investigate possible differences in perceptual variables between persons employing a person-oriented as opposed to a task-oriented type of nurse-patient relationship was influenced by insights from studies on the helping relationship discussed or reported earlier in this monograph. These studies have seemed to suggest that there are distinct similarities in helping relationships and that the helper's own attitudes and ways of perceiving himself and others may be far more crucial in fostering growth in the person being helped than are the particular technical procedures carried out by the helper. Believing that the nurse-patient relationship, when person-oriented rather than task-oriented, falls within the category of helping relationships as defined by these researchers, it appeared that a study of perceptual characteristics of person-oriented versus task-oriented nurses might be more fruitful than the traditional investigations of possible trait differences between groups have proven to be.

The perceptual variables investigated in this study were:

1. *Positive view of self or positive self concept* defined as general overall basic regard for the self and a notion of worth as a person. It is a fact of "being" alone and not "doing" that determines the individual's positive concept of self. Generally a person with a positive self-regard does "do" and "accomplish" but these are by-products of his more basic existence as a person of value.

2. *Identified with others* defined as feeling a part of the human race sharing all the problems, joys, and temptations of other human beings. This variable is the opposite to regard of self as different from or alienated from others.

3. *Perceiving others as able* defined as seeing another person as having the capacity to deal with his problems and believing he can find adequate solutions to his problems. This variable is the opposite of solving the other's problems for him and assuming control of his life.

The primary hypotheses of the study were that person-oriented student nurses would: (1) perceive themselves more positively than do task-oriented student nurses, (2) would perceive themselves as more identified with others than do task-oriented student nurses, and (3) would perceive others as more able than do task-oriented student nurses.

49

The study further tested three sub-hypotheses concerning relationships between the three perceptual variables under investigation and three behavioral characteristics of the subjects. This was accomplished by investigating the relationship between each of the primary perceptual dimensions and the behavioral dimensions of (1) openness to experience, (2) self acceptance, and (3) sensitivity to the feelings of others (empathy). It was theorized (a) that a person who perceives his self in positive ways also will be more open to his experience, self accepting, and sensitive to the feelings of others. Likewise it was hypothesized (b) that a person who can sense himself as identified with others will be characterized by the same behavioral traits, and (c) that one who perceives others as able rather than unable will be more open, self accepting, and empathic.

Definitions for the behavioral variables were:

1. *Openness to experience* defined as ability to assimilate accurately all perceptions of self, others, and the world with a minimum of distortion.

2. *Self acceptance* permits a person to acknowledge his basic humanness and remain content with this state. The self-accepting person can admit to failure and human mistakes because he is human. He does not need to be a superhuman because he is content to be human. He can live with what is and therefore experience the present while anticipating the future with joy.

3. *Sensitivity* defined as the empathic ability to see the world from the point of view of the related other. The sensitive person tries to place himself in the frame of reference of others and is generally acutely sensitive to the emotional world of others.

The Student Nurse Ratings

The student nurse groups were selected from the sixty students enrolled in the junior (second-year) and senior (third-year) classes of the Gordon Keller School of Nursing, Tampa, Florida. Gordon Keller is a three-year city-owned nursing school leading to certification as a registered nurse. It is fully accredited by the National Leagues of Nursing and is affiliated with a large (800-bed) metropolitan hospital (Tampa General). Primary responsibility for the

education of these student nurses lies with the staff of the nursing school. Duties of the instructors include active classroom instruction and floor supervision of the students. Thus, instructors have extensive opportunity to view students not only in the classroom but in interaction with patients. Among the ten instructors were four who had been with the training staff for at least two years and who had both taught and supervised each person among the junior and senior students. These four instructors were used to distinguish the person-oriented and task-oriented groups of nurses for the study.

First, they were given an intensive training period by the researcher devoted to defining the task-oriented versus the person-oriented approach to nurse-patient relationships so as to insure that the instructors would agree on the meaning of the terms. After they had reached a consensus on scoring these definitions each instructor rated each of the sixty second- and third-year students on a five point scale of approach to nursing care from task-oriented (low score) to person-oriented (high score). Thus, each student nurse had four independent ratings. Ratings were summed yielding a single score for each subject. From these scores the experimenter selected the twenty-three student nurses with the highest scores to comprise the person-oriented subject group and the seventeen student nurses with the lowest scores to comprise the task-oriented subject group. Although not statistically matched on these variables, students in the two groups were observed to be comparable in age (median age, twenty years; range, nineteen to twenty-seven years), general sociological background, and relative intelligence. Mean rating score for the task-oriented group was 9.6. Mean rating score for the person-oriented group was 16.5. The difference in these means is significant beyond the .001 level. Instructor agreement in rating was very high although no formal inter-instructor reliability coefficient was obtained.

PERCEPTUAL AND BEHAVIORAL CHARACTERISTIC RATINGS

Measurements of perceptual and behavioral characteristics of all subjects were obtained by use of judges from a battery of three projective instruments.

Thematic Apperception Test (TAT) *Cards.*—Responses were obtained to three cards of the TAT, 13M, 3BM, and 4. Cards were presented by the group method of projection on a screen while subjects responded in writing according to the standard Murray instructions.

Critical Incident.—This technique required the subject to describe in writing the most significant experience she had had in nursing to date indicating what the incident was, what happened, and why this was significant.

Structured Incidents.—Three structured incidents were presented to each subject in written form as follows:

1. If I were an unwed mother what would I do and how would I feel? What response could I expect from important people like friends, parents, and hospital personnel?

2. If I were assigned to a busy pediatric ward on which an eight-year-old girl was terminally ill of leukemia, what would I do and how would I feel? In what ways would I try to deal with the child's parents or would I at all?

3. What would be the best way to deal with a cranky, demanding old man who had been told he is soon to die of lung cancer after long years of smoking two packs of cigarettes a day?

Responses to TAT cards, Critical Incident, and Structured Incidents were obtained during a group meeting of the junior and senior nursing classes at which only the researcher was present. Anonymity of subjects was secured by use of a coding system so that subjects did not have to sign their names to their protocols. Although the sixty members of the classes responded to the battery of test instruments only the data obtained from the forty students comprising the subject groups of this study were analyzed.

Written protocols were typed and coded so that no judge was aware of the subject group to which a nurse had been assigned. Copies of the protocols were given to three judges for independent ratings on the perceptual and behavioral variables. All judges hold doctorates and are currently engaged in clinical and counseling work. In addition, each has had much experience in analyzing perceptual data gained from projective techniques. Judges were asked to rate each subject's protocol on a seven point scale for each of the six variables. During a training period with the researcher, judges came to agreement on definitions of the dimensions to be measured. Judges were requested to make ratings on a single one of the six variables at a time. Order of reading of the forty protocols was varied for each of the six readings and each judge followed a different order of variables in making the ratings. Judges were required to space their task over a two-week period.

Three months after the original rating each judge rerated the same protocols on a single variable with each judge rerating on a different variable. The rerating provided data on intra-judge reliability. Results of rerating showed that each judge varied, on the average, less than one rating point from one rating to the other. Inter-judge reliability was estimated by an analysis of variance technique. By this procedure a coefficient of correlation was obtained between the total rating on the six dimensions by one judge and the total rating by the other judges. The obtained coefficient was r=.72, indicating a high degree of agreement among the judges.

RESULTS

To test the hypotheses of significant differences between the two subject groups on the perceptual variables, estimates of the degree of relationship were computed by means of biserial correlations. Tests of significance by the "Z" score method were computed. In each case the biserial r=.00. Therefore, the data indicated no significant relationships between person-orientation and positive view of self identification with others or perceiving others as able. Thus, none of the primary hypotheses of the study was upheld.

Sub-hypotheses were tested by correlating (Pearson Product Moment) each of the three perceptual dimensions with each of the behavioral dimensions. The three judges' ratings on each dimension were summed, providing a total score on each dimension for each of the forty cases. Since these data were on a continuous scale, and each judge's score approximated a normal curve, use of the Pearson Product-Moment correlation method was justified. Results of these correlations are reported in Table 7.

The data of Table 7 indicate high positive relationships between the perceptual and behavioral variables. The student nurses who perceived themselves positively also tended to be open to their experience, self-accepting, and sensitive to the feelings of others. Conversely, student nurses who perceived themselves negatively were less open to their experience, less self-accepting, and less empathic in regard to the feelings of others. These same conclusions are also valid with respect to the dimensions of "Identification with Others" and "Perceives Others as Able."

In Table 7 the relationship found to exist between student nurses who are rated identified with others and self-accepting is represented by a correlation coefficient of r=.89. This correlation coefficient is exceptionally high but consistent with previous research of Stock,[4] Sheerer,[5] Fey,[6] and Suinn,[7] demonstrating an important relationship between self-acceptance and acceptance of others.

Findings recorded in Table 7 also suggest other relationships between dimensions of perceiving and dimensions of behaving.

TABLE 7. PEARSON PRODUCT-MOMENT CORRELATIONS BETWEEN
PERCEPTUAL AND BEHAVIORAL DIMENSIONS

Perceptual dimensions	Behavioral dimensions		
	Open to experience	Self-acceptance	Empathic
Positive view of self	.69[b]	.78[a]	.71[b]
Identification with others	.58[a]	.89[c]	.74[b]
Perceives others as able	.61[a]	.69[b]	.74[b]

a. Significant beyond the .001 level.
b. Significant beyond the .0005 level.
c. Significant beyond the .0001 level.

They indicate, for example, that persons who perceive themselves positively will demonstrate behavioral characteristics of openness, self-acceptance, and sensitivity to the feelings of others. These data add support to Combs' theory that behavior is a function of perception[8] and, further, that certain kinds of perception lead to certain predictable kinds of behavior.

4. Stock, D. An investigation into the interrelations between the self concept and feelings directed toward other persons and groups. *Journal of Consulting Psychology*, 1949, 13(3), 176-180.

5. Sheerer, E. T. An analysis of the relationship between acceptance and respect for self and acceptance of and respect for others in ten counseling cases. *Journal of Consulting Psychology*, 1949, 13(3), 169-175.

6. Fey, W. F. Acceptance by others and its relation to acceptance of self and others: A re-evaluation. *Journal of Abnormal Psychology*, 1955, 50, 274-276.

7. Suinn, R. M. The relationship between self acceptance and acceptance of others: A learning theory analysis. *Dissertation Abstracts*, 1960, 20, 3846-3847.

8. Combs, A. W., & Snygg, D. *Individual behavior*. New York: Harper and Brothers, 1959.

A Further Investigation

The nonsignificant relationship obtained in this research between person-orientation and the perceptual variables differed markedly from the studies reported earlier in this monograph distinguishing between effective and ineffective helpers in other professions. The author, therefore, carried out a second study, this time dividing the student nurses with respect to effectiveness as nurses instead of person- or task-orientation.

To obtain ratings of the effectiveness of the subjects, the author met with the instructors who had originally rated subjects on the person-oriented to task-oriented dimension. This meeting took place approximately one month after the original ratings. Each instructor was given a list of the forty students in alphabetical order. They were not told which students had been judged earlier as task- or person-oriented. The instructors now selected the twenty-three most effective nursing students by a consensus procedure. This involved a pretense by instructors that they were the hiring committee for the hospital and the floor supervisors. From the list of forty students they could hire twenty-three nurses only. They were reminded that they would not only hire these nurses but that they would work with them. They ranked the student nurses from one to twenty-three by arriving at consensus as to whom they would hire first, second, etc., up to the twenty-third student to be hired. It was then proposed that the judges complete the same procedure on the remaining seventeen students. They did so, producing as an end product ranks on all cases from 1 to 40. Students ranked high were assumed to be those most effective and those ranked low were assumed to be least effective.

The ratings for the perceptual variables obtained in the first experiment were then placed in rank order and compared with the effectiveness ratings by means of the standard formula for rho. None of the rho's obtained was significant at the .05 level of confidence. The rho (.27) obtained between effectiveness and identification with others was significant at the .10 level of confidence. Thus, no significant relationship between professional effectiveness and the three perceptual variables was found although there was a tendency toward a slight positive relationship between effectiveness and identification with others. The results of both studies thus show no significant relationship between perceptual organization and either effectiveness as nurses or person orientation. These findings are clearly out of line with the previous studies reported in this monograph. The implications of this disparity are difficult to assess. Among the reasons we have considered are the following.

1. Nursing is a helping profession dependent upon a different set of perceptual variables than teaching, counseling, or pastoral care. This is a possibility. We are loath to accept it, however, at this stage and prefer to await further research evidence before accepting that conclusion.

2. Our experimental techniques or our judging procedures were faulty. This may be the problem, but a painstaking review of our processes has provided no satisfactory answers.

3. It may be that a person who appears to concentrate on technological tasks rather than on human relationships may be just as psychologically healthy as one who seems more involved with human relations. For example, a scientist, more or less a recluse in a laboratory but working constantly to find a cure for a disease, may perceive himself deeply identified with other people, see others as able, and feel very positively about himself. In this research it appears that technological proficiency in a chosen field and the perceptual dimensions which have been studied seem not to be incompatible.

4. Perhaps students who enter nursing in the first place already possess a large measure of the kinds of perceptual organization we have investigated here. In addition, the further selection imposed by three years of exposure to a nursing staff valuing such qualities may have resulted in a distribution so skewed toward one end of the continuum as to make effective discrimination most unlikely.

Further research is clearly required to investigate these questions more fully.

The data obtained in this study show a clear relationship between perceptual organization and behavioral characteristics and thus lend support to the general hypothesis that perception is related to behavior. The exceptionally high relationship between student nurses who perceive themselves identified with others and student nurses who tend to accept themselves also provides further validity to the premise of Sheerer,[9] Fey,[10] and Suinn[11] that self-accepting people tend to be more accepting of others.

9. Sheerer, *op. cit.*   10. Fey, *op. cit.*
11. Suinn, *op. cit.*

7. PERCEPTUAL CHARACTERISTICS OF EFFECTIVE COLLEGE TEACHERS

by *Richard H. Usher*

This study was designed to explore the perceptual characteristics of selected college professors.[1] College professors are notoriously independent people and studies on the effectiveness of college teachers are extremely rare in the literature. Few institutions engage in any sort of systematic appraisals of their faculties. In the College of Education at the University of Florida, however, a comprehensive procedure for the rating of faculty members has been in operation for more than fifteen years. These unique data were made available to the experimenter by the administration of the college and members of the faculty for purposes of this investigation.

The major hypothesis of this research is that there is a significant positive relationship between faculty members' ways of perceiving and their ratings on various criteria of faculty effectiveness. The experimenter restated twelve of the original dimensions, prepared by the seminar described in Chapter 2, as hypotheses for this research. Accordingly, it was predicted that college faculty rated most effective would perceive:

A. Other people as:
1. more able than unable
2. more worthy than unworthy
3. more dependable than undependable
4. more internally motivated than externally molded
B. Themselves as:
1. more with people than apart from people
2. more wanted than unwanted

1. This report has been abstracted by Arthur W. Combs for purposes of this monograph from the original dissertation written by Dr. Usher. Proper reference to the original is: Usher, R. H. The relationship of perceptions of self, others and the helping task to certain measures of college faculty effectiveness. Unpublished doctoral dissertation, University of Florida, 1966.

3. more worthy than unworthy
4. more able than unable
C. Their task in terms of:
1. freeing rather than controlling
2. larger rather than smaller meanings
3. personal meanings rather than facts- or events-oriented
4. accepting rather than not accepting

DATA ON FACULTY EFFECTIVENESS

Within the University of Florida, College of Education, an unusual opportunity for research on faculty effectiveness was afforded. A comprehensive procedure for evaluation of faculty members had been in use for a number of years. These evaluations were obtained on each professor with respect to three phases of his work: (1) teaching, counseling, and ability to work with colleagues, (2) research and publications, and (3) participation in professional activities. Data concerning these matters were obtained every two years from the professor himself, from his students, department head, deans, and a committee of senior faculty peers. These data were then formulated into a series of ratings by the dean's office.

Fifty-five members of the faculty met the criteria for acceptance in the study; namely, a minimum rank of assistant professor and membership on the faculty at least two years. Of these, 27 per cent were unavailable for one reason or another and 5 per cent refused to be involved, leaving twenty-six subjects for the study. For each of these professors six ratings were obtained as follows.

Student Rating (SR).—The student rating form used in the college consisted of twelve multiple choice items covering various aspects of the professor's teaching. Only the first question from this form was used in this research. This question asked, "How would you rate your instructor in general teaching ability?" The five possible answers and points scored for each were: an outstanding and stimulating instructor, 5; a very good instructor, 4; a good instructor, 3; an adequate but not stimulating instructor, 2; a poor and inadequate instructor, 1.

The mean SR score for each teacher was found by summing the numerical values for each student's rating and then dividing by the number of students. Some teachers had been evaluated by only one class, other teachers by several classes. For one evaluation, the

58

mean score was that for only the one class. For several evaluations, the mean score was the mean of all student ratings for that teacher.

Department Head Rating (DH).—Every two years the department heads evaluated each faculty member in their department on teaching, counseling, and working with colleagues. Some department heads took into account the student ratings when making this evaluation; others did not. These evaluations were turned in to the dean of the college who sorted them into three groups scored as follows: superior, 9 points; middle, 6 points; least effective, 3 points.

Research and Publications (RP).—This evaluation made by the dean rated a faculty member according to the number and quality of publications he had. It ranged from a score of zero for a minimal amount to a score of four for the greatest amount.

Professional Activities (PA).—In this category staff members were rated according to the number of offices held in professional organizations and frequency of speaking engagements or program participation. The range was from 0 to 3.

Adjusted Total (AT).—The dean and selected senior faculty members reviewed the initial four ratings on each professor then added or subtracted points where it appeared ratings were unjust to the staff member in question. The total of these adjustments could range from -3 to +3.

General Effectiveness Rating (GE).—The SR, DH, RP, and PA raw scores were changed into standard scores. Each standard score was then multiplied by an empirically derived weight for that score to achieve comparability. Then the four weighted scores were summed into a General Effectiveness rating.

THE PERCEPTUAL DATA

Three judges, including the writer, were given training in the "self as instrument" technique of inferring perceptual characteristics from samples of classroom behavior. Judges made repeated observations of teachers in the classroom and were encouraged to utilize the full resources of their experience and sensitivity in making inferential ratings. It was stressed that the judges were to make inferences based on how it must seem from the *subject's* rather than the *observer's* point of view.

Judges started their training by careful discussion of each of the perceptual hypotheses, making sure there was general agreement as to the nature of the perceptual characteristic defined on the score sheet. Next, a series of practice observations were made on the faculty of the P. K. Yonge Laboratory School at the University of Florida. A percentage of agreement figure was tabulated by computing the inferences on which an observer agreed with the other two observers divided by the possible number of agreements. Agreement was defined as three judges not varying more than one point on the ratings for each dimension. Acceptable levels of agreement for the research were defined as agreement on at least 80 per cent of the items. The training session data revealed 83 per cent agreement after eighteen hours of practice. During the actual study the reliability of perceptual inferences was rechecked periodically by computing per cent of agreement between the writer and each of the other judges.

Each faculty subject for this study had indicated a class which observers could visit for two different one-hour periods. The writer and one other judge observed each faculty subject in the study for two different one-hour periods. Following each observation the writer and the other judge immediately and independently recorded perceptual inferences on a specially prepared score sheet. The perceptual score sheet contained the twelve perceptual continua of the investigation. Item one is reproduced to show how these appeared.

A. The subject's perception of other people and their behavior

1. Able—Unable

The subject sees others as having the capacities necessary to deal with their own problems successfully. He perceives others as basically able to make their own decisions and deal with their own crises effectively.

The subject sees others as being essentially unable to meet the crises in their lives and make their own decisions. His perceptions of the abilities of others are doubtful in nature.

Able 1 2 3 4 5 6 7 Unable _____
SCORE

Judges recorded their inferences by circling the appropriate number and also recording it in the blank to the right. A similar set of definitions for the other eleven hypothetical continua followed with a seven point scale for each. To reduce halo effect the twelve hypotheses were divided into two forms with six hypotheses on each of the two half-forms. When observing the first hour, the writer would fill out one of the half-forms, the other judge would fill out the second half-form. In the second observation period, the forms used were reversed. Though observing twice, each observer filled out only one complete score sheet for the twelve hypotheses. Sixteen perceptual scores were computed for each subject. Twelve were obtained from each of the twelve hypotheses. Four additional scores were obtained as follows: the four scores under the heading "Subject's Perception of Other People," were summed for a sub-total score. This was also done for the four scores under "Perception of Self" and the four ratings under "Perception of the Task." Finally, all twelve ratings were combined for a total score. Thus, there were twelve single scores, three sub-total scores, and one total score. To examine the relationship between the perceptual scores and effectiveness ratings, Pearson Product-Moment correlations were computed between the sixteen perceptual scores and the six faculty rating scores. Intercorrelations for perceptual scores and effectiveness scores were also computed.

THE RESEARCH FINDINGS

Significant findings from this study are as follows.

1. The characteristic ways in which these college faculty perceive themselves, other people, and their tasks are highly interrelated. From an examination of Table 8 it can be seen that intercorrelations of ratings on the twelve perceptual hypotheses are generally high and positive. This is consistent with perceptual self-concept theory which holds that an individual's behavior is at any moment the function of a highly interrelated, interactive field of personal perceptions of which the self-concept is the basic referent. The consistency of this correlation also suggests that a high degree of overlap may exist among these factors. Combs and Soper[2] have suggested in another study that significant and discreet perceptual characteristics may be fewer in number than we have supposed. They recommend the use of factor analysis techniques to explore this question in greater detail.

2. Combs, A. W., & Soper, D. W. *The relationship of child perceptions to achievement and behavior in the early school years.* Cooperative Research Project No. 814, University of Florida, Gainesville, Florida, 1963.

61

Table 8. Intercorrelations of Twelve Perceptual Hypotheses Utilizing Observation Inference Scores (N=26)

	A				B				C			
	1	2	3	4	1	2	3	4	1	2	3	4
Perceives others												
Able												
Worthy	.84											
Dependable	.85	.85										
Internally	.88	.90	.86									
Perceives self												
With people	.81	.85	.81	.86								
Wanted	.80	.74	.74	.83	.84							
Worthy	.70	.58	.62	.74	.77	.81						
Able	.76	.69	.72	.68	.79	.82	.80					
Helping task												
Freeing	.76	.84	.91	.85	.84	.71	.60	.71				
Larger	.80	.84	.84	.82	.84	.74	.66	.81	.89			
Meaning	.68	.81	.78	.80	.84	.70	.62	.68	.85	.91		
Accepting	.76	.88	.87	.84	.72	.59	.47	.56	.89	.78	.75	

2. Intercorrelation of ratings on the six measures of faculty effectiveness shown in Table 9 suggests that two very different aspects of faculty effectiveness are involved in the criteria used for faculty ratings in the college.

a) One aspect of effectiveness is represented by the student ratings (SR) and deals primarily with classroom teaching competence.

b) Another aspect of effectiveness is suggested by ratings on research and publications (RP) and professional activities (PA).

c) Department head ratings (DH) seem to be a compromise score somewhere between a and b.

TABLE 9. INTERCORRELATIONS OF SIX FACULTY EFFECTIVENESS MEASURES (N=26)

Effectiveness measure	Faculty effectiveness scores					
	SR	DH	RP	PA	AT	GE
Student ratings						
Department head ratings	.48[a]					
Research and publication	.23	.54[b]				
Professional activities	—.03	.38	.72[b]			
Dean's adjusted total	.44[a]	.87[b]	.81[b]	.72[b]		
Total general effectiveness	.69[b]	.86[b]	.77[b]	.56[b]	.94[b]	

a. Significant at 5 per cent level.
b. Significant at 1 per cent level.

These findings suggest that research, publications, convention attendance, consultant work, travel, etc., are not closely related to teaching competence, an observation many professors and students have long suspected. In this study we have accepted as our criteria of effectiveness items in actual use by this college. These results suggest, however, that two only slightly related aspects are involved, a. classroom effectiveness, and b. research, writing, and consulting activities. The first of these functions seems much more closely related to the interpersonal interactions characteristic of the other helping professions explored in these studies. The second is much more a matter of objective activity of a much less personal nature. It would thus appear, if these are valid criteria for judgment, that college teaching is a somewhat different task from the other helping professions. The helping function seems less central an aspect of the profession than is true for counseling, public school teaching, and pastoral activities if the effectiveness ratings used in this college are accepted as indicators of quality performance.

3. No significant relationships were discovered between faculty perceptual characteristics and research and publications, department head ratings, professional activities, or college dean ratings. The general hypothesis of the study that effectiveness of college

TABLE 10. CORRELATIONS BETWEEN TWELVE PERCEPTUAL HYPOTHESES AND FACULTY EFFECTIVENESS AS RATED BY STUDENTS (SR) (N=26)

Perceptual variables	Correlations with SR
Perceives others	.50[a]
Able—unable	.56[a]
Worthy—unworthy	.43[b]
Dependable—undependable	.39[b]
Internally motivated—externally molded	.49[b]
Perceives self	.39[b]
With people—apart from people	.36
Wanted—unwanted	.44[b]
Worthy—unworthy	.27
Able—unable	.33
Perceives helping task	.28
Freeing—controlling	.32
Larger—smaller	.29
Meaning oriented—facts, events oriented	.14
Accepting—not accepting	.32
Total perceptual rating	.40[b]

a. Significant at the 1 per cent level.
b. Significant at the 5 per cent level.

teachers is related to certain perceptual characteristics is not borne out, at least when effectiveness is determined by these factors.

4. Significant relationships were found between total perceptual ratings for faculty members and general effectiveness as judged by students. These correlations are shown in Table 10. The general hypothesis of the study that certain perceptual characteristics are related to the effectiveness of college teachers is thus borne out when effectiveness is determined from student ratings.

It will also be noted from Table 10 that, despite the appearance of a significant difference in the total rating, not all of the perceptual characteristics reach significant levels. In fact, none of the perceptual factors relating to the professor's perceptions of his task reach sufficient levels to be considered significant and only one in the self-perception area achieves significance.

5. Faculty members who perceive other people as basically able, worthy, dependable, and internally motivated are rated by students as more effective in overall teaching ability (Table 10). All four of the "Perceptions of Others" categories show significant relationships to student ratings of their professors.

6. The summed scores of all the items pertaining to "Perceptions of Self" show a significant correlation with student ratings in Table 10. Only one of the individual items in the category, "Sees Self as Wanted," however, achieves a significant level.

It may be that the perceptual organization of professors is more pertinent to the "human" and personal aspects of effectiveness in professional work than to the less personal aspects of research, publication, and professional activity. The present research is the first one in this series of studies to use indications of professional effectiveness not directly involved in human relationships. Further research is needed to determine what aspects of a person's perceptual organization may be of primary importance in determining success in objective pursuits like writing and research.

Previous researches which demonstrated a significant relationship between perceptual organization and effectiveness were performed with a sample selected on a "good"—"poor" basis, whereas the present study had a faculty sample that was strictly voluntary and whose spread on the effectiveness-ineffectiveness continuum was really an unknown quantity. In the present study, there was no attempt to create best-worst groupings of faculty members or to use only those faculty who were unequivocally one or the other on all ratings.

It may be that college teaching is simply a different breed of cat. Previous theoretical evidence which suggests that effective professionals are characterized by certain perceptions they hold about the nature of the helping task is only partly supported by the results of this research. The college teacher's helping task may be somewhat different from other helping professions studied. Much more research is needed before more definite conclusions can be stated.

Previous research on good teaching has repeatedly shown that correlation of methods, behaviors, etc., with effectiveness is low. Ellena et al., for example, conclude that no objective measure clearly indicates "goodness" in teaching.[3] The variability of results in the present research may be due to the fact that the effectiveness measures used are largely objective. This also squares with the fact that positive results were found with the more *subjective* student ratings of general overall effectiveness in the classroom and not with objective measures of research and publication. It may be also that there is a need to distinguish between teachers of primarily factual and content-centered disciplines and teachers who are expected to produce more personal changes in their students.

3. Ellena, W. J., Stevenson, M., & Webb, H. V. *Who's a good teacher?* Washington, D.C.: American Association of School Administrators, N.E.A., 1961.

Part Three
An Interpretation

8. AN OVERVIEW AND NEXT STEPS

What can we conclude from this series of studies and what directions do they suggest for further research? While these studies leave many questions unanswered and can hardly be regarded as definitive, they nevertheless provide additional support for basic concepts in perceptual theory, shed new light on the nature of the helping professions, and point the way to promising hypotheses for further research.

SUPPORT FOR PERCEPTUAL THEORY

The basic premise of perceptual psychology is that behavior is a function of the perceptual field of the behaver at the instant of action. Most research in human behavior has traditionally been carried on from an external point of view. That is to say, understanding of behavior has been sought from the frame of reference of the outside observer. The thesis of perceptual psychology, on the other hand, is that behavior can also be understood (and sometimes more effectively) when examined from the standpoint, not of the outsider, but of the behaver himself. The results of these studies tend to corroborate that position. They do more. Attempts to distinguish the behavior of professional workers in terms of objective criteria like knowledge possessed, or methods used, or behavior exhibited have generally been disappointing in the past. Several of the studies reported here, however, have demonstrated that significant relationships do, indeed, exist between perception and behavior. Even more, they suggest that a perceptual approach to the study of professional workers may provide us with more useful understanding of these persons than has heretofore been possible. Thus, these studies not only support the perceptual hypothesis, but suggest that this approach may be more fruitful in advancing our efforts to understand the helping professions. They seem to place in our hands a new and promising tool for further research.

A major difficulty in perceptual psychology is the problem of measurement. Measurement in more orthodox approaches to psychology can be a pretty straightforward matter of recording observations or counting responses. The study of perception is more

69

difficult since perceptions lie inside people and are not open to direct observation. Because perception can only be approached (at least, at present) by some form of inference, additional problems of reliability of measurement are posed for the researcher using this frame of reference. For some psychologists these problems have seemed so difficult that they have raised serious questions of whether such procedures can be dignified by the term "research" at all. The question requires an answer. The position of the perceptual psychologist is that techniques of inference can, indeed, provide reliable data if the researcher approaches the problem of measurement with the same discipline, care, and rigor demanded of science in any other field of exploration.

In these studies inferences about the perceptual organization of professional workers have been obtained from a wide variety of original sources including observations, interviews, "critical incidents," responses to problem situations, and stories told by the subject. Inferences were obtained by using the observer himself as an instrument of measurement. Observers also demonstrated in these studies that such inferences could be made with highly acceptable degrees of reliability and that such data could be effectively used for the exploration of an important aspect of human behavior.

The Nature of the Helping Professions

The Common Origins of the Helping Professions

The original impetus for these studies grew out of a suspicion that, while the various forms of the helping professions differ with respect to their purposes, clientele, and techniques, nevertheless, they are basically alike in the psychology through which they operate. It seemed to us that the crux of the problem of "helping" lay not in some mysterious special technique. Rather the various helping professions seem really to be expressions of a kind of basic "good" human interrelationship. That is to say, these professions appear to represent the concentration and crystallization of the best we know about human interrelationships for the sake of the person or persons to be helped. The helping professions seem to us not different fom life experience but selected from human experience. Within the limited sample represented by these studies, this thesis is given some support.

Ideally, the case for this observation would certainly be stronger had our studies investigated identical criteria with identical techniques in each of the professions we examined. Unfortunately, that is hindsight which suggests the need for further research, to be sure, but does us little good now. From the data we do have, however, there is sufficient evidence to suggest that the perceptual organization of persons who are effective helpers, at least for counselors, elementary teachers, Episcopal priests, and student nurses, have a number of common kinds of perceptions. Our original hunches seem to be supported and we are encouraged to continue exploring in these directions.

The Importance of Perceptual Organization
as a Distinguishing Characteristic

Our early theoretical consideration of these matters led us to the belief that the widespread failure of research efforts to distinguish between effective and ineffective workers in the helping professions was largely due to concentration on symptoms rather than causes. Observed behavior is the end of a process, an expression of it. As such, many diverse behaviors may occur as expressions of a single aspect of individual beliefs or perceptions. Conversely, different perceptual experiences can result in highly similar kinds of behavior. To distinguish clearly between effective and ineffective workers in the helping professions it seemed to us required penetration to the causes of behavior, a hypothesis supported by the observation of other workers that persons are often helped by highly diverse behaviors if the intent of the helper is positive. The accuracy of this reasoning is certainly given support by the findings of these studies. Our studies with elementary teachers, counselors, and Episcopal priests, especially, seem to lend credence to the importance of the perceptual variable in distinguishing between effective and ineffective helpers. The results for our college teachers, when effectiveness is judged by students, at least, also seem to corroborate our hypotheses. The findings of our study with student nurses, however, while not denying our original hypothesis, certainly did not corroborate it.

THE GENERAL FRAME OF REFERENCE OF PROFESSIONAL HELPERS

Three of our studies showing significant differences between effective and ineffective professional workers investigated the frame of reference in which the helper approached his task (Table 11). All these investigated the people-things dichotomy, two examined the internal-external approach dimension, and one further examined the perceptual-facts and the immediate-historical dichotomies as well. In view of the fact that the helping professions are designed to help people, it is not surprising to find that workers

TABLE 11. FRAME OF REFERENCE CATEGORIES SHOWING SIGNIFICANT
DIFFERENCES IN THREE STUDIES

Category	Counselors	Teachers	Priests
People—things	S[a]	S	S
Internal—external	S	S	NM
Perceptual—facts	NM[b]	S	NM
Immediate—historical	NM	S	NM

a. S=Significant difference.
b. NM=not measured.

who tend to be people-oriented are likely to be more effective. The remaining items explored in this category seem to represent a characteristic internal or perceptual approach which effective helpers take toward their students, clients, or parishioners. Such a characteristic frame of reference in the helper would presumably cause him to behave in ways that others would describe as sensitive or empathic, both qualities often described as desirable in counselors, teachers, pastors, and nurses.

THE HELPER'S PERCEPTIONS OF PEOPLE

It is apparent that effective helpers in all four of the professions indicated in Table 12 are characterized by a generally positive view of their subjects and a belief in the capacity of the human organism to save itself. It makes a great deal of difference whether helpers perceive their clients as able or unable. If a counselor, teacher, or priest does not regard his clients as able he can hardly permit them, let them, or trust them to act on their own; to do so would be a violation of responsibility. Apparently, effective helpers

tend to see the persons they work with in essentially positive ways
as dependable, friendly, and worthy people. This hardly seems like
a startling revelation. Indeed, it sounds like little more than good
common sense. It is necessary to remind ourselves, however, that
these are not factors which helpers *say* about themselves, but characteristic ways of perceiving inferred from their behavior. Effective
behavers do not simply verbally ascribe to these qualities; they
behave in terms of them.

TABLE 12. PERCEPTIONS OF OTHERS CATEGORIES SHOWING SIGNIFICANT
DIFFERENCES IN FOUR STUDIES

Category	Counselors	Teachers	Priests	Professors[a]
Able—unable	S[b]	S	S	S
Dependable—undependable	S	S	NM	S
Friendly—unfriendly	S	S	NM	NM
Worthy—unworthy	S	S	NM	S
Internally motivated—not	NM[c]	S	NM	S
Helpful—hindering	NM	S	NM	NM

a. Effectiveness determined from student ratings only.
b. S=Significant difference.
c. NM=Not measured.

THE HELPER'S PERCEPTIONS OF SELF

Two characteristics stand out in an examination of Table 13. In
the first place effective helpers appear to see themselves as one with
mankind, as sharing a common fate. Poor helpers, on the other

TABLE 13. PERCEPTIONS OF SELF CATEGORIES SHOWING SIGNIFICANT
DIFFERENCES IN FOUR STUDIES

Category	Counselors	Teachers	Priests	Professors[a]
Identified—unidentified	S[b]	S	S	NS[d]
Enough—not enough	S	S	NM	NS
Dependable—undependable	NM[c]	S	NM	NM
Worthy—unworthy	NM	S	NM	NS
Wanted—unwanted	NM	S	NM	S

a. Effectiveness determined from student ratings only.
b. S=Significant difference.
c. NM=Not measured.
d. NS=Not significant.

hand, have a tendency to see themselves as apart from others, as different from them. If the success of helping professions depends upon relationships established between helpers and helpees, as modern theory would seem to suggest, it is easy to see why this characteristic would distinguish between good helpers and poor ones. It is difficult to establish effective relationships with a helper unwilling to get involved.

A second major characteristic of a good helper seems to be the existence of an essentially positive view of self. Such views of self

TABLE 14. PERCEPTIONS OF PURPOSE CATEGORIES SHOWING SIGNIFICANT
DIFFERENCE IN THREE STUDIES

Category	Counselors	Teachers	Priests
Self revealing—self concealing	S[a]	S	NM
Freeing—controlling	S	S	S
Altruistic—narcissistic	S	NM	NM
Larger—smaller	S	S	NM
Involved—uninvolved	NM[b]	S	S
Process—goals	NM	S	NM

a. S=Significant difference.
b. NM=Not measured.

seem to be characteristic also of self-actualizing personalities as reported in the literature. A positive view of self provides the kind of internal security which makes it possible for persons who possess such views of self to behave with much more assurance, dignity, and straightforwardness. With a firm base of operations to work from such persons can be much more daring and creative in respect to their approach to the world and more able to give of themselves to others as well.

THE HELPER'S PERCEPTIONS OF HIS TASK

Effective helpers apparently tend to see their tasks more as freeing than controlling (Table 14). Such a finding certainly gives much support to the growth philosophy underlying most current counseling approaches and to the student-centered concept of teaching advocated by many modern educators. The concern of effective helpers with larger rather than smaller issues also seems to be consistent with the freeing purpose.

The self-revealing characteristic found in the effective helpers seems congruent with the identified-unidentified characteristic of self found in Table 14. Many writers have indicated that self-disclosure is closely related to healthy personality and the capacity to enter into intimate human relationships.

METHODS IN THE HELPING PROFESSIONS

In the original formulation of hypotheses for our studies of the helping professions our seminar listed seven continua which we thought might discriminate between effective and ineffective helpers in connection with the methods they used to carry out their tasks. None of these hypotheses has yet been subjected to test. In our earlier experiments this was because the problem was of less interest to us than hypotheses about the helper's frame of reference, perceptions of self and others, or perception of purposes. Later, we postponed further research on this question because changes in our thinking about the question of methods led us in somewhat different directions.

It will be recalled from our earlier discussion that a review of the literature had shown only very disappointing results with respect to distinguishing between effective and ineffective helpers on the basis of the methods which they used. In our early thinking about this matter it seemed to us we might find more clear-cut differences between effective and ineffective helpers if we looked, not at the methods they used per se, but rather, at the ways in which they were perceiving methods. Accordingly, our early seminar listed eleven continua for examination. As a consequence of our later studies, however, we have come to see the problem as follows. If the self as instrument concept of effective operation in the helping professions is valid, then the search for "right" methods is doomed before it begins. Since helpers as persons are unique, the hope of finding a "common uniqueness," by definition, is a hopeless search. It occurred to us then that perhaps the question of methods in the helping professions is not a matter of adopting the "right" method, but a question of the helper discovering the right method *for him.* That is to say, the crucial question is not "what" method, but the "fit" of the method, its appropriateness to the self of the helper, to his purposes, his subjects, the situation, and so forth. We now believe the important distinction between the good and poor helper with respect to methods is not a matter of his perceptions of methods, per se, but the *authenticity* of whatever methods he uses. There is already some evidence for this in our findings that good helpers are self-revealing, involved, and identified.

We suspect a major problem of poor helpers is the fact that their methods are unauthentic, that is, they tend to be put on, contrived. As such they can only be utilized so long as the helper keeps his mind on them. That, of course, is likely to be disastrous on two counts. In the first place it separates him from his client or student, and the message conveyed is likely to be that he is not "with it," is not really interested, or is a phony. Second, it is almost never possible to maintain attention to the "right" method for very long. As a consequence the poor helper relapses frequently to what he believes or his previous experience has taught him, and so the method he is trying to use fails because of the tenuous, interrupted character of his use of it.

We are about persuaded the question of the helper's perceptions concerning methods are of minor significance. Helpers will find the methods to carry on their tasks effectively if perceptions of self, others, purposes, and the general frame of reference are congruent with that of effective helpers. The validity of this position, of course, remains to be investigated. It is our hope that others will join us in exploring whether or not authenticity is truly the key question with respect to methods.

How Many Perceptual Factors?

In our studies of the perceptual organization of effective helpers we have so far demonstrated that at least twenty-one perceptual characteristics distinguish between good and poor helpers. In our original seminar we listed forty-three hypotheses for exploration. There seems to be no doubt that still others could be added to this list. There is an important question to be answered, however, concerning the number of truly significant variables involved in this matter. All of us engaged in these researches have the very strong feeling that there may, in fact, be comparatively few perceptual criteria related to effective and ineffective operations in the helping professions. In choosing hypotheses from our original list for investigation it became quite clear to us that some of these were duplications. They also seemed to vary considerably in terms of fundamental importance. Even among some of the perceptual characteristics we investigated in the studies reported here, it is apparent from simple observation that items overlap. In addition, in the factor analysis of children's perceptions carried out by Combs and Soper,[1] forty-seven of the forty-nine categories under investigation were reduced to one global factor which these authors called "a feeling of general adequacy." In order to determine the number of truly discreet perceptual characteristics involved in the discrimination of effective and ineffective helpers, we believe a factor analysis study of this matter is called for. Unfortunately, such a study would require a most expensive design and to this point we have not been able to find either the time or finances required to properly carry out such a project. Perhaps, some day, we, or someone else, may.

Ever since the various forms of the helping professions came into being the problem of discriminating between effective and ineffective workers has been a knotty one. We believe these investigations have opened some new avenues for understanding of the matter with broad implications for practical application. To this point we have been primarily interested in exploring these questions for their possible implications in the training of effective persons in the helping professions. This has already borne fruit in suggesting new approaches to the professional education of teachers based upon a perceptual approach to the problem.[2] Benton,[3] Gooding,[4] and Dickman[5] have touched slightly on the implications of their studies for the training of priests, teachers, and nurses. These are matters deserving much more speculation, experiment, and application.

To this point our researches have been primarily concerned with

1. Combs, A. W., & Soper, D. W. *The relationship of child perceptions to achievement and behavior in the early school years.* Cooperative Research Project No. 814, University of Florida, Gainesville, Florida, 1963.

2. Combs, A. W. *The professional education of teachers.* Boston: Allyn and Bacon, 1965.

3. Benton, J. A. Perceptual characteristics of Episcopal pastors. Unpublished doctoral dissertation, University of Florida, 1964.

4. Gooding, C. T. An observational analysis of the perceptual organization of effective teachers. Unpublished doctoral dissertation, University of Florida, 1964.

5. Dickman, J. F. The perceptual organization of person-oriented versus task-oriented student nurses. Unpublished doctoral dissertation, University of Florida, 1967.

exploring the perceptual organization of helpers in order to shed light on theoretical questions and to suggest areas of innovation for training more effective helpers in teaching, counseling, nursing, and pastoral care. The measurement techniques we have employed in these studies are at this stage still far less refined than we could wish. In time they will improve and new ones develop as well. If further studies continue the favorable trends we have seen so far, it is likely these measurement techniques may also contribute important new approaches to the selection and evaluation of effective helpers.

It is apparent that the studies reported here are little more than pilot studies. Like any research worthy of the name they raise far more questions than they have settled. For those of us involved in these investigations they have been exciting and stimulating explorations in what seem to us to be fruitful new directions.

We believe these studies represent but a small and tentative beginning of research into a most promising new approach to understanding the helping professions. What started as a series of hunches in 1957 has now become a conviction that we are on or close to the right track. If these concepts are not the truth, then we are encouraged by our studies to believe they are very like it. It is our earnest hope that this presentation may encourage others to join us on this path to further discovery.

UNIVERSITY OF FLORIDA MONOGRAPHS

Social Sciences

UNIVERSITY OF FLORIDA MONOGRAPHS

Social Sciences

THE
MOUNTAINS
BOW DOWN

Other novels by Sibella Giorello include

The Clouds Roll Away
The Rivers Run Dry
The Stones Cry Out

THE MOUNTAINS BOW DOWN

SIBELLA GIORELLO

H HARLEQUIN® LOVE INSPIRED® SUSPENSE

Recycling programs
for this product may
not exist in your area.

™ LOVE INSPIRED BOOKS

ISBN-13: 978-0-373-78785-2

THE MOUNTAINS BOW DOWN

Love Inspired Books/July 2013

First Published by Thomas Nelson, Inc.

Copyright © 2011 by Sibella Giorello

Author photo taken by Michael Good.

www.LoveInspiredBooks.com

Printed in U.S.A.

For my grandmothers,
Belle Goldstein Simpson
and
Frances Kennan Connor Worobec
Beauty with perseverance: Alaska pioneers

There's a land where the mountains are nameless,

And the rivers all run God knows where;

There are lives that are erring and aimless,

And deaths that just hang by a hair;

There are hardships that nobody reckons;

There are valleys unpeopled and still;

There's a land—oh, it beckons and beckons,

And I want to go back—and I will.

—from "The Spell
of the Yukon,"
Robert Service

ONE

With the trajectory of launched missiles, the mountains soared from the ocean. Smothered with evergreens, the steeps pointed to a sky so blue it whispered of eternity. Though it was June, snow on the granite ridges refused to melt despite almost twenty-four hours daily of sunlight. And where a liquid silver sea lapped the rocky shore, a bald eagle surveyed the cold water for fish.

First week of June: 5:00 AM in Ketchikan, Alaska.

It felt like falling in love.

That was a feeling I should've been familiar with, being newly engaged. That delicious sense of wonder, the dizzying sensations that came with standing on the threshold of new life—all that should have reminded me of my fiancé.

Instead, I was thinking, *Why doesn't my heart flutter like this when I think of him?*

Not the best thought for future marital happiness.

But it's part of the reason I was taking this cruise to Alaska *sans fiancé*. Hoping to get some perspective. Hoping to remember why, six months ago, I agreed to marry my high school sweetheart, a really nice guy named DeMott Fielding.

Only I wasn't gaining perspective on this ship. I was losing what remained of my mind.

We left the Seattle dock fifty-two-and-a-half hours ago—

but who was counting?—and I was suddenly surrounded by two thousand strangers, each of whom lacked any normal sense of personal boundaries. These people were crowders. Constant talkers. Swarmers and gatherers, they turned my dreams of solitude into a desperate need, like food or water. Among the passengers were my mother—never quite stable but not exactly getting sea legs—and my Aunt Charlotte, who genuinely believed rocks healed spiritual wounds, and my aunt's friend Claire, a self-professed psychic known as "Claire the Clairvoyant."

From day one, Claire made me want to jump ship, literally. But I was trying to be nice. Claire was my aunt's closest friend, and my aunt had given us these cruise tickets. Free. A gift.

Gifts always come with obligations. Always.

But on this morning as we sailed into the town of Ketchikan, I stole an opportunity to escape. Standing on the top deck, I took a deep breath of the freshest air ever tasted and scanned the mountains beyond the bow. The cruise's first port of call, Ketchikan was my first chance to get off the ship and I felt hope returning, sneaking back into my heart like a repentant runaway. My plans for today included a hike. Take in the view, collect some local rocks. Sit somewhere, alone.

It's all going to work out, I told myself. *The cruise, the engagement. Everything's fine.*

I lifted my hand to the sleepless sun and searched Deer Mountain. I was going to hike the trail that led to its summit, where a panoramic view displayed Tongass Narrows and these leviathan islands that broke through the Alaskan waters like pods of humpback whales. The town's dock was within sight, and that surveying eagle had landed on the pier, awaiting our arrival.

But then I heard three long bellows, blasting from the ship's stack.

Low and ominous, like warnings.

In the silence that followed, I held my breath and stared at the tiny houses snuggled against the mountainsides. Their windows glinted like burnished gold. When an amplified crackle shattered the still air, the eagle took flight.

A man's voice blared across the water, bouncing back from the granite steeps.

Every echoing word confirmed my sense of doom.

"Ladies and gentlemen, this is your captain, Oliver Roberts. We have encountered a situation that necessitates our immediate return to sea." He sounded British, his voice as clipped as a Bristol wind. "We will be sailing for an indefinite period of time—"

I leaned over the deck rail. As an FBI agent, I knew of only one "situation" that merited an immediate return to sea. I watched the water below as it churned into a milky froth, washing against the hull. The deck shuddered with vibrations, and when I looked up again, Ketchikan was receding, the golden windows slipping into the emerald trees. And my heart tumbled down, down, down.

No, no, no.

"We will be traveling south along the Inside Passage," the captain continued. "Please do not be alarmed by the helicopters."

Helicopters?

"We hope to return to our scheduled itinerary as soon as possible. In the meantime, thank you for your patience. As updates become available, I will endeavor to pass along the necessary information. On behalf of the entire staff of the *Spirit of Odysseus*, we appreciate your cooperation."

A raven crossed the sky, following the eagle's retreat, and the oily blackbird cawed happily at our misfortune. Taking a deep breath, I pushed myself from the deck rail and headed for the doors that led back inside the ship.

Back to the crowds. Back to the chattering noise.

"What kinda scam is this?" asked a man, hurrying beside me. He wore a baseball cap that declared his membership to the Phillumenists of Phoenix. "This cruise is a rip-off."

A petite woman gripped his arm and stared into his face with a tremulous expression. "Honey," she said with a tentative voice, "they did say something about icebergs. Maybe we hit one last night. You know, like the *Titanic*."

"Bitty, if we was sinking we wouldn't go back to sea." His aggrieved tone made clear he was burdened by the company of lesser minds. "They said we'd see Ketchikan. Guess what? We just did. Now we're leaving. Getting off the boat must be some technicality."

"Oh, honey, I don't think—"

Before I could grab the door, he caught the handle and spun toward me. "What d'you think?" he asked.

Several things, actually. None good. But my most insistent thought was, *My marriage better not be like this.*

Instead, I said, "The captain would rather dock than leave."

"What's *that* supposed to mean?"

I hurried inside.

"Hey, I asked you a question."

The air inside the sunroom was warm and smelled of chlorine, a sharp condensation coming from the nearby swimming pool. Picking up my pace, I hoped to lose the guy. But he stuck to my heels like tar.

"Don't you get it?" he persisted. "Now they don't gotta pay dock fees. We'll float around the ocean and they'll take our money and then dump us back in Seattle."

Conspiracy theories seemed to be fueled by everything but logic, which was why they were impossible to kill. Here was an obvious case: logic would say no self-preserving captain would bring two thousand people within kissing distance of Alaska, a lifelong dream destination for many, only to turn around and remain at sea with a village of now-mutinous passengers. The idea was idiotic. Ridiculous.

And one more reason why I craved solitude.

"Don't you got anything to say?" he demanded.

I zigzagged through the empty lounge chairs. "I'm sure the captain would like nothing more than for you to get off the ship."

"That's what *you* think," he replied, as if he'd never asked.

Once again the woman was clutching his forearm, her small shoes pattering across the tile floor by the hot tubs.

He told her, "Watch. They'll make us cough up more money to get on land."

Following me all the way to the elevators, he punched a tight fist into the Down button six or seven times and continued bolstering his crazy theory—"Notice how they even charge us for soda?" I was looking around for an escape route when my cell phone started playing "Ode to Joy."

I pulled it off my belt clip and stared at the caller ID. It was the ship's head of security. The bad feeling in my stomach tightened, and the elevator *bing*ed open. The angry man and timid woman stepped inside. Once again he held the door. "Aren't you coming?" he asked, annoyed.

I shook my head.

As the door closed, I sensed a sad certainty.

My vacation was officially over.

"What happened?" I asked.

Geert van Broeck only shook his head. It was a bald head, shiny and pink. Perhaps to compensate, he had grown an extravagant mustache that consisted of two long handlebars the color of snow. With the bald pate, his mustache made him look like a vandalized pumpkin.

"No questions here," growled the ship's head of security. We had walked away from the elevators and now headed into the Salt Spray restaurant. A buffet-style eatery, it was perched on Deck Fifteen, the ship's top floor, and it smelled of scrambled eggs and fried ham, onions and potatoes. My stomach growled but otherwise I kept quiet and followed the man who had taken my gun from me at the Seattle dock. Ship rules. No firearms. Not even for FBI agents, though Geert assured me my Glock would be returned whenever we came to American soil. I was going to retrieve the gun this morning. I promised my fiancé I wouldn't hike without protection. Already DeMott had left three messages on my cell phone, worrying about aggressive bears.

But then, DeMott worried about most everything these days.

"It is not good," Geert said, when we emerged from the restaurant to the open deck. His thick Dutch accent made him sound perpetually angry. Maybe he was, stuck on a cruise ship. "We got a passenger missing."

"Missing, as in, fell overboard?" I asked. "Or missing, you suspect foul play?"

"Is this how they train FBI—ask stupid questions?"

Three days ago, when Geert took my gun, I learned that he had been trained by the Dutch elite police, the Royal Marechaussee. That tenure infected him with an enflamed sense of superiority, and his "stupid question" comment was his fourth dig at the FBI since Sunday. I tried to stop counting, but not hard enough.

"Do you have an identity for the missing person?" I asked, teeth clenched.

"Woman." The word sounded derogatory with his accent. "Husband reported it."

The white handlebars of his mustache twitched.

"You don't believe the husband?"

"This is not my first trip through the tunnel of love. Husbands, they are trouble. Once, I find the wife did it. Some woman hurrying the death-do-them part."

I was ruminating on my next stupid question when his large face suddenly broke into a radiant smile. The skin around his blue eyes crinkled, the mustache rose like a biplane.

"Nice sun we got, yah?" He stopped dead in his tracks, greeting an elderly couple coming toward us.

"Whole lot nicer if we landed on shore," the old man said. He had a curved spine and stabbed the teak deck with a pronged cane. "What happened, somebody take a leap off their balcony?"

Geert's forced smile completed his head's jack-o'-lantern appearance. "We gonna get to Ketchikan, not to worry. Not to worry!"

The elderly woman leaned forward. Her navy windbreaker was from the Phillumenists of Philadelphia. *Burning with Brotherly Love.* "Are they serving breakfast?" she asked.

From the chest pocket of his white officer's uniform, Geert pulled out a piece of paper and scrawled his name on it, handing it to them. "Bloody Marys. Free."

The old man narrowed his eyes. "Must be bad, whatever happened."

Geert gave a chuckle. "Nothing, nothing is wrong."

"Now I'm really worried," the man said.

"Coffee, danish, sunshine. Enjoy the day. We talk later, yah?"

Giving a quick wave, Geert hustled across the deck. When we were out of earshot, he muttered, "Big-time cruisers, gotta keep them loyal to the line."

"This missing woman," I said, redirecting. "I take it she's an American."

"Yah. American."

"American" sounded worse than "woman."

He stood at a door next to the blinding-white smokestacks and tapped a numbered code into the security keypad, pulling the heavy latch.

"We looked everywhere," he said. "Every deck. Fore and aft. Port and starboard. We checked their cabin, their friends' cabins, the open bars. Now we gotta turn around."

I knew enough about the situation to know it had its own acronym, MOB. Man overboard. And I knew the laws were fairly straightforward. As soon as a passenger was officially missing, the cruise ship must immediately return to its location corresponding to when the person was last seen.

I asked where that was.

"In the bar," Geert said.

"You know what I'm asking."

He was walking down a long narrow corridor of painted steel. It was gunmetal gray with curved cabin doors marked by single digit numbers. Officers' quarters, I assumed.

"Until midnight, she was in the bar with the husband," Geert said, finally. "He stayed. She went back to their cabin." The mustache twitched. "The husband stumbled back to their cabin around 3:00 AM. Wife not there. He went back to the bar. For a drink."

"It was still open—at 3:00 AM?"

"Open all night. Nobody's driving, yah? Husband has another drink, *then* comes to the concierge." His white eyebrows were as snowy as the mustache and they lowered with contempt. "Four this morning, we start looking. Look and look. Can't find her. I call the captain, tell him MOB, then I remember. We got FBI on board."

His last sentence dripped with sarcasm. I waited silently as he tapped two codes into two separate security pads. The sign beside the door read Captain's Bridge, Authorized Personnel Only.

"Does this mean I can have my gun back?" I asked.

"No way." Geert pushed open the door to the bridge. "I don't trust Americans."

Oliver Roberts, the captain, was English. His teeth proved it.

I extended my hand. "Raleigh Harmon, special agent, FBI."

Captain Roberts gave a brisk shake, then clasped his hands behind his back and rocked on his heels. "Geert told me we had an FBI agent on board. Rather excellent luck, that. The Coast Guard and Civil Air Patrol have been alerted as well."

The bridge had floor-to-ceiling windows and as we headed out of Ketchikan, the sun-dappled ocean looked like liquid silver. Up ahead, where mountains sliced into the pool of molten metal, three Coast Guard tugboats chugged down the channel toward our ship in a triangular formation. From ten stories above, they looked like toy boats in an enormous bathtub. Two of the tugs shifted to each side—one starboard, one port—while a third bobbed out of our path, waiting to follow aft.

"The helicopters should be joining us momentarily," the captain said.

"You were able to pinpoint the location where the woman went missing?" I asked.

Hands still clasped behind his back, the captain strode to a bank of computers split into two sections and watched by four crew members. Between the counters, a white-shirted officer stood and lightly touched the ship's wheel. I looked at the thing twice. Its diameter was no more than eight inches and seemed much too delicate for guiding a vessel whose length extended nine hundred feet. Under my feet, I felt the engines rumbling.

"Twenty-two knots, Captain," one of the crewmen called out.

"Tell them to keep it there until we clear the channel," replied the captain. "Then pull back to fifteen."

The crewman picked up a black telephone and murmured something as the captain pivoted like a soldier. He pointed to a nautical chart displayed on the largest monitor. Alaska's rugged coastline glowed like a radiated snake, bulging and shrinking around the deep coves and carved fjords of the Inside Passage. The ocean was represented by a wash of black while our ship was a small red rectangle, blinking south along the bright-yellow coast.

"The husband claims he last saw her at twenty-four hundred hours," the captain said.

"Midnight," Geert said, for my benefit.

"At that hour, we were in Canada, not the United States." The captain turned to look at me. He had rheumy English eyes, clouded by years at sea. "That circumstance brings some rather complicated jurisdictional issues to this situation. Are you aware of that, Agent Harmon?"

"Yes, sir." I felt another ladder-drop of emotion. Either nautical laws were simple—such as *MOB, turn around*—or they were as tangled as beach kelp. Suddenly I could smell the seaweed. If a person went missing within three miles of the US coastline, the case went to that state's trooper division. But within one mile of the Canadian coast, the Mounties rode in. The FBI was supposed to investigate any missing Americans, whether in foreign or domestic waters, but our field offices were known to squabble over which city the case belonged to—port of departure; port nearest the disappearance; or the city where the missing passenger claimed residency.

And over all of it, the ship's captain had ultimate and absolute authority. He even had authority over the United States government.

Staring at the bright flashing sea, I felt a headache coming on. "Which state is the woman from?" I asked.

Geert said, "Caw-lee-for-knee-ya."

California sounded no better than "woman." Worse than "American."

"Los Angeles, specifically," the captain said. "She's the wife of a rather famous movie star. Milo Carpenter."

My blood went cold.

"He's on board shooting a movie," the captain continued. "Are you familiar with his films?"

I nodded. More than familiar. Milo Carpenter was my ticket on this ship because my aunt was hired by...*oh, Lord, no*... Mrs. Carpenter hired my aunt. The woman. The MOB.

I turned to the captain, preparing to unravel the complications one at a time, but the bridge suddenly erupted with a loud squawk. It came from near the computer consoles.

"All stations, all stations, all stations! This is the Alaska Coast Guard, come in, *Spirit of Odysseus*. Over."

The captain lurched, yanking a radio from the computer counter and squeezing the side button. "This is the captain of the *Spirit of Odysseus*. Over."

"Captain, we see your MOB."

"Stop the engines!" the captain yelled.

The crewman grabbed the black phone again.

The captain squeezed the radio button. "Coast Guard, exact location please. Over."

I stepped closer to the picture window and felt the engines losing power until the sound dropped to a low growl, almost inaudible. Down below, to the port side, the Coast Guard tugs bobbed in our wake. A guardsman stood on the snout-nosed deck wearing an orange search-and-rescue suit. He held a set of binoculars to his eyes, then turned, yelling toward the tug's small cab.

The radio crackled.

"Captain," the Coast Guard said. "The MOB is not in the water. Over."

"Say again? Over," the captain said.

"I say again, MOB is not in the water. Over."

The captain frowned. "Specify, over."

"The MOB is hanging off the top rail, Captain," the voice said. "And she's in a noose. Over."

TWO

Geert burst through the steel door to the top deck and I raced behind him. Sea air slapped my face as we ran under the bridge toward the aft, following the directions the Coast Guard had given.

All three tugs had come around port side and the guardsmen crowded the prows, their search-and-rescue uniforms bright as burning flames. They waved their arms and pointed, and the Dutchman gazed around the deck, taking in the painted steel rail, the teak, the back deck leading into the ship.

I glanced down at the tugs again. The sailors seemed to want us to move across the deck, their gestures like some horrible version of the game of "warm, warmer—no, now colder."

Suddenly Geert bolted toward a small alcove that extended over the water like a princess balcony. A thin chain blocked entrance to the short platform, and a small sign warned passengers to keep away. A thick gray rope puddled on the deck beside the half wall.

The Coast Guard started waving excitedly.

Unhitching the chain, Geert stepped over the disheveled rope and stared down the ship's side.

"Ach," he said, drawing back.

I walked over and looked down.

Blond hair blew across her face like sheaves of wheat. Her face looked down the vertical column of her body, as though watching her bare feet as they bumped against the white hull. Her feet kept syncopated rhythm with the rocking motion of the ship, and on the upswing I could see her toes. The nails were painted blue and the color nearly matched the ocean. Eerily, the polish now matched the color of her cold skin.

"Dead," Geert said.

I shifted my eyes to the rope strung around her neck. It was orange and made of nylon or polyester. Extending from the nape of her neck, the rope ran like a fuse to the rail, then slipped through a six-inch opening at the base of the half wall. From there it continued to the gray rope that puddled at our feet. The gray rope was sodden, bloated with rain and seawater from our journey from Seattle.

"Do you have a crime kit?" I asked.

"Stupid question." Geert unclipped a small black radio from his belt. His Netherlandish accent sounded sterner than ever as he ordered someone to bring the crime kit to Deck Fourteen, aft.

"And find the husband," he said. "Use the back stairs, bring crew with barrier cones. I don't want no lookie-looks around."

Next, he radioed the captain.

"Ach," Geert said. "Suicide."

I stepped back, moving carefully around the two ropes and wondering how much evidence the wind and rain had washed away.

Maybe all of it.

The gray rope soaked with rain was knotted around a steel post. The rest of it had bunched up, unable to pass through the small opening where the thin orange line dropped. A long rope, the disheveled coil measured three or four feet in diameter, even dislodged. Perhaps a foot in height. No scuff marks had been left on the small balcony, no footwear residues.

But something didn't look right.

"My men are bringing the husband," Geert told the captain. "I will call the undertaker."

"Excellent," replied the captain. "Let's remove her body from public display as swiftly as possible. Need I remind you of that blasted Nancy Grace? She ran those pictures of the bloody balcony for weeks."

I slipped off my small backpack and dug around for my Nikon. The camera was full of fresh batteries for my hike up Deer Mountain Trail, but when I raised it, waiting for Geert to step out of the way, he ignored me.

"Yah," he said, continuing his discussion with the captain, "I make sure we have no lookie-looks."

Despite his obvious disapproval, I began photographing the scene. The dislodged gray rope. The thin orange strand tied to its base. Zooming in, I saw how her body weight had cinched the knots in the nylon so tightly they nearly disappeared into the braid. When I leaned over the balcony, her body hung like a high bumper waiting for a dock. I completely understood the urge to grab the line and hoist her from view. But first came evidence, and since the laws of the sea gave me almost no jurisdiction, I kept taking pictures, closing down the aperture against the sunlight bouncing off the water and reflecting on the ship's white hull. The wind continued to blow through her pale hair. It looked alive.

I scanned the side of the ship. No balconies. Only small portholes, the rims protruding. But these were at least five yards beneath her feet. And much too small for a grown-up to crawl through.

I glanced over my shoulder. Geert watched me, twirling an end of the white mustache.

"The gray rope," I said. "What is it used for?"

"Rough weather. Crew throws it to the dock. Extra mooring."

"And the orange rope?"

"Keeps the mooring line together." He pointed a shiny black shoe at the disheveled line. "She untied the thin rope. Now it's all come undone."

Behind him two Asian men came toward us. They wore black slacks and black sweaters, their shoulders adorned with discrete gold epaulettes. The taller one carried a titanium case that he set on the deck, then popped open. He offered Geert latex gloves. When I held out my hand, he glanced at Geert, hesitating. At his boss's nod, he gave me a pair while the second man photographed the crime scene, more quickly than I had. They placed red traffic cones across the deck.

I glanced at my watch. 5:43 AM. The public had not yet appeared.

"The husband is coming?" Geert asked.

The tall Asian man nodded. Both of them worked silently, taking gestural cues from Geert—nods, shakes of his bald head—so that with the solid black clothing, they reminded me of ninjas.

Geert squatted, lowering himself to the deck, and placed his big feet on either side of the half wall's small opening. Taking the orange line in his gloved hands, he leaned back and pulled. The Ninjas gathered behind him, also pulling, while I took more pictures and listened to Geert's breathless mutters. They sounded like Dutch curses.

Though the Ninjas strained, they remained silent, and her body came up by inches. The sound that caused me to glance away, nauseated, was her feet banging against the hull. When I looked back to the retrieval, the bow thrusters were once again shuddering through the deck. The ship turned as if placed on an axis. Inside the steep and narrow channel, we pivoted and the precipitous blue mountains shifted by degrees until we once again pointed toward Ketchikan.

But with the turn, I realized how clever it was that she

hung off the port side. As we sailed into town, no one would have seen her. Ketchikan's harbor greeted ships on their starboard. The harbor, the tree houses. The marina full of fishing vessels and sailboats. It wasn't until the Coast Guard sailed down the channel on our port side that her body was seen.

His bald head beaded with sweat, Geert clutched the rope as the Ninjas raced to the railing, reaching down. They pulled her over the side and Geert scrambled to his feet. She rolled over the steel bar and the Dutchman tugged down her palazzo pants, pulling them over her exposed legs, as if to preserve one last shred of propriety.

The Ninjas laid her on the deck. One of them pressed his fingers into her neck, searching for a pulse. A formality at this point. Her eyes were half-closed, her skin the grayish blue of death. She looked asleep, and cold. All except her tongue. It was purple, and it protruded from her parted lips as though she was making a face. Somebody sticking out their tongue to mock a photographer.

But what bothered me more was her neck. The string of bruises circling her throat looked like violet pearls. And the "noose," as the Coast Guard said, was not that at all. It was a tight double knot. I was rushing to take pictures of both her neck and the rope because the Ninjas had already begun covering her with a tarp from the crime kit.

Geert opened his cell phone and I heard three notes, presumably 9-1-1 because a moment later he asked the state patrol to meet the *Spirit of Odysseus* at the Ketchikan dock.

"No sirens," he ordered. "Suicide. She's dead. Done." He paused, then repeated, "No sirens."

The taller Ninja packed up the crime kit. More crew were arriving to form a human barrier behind the red cones, as passengers began leaking out of the nearby restaurant, drawn perhaps by the ship's sudden turnaround. Or because word was out about the MOB.

Geert made a second call, asking information for the number to the Ketchikan funeral home.

I leaned over the half wall. Squinting at the bright water now rushing past, I tried to measure the distance from the rail to where she had been hanging. Twenty feet, I guessed. Maybe thirty.

I turned back to the tarp, lifting the edge and examining her neck.

"First one of the season," Geert said to someone on the phone.

I did a visual search of both ropes, looking for any foreign fibers, stray hairs, anything that might make sense of this sight.

"No, not old," Geert said. "What do the Americans say— the middle age?"

I picked up the gray mooring line, thick as a man's forearm, dense with water. Shifting what remained of the coil, I searched for the place where the orange line began and reached into the ropes. I saw something glint in the bright morning light, flashing like a new copper penny. I worked my hand through the layers of line, then touched the cold steel deck. I slid my hand around, feeling blindly for the object. When I touched something sharp, I pulled it out.

It was a bracelet. The blue stones stopped my breath. Dangled in the sunlight, the facets sparkled like beads of seawater, the color shifting from ultramarine to cerulean blue to a hue that was almost purple. As a geologist, I'd seen my share of gems and my first guess was that these were sapphires. But when the blue suddenly flashed again, I wondered if they weren't something even more precious.

Tanzanite, a rare blue stone found only in Africa?

Blue diamonds?

Whatever these gems were, the bracelet was worth money. Buckets of money.

Still on the phone, Geert's eyes fixed on the jewelry.

"No, nothing suspicious," he was saying. "Just some lady who decided to kill herself. But keep it down. Husband's a movie star."

"Movie star" joined the other derogatories: Woman, American, California.

He reached out, opening his hand. I hesitated.

But I had no jurisdiction.

I dropped the bracelet into his palm, and he closed the phone.

"Now you can go back to vacation," he said.

"I don't mind hanging around," I said casually.

"You can go. I'll wait for the state troopers." He gave me a flat expression. "Go, have some fun."

I smiled. "That's all right. Fun can wait."

THREE

Geert stayed with the body while I walked though the barrier of crew and plastic cones, crossing the Astroturf strip that was the ship's putting green. I climbed the stairs to a short deck offering a netted basketball court. Beyond that, a crewman was lowering a diagonally divided red-and-yellow flag from the mast. The "O" flag. *O* for "Overboard."

Stepping onto the basketball court, I opened my cell phone, ignoring two missed calls from DeMott and an incriminating sparkle the sun kicked up in my engagement ring. I scrolled through my phone book until I found the number for Alex McLeod, my former supervisor in the FBI's violent crimes unit of the Seattle field office.

Taking a deep breath, I prepared the urgent petition inside my head.

He answered on the first ring. "McLeod."

"Sir, it's Raleigh Harmon."

"Raleigh! Tell me you're calling to come back. I've got an assignment here with your name written on it."

Last year a disciplinary transfer sent me from Richmond to Seattle. McLeod turned out to be a decent boss, but when my punishment was lifted several months later, I ran straight home to Richmond. And to DeMott.

"Actually, sir, I'm on a cruise ship. In Alaska."

"Vacation? Good, Raleigh. You need it."

I hesitated, wondering how much to tell him right away. How much he would believe. "Yes, sir, vacation. But there's one problem. A woman was just found hanging off the back of the ship. The cruise line is ruling it a suicide."

"You want me to notify the Alaska office, is that it? So it's on record?"

I turned a slow circle, making sure nobody could overhear my words. Three basketballs were rolling across the sports court, spinning with the sea swells. "Sir, I don't think it's a suicide."

"Why?"

"She was hanging at least twenty feet from the deck by a thin nylon rope. Maybe thirty feet. There's no ladder. Which means she had to jump."

"Okay, she jumped. People jump overboard."

"But a jump like that, with that rope, would've practically decapitated her. The rope would rip right through the skin and tissue. When they pulled her up, her neck showed only minor bruising. She looks like somebody taking a nap."

"Raleigh…"

I knew that tone of voice. I heard it daily in Seattle, after I insisted a missing persons case didn't look right.

"Sir, I also found a piece of jewelry," I pressed on, trying to bolster my argument. "A bracelet, buried under another rope. Eight or ten stones, a total of about fifteen to twenty carats. And they don't look fake."

"She jumped, it fell off."

"Respectfully, sir?"

"Go on." He sighed.

"This suicide required the kind of planning that goes down to the last detail. If somebody prepares that much, how would they forget to take off a bracelet worth at least fifty grand? For that matter, why wear it at all?"

During the long pause that followed, the wind swept over my phone, the static sounding like a distant storm.

"Where's the ship?" McLeod finally asked.

This was what I liked about the guy: he always listened. Didn't always agree, but he trusted agent instincts.

"The ship turned around, thinking she was overboard. Now we're heading back to Ketchikan."

"We have no jurisdiction, Raleigh."

"Yes, sir. I realize that. One more thing?"

"What?"

"Her husband's Milo Carpenter."

"The movie star?"

"Yes, sir."

"Milo Carpenter—he's on your ship?"

"He's filming a movie. He plays an FBI agent." *Badly*, I wanted to add. *Very badly*. "And, well, here's the last thing. I'm onboard as a consultant."

"That's not a vacation, Raleigh."

"Yes, sir."

Another silence followed. "You need a vacation," he said.

I imagined McLeod, sitting in his glass booth of an office surrounded by the violent crimes squad. He would be wearing his standard white shirt and dark slacks, his red suspenders freckled with oily stains.

"Sir, I wouldn't be calling unless—"

"The cruise ship has no suspicions?"

"Suicide, no questions asked." I described for him how the body was pulled up before any substantial evidence could be collected. How Geert already called the cops, the funeral home, and labeled it a suicide before the autopsy was done. "The Alaska State Troopers are coming to close out the scene. No sirens. That was the order."

"Okay, we let the troopers handle it until later—"

"No, sir."

"What?"

"I'm sorry, we can't. The crime scene's compromised already, and I doubt the troopers will recognize the impossible physics of this thing. In addition to having no major damage to her neck and throat, she'd have to be an acrobat to climb down there with a rope. At night. On a ship. You see where I'm going? If the FBI doesn't pursue this, somebody gets away with murder."

"And you're willing to take it on?"

The rub.

"I might have a conflict of interest, given my consulting job with the deceased's husband. And, well, here's another thing."

"You just said you told me the last thing."

"The dead woman hired my aunt to do some consulting on the movie as well."

Judy Carpenter, I explained, wanted my aunt to teach the movie crew about the healing powers of rocks. That part I didn't want to explain to McLeod. To anybody.

"Sir, you know I'd take it, but given the circumstances…"

"Another way to look at this is, you've got an inside line."

"Yes, sir. But could you contact the Alaska office, ask them to take it?"

"Because it's you, Raleigh, I will. You've extinguished yourself before."

Along with food freckling his suspenders, McLeod dropped malaprops whenever he opened his mouth. I had neither the bad manners nor the courage to correct him and simply inserted the right word in my mind. Here, I replaced "extinguished" with "distinguished."

"Thank you, sir."

"I'll see if they can send an agent on board. Then you can go back to your version of a vacation. In the meantime, stick close to this until you hear back from me. Maintain procedure as much as possible. Talk to the husband. His statement might not be admissible later but it'll help whichever agent gets assigned to the case." He paused. "What's he like?"

"Sir?"

"Milo Carpenter."

"He's a drunk."

"I'll tell my wife," he said. "She sees that guy in a movie or on some magazine and she's tinkled pink."

I did the substitutions—"tickled" for "tinkled"—then thanked him for listening. It was more than my boss in Richmond would have done.

"You're welcome," McLeod said. "I'll call as soon as we hear back from the Alaska office."

As I walked back along the steel rail, tasting the salt that rose from the ocean, I could see Geert and his bald pate reddening in the sun. He stood over the tarp-covered body like a man guarding a good parking space.

"You called the FBI?" he said.

I nodded, not surprised by his question. Cruise ships hired the best security money could buy. As he said himself, this wasn't his first trip through the tunnel of love. But as we stood there with her body between us, I sensed borders forming, the boundaries that divided our disputed territories. I wanted truth. Geert wanted protection—protection of the ship's reputation.

"While you called your people, I hunted down the husband," he said, as if his choice trumped mine.

Led by two Ninjas, the movie star passed though the human security line. Every head swiveled to follow him, until Geert gave one quick shake of his head. The tall Ninja pivoted and turned to the crew. The employees whipped back around, facing the deck's public area.

Milo, meanwhile, was staggering toward us. Like most

movie stars, he seemed smaller in person, even with his six feet of height. There was something compact about him, so that the broad shoulders seemed out of proportion with his narrow chest and slender hips. His face was rough-hewn, ruddy from booze. His strongest feature was bright green eyes. They were glazed this morning. They'd been that way since we left Seattle. But the varnish looked different now. Perhaps from shock.

Perhaps not.

Geert said, "I am sorry."

Slowly the Dutchman leaned down, pinching the edge of the tarp. "It will seem rude, but I must ask."

He paused, seeking permission.

Milo nodded.

Geert pulled the plastic all the way back. "Is this your wife?"

The actor seemed frozen. When he finally moved, his feet were leaden, moving closer to the body, walking like a man condemned. His green eyes once again found Geert, but they seemed dull, unable to see.

"I felt the boat turning around," he said, wooden. "I thought you found her. On board. Not…" The words trailed away as he stared down at the noose still around her neck.

Geert waited. "I am sorry, Mr. Carpenter."

Milo's eyes shifted. They went first to the steel half wall, then the mooring line. He followed the thick rope from where it wrapped around the steel pole, to the orange rope that snaked around her pale throat and the strand of purple bruises. Her fatal necklace.

And then suddenly his face fractured. It broke with pain and revulsion and fear.

Plenty of fear.

Geert quietly offered some abbreviated details. Coast Guard called, found hanging, clearly a suicide. Silently I begged him to stop talking. But it was not the FBI's investigation.

Not yet.

When a commotion broke over at the security line, we turned to see a stout man trying to break through. The man began yelling.

"Sandy…" Milo said in a weak voice.

Sandy Sparks, one of the film's producers. My aunt introduced him the first day, making sure I understood that Mr. Sparks helped pay for our tickets, for our consulting services.

"Would you like him to come over?"

The movie star nodded.

Geert flicked his eyes at a Ninja who gave a hand signal. The human barrier immediately parted.

"Did she—" Milo swallowed, his Adam's apple bobbing. "Did she suffer?"

Rather than answer, Geert watched the pudgy man. Short arms pumping, he approached us as if running, though he looked like someone who had never run anywhere, ever.

"Did she suffer?" Milo repeated.

Geert continued to pretend he couldn't hear him.

I cleared my throat. "Mr. Carpenter, was your wife depressed?"

He turned, recognizing me. Then he looked confused. "Why are you here?"

"I'm with the FBI."

"But you're—you're with us." He pointed to his chest, implying the movie production. Then he turned to Geert. "Why do you need the FBI here?"

"She was on the ship," Geert replied, in a tone that said I was some unwanted accessory, free of charge, like an extra ashtray in a new car.

"I'm very sorry for your loss," I continued. "Was she upset about something, depressed in any way?"

His broad shoulders hunched. He gave a small nod.

"Did she give any indication she might do something like this?"

The green eyes flashed like emeralds. "If she had, you think I'd let her come on this ship?"

Geert twirled the mustache. *Stupid question.*

But I had another one. "Did she have any knowledge of knots?"

"Knots?" Carpenter said, even more confused. But then his eyes dropped to the orange line and I watched the successive layers of comprehension explode inside his mind, detonating with the well-tied knots. When he looked up at me, the veneer was shattered.

The pudgy man arrived, crying out his name. "Milo! Milo!"

The actor was too tall, his shoulders too wide, for the shorter man to grab, but Sandy Sparks reached up anyway. It was an awkward hug. Milo looked like an overgrown boy craving parental comfort.

"Sandy," Milo said. Tears were coming now. Tears whose absence had me wondering. "Sandy—Judy is dead."

"I heard. I'm sorry, Milo. I'm sorry."

"She hung herself, Sandy!" He pointed to the tarp that Geert had once again pulled over her body.

The chubby man nodded, gazing at the lumpy shape. Then he glanced at Geert. "He saw her?" he asked.

Geert nodded, grimly. "I wanted her identified here. He tries to go to the funeral home, the lookie-looks will take photos."

Sparks looked around, suddenly assessing the risks. He stared at the human barrier. "Wow, thank you."

"Most welcome." Geert nodded. "We are here to help."

Sparks turned to Milo. "I know this is bad, man, but you need to get out of here. If anybody takes a picture, it's the cover of the *Enquirer*. And that rag has enough pictures of you."

Milo straightened.

"You hear what I'm saying?"

Milo wiped his face, as if pulling himself together, then allowed Sparks to lead him away while Geert signaled to the tall Ninja who was hovering near us, ever silent.

"Escort Mr. Carpenter back to his room," Geert said. "Keep them on the back stairs."

I started to say something.

But he glanced over, cutting me off.

"And guard his cabin door," he told the Ninja. "Just in case."

FOUR

Luck doesn't exist.

Scientifically, that theorem wasn't provable but I've believed it since I was a little girl. Now, heading down the ship's gangway to the Ketchikan dock, I had no reason to change my mind. Behind me, the mortician guided the metal cart loaded with Judy Carpenter's body, and I kept my hands in back, helping with the weight on the slanted ramp. Geert had assured us that all tour-taking passengers were gone—including my mother and my aunt—but as "luck" would have it, my mother stood at the bottom of the gangway.

There was one person who shouldn't see this corpse, and it was my mother.

My sense of dread turned to stone.

Head down, she searched frantically through an oversize handbag, and for one split second I considered reversing direction, turning around and pushing the mortician and the dead woman back into the ship. Hide out until the coast was clear.

But his cart clattered like twenty tin soldiers coming apart, and when she looked up at the noise, I let go of the handle behind my back.

"Hey—!" the mortician said.

Her already troubled eyes filled with questions. Questions I couldn't answer truthfully.

"Raleigh Ann?" She leaned to one side, trying to see around me. On the cart the black body bag looked ominous with bulk. Almost as bulky as the mortician. He was clad in black fleece, resembling an overfed polyester lamb.

Her purse hit the ground.

"Oh my word!" she exclaimed. "Did somebody *die*?"

I turned, feigning surprise at the man and the cart.

The mortician was scowling, and now that I'd let go, he was straining to hold the cart against the gangway's descent.

"You gonna help me?" he demanded. No longer lamblike, he puffed, an ornery bull.

I pressed a shaking hand against my beating heart. "Me? You want *me* to help you?"

"You said—"

"Did somebody die?" My mother's voice was trembling.

Nadine Shaw Harmon, authentic Southern belle, might be politely described as "a bit touched." Her bouts of paranoia struck with the sudden fury of August thunderstorms, and the torrential aftermaths kept me from telling her the truth about my job. Before becoming an agent, I spent four years in the FBI's forensic lab, and both my dad and I agreed she didn't need to know everything. My forensics work was in mineralogy; we told her I was a geologist. That was true. True enough. But one day somebody decided to shoot my dad, cutting him down in cold blood. His murder has never been solved, and I decided the most productive way to fill this gaping hole in my heart was to join the hunt for bad guys. When I graduated from Quantico, fatherless, with no mother in attendance, my personal life became one long covert op.

Taking in the horrified expression on my mother's face, I stepped aside and allowed the portly mortician to clatter past us with the dead body. He grumbled as he passed, and I geared up for my first whopper of this vacation.

"I have no idea what that's about." Quickly I changed the subject. "Aren't you supposed to be sightseeing today?"

But her jasper-hued eyes remained on the mortician. He pushed the rattling conveyance across the conglomerate pavement that formed the ship's dock. The rough pebbly surface made his progress sound like a train of broken-down shopping carts. At a black Suburban that was coated with winter dirt, he snapped open the back barn doors as if the handles were hot. Taking hold of the cart again, he rammed it against the vehicle's dented chrome bumper. Its legs buckled, sending the entire contraption flying into a dark space gutted for transporting passengers who would never complain.

"And on a vacation too," my mother said sadly.

The mortician slammed the doors and whisked his pudgy palms across one another, finishing off the job.

"Wasn't there a trip to Misty Fjords today?" I asked.

Her skin was like Carrara marble, and when she closed her eyes, bowing her head, she looked like an angel. In her sweet Southern voice she began praying, calling out to heaven with heartfelt pleas. Though I closed my eyes with her, I couldn't help listening to the Suburban's rumbling muffler, or how it harmonized with the tour bus convoy pulling away from the dock. I opened one eye and saw that a single bus remained. Closing my eyes again, I tried to concentrate on the words seeded by Scripture, watered with Dixie, and rising to their intended destination in a voice that trembled.

But another voice intruded.

"Hey, what're you guys doing?"

Claire, the self-professed clairvoyant, walked toward us wearing a bright-yellow raincoat, despite persistent sunshine. Her spiked hair was ashen, like asbestos, and although she claimed to see into the future, my experience had been that she barely stumbled through the present.

Claire hooked a thumb at my mother, then whispered, "What's she doing?"

"Nothing you'd be interested in." I glanced at the Suburban. The mortician glowered, waiting. I suddenly wondered what Claire and my aunt would say when they discovered Judy Carpenter was dead.

"Is she okay?" Claire whispered, narrowing her already beady eyes.

"She's fine."

"Okay, then tell her to wrap it up. The bus is waiting."

This was my sister's fault. My sister Helen was supposed to come on the cruise. But at the last minute she claimed work would keep her in Richmond. My aunt gave the ticket to Claire, and I added another entry to my long list of Helen's infractions.

"Amen," my mother said.

She looked calmer, marginally, and I guided her gently toward the last remaining tour bus, now belching diesel fumes at the curb.

"Take plenty of pictures," I told her. "I hear those fjords are beautiful."

"Why aren't you coming?" she asked.

"Hiking, remember?" Except now it was a lie. Another lie. "I told you. Deer Mountain Trail."

"DeMott said to make sure—"

"Yes, I know, don't worry. I'm going with a group."

Lie number two. Or three.

Suddenly the mortician honked his horn. My mother jumped. I looked over. He was staring out his window with an expression that said his best friend was the grim reaper.

"Why is that man staring at us?" my mother asked.

Because I asked him for a ride to the funeral home.

"He must be waiting for somebody." Three lies, in less than a minute. A new record.

Claire trundled beside us. "Did that guy just roll a body bag down the gangplank?"

"Gangway," I said.

"But I saw him. He shoved a body into that car, right? Last night I had a dream somebody died. I woke up this morning, knowing it would come true."

"What?!" my mother cried.

"Nadine, I can see into the future. Especially when it comes to death."

"Don't you need to get somewhere?" I gave Claire a frigid smile.

"What d'ya think I came over for? Charlotte's saving seats on the bus but some guy just whacked her with his cane. Your mother's holding up our whole tour."

"Oh, I'm so sorry." My mother hurried, following Claire through the gray clouds of exhaust. Like people passing through a veil, all I could see was the yellow raincoat and my mom's new pink tennis shoes. She was accustomed to high heels that pitched her forward like a ski jumper, and the tennis shoes gave her a flat-footed walk. When she climbed aboard the bus, she glanced back.

My smile was ready, waiting. I waved.

Once they were inside, I glanced back at the mortician, giving him a signal that it would just take one moment more.

But the bus didn't leave.

Walking up and down the middle aisle, a tour guide handed out papers. As the moments stretched on, I unclipped my cell phone and tapped out the cell number Geert gave me, in case I had any more "stupid questions."

Here was one: "What's the mortician's cell number?" I asked.

"He is with you," Geert said.

"I need to call him."

An incriminating silence followed and I walked to the

edge of the pier. The harbor smelled of kelp, and calciferous barnacles clung to the wooden pylons. Water lapped against the pier, and I memorized the ten digits Geert offered, beginning with area code 907.

I dialed the number. The Suburban's window slid down and the mortician's round face peered out.

"You can't just walk over here?" he said into the phone.

The bus still hadn't moved. And any moment some idea could pitch its tent inside my mother's paranoid mind, prompting more terrified questions.

"I'll meet you at the funeral home," I said. "Is it far?"

I heard a low guttural sound in the phone.

"You're in Ketchikan," the mortician said. "Nothing's far."

Downtown Ketchikan looked as if organized landslides laid out the streets. On the mountain's upper levels, wood-frame houses notched the mountainside while a commercial district descended in waves along winding and narrow streets that eventually dropped to a final row of storefronts hanging over the ocean on piers.

Hurrying down Front Street, I followed the mortician's directions. On my right, Deer Mountain loomed three thousand feet above town. I still had my rock hammer in my backpack, hoping to sample some local geology, and the mountain's patient beauty seemed to mock my sudden change in plans. At Mission Street, I looked for St. John's Episcopal, remembering it because it had the same name as my parents' church back in Richmond. The resemblance stopped there. Even with the bright June sun shining on the lap siding, the building looked soggy. The graying boards testified to America's heaviest annual rainfall, precipitation that was measured in feet, not inches, per year. Ten to twelve feet, on average. The other difference? A totem pole across the street.

From Mission, I crossed a footbridge that became Creek

Street. Water from the mountain rushed under the creosote-soaked boardwalk, pummeling the dark granite boulders and sending up a spray of mist that the morning sun turned into faint rainbows. Trotting across the boards, my steps sounded hollow. I passed a pretty Native girl standing in the doorway of a nineteenth-century wooden building. Her sequined dress didn't quite reach her dimpled knees and the sound of rushing water drowned out her greeting. Back in the early 1900s, this boulevard was Ketchikan's infamous Red Light District. The "houses of ill repute" had maintained a steady stream of miners and lumberjacks and merchants who got rich selling picks and shovels to fortune seekers. And now, in the era of Internet porn and MTV, a historic whorehouse seemed quaint.

The mortuary sat at the end of the boardwalk. An old wood-frame building painted a muddy-yellow agate was tucked so tightly against the mountainside that the upper floor had doors to different roads, matching up with the switchbacks carved into the mountainside. Under the second story eaves, the Suburban's dented bumper was backed up to wide doors.

A bell rang when I opened the door on the first floor. I smelled the unmistakable odor—Eau de Funeral Home. They all smelled like this, like rose petals marinating in formaldehyde. But the receptionist was something different. Green tie-dye shirt. Long white hair cascading over bony shoulders.

She lowered the paperback she was reading—a murder mystery.

I introduced myself.

She smiled wickedly. "He's dying to see you."

Before I could reply—if I could reply—she leaned back and threw her voice at the ceiling. "Bobby! She's here about the body!"

His reply was two stomps. The pendant light shimmered with dust.

"Go right up." She picked up her book.

The stairs were narrow, beveled from wear, and I could see why the body was unloaded upstairs. The mortician waited at the second-floor landing, tying a rubber apron around his substantial girth. It was green. A plastic face shield was lifted to his sweating forehead. I changed my mind. Not a lamb. A crocodile.

"What'd I tell you?" he said. "Nothing's far in this stinkin' town."

He lumbered down a paneled hallway, passing a room to our left that displayed caskets. Stacked three high along the wall, one was propped open in the room's middle to display the benefits of eternal satin rest. The mortician shoved open a set of hinged double doors on our right, letting the flaps swing back on me.

On a stainless steel table, the black body bag lay with thick nylon straps running under its lumpy contours. The straps were connected to a metal pulley system secured to an exposed I-beam on the ceiling. This, I presumed, was how he worked alone. Rolling carts, straps, pulleys. Even after rigor mortis set in, he could move a body by himself. Above a stainless steel sink hung a small certificate, a state license to embalm, while another document beside it gave him permission to perform autopsies. The stainless steel counter, four feet at best, displayed his tools. Clamps. Hooks. Scalpels. Nothing fancy. Once somebody died, finesse was wasted effort. Not that this particular mortician was concerned with finesse, ever.

"If you're planning to stay for the show," he said, "I gotta get permission from the family. State law."

"No, thank you, I don't need to observe the autopsy," I said. For one, my presence would trigger suspicion in Milo Carpenter and I wanted the actor completely unprepared for any upcoming interviews. "I'm interested primarily in cause of death. You heard how she was found?"

"Yeah," he said. "Finally something different."

"Pardon?"

"The cruise ships send me newlyweds and nearly-deads. I get honeymooners who got drunk and fell overboard, or old folks who screwed up their medications for the last time. Sometimes a heart attack, since everybody wants to see Alaska before they kick the bucket. You might've noticed?"

"Noticed what?"

"Most of these passengers are one foot in the grave."

I had noticed a certain demographic. At thirty, I was among our ship's youngest passengers.

"Do you have much experience with suicides?" I asked.

"Four this year."

"In Ketchikan?"

He walked over to the sink, checking out the scalpels. "Teenagers. Boys. They watch that YouTube video."

"What video?"

"The one that shows how to wrap a cord around the neck for a sexual thrill. Autoerotic asphyxiation. Cuts off the oxygen while they're masturbating." He picked up a knife. "Problem is, the point of no return doesn't take long, a minute or two and they pass out with the cord still around their neck. Last month I flew into a Native village. Place doesn't even have one paved road. But they get the Internet. They have computers. One kid, one belt, and YouTube. And he was dead."

"That's awful."

He shrugged and examined the scalpel's triangular blade, like a hostess checking the cutlery for water spots.

"Have you ever seen a jumper's body?" I asked.

"We don't get much jumping in Ketchikan. With all the rain, we're more head-in-the-gas-oven type people."

His smile was ghoulish and I suddenly wondered if I should stay for the autopsy. "Her body was hanging about twenty feet below the deck. There's no ladder down there."

"I got it, she jumped."

"Look carefully at her neck."

His dark eyes shifted to the body bag.

"The rope was thin nylon," I continued. "A jump from that height should've done major damage to the neck and throat. At the very least, the rope would've sliced into her windpipe."

"I hear she's famous."

"The husband's famous. Milo Carpenter, the actor."

He nodded, picking up his rubber gloves. "Sure you don't want to stay?"

I thought of Milo's face from this morning, when we stood near the body. He showed fear. But fear of what, discovery? If he knew I suspected something, he'd probably lawyer-up. After that we'd learn nothing. "No, thank you. How long will your exam take?"

"Depends."

"On?"

"On what I see," he said. "Go wait in the chapel."

Another set of narrow stairs led to the third-floor chapel. The narthex had a front door that opened to a mountain road curved like an S and I tried to imagine how this worked. The bereaved came in on the first floor, the dead were embalmed on the second floor, and all of them were driven up the mountain in order to walk into the chapel on the third floor.

And it got weirder inside the chapel, whose entry was a pair of louvered pine panels, like saloon doors from a western movie. The sunlight that streamed through amber stained glass windows barely illuminated the room. Everywhere was dark wood, almost black. The floor, the wall, the peaked ceiling. And the straight-backed pews, rows of dark wood, resembled open coffins. Above them, tarnished brass sconces held white candles gummed with dust.

This place felt haunted.

I was turning to leave when my cell phone rang.

Allen McLeod. Calling from Seattle.

"The Alaska office wants us to take it," he said.

I dropped into a pew. "May I ask why?"

"Nobody's available. It's that simple. Our closest office is Juneau, and that's just a resident agency with two guys covering all of southeastern Alaska. They're both working urgent cases. And Anchorage can't spare anybody either. So if this thing turns into a case, Raleigh, it's yours."

Resident agencies were FBI outposts in the hinterlands, where agents handled everything from mail delivery to mail fraud to murder.

"They don't have anybody?" I asked.

"The SAC"—Special Agent in Charge—"pointed out that you're already on the ship. Plus it left from Seattle, and it'll return here too. Technically, he can make the argument that the case would belong to this office."

I could smell dust in the chapel air and the acidic scent of old stained wood. When I didn't reply, McLeod said, "Look on the bright side, Raleigh. Maybe she killed herself. Anything from the coroner?"

I told him what Geert explained to me: Nautical law dictated that a cruise ship go to the first port with a funeral home. In this case, Ketchikan. If the death was deemed suspicious, the body went to that state's medical examiner. In Alaska, that meant Anchorage. "I'm waiting to hear if the mortician agrees this looks suspicious."

"Okay, if it's not suspicious," McLeod said brightly, "you can go back to your vacation."

Dread buckled down on my neck. "Yes, sir."

"I see you've still got that 'sir' habit."

"I'm sorry, I'm—"

"From the South, I know. But whenever you call me 'sir,' I feel like a country pumpkin.".

Mentally inserting "bumpkin" for "pumpkin," I promised to call when the mortician finished the examination.

Closing the phone, I walked down the chapel's middle aisle, fingering dust on the candles, taking in the place's muted amber glow. And I tried to kick self-pity to the curb. My last vacation was six years ago, the summer before my father was murdered. We went rock hunting in North Carolina, searching Pressley Mine for sapphires. Now here was Alaska, every geologist's dream, and I was stuck in some funeral home lifted from the Twilight Zone, awaiting a verdict whose conclusion I already knew: her death *was* suspicious. The issue was jurisdiction: I had none.

Stepping through the translucent beams of dusty sunlight, I glanced at my watch. My heart tightened. I hated this feeling. This pity for myself. Willing myself not to check the time again, I stared at the cavernous pulpit. After several excruciating minutes, I sat down and picked up a hymnal from the bench. I fluttered the pages, feeling the soft, almost slippery pages. They had the atmospheric damp of books stored in wet basements. After several more minutes, I grabbed the Bible next to it, impatiently fluttering again until I saw the words. They had no phonetic resemblance to English. I flipped to the front and saw that it was a translation into Tlingit, the local Native language. The book of John read, *Dikée Ankáwoo doo Yéet dàt John-ch kawshixidee Yoox'utúnk.* Searching for other passages, I found a small scrap of paper in the book of Habakkuk. The crude handwriting flowed with divine wisdom.

Sometimes We gots to Wate, it said.

Not a bad summary of Habakkuk, I decided. And a fair comment on my own circumstances. But self-pity told me

I'd been waiting forever. Waiting for my mother to get well. Waiting for justice for my father. Waiting for love.

I shook off the next thought—did I really love DeMott, or did I love the idea of settling down?

The saloon doors swung open and dust motes exploded through the amber sunlight. The mortician strode down the aisle wearing rubber boots and his apron. The doors squeaked back and forth behind him, making him seem like some demented gunslinger.

"She had a face-lift," he said, as though uncovering the real crime. "I found scars behind her ears. It wasn't a bad lift. Somebody also cauterized the capillaries around her eyes, you know, lasering off her bags."

To emphasize his findings, he pointed to the shiny pouches beneath his own eyes. Avaricious eyes.

"So we can rule out the idea she killed herself over wrinkles."

"How do you know she didn't lower herself down there? She could've hung there until it was lights-out."

"Climbing down there would require superhuman upper-body strength. And she's not a small woman."

"One hundred seventy-two pounds."

"At night, on the open sea."

He wagged his head, as if still not ready to concede suicide. "Stick your head in some rope, hang a minute, you're about done. That's what those teenagers don't realize, going for the cheap sex thrill. Not that there's another kind in Ketchikan."

"What about her neck?" I said, trying again. "How much damage did you see?"

"Not much," he agreed.

"That doesn't strike you as suspicious?"

"But I'm supposed to say if it's possible she killed herself. The answer is, yeah, it's possible."

"Possible is not the same as likely." I felt my temper rising. The man was both morbid and obstinate. "And it isn't probable either. What I'm asking is, after what you saw, is it *probable* she killed herself?"

"I don't want to be in the middle of this."

"The middle of what? She's dead."

"But famous."

"The *husband's* famous," I clarified, hoping to encourage his spine.

"Okay, whatever. It means they'll run something about it on television, one of those shows about celebrity deaths. And they'll make me look like an idiot, some hick mortician in Ketchikan. What do you think people do around here when it rains all year? They watch TV. I'll be the biggest joke in town."

I restrained the urge to tell him he probably was already. "You're saying the exam was inconclusive?"

"No. I'm saying I got second thoughts. Let the medical examiner in Anchorage go on the line. Let him deal with the reporters." He pointed to the floor. "I just put her in a shipping container. If the weather holds, a plane can get her out today."

On the one hand, I agreed with his decision; I'd rather have an ME's ruling. But the greatest enemy for solving any crime was time. And this invertebrate was wasting time, all but admitting Judy Carpenter's death was highly suspicious—but he didn't want the responsibility of saying it. He would still collect his pickup fee from the cruise line, and I suspected he might call the *Enquirer* later, to find out how much they paid for an anonymous description of her cosmetic surgery.

"How long does that take, sending the body to the MEA?"

"A day to fly it up there, then it goes to the morgue. A real morgue, like what you got in the lower forty-eight."

Five days remained on the cruise. Five days to figure out what happened to this woman and who did it. But with the body transport, it left four days. Two thousand passengers, and a husband who was an actor. A man paid to pretend.

"Once her body gets to the medical examiner, how long then?"

"Then it's get in line." He shrugged. "All those tourists want to see Alaska before they die, so the morgue's a busy place."

I jogged down Creek Street's creosote timbers, darting around tourists who carried bulging plastic bags filled with souvenir hats and shirts. When I reached Mission Street, I slowed to a walk, then stopped at Whale Park and called McLeod. I told him about the body being shipped to the ME in Anchorage.

"So her death is suspicious," he said.

"Not officially."

"What's that mean?"

"It means the mortician is a coward. He won't come right out and say it's suspicious. And I don't expect anyone from the cruise line to disagree. Murder doesn't exactly make you want to get on board the ship."

"Neither do suicides," McLeod pointed out.

"Except suicide isn't seen as the ship's fault."

"Good point. What about next of kin?"

"No children." This was something I'd asked Geert. And it *wasn't* a stupid question.

"Did you get to talk to him?"

"Carpenter? I asked if she'd been depressed." I described the rest of this morning's scene—Carpenter staggering to the body, showing shock and sadness, comforted by Sandy Sparks, the producer, then being whisked away so photographs wouldn't show up in the tabloids. "His reaction wasn't what I'd expect from a man whose wife was just found dead."

"So right now, the only person who thinks she was murdered is you?"

I stared at the mountains. Steep forests layered their sides. Ocean water curled like liquid mercury around their feet. McLeod sighed. A man of prodigious sighs, his lungs moved air like ancient leather bellows.

"Sir, I'd like nothing more than to tell you this woman ended her own life. But facts say otherwise. A killer is on that ship and if we don't find him, he walks away a free man." I stopped, afraid my voice sounded strident.

"Don't ever change, Raleigh." The air bellowed again. "It's good you're like this. Good for us. Not so good for you."

"It's fine, sir."

"That's what you always say. But I want to send you some help on this."

I felt the weight lift from my shoulders, the tension in my neck easing. "Thank you, sir. I'd appreciate some help."

"Great. Jack can be there by this afternoon."

"What—pardon? Jack?"

"I sent out a squad e-mail after the Alaska office passed. Said it was a free cruise to Alaska, which it sort of is. Jack was the first to reply. His plane's ready to go."

I felt sick. "Plane?"

"He's a Bureau pilot. Didn't you know? Keeps his own plane."

What I knew about Jack Stephanson was this: he was a complete jerk. During my disciplinary transfer to Seattle, Jack was assigned to help ease my transition into the new field office. Help the new kid. Instead he hazed, harassed, and mocked me, before finally admitting his initial goal was to flush me from the FBI. And if that wasn't enough, before I went back to Virginia, he'd had the gall to ask for a date.

"He needs to know when your ship leaves Ketchikan."

We leave in five minutes, I wanted to lie. *Don't bother sending him.*

Lifting my face to the sun, feeling the sting of self-pity in my eyes, the happy tourists flowed like a river around me. Across the street, on the totem pole, a raven perched and cawed with harsh laughter. I agreed it was quite the joke: my "help" was Jack Stephanson.

"Thank you for offering, sir, but on second thought, it's better if I handle this myself."

"Nonsense, Raleigh. You're looking a gilt horse in the mouth."

I had rules about lying. Really. In their way, they were strict rules. It was permissible to lie in order to protect my mother's mental health. Or if the Bureau sent me undercover. Otherwise lying still ranked with the other nine commandments.

But right now, the truth tasted as bad as Eau de Funeral Home.

"Six o'clock." I swallowed. "The ship leaves Ketchikan at six tonight."

"Plenty of time! Make sure their security knows Jack's coming on board. If they give you any grief, call me. A retired agent runs their corporate security."

I wanted to say something, but words refused to leave my mouth.

McLeod continued, "Jack says meet him at the marina. You know where that is?"

I stared at the marina. The wooden masts and towering fishing vessels rocked softly along the base of Deer Mountain.

"I can find it," I told him.

"You can always count on my help, Raleigh," he said. "I'll never leave you up a creek without a saddle."

FIVE

At the cruise ship gangway, the big bald Dutchman waited with one hand stretched out.

Making sure nobody could see, I reached into my back-pack and surrendered my Glock 22, pushing away the vulnerability that always swept over me whenever I wasn't armed.

"The undertaker called," Geert said, walking up the plank with my weapon concealed in a nylon pouch.

I figured the mortician probably started tattling before I was halfway down Creek Street. Shrugging off my backpack, I followed Geert to the security arches. He stepped around them while I scanned my room's keycard in a computer by the entrance, then sent my pack through the X-ray machine. I waited for the inevitable query about my rock hammer, which Geert vouched for—one of his abrupt nods that nobody questioned. He and I proceeded across the atrium where a chamber quartet played Vivaldi for people who stayed on board, their reasons completely beyond my comprehension.

"The mortician says—"

"In my office." He suddenly broke into one of those large smiles never intended for me and stopped to chat with an elderly couple. To the strains of "Spring," they asked him about the ship's turnaround this morning. Geert glossed over the details and I stared at the floor. It was stone, red stone. Rouge

Royal, I decided. The distinctive limestone from Belgium, threaded with white veins. Almost as hard as Geert.

"Hope to see you tonight." He waved to the couple and started walking again, assuming I'd follow. An obedient puppy.

We took a sharp right from the atrium and cut through the casino. The place was empty. But the acrid odor of cigarettes seeped from the green felt poker tables and the carpeting patterned with tumbling dice. We came out the casino's other side to a dark hallway with padded blue walls.

Geert took a small remote from his front pocket, pressed a button, and a section of the padded wall swiveled open.

I counted four rooms inside the hidden chamber, each empty. Geert's office was at the far end. A porthole above his desk framed a bright circle of reflected light, shifting with the play of water. He stepped to the interior wall, opened a wooden cabinet, and spun the dial on his safe, shifting his large body to block my view. I gazed out the porthole, preparing myself for another conversation that would sound like clomping wooden clogs. When the safe popped open, he deposited my gun inside, slammed the door shut, and gave the dial another spin.

In his thick accent he said, "The mortician did not say suicide."

"The mortician wants a second opinion," I clarified. "Obviously something was suspicious or he'd just say she killed herself."

"What's so suspicious?"

"The bracelet, for instance."

I was certain this was a test. His long background in law enforcement surely gave him radar. And this morning's scene must have triggered one or two signals. When he turned toward the porthole, his Dutch-blue eyes seemed translucent.

He twirled the handlebar mustache. "Now we got real problems."

"Because it's murder?"

"Because you want to stir up our guests. You can't run around talking about murder. People pay money for this trip. Lots of money. Right now, the woman is a suicide. Caw-lee-for-knee-ya suicide. Everyone believes it but you."

"And you."

His eyes gaped. "I said no thing like that."

"You don't have to." I wanted to point out the neck bruises but didn't know this man's full motives. Maybe he wanted to cover this up. Maybe somebody paid him to cover it up. "With your esteemed background in law enforcement, you can't be comfortable with how well preserved she looked."

He gave a Netherlandish shrug. "We get all kinds on ships."

"Including murderers."

"Who sees a murderer? I see happy people, all over."

"Happy on the outside. But inside, somebody's a monster."

"You say."

"Yes, and I'd like to see the complete passenger list. Along with the crew list."

"Crew?" The blue eyes widened.

"I'm going to run background checks."

"What, you think I hire them from calling their mommy? I check backgrounds. Nobody works this ship unless they are clean like whistles."

"Then the passenger list. Please."

"You don't talk to nobody before you talk to me."

I hesitated, then lifted my head arrogantly. "I'm bringing aboard another FBI agent."

I said this with as much haughtiness and bravado as possible. My hope was the tone would tick him off, along with somebody of no authority giving him an order. Then he would deny Jack coming on board.

But luck doesn't exist.

Picking up his desk phone, Geert stabbed ten numbers and spoke to somebody by the first name of Candice. He slathered on the charm and I learned that Candice's son in the military was doing fine; the weather in Florida was great; and Geert was taking her for a drink next time he was in Orlando. I gazed out the porthole until he asked Candice if there were any empty cabins.

He glanced up, speaking to me like an interrogator. "What is the name of this person?"

Satan.

"Jack Stephanson," I said.

He thanked Candice, then hung up.

"Nice cabin. Ocean view with a patio. Living room, the whole thing."

Sure. Jack gets the suite. Meanwhile I was practically in steerage.

"You know what would be nice," I said, feeling a sinister hope. "If you could find some poor deserving people and give them the deluxe cabin. The agent could take their cabin."

"Yah, what I'm doing. The agent will be next door to you."

I suppressed a sob.

"What is wrong?" he asked.

"Nothing. Do you still have that bracelet?"

"Stupid question. It is in the safe."

"May I borrow it?"

The white eyebrows avalanched into a frown.

"I noticed that you didn't show it to the husband."

"I am waiting," he said.

"For what?"

"For when he is not drunk."

"That might take awhile," I said. "May I show it to him, to see his reaction? I can bring it right back."

He thought about it before swiveling toward the safe and

once again opening it. He handed me a clear plastic bag. An evidence bag. Which told me he did have suspicions.

Even in the mundane bag, the blue gems glittered, luscious with wealth. *Sapphires or tanzanite?* I wondered again.

"You know where he is?" Geert asked.

"Carpenter? No."

"He is in the Sky Bar," Geert said. "And he is drunk."

The Sky Bar perched over the ship's aft with a space-age design full of sleek picture windows and skylights. Even parts of the floor were Plexiglas, and as I walked over to the movie star hunched over his drink at the bar, the view of the ocean below inflicted mild vertigo. Since we left Seattle, Milo Carpenter had worn sunglasses, even indoors. Here, it made sense. So much white light flooded the place everything looked like an overexposed photograph.

I took a stool beside him. The famous firm jaw was whiskered gray and brown, his skin slack. Shock did that. Lack of sleep. Too much alcohol.

Or the strain from covering up your wife's murder.

The bartender kept silent watch over his lone patron, washing and wiping glasses. The brass name tag on his uniform said "Corey, The Philippines."

"You're open, right?" I said.

"Yes, we are closed," Corey said.

I looked at Milo. No reaction. "I'm with him," I said.

The actor looked up. His dark Wayfarers were like black panels over his eyes. His forehead suddenly wrinkled with curiosity. During my two days consulting on the movie, I'd noticed curiosity never lasted long.

He went back to his drink.

"What you like?" Corey asked me.

"Coca-Cola, please. With ice cubes, no crushed ice."

"Yes, crushed ice."

"Yes. Cubes."

Milo bent his elbows on the bar, guarding three fingers of bourbon. The bartender walked away and I no longer cared what was in my Coke.

"You doing all right," I asked Milo, "considering what happened?"

He smiled. A perfect smile. Teeth like a Steinway.

"Here, you can have this." He grabbed a pen beside his tab, then picked up the white coaster Corey set down for my Coke. Scrawling his name on the cardboard, he offered it to me. "Auction my autograph on eBay, you'll make good money."

The *M* looked like a ragged mountain range. The *C* was an *O* with the middle bitten out.

"I wanted to talk to you about this morning." I placed the coaster back on the bar. "Can we go somewhere private?"

"Talk, like, an FBI agent?" The perfect smile disappeared.

"Right." I nodded. "Not for the movie."

The bartender turned discreetly and puttered toward a back sink. Milo stared at the man's back, then unsaddled himself from the bar stool, slowly making his way across the room. The tables and chairs were more clear plastic. Looking through them, the objects on the other side looked bent and melted. Like being trapped inside a Salvador Dalí painting.

"I'm sorry about your wife." I took a seat at the Plexiglas table that made our feet below look like clown shoes. "She seemed like a nice woman."

"My wife was the greatest." His voice sounded tired, croaky. "There was nobody greater."

Judy Carpenter had stayed behind the cameras on the movie set. Milo was the center of attention. Good and bad attention. From what I'd seen, he stayed so inebriated that even the simplest scenes required ten or fifteen takes. The movie didn't need an FBI consultant; it needed a Betty Ford counselor.

"How long were you married?"

"Twenty-two years." He shook his head. "The greatest woman, ever."

"Twenty-two years is quite an accomplishment."

"In Hollywood that's an eternity."

"Was it a happy marriage?"

He stared at his drink. The sunglasses had slipped down the bridge of his nose. A good nose. Not too small. Not too big. Maybe even real. He pushed the sunglasses back up before looking at me.

"I'll start from the beginning, so you get the clear picture," he said, with a trace of hostility. "I was a skinny unemployed actor and she—" He laughed. It turned into a sob. I waited. "She was sewing costumes for ice-skaters. Ice-skaters! Whatever money she made, she spent on sending me to auditions. She never gave up, never stopped believing. She—" He caught another sob, drinking through it. The ice clicked on his perfect teeth.

"So she's been with you the whole way."

"You have no idea. What we went through… My first jobs went straight to video. No character development. They never gave me time to figure out who I was playing."

During my time giving him advice on FBI procedures— most of which he ignored—I noticed that every conversation came back to him. It wasn't really a surprise. Acting was a narcissistic profession. From what I'd seen, Milo Carpenter was born for it.

"Then I got this one character," he continued. "I really dug him. I knew I could nail his personality. I knew it. But those low-budget jerks, they just wouldn't give me the chance. I came home from the set one night feeling really low. I was ready to quit, go back to moving furniture. You know what Judy did?"

I shook my head.

"She made me a giant fat suit." His gleaming smile reappeared.

"That was thoughtful," I said, for something to say.

"No, see, my character was a burglar but he was too fat to get through any windows or doors. Comedy, get it?"

"Yes. Of course. Comedy."

"But that production was too cheap to let me take the fat suit home. I wanted to really get into the character. But they were afraid I'd rip it or something. So Judy made me one. Every night I could walk around our dumpy apartment in West Hollywood and stay in character. And she didn't spend one dime on it—that's how good she was. She took this foam thing off our bed and cut it up. Then she used the scraps from those ice-skater costumes. When the reviews came out, every single one said I was the best thing in a bad movie. *That* was my break." He looked into the drink again, then downed the rest of it. "That's all you need to know about my wife. The woman was a real saint."

"Did the saint happen to leave a suicide note?"

He froze.

I wasn't his buddy. I wasn't interested in his charm. And somebody killed his wife.

After a moment, he shook his head, indicating she left no note, and I pulled the plastic bag from my pocket. With the room's intense illumination, the blue gems glowed like tiny gas flames. Hypnotic pilot-light jewels. "Did this bracelet belong to your wife?"

He pulled the sunglasses off his face. The famous green eyes were bloodshot, bagged with dark circles. "Where did you find that?"

"Did it belong to your wife?"

"You found that on her?"

I left the bag on the table. Light poured into the facets. But the colors kept shifting from light blue to navy to that fierce

violet hue. I'd seen sapphires do something like that, but
only really nice ones. Amethyst could also color-shift, despite
its classification as only a semiprecious stone. But maybe
the idea of amethyst came from the sharp scent on the actor's breath. The ancient Greeks named the purple stone *am-
ethustos*, meaning "not intoxicated." Believing violet quartz
protected against drunkenness, the Greeks even made their
drinking vessels out of amethyst.

Milo Carpenter grabbed the bag and started to tear open
the taped seal.

"Don't open it," I said.

"Why not?"

"It's evidence."

"Evidence."

I didn't reply.

He leaned forward, almost sneering. "You need more evidence she's dead?"

I kept quiet, to keep him talking.

"What more!" he yelled. "What more!"

"One more?" Corey called from the bar.

Signaling a round for himself, Milo lowered his voice.
"You better start talking. Why do you need more evidence?"

For once, he looked genuinely curious.

"Mr. Carpenter, are you certain your wife committed suicide?"

The glaze over his eyes made it difficult to tell if he was
thinking, or not thinking. Or trying to sober up enough to
think. Or to lie.

"Who wanted your wife dead?" I pressed on. "Someone
on the movie crew?"

"Everybody—"

"Everybody?"

"Nobody," he said, addled. "Everybody loved Judy. They
loved her."

The bartender appeared, setting the fresh drink on a new coaster. Milo shook his head.

"Not right drink, yes?" Corey asked.

Picking it up, the actor gulped like a man dying of thirst. He handed the glass back to the bartender.

"One more, yes?"

Milo nodded. The bartender walked away.

"You told me this morning she was depressed." I leaned forward. "Was she taking medication for the condition?"

"You think I killed her." His voice was flat, uninflected.

"Mr. Carpenter, I don't know what happened to your wife. But if she killed herself, there must be some reason. And if you know what it is, please tell me."

He grabbed the sunglasses from the table, sliding them over his face. Then he stood, swaying for a moment before he squared the wide shoulders and tried to walk out of the bar, bumping into the plastic chairs. Like a drunk.

That part, I decided, was no act.

SIX

The thin woman who answered the door to the ship's penthouse had a pile of platinum hair. Her name was Larrah Sparks and her bikini was so small it could've belonged to the real Barbie, whom Mrs. Sparks closely resembled.

I showed my FBI credentials, reminding the producer's wife.

"Huh," she said. "Is this something with the movie?"

"No."

"Did I ever tell you I did two movies that had FBI agents in them?"

Three times. "Yes, you did."

"None of the agents was female," she continued once more. "If I'd played the agent we would have made money."

I gave my official smile, an expression Quantico issued on graduation day. "Is Mr. Sparks available?"

"You know how to spell my name, right?" She spelled it. "Rhymes with 'Harrah.'"

"Got it." Larrah-Harrah. Scarrah.

After Milo had staggered out of the bar, I went to ask Geert if the movie's producer was taking any tours in Ketchikan. The ship's computers at the gangway tracked each passenger's boarding and reentry. Sparks had stayed on board.

"He's in the tub," Larrah said over her shoulder, walking across the apartment-size cabin. "We was just taking a little splash."

The view from the patio was so beautiful it could have been a movie's fake backdrop. Gravity-defying slopes, white-capped peaks, glistening ocean under a sparkle of sunshine. Sitting in the hot tub, Sandy Sparks was speaking on his cell phone, his back turned to the glory of Alaska.

"You tell that jerk he'll never find another gig in LA," Sparks was saying. "I'll make it my full-time job to cut him off."

The nubile Mrs. Sparks climbed the four steps to the edge of the hot tub, then made a slow descent into the water. Perhaps it was the pile of vanilla hair on her sticklike body, but she reminded me of an ice-cream cone dipping itself in melted chocolate.

"Just get it done." Sparks slammed the phone shut.

When I held out my card, his wet fingers placed it on the edge of the hot tub. "What's with the card? I know who you are."

I asked if we could speak alone.

"Yeah, sure." He looked at his wife. "Hey, Laurrie, give us a minute, would ya?"

Laurrie—which I guessed was Larrah's real name—glared at her husband before standing and climbed back out. She stomped over to the patio door. Her bare feet left surprisingly large footprints on the patio floor.

She closed the sliding door behind her, hard.

"Did I ever tell you I produced a couple other movies with Fed characters?" Sparks said.

Twice. "Yes, you did."

"Only we didn't cast women as agents. Laurrie thinks that's why they tanked."

Each time they told me about their previous "Fed" experience, it was as if the previous conversations never happened.

Once more I brought out the official smile. "Mr. Sparks, I wanted to talk to you about Judy Carpenter."

"Judy, yeah. That's some crazy stunt she pulled. Amazing. Unbelievable. Did you know she made Milo a star? Seventeen years they were married."

"I heard twenty-two."

"Twenty?"

"Two. Twenty-two." These people didn't listen to anybody but themselves.

"That's like two centuries in LA. They had the longest marriage I know. I was just talking to a producer friend"— he nodded at the cell phone resting beside my card—"and he couldn't believe Judy checked out like that."

"It's best if you don't talk about it. Not yet."

He lifted his hands, inadvertently splashing some water on my shoes. "Hey, I wasn't talking. I was just asking if he'd heard anything. My publicity people are working on an official statement, before the paparazzi come parachuting in."

"An official statement that says…?"

He scratched his rounded shoulders. The wet black hair lay as flat as a pelt on his pale skin. But he was a man who stayed in motion. Since I'd come on deck, he'd already scratched his shoulders twice, his face once, and nodded at the end of all my sentences, anxious to speak before the other person finished.

"We're still trying to figure out a way to spin this, so it doesn't sound so bad. To most people. That nutty crowd of hers would believe anything. We could say she got abducted by aliens and they'd believe it. No offense."

"None taken."

That "nutty crowd" included my aunt Charlotte. Judy Carpenter agreed with all her ideas about crystals and reincarnation and all the other New Age claptrap. It was Judy who insisted my aunt work with the movie crew.

"Did Mrs. Carpenter seem depressed to you?" I asked.

He shrugged. "I wasn't married to her."

"But did anything seem different about her in recent weeks?"

"To tell you the truth"—he scratched again—"she seemed a little down this past year. Menopause, what I thought. She got fat, started getting emotional about everything. It wasn't like her, so I figured it was hormone hell. You know, female stuff." He looked at me. "You saw her. What'd she seem like to you?"

During the two brief days I'd known her, Judy Carpenter never seemed completely there. Not so much a thousand-yard stare, but three hundred yards and looking at a different field altogether. "Distracted," I said. "She seemed distracted."

I thought that had to do with work, with coproducing a movie. With a boozed up lead actor who was her husband.

"She was a hard worker. You know she produced rock bands too? That's how this whole crystal thing came into our movie." He picked up my soggy card, reading it. "You're Charlotte's daughter?"

"Niece."

He nodded, as if committing the fact to memory. "Judy really wanted Charlotte to come on this trip. She swore that if we did what Charlotte said, the movie would be a hit."

My dad's sister owned a New Age boutique called Seattle Stones. Last year she stumbled upon the idea that crystals emitted distinct vibrations, and each vibration matched a certain type of music. Tiger's eye kept a hip-hop beat. Obsidian had the dark energy of heavy metal rock. Turquoise harmonized with folk. To test her theory, my aunt loaned some crystals to several Seattle bands. Two of them scored their first rocket hits on the Billboard chart. Other bands began packing clubs. One of those hit bands had an LA producer, Judy Carpenter. When she heard about the "rocks that rock" idea, she immediately called my aunt. Not surprisingly, they hit it off, and later Judy convinced Charlotte the rocks could work with acting too. And she had just the movie to try it out on. Did Charlotte want to come on a cruise to Alaska? Never shy, my aunt asked to bring her family. Four tickets. That was Charlotte's fee. And when my aunt learned that Milo was playing an FBI agent, she offered my consulting services. That detail we kept from my mother.

"Nobody worked harder than Judy," Sparks was saying. "Back in the spandex-rock days she sewed outfits for some big-hair bands."

"I heard it was ice-skaters."

"Skating, yeah. That came first. The Mommie-dearest types really forked over some cash. But making the band outfits was how Judy got into the music biz. Then Milo started making money in action flicks, and since they didn't have kids, Judy adopted bands. She had an ear. She made money. So when she told me about those Billboard hits and those stones from your mom—"

"Aunt."

"—I was like, 'What is this, Jack and the Beanstalk?' She goes, 'No, I'm serious. This woman in Seattle, she gets you in tune with the universe and everything just falls into place.'"

I stared out at the water, resisting the urge to roll my eyes.

"Between you and me, I wasn't so excited. But Judy was desperate for Milo to make another hit." He rubbed his ear, rapidly. "So I listened to her. Milo's an old friend, and he's on the skids. By just hiring the guy I'm out on a limb, but it's a sequel. What can I do—cast a different actor? Never works. Okay, maybe with a part like James Bond. But Milo's no Sean Connery. Not even Pierce Brosnan. He's not even Tim Dalton."

"Judy was the film's coproducer, is that right?"

He nodded. "She offered to help fund the movie. I think

she offered so we'd actually make the thing. But the deal breaker was we had to use these rocks from your mom—"

"Aunt."

"—so we could find everybody's wavelength. In the end I decided, what the heck? Rocks, what can it hurt? Hours at sea. And with Milo in the lead, we need all the help we can get." He shrugged a hirsute shoulder. "And now it feels like a curse."

"What does?"

"All of it. Her suicide. That's like a curse." He ran a wet hand over his thinning hair. "All we can hope for now is that she created some buzz at the box office."

I gazed across the patio to Ketchikan's harbor. Seagulls perched along the dock rail, waiting for food. When I looked back at the producer, he had opened his cell phone again.

"Mr. Sparks, one more question. If she wanted her husband's movie to succeed, why would she ruin it by taking her own life?"

He snapped the phone shut. "Okay. The truth?"

I nodded, wondering what we were talking before.

"Judy was madly in love with Milo."

I waited. "So she killed herself?"

"He's getting too old to play action. His career's in the toilet. It's not like he's Bruce Willis. Or Nic Cage. He's no Sly Stallone—"

"I see, but how does that relate to her suicide?"

"You Feds are sworn to secrecy, right?"

"Confidentiality?"

"Yeah, right, confidentiality. You can't go to the tabloids, who have enough on the guy?"

"Even if I could, I wouldn't speak to the tabloids."

He considered my statement. "Here's the bottom line: Milo's an alcoholic."

I shifted, impatient. "No offense, Mr. Sparks, but that's not news."

"Ten years ago, peak of his career, Judy got him dried out. The guy had started believing his press. It happens. Some not-too-smart actor decides he's a genius because a writer put good lines in his mouth. After he got clean, Milo figured out he can't drink. He's a raging alcoholic."

"He's drinking now."

"That's what I'm saying: he fell off the wagon."

"So she killed herself?"

"Oh, wait, I got it. You don't read the tabloids. Milo, with the babe? It's all over the *Enquirer*. It tore Judy apart."

"He's having an affair?"

"What did I just tell you? She was madly in love with him."

It didn't add up. I pulled the plastic bag from my pocket and handed it to Sparks. He squeezed the bag, staring at the stones. "Something from Charlotte?"

"Did Mrs. Carpenter ever wear this?"

He drew the bag close to his face, getting a good look at the jewelry. "This is nice. Where did you get this thing?"

"Did you ever see her wearing it?"

He handed it back to me, shaking his head. "She could probably even afford it. But I never saw it on her."

Behind me, I heard the patio door slide open. Larrah Sparks had donned a white terry cloth robe, draped around her shoulders. In one hand she held the cabin phone, in the other was the receiver.

"It's for you," she told her husband.

"You can't bring it to me?"

With cold nobility, the terry cloth like a royal robe, she bore the phone across the patio.

"You're sweet," he said sarcastically.

Dropping the robe on the decking, she climbed the stairs and lowered herself inch by inch into the hot water.

"Sandy Sparks…" he said into the phone. "Yeah, that's my dad…"

Suddenly Sparks shot up from the water. "She did *what*?"

"Oh great," Larrah mumbled.

"I'll be right there." He slammed the phone into the receiver and churned toward the tub stairs.

"What happened?" his wife asked in a bland voice.

"Shopping for souvenirs. He turned around for one second and she was gone. They can't find her."

He padded quickly across the patio, swimsuit dripping, then into the penthouse. He didn't close the door.

I looked at Larrah. "What's all that about?"

"His parents are on the cruise with us." She sighed. "His dad got some convention going on, something to do with his matchsticks."

"The phillumenists?"

She looked up, surprised. "Yeah, them phillum-a-what-evers. But Sandy wanted his mom to see Alaska before she loses all her marbles." Larrah pointed to her head. "She's got that old-timer's thing, where she can't remember anything? I told him she'd be trouble. Sure enough she locked them out of their room and lost his dad's wallet on our first day. The first day! We hadn't even left Seattle. I told him to leave her there with somebody, but does he listen to me? No. All I hear is, 'Laurrie this and Laurrie that.'" Wiggling back against the hot tub jets, she stretched out her long neck. "I want to play an FBI agent. It seems exciting."

I turned, staring into the penthouse. A half-dressed Sandy Sparks was racing across the cabin carrying his shoes and socks. Within seconds he was out the cabin door, into the hallway.

"See what I mean?" his wife said. "He didn't even tell me good-bye."

SEVEN

That afternoon, as the tourists came streaming back to the cruise ship, I swam against the current like a spawning salmon, walking along Front Street, where the road literally ended at the water. Abandoned crab pots dotted the rocky beach, the scent of rust rising in the warm sun. Farther out, fishing vessels chugged for the marina and seagulls circled, calling out for dinner. On one prow, a burly man in hip waders threw a line to a man on the dock. He kneeled, knotting the rope to a steel cleat.

I thought of Judy Carpenter's rope.

Whoever killed her picked an ideal location. Far from the captain's bridge at the other end of the ship. No cabin windows. No security cameras. And that bracelet. I wasn't sure what those gems were, except that they looked valuable— but valuable enough to cost Judy Carpenter her life? And I wondered why it was left behind.

Lifting a hand, I shielded my eyes from the sun that refused to fade. No planes crossed the sky. I checked my watch. Thirty-five minutes. If he wasn't here in thirty-five minutes, the ship would leave without him.

Please.

I climbed down from the pier and walked the coarse sand beach. Afternoon high tide was creeping up the shoreline, darkening the green sand until it looked black. Geologists have a term for the places where certain rocks or rock formations are initially discovered. It's called "type locality," and Ketchikan's was a relatively recent volcanic basalt called the Gravina Belt. With heavy deposits of chlorite and epidote, two green minerals, the basalt produced beaches of dark sand. I pulled away the ribbons of rubbery sea kelp and dug my bare hands through the coarse sand. My hike was gone but there was still time to find some type locality samples for my rock collection. I rinsed the best candidates in the tide, the ocean so cold my fingers went numb. Later I couldn't say where the time went, but my daydreams were shattered by a sound like a faraway buzz saw.

I looked up. The wind blew my hair across my eyes, but I saw the plane turning sharply within the steep and narrow channel, then dropping through the air until the pontoons splashed on the glittery water.

The window behind the rotating front blade was dark.

The man who caught the rope earlier walked to the outer birth, waving in the plane and directing it to the outer bumpers. The plane taxied for the dock, where the man tied it. I held my breath as the cab door opened.

Looking like an aviator sent from central casting, Jack Stephanson stepped out wearing a brown bomber jacket, Ray-Ban sunglasses, two days' scruff of beard, and a smile that competed with the sun. He tossed a canvas duffel bag on the dock.

And everything seemed to hurt. Even my feet. I looked down.

The water had risen over my toes, cold and aching.

Dropping the Gravina Belt samples in my pocket, I walked up the beach to the pier. My shoes made hideous squishy sounds, wet and flatulent. Across the water Jack was handing the harbormaster a piece of paper, then pointing to the cub plane before clasping the man's shoulder like an old friend. He picked up his duffel and strolled down the dock, glancing around. Mr. Casual.

I didn't move.

When he didn't see me, he stopped. Searching the street above, he moved slowly, scanning the area with evident concern.

Harmon, I told myself, *run for your life.*

One half second can feel like an eternity. He glanced over at the pier and his tan face broke into that wide grin.

I knew that grin. I had to look at it every day I was stuck in the Seattle office. Every day that Jack toyed with information, or sent me on some schoolgirl errand, or challenged my procedures based on minor technicalities. Watching him jog up the gangway from the marina to Front Street, every one of my old resentments stormed to the surface.

He was still smiling when he reached me. "Harmon," he said, "you look as wound up as ever."

"If you came here thinking you're going to save the day, scrub the idea from your struggling brain." I headed down Front Street, feeling righteous. But my squishy shoes ruined any sense of superiority.

Jack ran to catch up. "You figured out who killed her?"

"No. But I don't need your help."

"Excellent, I'll kick back by the pool." He grinned.

A string of nasty words begged my tongue for a chance to wipe that smug expression off his face. But when I opened my mouth, the ship blew its horn, signaling departure.

"That must be the Love Boat," he said.

I turned and walked away.

The Ninja who met us at the gangway had a pencil-thin mustache. Without a word, he took our guns, then waited off to the side as we crossed through the security arches.

Jack still triggered the alarm, and a dimple-cheeked young woman brandished the security wand. Jack lifted his bomber jacket, winking at her. "My belt buckle's a deadly weapon."

She giggled.

I gagged and waited with the Ninja while the girl practically drooled on Jack, taking her time moving the wand over his muscular outstretched arms, then down his legs. When she was finished—mistakenly pronouncing him harmless—the Ninja led us across the atrium. This afternoon the entertainment was a beautiful showgirl in a red leotard twirling a silver baton. Every man on board had gathered to watch her fling the baton through the four-story atrium, cart wheeling before she caught the thing right before it struck the marble floor. Jack applauded as we turned right into the casino. Red-vested dealers glanced up from stacking their poker chips on the felt tables.

"How ya doin'?" Jack asked.

I gritted my teeth as we came out the other side. The Ninja pulled out the remote control, opening the upholstered wall.

"What's this," Jack said, "the Bat Cave?"

We ignored him.

Geert was sitting behind his desk, perusing some kind of ledger, but when he looked up, his Dutch-blue eyes iced over. Taking our guns from the Ninja, he swiveled toward the safe, once again blocking the view with his back.

"The producer says you asked a lot of questions." He deposited the guns in the safe, shut the door, spun the dial. "If you think she got murdered, look at the husband. Most of them just push the wife overboard. Maybe this one went to some trouble. If it's not suicide."

"It's not suicide." I performed the introductions between the men. Their handshake was so tight their fingers went momentarily white.

Geert sat down and twirled his mustache. He used his left

hand, I noticed, the hand that didn't shake Jack's. "What did the husband tell you?" he asked.

"Not much. He got hostile."

"You think he killed his wife, you want him to thank you?"

"That's not what she's saying," Jack said.

"Yah. It's your problem. But don't make it my problem." Jack narrowed his eyes. "What?"

Geert lifted both hands, offering some Netherlandish gesture that managed to combine ennui with existential bleakness. "We got some lady who kills herself. Or maybe he kills her. I don't say no to that. But either one means I don't got no serial killer on my ship. I don't want no panic breaking out because of you and your questions."

"So you don't care what happened or who did it?" Jack asked.

"I care about other passengers," he said. "Suicide, it's done. If it is not suicide, the target was her. I'm gonna let you FBI people look into it only because—"

"Hold it." Jack raised his hand, the palm open to signal *stop*. "You're going to *let us* look into it?"

Geert stared at him with unveiled animosity. "Yah."

"Let me explain something to you." Jack pointed at me. "This isn't some Girl Scout. If she says this death looks suspicious, then it's suspicious. Period. And you can either cooperate with her investigation or I will file enough paperwork to stretch from here to Antarctica, all of it alleging this cruise line covered up a murder." He smiled. An official smile. "I'm making it your problem. Are we clear?"

Geert's bald pate seemed to blister. His ice-eyes shifted to me, but I had nothing to say. The last person I expected to defend me, especially like that, was Jack. I was speechless.

"I want promise," Geert said. "No passengers disturbed, unless I agree. Nobody but the husband. Him, you can go ahead and bother."

"Because?" I asked.

"Because the husband always kills the wife. Always."

I keyed open my cabin, studiously ignoring Jack two doors down the hall, and found a room bustling with perfume and that peculiar electricity produced by women ramping up to full female regalia.

"Hurry up!" exclaimed Aunt Charlotte. "It's formal night!"

Her pleasantly plump figure was layered with diaphanous pink silk, and she floated across the room like an underwater sea creature, drifting through the door that linked our cabins. My mom and I shared this room; Aunt Charlotte and Claire were next door. I wanted to pull my aunt aside and talk about Judy Carpenter, but my mother was here, watching. Another undersea creature, she wore a beaded red sheath that amplified her sultry curves. But her jasper eyes were charged by some neurasthenic current.

"How were the fjords?" I asked.

She nodded. "They were nice."

Nice? Misty Fjords, among the world's most spectacular landscapes. And all she could say was *nice*?

"Mom, are you feeling okay?"

"I'm a little tired." She dropped her voice to a whisper. "She talked the entire time."

"Who?"

"Claire, on the bus. She sat next to me and talked the entire time."

Claire, our cross to bear.

"I'm sorry."

"How was your hike?" she asked.

I almost said *nice*. "Good. It was good."

"You better shower," she said, staring at the green sand under my fingernails, my wet shoes.

In the shower I scrubbed my fingernails and hummed that

tune from *South Pacific*, about washing that man right out of my hair. When I stepped out, I felt renewed and cracked the door to release the steam that turned the mirror opaque with mist. The bathroom was the size of a broom closet.

And I heard the voice.

"I'm not making it up," Claire was saying. "It's true."

"But…how…?" My aunt. Her words stalled. "When…?"

"This morning. Remember the fat dude with the body bag? That was Judy. They found her hanging."

"Hanging!" my mother cried.

"Yep. Hung herself last night."

My mother gasped. "Oh my lands."

I grabbed a white towel, pressed it to my mouth, and screamed.

Claire continued, unabated by the panic in my mother's voice. "Must have planned the whole thing. The trip, our tickets. That's what suicides do, you know. Plan everything down to the last detail. When people ask me to contact somebody who killed themself, I say—"

"Claire!" I wrapped the towel around my body, kicking open the door. "May I speak with you?"

There was a pause.

I came around the corner. "Claire?" They stood in the middle of the room, aquatic creatures lost at sea. Aunt Charlotte had the startled expression of somebody who just got bad news and was trying not to freak out. I looked at her, holding eye contact, waiting until she got my signal.

"Nadine," she said to my mother. "I need your opinion."

"About what?" My mother sounded scared.

"Which jewelry goes with this outfit." My aunt gently led her through the door between our cabins. "You have such an eye for style."

I closed the door.

Claire's curry-yellow Indian sari was three inches too long.

She looked like bleached kelp. And for some reason she had a pink stone stuck to the middle of her forehead. It looked so weird I couldn't take my eyes off the thing.

"My third eye." Claire tapped it with her finger. "But, boy, does Superglue sting."

"You Superglued that to your forehead?"

"Be careful. Stare at it too long, you'll get hypnotized."

I closed my eyes for different reasons and drew a deep breath. The room smelled of patchouli and my mother's panic. "How did you hear about Judy Carpenter?"

"Milo told me."

"Milo. When?"

"When I went up there."

"Up where?"

"To his room. Judy booked a reading for this afternoon. When she didn't show up I went to get her, and Milo totally broke down. Just lost it. He told me what happened and I decided she made the appointment so she could talk to him. You know, from the hereafter."

Concrete wasn't this dense.

"But I don't think she's reached her final destination."

"Pardon?"

"I told him we should try calling tomorrow."

It was too much. The voice that sounded like a metal spoon banging an empty pot. The yellow outfit that made her squat body look like an emergency life raft. This whole idea that she could call the hereafter, like AT&T for the dead. I was drawing another deep breath, trying to measure my words, when Claire jumped into the silence.

"It's those people next door. I haven't had one good night's sleep since we got on this boat."

"Ship."

"What?"

"This is a ship, Claire. Not a boat."

"Okay, whatever, but somebody needs to tell them to stop partying. I'm about to lose my mind."

I let that one go.

"Claire." I spoke slowly, the way Quantico taught us to talk to belligerent drug addicts. "I need a favor. A really big favor."

She frowned. Her forehead buckled around the pink rock.

"Don't talk about Judy's death, to anyone. But especially not in front of my mom."

She reached up, massaging the skin around the pink stone. "What's wrong with your mom anyway? I'm not being nosy. I just want to be prepared in case she's another suicide waiting to happen."

"Nothing is wrong with her."

"Then why's she so jumpy? And sometimes I can't understand a word she's saying."

My mother was too nice to tell her to shut up. Instead, she was probably showering her with Southern platitudes and blessing her heart all over the place. But those manners came with a price. The strain was all over my mother's face.

"Claire, don't you think Judy would be way upset about you talking about her, instead of to her?"

She gave another frown. "You think that's why she didn't make contact?"

I released the official smile.

"Because I'm talking too much? Hey, you know, that's an idea. I need to *listen*. Okay, now I feel better."

"And that's what matters."

"You know, if you ever want to get in touch with your dad, just say the word."

Feeling a shiver run up my spine, I opened the door separating our cabins. Claire trundled away. Airy flute music was playing in my aunt's cabin, some South American woodwinds, and the volume was turned up to block my mother from overhearing my conversation with Claire. I caught Aunt

Charlotte's eye, silently thanking her. My mother sat on one of the twin beds, watching her sister-in-law model jewelry.

I pulled on a sleeveless black velvet tank with black pants and three-inch black heels. Stepping into the bathroom, I combed my wet hair into a sleek ponytail, added mascara and pearl earrings. I was no girlie-girl, but I loved being a girl. I was finishing my lipstick when somebody knocked on the door. "I'm almost done!"

"There's somebody here for you," my mother said.

Once again the three women stood in the middle of the cabin. Only now they gaped at the open cabin door.

Turning, I followed their gaze.

The black tux was tailored to his muscular frame. I hated to admit it, but he looked good. No. He looked *amazing*. He'd even shaved and combed his hair, and I was trying to figure out how he got that tux into his duffel bag without wrinkling it when Aunt Charlotte breathed her own declaration: "Yum."

My mother simply stared.

Amid the hail of hair spray and evening attire—not to mention Claire—I forgot to deploy my latest fabrication. With a smile plastered on my face, I introduced each of the ladies to Jack. It was discouraging to see that his manners were impeccable.

"How do you know Raleigh?" My mother shook his hand.

"We used to work together," I interjected. That was true. "We ran into each other this afternoon."

"On the hike?"

"Right," I said, before Jack could reply.

"You're a geologist?" my mother asked.

"Geologist? No, ma'am. I'm a special a—"

"A specialist on glaciers." I grabbed my purse. "Jack's specialty is glaciers. He's a glaciologist. Freezing cold atmospheres. So cold, it's cruel." I leaned down, kissing my mother's soft cheek. Her beautiful eyes were confused and stabbed my heart. "If you need anything, I have my cell."

"You're not eating with us?" she asked.

"Jack needs some help with his research on Alaskan glaciers." I waved good-bye, shoving Jack into the hallway, slamming the door shut.

"What was all that about?" he asked.

I jogged down the hallway. When necessary, it is possible to run fast in three-inch heels.

"Harmon, what's going on?"

"Just stick to the story, okay?"

"But your mom thinks—"

I picked up the pace.

But he stopped.

When I turned, he was standing in the hallway, looking genuinely shocked.

"She doesn't know," he said. "Your mother. She doesn't know you're an FBI agent."

Unable to speak, I headed for the elevators and kept my head down, sending up more desperate prayers for forgiveness, wondering when God would get as tired of me as I was.

EIGHT

"You look nice," Jack said.

I lifted the menu, hiding my face. My cheeks felt hot, suddenly. It was the run in heels, I decided. That's all.

"What are you going to order?" he asked.

The same thing I'd ordered two nights in a row, though I pretended to scan the menu until our waiter appeared. His name was Paolo, from Naples. He asked us what we'd like to drink.

"Coke, no crushed ice."

"Club soda," Jack said. "Two limes."

That happened to be my second-favorite drink.

"Would it be possible to order dinner now?" I asked.

"Certainly," said Paolo. "I thought you wanted some time with your fiancé."

He smiled, full of Mediterranean romance, and glanced discreetly at my engagement ring. I was about to explain—Look, buddy, my fiancé's in Virginia—when I suddenly wondered if Geert had come up with some ruse to explain Jack's presence onboard. One more way for security to cover up the FBI investigation.

"Thank you, but we're in a hurry to get somewhere tonight."

Paolo slid his eyes toward Jack, then lifted his eyebrows with insinuation. "Tonight," he said, "we have oysters."

"No thanks," I said. "Filet mignon, medium rare. Baked potato, loaded."

"And for the vegetable?"

"Chives on the potato."

Paolo hesitated.

"They're not a vegetable," I agreed. "But they're green."

"Very good, miss." He turned to Jack. "For you, sir?"

"The same."

"Excellent." Collecting our menus, Paolo bowed and left.

I took one of the warm rolls from the bread basket.

"I'm a geologist," Jack said. "And I'm your fiancé. This trip gets better and better."

Tearing the bread in half, I thanked God, even for annoyances. I slathered two pats of butter on half a roll.

He said, "Do you prefer 'sweetheart' or 'honey'?"

"Here's the deal, Jack. My mom doesn't know I'm an agent—"

"Why not?"

"If you'll be quiet I'll tell you. She worries, and I don't like her to worry."

"So you told her you're a geologist?" he asked, incredulous.

"I have a degree in geology. I worked in the mineralogy lab."

"Harmon, almost true is not true."

"You want to help me?"

"Yes."

"Then for the next couple days smother that huge ego of yours and pretend you're a humble geologist instead of some hotshot violent crimes agent whose belt buckle is a deadly weapon."

He smiled. "Where have you been all my life?"

"Hiding from you."

"I've missed you."

"I'm serious, Jack."

"So am I."

Reaching into my purse, I took out the copies of the passenger list, courtesy of Geert. Paolo arrived with our drinks, and I sipped and drew circles around the names associated with the movie crew.

"How's life been in Virginia?"

I looked up. His blue-green eyes seemed brighter than I remembered.

"There are twenty-two people on this ship who are working on the movie," I said. "They all knew Judy Carpenter, or knew of her. If we divide them equally, prioritizing interviews, we can knock this out quickly. I already talked to the producer and his wife. He says Judy Carpenter killed herself because Milo's a philandering drunk, some tabloid ran a story about it. Except we know she didn't kill herself, so our main suspect remains the husband, Milo. I tried. Now it's your turn. See if you can confirm his alibi. He claims he was—"

"That's a nice ring, something for our undercover work?"

I glanced down at the thin gold band encircled with yellow and green gems. Citrine and peridot, two of my favorites.

"I'm engaged, Jack."

"You can't be."

"Judy Carpenter had to know her killer. There were no signs of struggle at the crime scene. I didn't see any defensive wounds and the mortician didn't mention any. Again, that points to the husband."

"What if the killer got off the ship in Ketchikan?"

"Everybody who got off came back on, according to Geert."

"That crazy Dutchman can track everybody?"

"The room keys. They're scanned into the computer whenever anybody leaves or comes back. One key per person."

"What's he like?"

"Geert's tough but I think—"

"I meant your fiancé."

Looking away, I hoped to sever this line of questioning. I didn't want to talk about DeMott, especially not with Jack, but something even more disturbing was barreling through the dining room like a giant yellow Nerf ball.

"Oh no."

Claire pointed at Jack. "I've seen you before!" Her metallic voice silenced the conversations at the other tables. People turned, staring. "I knew it! You're that guy from the mountain!"

Jack looked at me. "I was waiting to bring this up, but what is she doing here?"

Last fall Claire decided to "help" me with my missing persons case. When she showed up on Cougar Mountain, tracking the killer in her mind, Jack basically told her to go find her aluminum hat so the aliens could find her.

"I warned you about this guy, Raleigh. He's totally toxic."

Jack squinted. "Is that a zit on her forehead?"

"Two nights ago I had a nightmare about sharks," Claire continued. "Sharks were attacking us. We all died. It was a sign. Predators among us!"

"Claire, you're causing a scene."

"I'm going to figure out what's going on here." She pointed to the pink stone. "You can't fool me. I'm a clairvoyant."

"You mean crackpot," Jack said.

The other diners continued to stare. Gentlemen in tuxes and festive red bow ties, the ladies in luxurious gowns. And here came Paolo, rushing across the room, hurrying past the white-clothed table where my mother sat beside my aunt. My mother was watching this, looking disturbed.

"Claire, sit down."

"I know you two are up to something."

"Sit down or I'll—"

"I heard what you told your mother. You're a liar. Glaciers?" She pointed at Jack. "He's an FBI agent. No wonder that poor woman—"

I jumped up. "One more word and I'll—"

"Are you threatening me?"

"Yes. Say one word to her and you will regret it for the rest of your life."

"Don't think you can push me around." She spun on her heel, tripped on the long sari, then picked it up and stomped back to my aunt's table.

Paolo stood beside our table, wringing his hands. "Everything is all right?"

"Everything is fine," Jack said. "Can we send a drink over to that woman?"

"But of course." Paolo bowed. "What would you like to send?"

"Hemlock."

"*Scusa?*"

I sat down, my heart pounding. "Never mind, Paolo. We're fine, thank you."

With another discreet bow, he walked away. Several people stopped him, asking questions. I waved at my mother, smiling. She nodded, then stared down at her silverware.

I took another roll from the basket. Three pats of butter this time.

Jack said, "Let's talk about this guy."

"Milo Carpenter is basically a—"

"No, the guy you think you're going to marry."

I bit the roll. Chewed. Then bit again.

"Harmon, I flew up here on a moment's notice. The least you can do is tell me about your fiancé."

"I didn't ask you to come, Jack." I glanced at my wristwatch. "Right after dinner, my aunt's giving one of her crystal seminars for the movie people. I don't expect Carpenter to show up. Maybe you can get him to talk."

"Life is boring without you."

I buttered another roll and stared out at the room, waiting for my steak. If I had to, I could eat my way through this mess.

Oh yes.

I could.

After a perfect filet marred only by Jack's company, I walked through the ship's thematic wonderland designed to stave off midsea boredom. Every public area had a grand theme, from dining rooms that resembled Italian trattorias and Japanese sushi gardens to outrigger lounges and leather-scented English pubs.

There was even Pharaoh's Tomb, where my Aunt Charlotte was holding her seminar. Appropriately cavernous, the tomb room had pillars painted into leafy palm trees and gilded sphinxes that bookended a low wooden stage where, according to the ship's daily schedule, a standup comic would appear in the blue hours.

Unfortunately, the audience here now didn't understand what a joke this show was too. Sitting in the front rows, the beautiful movie people stared at the table on stage draped in velvet and displaying dozens of polished crystals. Under the lights, each stone gleamed with promise. My aunt stood beside them, proud as their earth mother.

Next to her Sandy Sparks held a microphone and spoke in a somber voice.

"This is a tragedy," he was saying. "Nobody saw her suicide coming. And Milo, obviously, the man's devastated. I've spent some time with him, and I've been trying to decide where this leaves us with the movie."

He paced the stage. My aunt still wore her formal wear from dinner, but Sparks was dressed like a little kid. T-shirt and jeans, tennis shoes and a bright-blue baseball cap with some kind of Roman warrior over the bill.

"Nobody worked harder than Judy to get Milo where he is today. Not even Milo. If that sounds crass to you, you didn't know the woman. She wanted Milo to own the box office."

I glanced around the room. In the deep shadows a bar ran along the back wall. I walked over, still listening to Sparks, and asked the Filipino bartender for a club soda with two limes.

The movie people seemed to hold their breath as Sparks spoke, waiting on his next words. Only his wife wasn't listening. Larrah cupped a hand over her mouth, talking into her cell phone while Sandy glared at her.

"I've decided to keep filming," he said. "It's what Judy would have wanted. We're going to honor her life by not quitting."

The applause continued for several moments, until Sparks held up his hand.

"But one condition. And I'm serious about this. If anything leaks to the press about her suicide, or anything about Milo's condition, I'll know where it came from. When I find out who's talking—and I will—you won't be able to collect garbage in Hollywood. Is that understood?"

Nods all around. Except Larrah. She was still on the phone. Sparks lifted the warrior baseball cap, running a hand over his thinning black hair.

"Another person Judy believed in was Charlotte Harmon and her work with crystals. Judy said this movie could reach number one at the box office if we just followed Charlotte's direction." He smiled at my aunt. "Are you ready?"

My aunt's face looked drawn and sad, but she took the microphone. Larrah Sparks snapped her phone shut, then raised her hand.

"You have a question?" Aunt Charlotte asked.

"I feel sad about Judy," she said. "Do you have a crystal for that?"

My aunt nodded. "Grief. I feel it too. And I do happen to have some…" She paused. "Judy asked me to bring…"

My aunt gazed at the crystal display, unable to finish what she was saying. After a long uncomfortable moment, she looked up. Under the stage lights her tears were white. "The stone is called Jet. It has a lot of healing properties. Judy asked me to bring some. I thought it was in case people got sick."

She dabbed her eyes with the sleeve of her tunic. I heard sniffles from the crowd. But then she lifted her face.

"Sandy's right. We're going to carry on. For Judy. It's what she would want. Who's ready to start?"

Larrah Sparks was first on the stage. My aunt handed her a piece of Jet.

"But it's black," Larrah said.

"Yes, the Victorians wore it with their mourning clothes. It's excellent for grief."

"But black washes me out." Larrah held the stone as if it was fungus. Polished to a high shine, the stone reflected light like a mirror. "Don't you have something bright and happy? You know, not so gloomy?"

"Jet's been used to ward off evil spirits as far back as the Middle Ages."

I picked up my drink. There was nothing "magical" about Jet. It was fossilized coal. But the lovely lemmings continued to crowd the table.

All except one.

She headed toward the bar as if in a hurry, her wild black hair spilling like ink over a soft Bohemian-blue dress.

"Close your eyes," my aunt was saying to Larrah. "What do you feel?"

Larrah's pale hand clutched the black rock. My aunt waited for a response, then continued her tutorial.

"The vibrations within these crystals will tune you into

the universe. Once you're on that cosmic vibration, nothing can hold you back as an artist. I've seen this again and again."

They listened like children hoping a fairy tale would finally come true, rapt and captivated by the promise. But here's what was true. Minerals could emit vibrations, most notable being atomic energy. And the cells inside our bodies rely on energy, including the electricity that signals complicated processes such as insulin secretion or the production of white blood cells. But to believe that mineralogical energy could be matched to human emotions and produce hit music and great performances was an idea that made Claire seem like a left-brained skeptic.

"When we discover which crystal matches your movie character," Aunt Charlotte continued, "you're going to experience a total transformation. Now, Larrah, what role are you playing?"

"I'm playing the victim." She said it with no trace of irony. "So my vibration should go with her vulnerability. But I'm going to show this character has interior strength too, you know what I mean?"

I turned to the woman in the blue dress. She was ordering a Sprite with lemon and lime.

"Yes, lemon," the bartender replied.

"And lime."

"Yes, lemon."

"No, and lime."

"Yes, lime."

"I want both, one each."

"Yes," he said as if he had no idea what she was talking about, then left to make the drink.

"Not interested in this?" I asked in a low voice, nodding at the stage.

She glanced over, giving a shy smile. "I like my feelings the way they are. And besides, I'm not really an actor."

"You're part of the crew?"

"I'm a musician. I play the piano player in the movie, but since that's my real-life job, it's not really acting."

I extended my hand. "Raleigh Harmon."

"MJ," she said, shaking. "I've seen you around the set."

"I'm related to the crystal lady."

"Oh—I'm sorry, I didn't mean—"

"I think it's a crock."

She looked relieved, then glanced back at the stage. Her hazel eyes, along with her mouth, drew down at the outer edge, giving her a wistful expression. "Last time it was worse," she said. "We had to do past life regression."

"Last time?"

"Judy was really into this stuff." MJ sighed. "It was for another movie, and I played another musician. Really stretching here, you know? But Judy brought in this guy who wanted us all to settle our past lives, so we could move forward. Make peace with all that stuff you supposedly did before you were yourself."

"You knew Judy pretty well?"

"She produced my CD. Then she put me in movies so I could make some money. I didn't agree with all her ideas, but she sure took good care of me."

Her drink arrived with two limes and one lemon. She thanked the bartender and stabbed the plastic straw through the ice, forcing carbonated bubbles to explode at the surface. Her hazel eyes became as watery as opals.

She almost whispered. "I can't believe she's gone."

"You were surprised?"

She hesitated. "Sandy said we're not supposed to talk about it."

"I agree with him. I'm just curious. I didn't know her long, but she sure didn't seem like the type to commit suicide. Especially like *that*."

MJ continued to stare into her drink. "Are you a cop?"

"Pardon?"

"You sound like a cop." She looked over, leveling me with her eyes.

"I'm helping Milo with his role. I'm an FBI agent." I paused. "But I still wonder why Judy would kill herself."

Without a word, she picked up her drink and walked back toward the crowd. Only she hovered at the edges, some lovely butterfly with a broken wing, while Larrah Sparks tried to find the right crystal, the accurate vibration for Barbie as a victim. Aunt Charlotte placed a violet-blue stone—fluorite was my guess—in the actress's thin hand.

"Feel anything now?" my aunt asked.

"Maybe..."

I felt something, and it was gripping my shoulder.

Claire had changed from the yellow sari into gray sweats. The pink stone was still glued to her forehead but the adhesion was giving way. The crystal tilted, the third eye of a drunken cyclops.

"I just figured it out," she said, letting go of my shoulder. "You think somebody murdered Judy. So Mr. Toxic came on board to help you."

Here was another problem with Claire. She had busted-watch accuracy. Twice a day she managed to be right.

"Where did you get that idea?" I asked.

"Raleigh, I'm a clairvoyant." She leaned in with the inebriated third eye. "You can't fool me. I know when something's going on."

I wanted to push her back, get her out of my personal space. Instead, I praised her. "Your clairvoyant skills are excellent, Claire."

As expected, the compliment confused her. She took a step back, relaxing. "I probably came on a little too strong at dinner," she admitted. "But it's because I feel responsible."

"For what?"

"For Judy. I tried to tell Charlotte."

"That Judy was suicidal?"

"No, about the vibrations. In the crystals. They're not the same. I told Charlotte we're getting too close to the North Pole. I told her how magnetic forces can make the needle on a compass go crazy. I think that's what killed Judy. This crazy magnetic energy."

"It's crazy all right."

"Are you calling me crazy?"

"I'm saying there's no wa—"

"You think I'm crazy!" Shouting again.

The pretty people on stage turned around. I waited, holding my peace, until the lemmings returned to their tutorial. My aunt was explaining how the Pueblo Indians buried their dead with Jet so they had protection in the afterlife.

"Claire, you can let yourself off the hook. The crystals can't make people want to kill themselves."

"You're wrong. You watch. Watch me and my third eye. I'm going to break this case wide-open." Her voice was rising again. "You can make fun of me, go ahead." Yelling now. "I'm going to find out who killed Judy."

"Claire, keep it down."

"And when I'm done, the whole world will know about Claire the Clairvoyant. The FBI won't make fun of me then!"

Shielding their eyes against the stage lights, the movie people peered into the tomb.

Claire stabbed her finger into my shoulder. "Just because you're an FBI agent doesn't mean you can insult me. You cops get so arrogant. But I know all about you, Raleigh. I know how you lie to your mo—"

"Shut up."

"What did you say?"

I stood up. In three-inch heels, I towered over her. "Shut up or I will—"

"You're threatening me! Again!"

"My life is none of your business."

She turned to the bartender. "Make a note."

"Yes. What kinda drink is that?"

Claire turned toward the stage, bellowing, "Charlotte! Your niece the bully is doing it again. She doesn't want me to figure out who killed—"

"Stop it, Claire." I grabbed her arm.

"Police brutality! Help! She's beating me up!"

Aunt Charlotte practically jumped off the stage. I wasn't holding Claire's arm anymore, but she continued an incoherent screed about police brutality and forces of darkness and she wouldn't go peacefully and I was backing away when I caught my heel on the bar stool. Lunging for the bar, I accidentally bumped Claire's arm.

"She hit me!"

My aunt rolled up like a frantic ball of silk. Sandy Sparks was right behind her, followed by the flock of lemmings.

"She carries a gun," Claire said, pointing at me.

Their collective gasp sucked every ounce of oxygen from Pharaoh's Tomb.

"I am not carrying a gun," I said. "And I didn't hit her. I was trying to move away when my heel caught and…"

It was no use. Nobody was listening. Nobody cared. And every mind was already made up. Forming a crescent around me, the handsome faces showed disdain, and fear. I glanced at the bartender. He was wide-eyed, a man who doesn't know whether to duck or serve drinks.

"I am not carrying a gun," I said again.

Claire was sobbing. "She hit me, Charlotte."

"I did not hit her."

"You did!" Claire pushed up her sweatshirt sleeve, showing her forearm. "Look!"

The skin *was* red.

"It was an accident," I said. "I fell."

Claire tucked her face into Aunt Charlotte, who patted her back. "I know, Claire, I know," my aunt murmured. "We're all hurting right now."

The crowd stared, gorgeous zombies waiting to attack, but my aunt's forehead was notched with worry. I knew that expression from my dad. Her brother. This was how he looked whenever my mother's mind refused to reconcile with the real world, a look of pure love—and adamantine resolve.

It meant: stop the suffering, by any means necessary.

"Raleigh, you need to leave."

"Aunt Charlotte, I didn't—"

She held up her hand, silencing me. "I heard what you said in the dining room." Her voice was firm, scolding. "This behavior is unacceptable. Now go. Please."

The beautiful crowd shuffled back, clearing a path for my exit, an angry Red Sea parting so the apostate could be exiled from Pharaoh's Tomb.

NINE

Meanwhile, Jack was mano a mano with Milo.

"We're shooting the breeze." His voice sounded cockier than usual. "You want to stop by? We're in his cabin. Just tell No-No to let you in."

"No-No?"

I rode the elevator to Deck Fourteen where recessed lights illuminated coved doors that led to the ship's most expensive cabins. The penthouse was farther down the hall. Deck Fourteen was also where Judy Carpenter was hung.

The Ninja standing outside Carpenter's cabin watched me approach, his face blank as a mask.

"Let me guess," I said. "No-No?"

He raised an eyebrow.

"Jack Stephanson told me to stop by."

As though hearing some password, No-No opened the door.

The deluxe cabin was not as opulent as the penthouse but had a small living room with a couch, two chairs, and a flat-screen television, which was being watched by a beefy fellow whose forehead hung over his eyes like a mansard roof. I'd seen him around the set; he kept the public at bay, some kind of bouncer. But we'd never been introduced.

He lowered his head with suspicion. The heavy brow cast shadows over his eyes.

"Raleigh Harmon, FBI."

"I know who you are."

He left it at that, giving no name.

"Is Jack Stephanson here?"

"In there." He pointed to the closed door. "They know you're coming?"

I nodded.

Milo Carpenter sat cross-legged on a king-size bed, a floral coverlet bunched beneath him like a ruptured garden. With both hands, he clutched a bottle of Jameson's whiskey, half gone. Both bottle and man, half gone.

Beside the bed, Jack stretched out in a chair. Mr. Casual, still.

"Harmon, you're just in time. We need a woman's opinion."

I glanced back at the man with the mansard forehead. He was absorbed in an ultimate fighting match on TV. I closed the door.

"We were talking about how unreasonable women get," Jack continued. "Women take everything to the outer edge of reason."

Milo's blond hair looked dull, like rye stripped by a hard wind. His face was flushed, the workaday charm of it, the thing that drew men into movie theaters, was somewhere inside that bottle. Swigging, he offered it to Jack.

"Thanks," Jack said, "but no drinking on the job."

"That stinks, you should become an actor."

Jack's eyes sparkled. He was enjoying this. The creep.

"So you want to hear what happened?" he asked, before suddenly turning to Milo. "Oh, do you mind if I tell her?"

"Might as well." Milo pulled a thread on the coverlet, gathering the print into a rayon bouquet. "People are gonna hear it soon enough."

"It's because of his affairs," Jack said. "She found photos.

Pictures of Milo with other women. Just devastated her." He looked at Milo. "Mind if I show her?"

Still gazing at the bedspread, Milo shook his head and Jack stood, picking up a manila folder from the nightstand. I watched a tear run raggedly down the actor's unshaven cheek.

I expected grainy surveillance photos. The sort taken at night from a great distance with a long lens. But these were color. In focus, well-lighted, and all of the women seemed aware of the camera. Dressed in Frederick's of Hollywood, they relished the pornographic "art."

I closed the folder, feeling disgusted.

"She found them when she was hiding my Christmas present." Milo's voice rasped. "Wasn't much of a Christmas."

"How many women were there?"

Milo glanced at Jack, who shrugged.

"What did I tell you? It matters to them." Jack turned to me. "That was Judy's first question, how many women."

"It's a legitimate question," I said.

Milo gave a mirthless smile. "How many? How high can you count?"

"You not only cheated on her, you kept evidence of it."

"You want to judge me? Fine." The glass-green eyes were shining. "But you don't know everything. We were living like brother and sister for years. She said she was okay with that. I loved her—" He stopped, seeing the disbelief in my face. "I did," he insisted. "I loved her. That's why I kept all those affairs secret. I didn't want to hurt her. But she found the pictures, then demanded we go to counseling. And the tabloids ran with the story."

"Marriage counseling?" *Or rehab*, I wondered.

"Sex addiction. She thought I had a problem."

Jack cleared his throat. "He finally asked her for a divorce and she came apart."

"Really?" I said. "But you go on a cruise together."

"I filed papers," Milo said. "You don't believe me, check the courthouse in LA."

"And get a room with one bed."

Jack scratched his chin. "One bed. That is a good point."

Milo swigged from the bottle, then drew his wrist across his mouth. "She begged me, okay? Said all we needed was some romance."

"That's what you call staying in the bar all night?" I said. "Romance?"

He glared at me. "I stayed in the bar because I didn't want to sleep with her."

"Very thoughtful."

"Hey, I could've had any woman in that place, but I didn't want to humiliate Judy. And not when she's working on the movie." He looked at Jack, trying the line again. "I wasn't going to humiliate her like that. You believe me, don't you?"

"Yeah." Jack nodded. "What time did you come back to the cabin?"

"Around three. I think it was around three."

"Was she here?" I asked.

"No. And I knew I'd hurt her." He was almost pleading. "I loved her, I swear. I just wasn't *in love*."

"So she wasn't in the cabin," I said, prompting again.

"I decided she was walking around, getting some air."

"She got some air all right," I muttered.

He didn't seem to hear me. "I was going to tell her we'd always be friends and some day she'd meet a guy who really appreciated her, loved her the way she deserved. But I went back to the bar because I couldn't find her. I had another drink, then got a bad feeling, and went to the desk to ask them to help me find her."

The bedroom door swung open. There was no knock. A plain woman appeared. Brown hair the color of tonight's baked potato; skin the color of fat-free milk. I'd seen her around the set and with the zombies tonight in Pharaoh's Tomb. She always held a clipboard and reminded me of a winter sparrow, the way she quirked her head. Her voice wasn't chirpy, though. It was flat, packed down like sandstone.

"What are you doing here?" she asked.

"I was invited."

She quirked her head at Milo. "We just had a scene."

"One of my scenes?" Milo asked.

"*A scene.*" She pecked her head toward me. "She made a scene. At the crystal seminar."

I glanced at Jack but his eyes were watching the Bird Girl.

"Sandy's afraid the paparazzi are going to find out. He wants a press release so it doesn't get blown out of proportion." She lifted the ever-present clipboard, waiting for permission.

"Read it." Milo dropped his head.

She looked at Jack. Then me.

"Read it, Betsy."

"'Judy Carpenter, wife of action-adventure star Milo Carpenter, died early Tuesday morning while on a cruise to Alaska with her husband. Mrs. Carpenter was a music producer of popular bands including recent breakout artists Stress Test and Peculiar Utterance. She committed suicide.'"

He looked up. "That's it?"

"No. 'Milo Carpenter is devastated by the loss of his life partner and wife of nineteen years.'"

"Twenty-two," he said. "We were married twenty-two years. Our anniversary's next month."

She scratched her pen on the paper, then read again. "'During this difficult time, Mr. Carpenter hopes his many devoted fans will respect his need for privacy. But the public is encouraged to post thoughts and feelings at www.milocarpenter.com. Mr. Carpenter plans to read every single note.'"

"What?"

"I'll read them," she said. "'To honor his wife's dying wishes, Mr. Carpenter will continue with his blockbuster movie *Northern Decomposure*, a sequel to his blockbuster hit *Nice Death*. The new movie will be in theaters later this year.'"

"We have a release date?"

She shook her head. "Sandy says keep it open. You never know with editing and production delays. I'm sending the release to the majors, *Variety*, *ET*. You want to take calls?"

"No."

She pecked out a nod, then left.

Jack stood up. "We should get going too. Thanks for your time, Milo. It takes a real man to deal with something like this."

Still playing Bad Cop, I waited by the door while the movie star got up to hug Jack. I was surprised when Milo turned to me with something like apology in his eyes.

"Sorry I didn't tell you all this earlier," he said. "This whole thing. I mean, she's dead. You know?"

Yeah, I knew. And my father was murdered and I'd spent years dealing with other people coping with violent loss. In all that time, I'd never seen anyone who could've listened to a press release about their next business venture.

He waited for me to say something.

Anything.

"Yes," I said. "I'm sure this has been quite a shock."

Neither Jack nor I said another word until we had turned the corner and stood alone by the elevators.

"You're buying this?" I said.

"You saw those pictures. Women throw themselves at that guy."

"I hear envy."

"Probably."

He said it so calmly it deflected my blow. Which only annoyed me more. "Jack, I saw her. She wasn't some weeping willow. That woman took herself—and her worthless husband—from rags to riches, literally."

"And the pictures upset her. Can you imagine the pain she must have felt?"

"Then why bring them on board?" I hit the Down button.

"I don't know. But I checked his bathroom. He's got a monster prescription for Viagra and that stuff for thinning hair. She was taking Ambien, which might have made her spacey but not suicidal. I also checked the garbage."

"Thank you," I said begrudgingly.

"I don't think he killed her, Harmon. He truly believes she took herself out because he didn't love her anymore."

"But sends out a self-glorifying press release."

"He's an actor."

I reached past him, pressing the button again. "He's practically dancing on her grave."

"Actors are narcissists."

"They lie for a living."

"Have you ever seen one of his movies?" Jack asked.

"No."

The elevator *bing*ed, then opened. It was empty.

"Watch one of his movies. He's not that good a liar. And he's a drunk. He would've messed up the story by now. But he's repeating it word for word."

"Rehearsed."

The elevator stopped at Deck Twelve and two couples shuffled inside. One of the men used a walker. Jack and I pressed ourselves to the mirrored back wall. As the door closed, Jack leaned over, whispering in my ear.

"You're dying to know how I got him to talk."

"I can imagine."

"I apologized."

Staring at the numbers above the doors, feeling his breath on my hair, I decided this was the world's slowest elevator. "Apologized for what?"

"For the way you treated him."

I turned. "You did what—?"

His face was inches away and he was grinning. "They're all narcissists. I told him he was right and you were wrong and he opened like a spigot. Spilled everything."

Our next stop was Deck Ten, where two more couples got on. They wore phillumenist name tags.

"Five, please," said a gray-haired woman.

"We're all going to five," shouted the man with the walker.

Jack scooted closer, making room for the woman on his right side. "Why did you get engaged?" he asked.

I stared at the numbers, wondering if the elevator was defective.

"You won't tell me who he is?"

I did the calculus. The number of people onboard, divided by the number of elevators, then factoring in the disproportionately high percentage of passengers eligible for AARP—all the people who couldn't use the stairs—and when the door opened, we had only reached Deck Nine. Two more couples shuffled inside.

No more elevators, I decided.

Since I wasn't talking, Jack had struck up a conversation with the elderly woman next to him. She kept nodding at what he said, her trifocals flashing under the lights.

"And I'm heartbroken," Jack was saying. "She went and got engaged to somebody else."

Her wrinkled face melted with pity. "Oh, you poor thing!"

My face was enflamed, my lungs begged for air. When the elevator finally opened on Deck Five, the men turned, helping their wives out while Jack held the door for them.

"Hot dog!" exclaimed a man named Bill. His name tag said he was a phillumenist from Florida. Snapping his fingers, he escorted his wife to the atrium where a swing band played to a sea of white hair. "Listen to that, honey!"

Jack and I waited for the last of them to leave.

"Want to dance?" he asked.

"No. I want to know what's wrong with you."

"I can tell you over a drink."

"Over my dead body."

"On this cruise, Harmon, that's not a joke."

I checked my watch. Geert's curfew was 10:00 PM—no "bothering" passengers after that. It was now four minutes to, and the ship docked tomorrow in Juneau at 5:00 AM.

"Did you call the Juneau office?" I asked.

But he was watching the old folks dance, a faint smile on his face. The music played like oscillating ribbons of sound.

"He's an old pal from Quantico," Jack said finally. "He said he'll meet us at 6:30. Come on, Harmon, one dance?"

"He'll have background checks on the movie people?" I asked.

"Harmon, listen to that." He moved his head to the beat. "That's 'Mack the Knife.'"

"And this is Good Night Jack."

His reply was cast to my retreating back and I almost turned around. It was what he said and how he said it.

"Sweet dreams, Harmon."

But I kept walking, past the art gallery closed up for the night, and the pastry café, and though the music began to fade, I could still hear the singer looping back to the song's chorus, going over those shark teeth pearly white, how Mack he keeps them outta sight. And as I headed to my cabin, I rubbed my hands over my bare arms, smoothing down a sudden case of goose bumps.

* * *

In the great white north in June, ten o'clock at night wasn't really night. Around the edge of our blackout drapes, the sun drew a golden line, reminding me that the world beyond was still glowing.

Beneath the window, my mother snuggled under a white duvet, her back turned to the nightstand between our beds. The phone blinked with messages and a slip of paper was stuck under the phone's base. Leaning into the window's ambient light, I read my mother's graceful handwriting. *Where are you? Where. Wear. Ware.*

I stared down at her curled form. Her breathing was steady, slow enough to tell me she was gone to the world. Her word riddles, the lettered solitaire, was no game. Her mind was fracturing, and I vowed to spend time with her tomorrow.

Picking up the phone, tiptoeing through the dark, I stretched the phone cord to our small closet and pushed the message button.

It was DeMott. And his voice sounded close, as if he was hiding here with me.

"I'm trying the room phone," he said, "since you're not answering your cell."

At first I didn't mind when DeMott began calling my cell phone several times a day. I was just grateful he agreed I should take this vacation by myself. But his need for constant contact began to remind me why I wanted to get away. The relentless questioning, the dismay when I needed solitude. The inability to appreciate FBI work. And now, with Judy Carpenter's death, I had a legitimate reason for not returning his calls—but couldn't tell him. It was an open case, and DeMott complained that I worked too much, that I didn't know how to "just live."

"Richmond's on high broil," he drawled. Weather was a favored topic, probably because nothing else changed at

Weyanoke. Occupied by Fieldings since the early 1700s, his family's plantation on the James River was a fabled estate, where Robert E. Lee once danced the Virginia reel across the walnut floors and where a Confederate cannonball still lodged in the dining room's brick wall. DeMott wanted us to get married on Weyanoke's lawn. But the battle over that was nothing compared to the fight over where we would live as man and wife. Just the thought of living at Weyanoke made me hyperventilate.

"And we've got fireflies at night, your favorite," he continued. "I sit out on the porch and watch them light up the dark, and I think of you."

His desultory Southern voice never rushed, never sounded urgent. The voice that turned weather into a narrative. And now, listening to him describe the night, I pressed the phone to my ear. I loved his voice.

I loved him.

"Tell your mama her dog's happier than a pig in mud," he said.

Madame, my mom's dog. DeMott was taking care of her while we were away.

"That creature loves running these fields, sniffing out the rabbits, jumping in the river." He paused. "Raleigh, you're going to love it too. I promise. It'll be different than what you think."

I dropped my head. My heart ached.

"I've put pressure on you," he said. "And I'm sorry. We don't have to hurry. You just enjoy your vacation. I mean it. And when you come home, I'll be waiting. I love you. Call me. Bye."

The arid sound of a dead line rushed past, the nothingness of nowhere. And nobody. Still, I held the phone to my ear and calculated the time difference. Four hours ahead of Alaska, it was past 2:00 AM at Weyanoke. His sister Mac would say

I had no manners, then harp on it for days. Yet another hurdle for us: Mac, his sister who kept me atop her enemies list.

Replacing the phone on the nightstand, I stuck to the bedtime routine. Brush teeth, wash face, and ignore that question begging for an answer. *You can't return your fiancé's call and you're relieved. Wasn't that another bad sign?*

I pulled the covers up tight and listened to the ship sliding through the Inside Passage. The ocean brushed against the side, whooshing and splashing, and once again I thought of Judy Carpenter.

I wondered if she was completely dead when she was hung there, or if her last moments were spent listening to this cold brush of sound, the silver splash of ocean as it escorted her to an end of days.

TEN

At 6:15 AM Wednesday morning, the Juneau gift shops were already open, offering passengers the souvenir T-shirts and baseball caps and jewelry and native Ulu knives.

But I was looking for a place called the Hurff A. Saunders Federal Building.

"I know where it is," Jack insisted. "If we hit Evergreen Cemetery, we've gone too far."

Under the sun shining as though clouds didn't exist, Juneau clung to the bottom of two mountains, Mt. Roberts and Mt. Juneau. Near ninety degrees, the slopes fell with the long and lush lines of weighted skirts. Between the shops along the waterfront, strips of wooden stairs stitched up the hillsides, embroidering small houses to green forests. On the other side, across a wide band of water called Gastineau Channel, another mountain rose to an island, Douglas Island, and as Jack and I climbed the hill that was Main Street, I gazed at the beige sand rimming the shore. This landscape of fjords and steep mountains was far too young for such fine beaches. More likely the sand was a byproduct of the town's once-prodigious gold mines, when the bedrock was crushed and pulverized to release the precious metal within. But the beach reminded me of another hike I planned and wasn't taking, to the abandoned Perseverance Mine.

When I saw the federal building, it didn't exactly lift my spirits. The place was an aesthetic crime, especially amid such fulsome natural beauty. A block of steel the color of tarnished brass, the rectangular building rose nine stories from the street like some sick advertisement for all the soul-deadening bureaucracies inside, all those government agencies whose acronyms could be strung together like boxcars. EPA. DEA. OSHA. NOAA.

FBI.

Jack held the door. "It's called the SOB."

"Pardon?"

"State Office Building. SOB."

The FBI's resident agency occupied a corner of the ninth floor. A messy ten-by-ten room with two desks, the dark brown carpet couldn't hide the coffee and mud stains, or the winter salt-melt that covered it like dingy doilies.

Agent Kevin Barnes slapped Jack on the back—hard. Facial hair was rare among agents, unless they were working undercover. But the beard on Barnes's face was so thick his gray eyes seemed to peer from a brown fur mask. Dry mud coated the bottom of his jeans and his black sweater frayed around the collar.

He plunked down in a chair behind his desk. The seat was crisscrossed with duct tape. "How long have you known Romeo here?" he asked.

"Long enough to know he's trouble."

"Barnes." Jack said, "did you run the background checks or not?"

"Have you seen his plane?" Barnes kept his gray eyes on me.

I nodded.

"The paperwork?" Jack said. "You didn't do it, did you?"

"I did it," Barnes said. "NCIS and CCH."

National Criminal Information System, for outstanding

warrants. And Computerized Criminal History, to reveal any arrests, convictions, sentences served, date of release from prison, etc. The CCH would also give us physical descriptions and personal data such as birth records and social security numbers.

"Thank you," I said. "That's really helpful."

"My pleasure." His smile was an amber tear across the fur mask. "I also called a friend who's a detective with LAPD. Before I escaped to here, I worked in the LA field office." He leaned back until he was almost horizontal, then suddenly lifted his feet, catapulting forward. At the last second, he grabbed the edge of the desk, preventing a collision with his computer monitor. "After working in LA, I can tell you for a fact that movie people are prone to doing all kinds of stupid stuff. So these records are long, and eventually boring. Speaking of which, you know Jack's reputation, right?"

Jack said, "What did LAPD tell you?"

"They told me to call back." Kevin kept his eyes on me. "Raleigh, can I give you some advice?"

I smiled. "Fire away."

"Don't get in Jack's plane. You're as good as gone."

"Bad pilot?"

"I'm not talking about that kind of gone."

"Barnes." Jack's jaw was set. "All we need—"

"If I didn't warn you, I couldn't live with myself."

"You can't live with yourself now, you sorry sack of—" Jack stepped forward.

He was only three steps from the computer, but the path was blocked by a dorm-size refrigerator, several stalagmites of FedEx envelopes, state torts, and FBI documents, along with some vacuum bags. The vacuum itself standing next to Barnes's duct-taped chair.

"We're in a hurry," Jack said, kicking the vacuum bags.

Barnes kicked them back. "He seduced every woman at Quantico."

"Every one?" I glanced at Jack. His jaw was knotting.

"Well, that gal from Utah got away. But she turned out to be a lesbian."

Jack lunged for the computer's mouse.

"Click it and you die, Jack."

"Take your best shot!"

They began wrestling for the mouse and I glanced out the window, suppressing a sigh.

The tiny resident agency lacked every amenity, including one decent chair. But the picture window redeemed it all. Below, I could see the gray-green channel as it coursed past Douglas Island. And the mountain forest looked like a quiver of emerald arrows, aimed for a cerulean sky that leased eternity. Just looking at it, my heart skipped a beat.

"That's what keeps me here," Barnes said.

I looked over. They were still shoving each other, locked in some testosterone-fueled standoff. "No matter what kind of day I'm having"—he elbowed Jack's ribs; Jack winced— "even Romeo here showing up, I can look out that window. Nobody in the Bureau has a view like that."

My desk in Richmond was hunkered beneath a heating vent next to an echoing stairwell. The tight spot was chosen for me by my supervisor, the same woman who sent me on a disciplinary transfer.

Jack hip-checked the chair, slamming Barnes into the vacuum.

"What did you find on the movie crew?" I asked.

Picking himself up, climbing back into the chair, Barnes gave Jack one final shove before placing the keyboard on his dusty jeans. "So glad you asked." He typed quickly.

It finally seemed safe to lean in closer. "Right now," I said, "this does not look like a random crime. We're concentrating on people who knew the victim, worked with her, or had access to her. I'm especially interested in the husband."

Barnes clicked a final command, opening the document. "Hollywood is a food chain for deviants. Down at the bottom, they're mostly drug addicts. Pot, coke, Ecstasy. You'll see some busts for possession, but I did find one distribution case, sentenced as a felon."

I opened my notebook.

"Female," he continued. "Martha Jane McTavish. Age 27. She rents a place in Venice Beach, owned by your victim."

I leaned over his shoulder and stared at the mug shot. The long black hair was still wild, but fear had widened her eyes. MJ, the girl in the bar last night. No wonder she pegged me for a cop.

"Any other details?" I jotted down the dates.

"Plenty. She ran a heavy marijuana operation around the San Jose area. It was another rental but the local PD got tipped off when the electric bill exceeded occupancy by about three dozen people. Place was a greenhouse. Hundreds of thousands of dollars in plants. She served two years and got paroled on good behavior."

"What's her connection to the movie?" Jack asked. The fight was over. It was all about the case now.

"She plays the musician," I said.

They looked at me.

"I met her last night. Judy produced her CDs. She wouldn't talk about the hanging. Did you see anything besides the Venice rental that connects her to the Carpenters?"

Barnes scrolled down the list. "Nothing here, but the Carpenters have their own problems. Four DUIs between them. Hers was almost twenty years ago but he lost his license. Two years ago he got picked up for L&L in some bar."

Lewd and lascivious.

"Nice guy," I said, looking over at Jack.

"LAPD found trace amounts of marijuana on him," Barnes continued, "barely enough for possession. Most of them smoke pot, or do something else destructive with all that money."

"What else flipped your radar?" Jack asked.

"Money. The biggest troubles involve money. On that count, the Carpenters seem okay. But most everybody else has some kind of tax lien, overdue child support, or alimony due for multiple ex-wives. They're running on borrowed funds. And you'll want to check out Martin Webb." He glanced at Jack. "Remember that flick *Dodge and Ram*? He directed it."

"He did that?" Jack asked.

"Yeah, but he also directed that one where Milo Carpenter played a Special Ops guy."

"That was weak."

"That scene, when he cried? I walked out of the theater."

"I caught it on cable and it was still *bad*. You can't have a guy—" Jack glanced at me.

"*Anyway*," I said. Men and movies were almost as bad as men and cars. And to be fair, women and shoes. "Can we get back to the list?"

Barnes nodded at the monitor again. "Martin Webb's got two foreclosed mansions and California's garnishing his wages for child support."

"A *really* nice guy," I said.

"It gets even better. An assistant filed rape charges against him, then settled out of court."

"He paid her off, that's why he's broke?"

"I doubt it. Working in LA, I learned how they all play games. I'm not saying her claim's necessarily frivolous, but everybody wants fame. She probably got some movie deal. But there's a judge here ordering Webb to take anger management classes." He glanced over at Jack. "I wonder if that's where he got the idea for that scene in *Tight Corner*, remember? Where the guy goes to an anger management class—"

"And trashes the place," Jack said. "He picks up the table and says—"

"'How's this for behavior modification?'"

They laughed, quoted more lines, and I sighed.

"Do you have any photos of Webb, for Jack?" I asked.

Barnes clicked the mouse. Martin Webb's face was handsome but petulant; clever eyes were surrounded by dark lashes and a narrow chin anchored by an oddly voluptuous mouth, almost feminine. In the mug shot, his mouth clamped with fury, just like I'd seen it around the set whenever Milo flubbed his lines for the tenth time.

"What is he, about forty?" Jack asked.

"Thirty-eight," Barnes said. "Young for how much he's done. Good and bad. But his career's really gone downhill fast."

"Did he have any connection to Judy Carpenter?" I asked. "Other than this movie."

"I didn't see anything, but remember he directed Milo Carpenter in other movies, years ago."

"Maybe the director hated her," Jack said.

"Or maybe that bracelet was supposed to pay off some bills."

"What bracelet?" Barnes asked.

I described the jewelry, fallen between the rope coils, and Barnes asked questions about the crime scene, homing in on my description of her neck, the strange way her tongue stuck out.

"Come on, that rope would've broken her neck," he said. "That whole thing sounds staged. Or should I say, *directed*." His gray eyes glinted from the fur mask. "You're making me wish I'd taken this case."

"But you didn't." Jack's voice was so territorial I turned

to look at him. But he kept his eyes on the monitor. "Who else?" he asked.

"Check out a guy named Vinnie Pinnetta. Also gets violent with women. He worked as a bouncer in a Vegas strip club, after serving time for breaking and entering, and then kicked his pregnant wife. He served time for both."

"Such nice people," I said. "How'd he get to Hollywood?"

"Bodyguard."

I leaned over Barnes's shoulder. In the mug shot, the police camera's flash made the mansard forehead seem even more pronounced. Vinnie Pinnetta's eyes were like shadows. When I turned around, Jack was leaning in so close I could smell his cologne. Citrus and light musk.

"Remember him," I said, "from Milo's last night?"

"Who could forget a teddy bear like that?"

I looked at Barnes. "He's *Milo's* bodyguard."

Barnes raised his bushy brown eyebrows.

"Too simple," Jack said. "Carpenter really believes she committed suicide over his affairs, and because he filed for divorce."

"Yes." I nodded. "He was dumping her after more than twenty years of marriage. He and Jack are like best buddies."

Barnes gave a ragged grin. "I'm not worried about you, Raleigh."

"Listen to me," Jack insisted. "He's acting guilty because he feels responsible. He's a total narcissist."

"No wonder you hit it off with him," Barnes said.

But Jack was shaking his head. "I'm telling you, he didn't do it."

"Here's something to consider." Barnes leaned back in his chair again. "California's fifty-fifty when it comes to divorce. Now he doesn't have to split anything, Milo gets to keep all of it. And there's a lot to keep. Not like your ex-wife, Jack. She got half of nothing."

His *ex*?

Jack looked ready to give Barnes another smacking, but the agent was busy lifting a paper pile from his desk.

"Here, I printed you a hard copy."

"Thank you," I said.

"Yeah," Jack growled, "thanks for the *help*."

"Raleigh," Barnes said, ignoring Jack, "this your first trip to Alaska?"

I was already fanning through the pages, stopping to stare at the mug shots. "Yes, this was supposed to be a family vacation."

"Sorry about that."

"I'll come back someday."

"We've got an opening."

I looked up.

"The other agent wants to move back to the States."

Jack laughed. "Hey, genius, Alaska is a state."

"That's what you think." Barnes turned to me. "No squad commander. No supervisor. And it's never boring. I can put in a good word for you."

"You don't even know her," Jack said.

"I see she handles you just fine, Romeo."

They were bickering again and I flipped through the report, when suddenly a mug shot seemed to leap off the page. I turned the report so Jack could see her face.

Claire.

"Don't tell me," he said. "She got busted for building a spaceship without a permit."

She had several different names. Claire Rainmaker. Claire Waterwoman. Finally, Claire the Clairvoyant. In 1999, she was arrested at the World Trade Organization riots in Seattle. Maybe that's where she learned to screech about "police brutality." She was later busted for not having a business license for her psychic palm reading operation on Aurora Avenue. But the capper was two hundred and forty-three parking tickets, still unpaid.

I pointed to the number, showing Jack.

"Two hundred and forty-three?" He whistled. "That nut's more ambitious than I thought."

ELEVEN

The wind whispered though the spruce boughs on Calhoun Street, filling the air with a cold crisp scent, like spring snow. A steel handrail ran alongside the buckling sidewalk—something to grab during icy winters—and I tried to imagine what life would be like here. Minutes to the mountains. Fresh air. Ocean water. And no boss.

"Who should we check first?" Jack asked.

"The bodyguard."

"Then you agree Milo didn't kill her?"

"No. I agree it's very convenient to have a bodyguard." I glanced up the street as an old Volvo came slowly down the road, in no particular hurry. "Who do you suggest we look at?"

"Claire."

I stopped.

"I want to arrest her," he said, "so she'll leave you alone."

On our right, the Alaska governor's mansion stood out like a Southern thumb. It was a bright white neoclassical house with columns framing a portico. Beautiful but more suited to a Southern plantation. It made me wonder if the street's name—Calhoun—was for the fiery orator from South Carolina, the seventh vice president of the United States, and the first to resign from office. Odder still was how the house was positioned so close to the sidewalk. We stood not ten feet from the front door, with no guards, no gates, as if we were expected to walk up and ring the doorbell. While I opened my cell phone to call Geert, Jack circled the house, marveling.

"What," Geert answered, gruff as usual.

"Are the movie people still on the ship?"

"They went in helicopters. Touring some glaciers."

"What time are they expected back?"

"Late. They wanted a salmon-bake on the river."

So he was checking on them. Good. He suspected something too. "Did Milo Carpenter go with them?"

I heard the plastic clacking of a keyboard and watched Jack strolling around the house.

"One guy stayed," Geert said.

I waited. He waited.

Fine. I'll ask.

"Do you have his name?"

"Of course. Webb. Martin Webb."

My heart rate kicked up. "Keep an eye on him until we get back to the ship."

"He's gone."

"You just said he stayed."

"Neen. I said he didn't go with them. He bought a ticket for the tram ride from our concierge."

"When?"

More clacking. "Eighteen minutes ago."

"Thank you." I closed the phone and jogged to where Jack stood gazing at the white column portico. The place looked like Tara, airlifted to the Last Frontier.

He said, "I just realized who you remind me of. Remember that governor who ran for vice—"

"Webb didn't go with the rest of the movie crew. He bought a ticket for some tram ride."

Jack pointed down the hill. Juneau's downtown spread

across the short basin, stopping at the water's edge. "There's only one tram. Over to the left, see it?"

Three enormous cruise ships floated in the channel and from the shoreline a twin set of cables rose, pulling up the mountain something that looked like a red box. Above the treetops, the wind that rippled the channel's gray-green water also swung the car slightly.

"It runs every ten or fifteen minutes," Jack said.

"How do you know?"

But he was already on his cell phone, asking information for the Mount Roberts tram.

"Yeah, hi," he said. "Two tickets for the next tram up." He paused. "Okay, thanks anyway." He closed the phone. "Sold out."

"What's up there?"

"A restaurant with a view that steals your breath. A wild-life center but—"

"How do you know?"

"—but from what Barnes just told us, Webb doesn't sound like a nature lover." He stared at the summit of Mount Roberts, squinting against the sun. "Maybe I've seen too many action movies."

"What?"

"Theoretically, a helicopter could land up there."

"Theoretically."

"The summit's got a flat ledge." He pointed. The mountain had sides steep like walls. But I could see a short plateau near the top.

He said, "Canada's only a few miles away. It sounds crazy, but so was hanging Judy Carpenter like that. And suppose she had more jewelry on her? Suppose he wanted to take off with it?"

"I get it, but how do you know about—"

"You're a runner, right?"

"Yes."

He looked at his watch. "Then c'mon, let's run."

On the forest floor, yellow flags of skunk cabbage waved when Jack ran past. I watched bouquets of green ferns sway like palms crying out Hosanna. But ten paces behind him, I was struggling, my lungs searing on every intake.

He yelled down the trail. "You okay?"

I nodded, too breathless to speak, and when I looked up, he was glancing back to see if I was all right.

The expression on his face stopped me. One split second. But I saw it.

Tenderness. Concern.

And then it was gone.

"You went soft down there in Dixie," he said. "Must be that fiancé."

He took off, and the trail got steeper.

This was not the hike I had in mind. But the geology was an epic crime scene. Before this quaint town laid itself across the foot of these mountains, some catastrophic event had lifted layered rock miles toward heaven. For untold years, wind and rain pummeled the rock while the shifting tectonic plates continued to grind at the fault lines that cut through the channel below. When the Ice Age blanketed the entire region, it scoured the stones, leaving frigid striations still visible on the dark boulders I passed at every switchback, leaning on them for rest.

When I finally caught Jack, he stood next to a large wooden cross. Waiting for my pulse to drop from heart attack country, and not wanting Jack to know it, I turned my back to him and read the sign beside the cross. It described a missionary priest who cut this trail and raised this marker, reminding every hiker who built the mountain and designed the trees and bestowed each of us with our laboring breath.

"Thirsty?" Jack asked.

Parched was more like it, but he opened his hand, presenting something like green snails, and popped one in his mouth.

"Fiddleheads, the tops of ferns. Keep you hydrated." He grinned. "I promise, it's not poison. Harmon, live a little."

A texture like Bibb lettuce, a taste like chlorophyll, and he was gone before I could ask how he knew where we were going. Up the rest of the trail my quads burned as if my thighs decided to host the phillumenists' convention. Jack slowed down enough that I could keep an eye on the back of his shirt, spined with sweat, but mostly my head stayed down as we pumped up the mountain.

Then, as suddenly as it appeared, the forest fell away.

We stood on a rocky plateau. Across the channel snow-capped mountains extended as far as my eyes could see, endless white rows. They sliced at the clear sky purged of particulate, offering a vision both beautiful and chilling. Chilling, because it was a place man could not survive. When I looked down, blue blossoms of forget-me-nots shook in the wind. I plucked one, marveling that such delicate flowers could survive high summit weather. The rock was some green gabbro, a metamorphic mix of stone churned and spewed from the earth's deeper layer. Both flower and stone went into my pocket before I shrugged into my jean jacket. Jack stood at the edge, pulling on his brown sport coat. He ran his hand through his hair, the golden ends glistening with sweat. And he surveyed the crowd of people.

So many people. Hundreds, maybe thousands. A complete contrast to the forest's quiet solitude, the tourists snapped pictures and followed guides who wore orange vests and pointed to the cages set on four-foot timbers. One guide carried a bald eagle, leashed to her metal wrist cuff.

"You see Webb?" Jack asked.

When I shook my head, Jack pressed into the crowd. Once

again I tried to stick close but he was faster. I lost him when another man stepped between us. He wore a canvas bucket hat and smiled at me.

"Excuse me," I said.

"Excuse me," he replied.

Locked in that side-to-side hopping dance, we kept blocking each other as we tried to get out of the way.

The guide to my left was saying, "Eagles mate for life, and it's tragic when a partner dies and we find—"

Suddenly I felt a hand grab my wrist, pulling me through the crowd. I bumped into people, sputtering apologies, then popped out the other side. Jack held my hand, still walking forward, dragging me along. But when I looked down, his fingers had entwined with mine. Adrenaline shot from my heart, flying down my arm. Pulling my hand away, I tucked the tingling fingers into my pocket and kept following. He never turned around.

"This beautiful cat has been with us for about three months," said another guide. She was pointing to a six-foot cage where a buff-colored animal limped across the container. "He's a lynx and his leg was crushed." There were other cages, all set on timbers. A black bear cub was missing an eye. A grouse's short legs were crooked.

Jack turned, whispering, "Six o'clock."

Directly across from us, Martin Webb hovered at the edge of the crowd. A tall man—six one, according to the background check—his elongated face looked gaunt and I was struck again by his features, how the full lips consumed that narrow chin. But now those clever large eyes darted side to side, furtively.

"We had to sew up his ear," the guide continued, pointing into the cage. "See how it's torn?"

The crowd pressed in.

Webb stepped back, then turned toward the forest. The

trees stood like an emerald curtain behind the wildlife display and his black sweatshirt and black jeans blended with the dark evergreen boughs.

Jack opened his hand, signaling for me to circle the crowd, using the bodies as cover.

When I came up at nine o'clock, Webb was already pushing away the tree limbs. I didn't see Jack.

The guide said, "In this next display, you'll see an example of our work with wounded birds. This puffin was found bleeding..."

The crowd shuffled to the right and Jack popped up, signaling for me to follow Webb. I partially opened the fanny pack, making sure the Glock was accessible, then lifted my arm, protecting my eyes from the branches that scratched at my face. Inside the trees, sunlight turned to alchemy, the branches of hemlock and spruce turned the golden beams to silver. Sticks were snapping to my right. I crouched, squinting through the brushy limbs. His black figure slashed through like an iron sword. Racing after him, I shoved away the branches—only to have them bounce back, full of life and spring. Suddenly he looked back. His face was white against the forest, panting, struggling.

And then he was gone.

I raced faster and found him lying on the ground. Jack stood over him, a hunter bagging the white hyena.

"Are you Martin Webb?" Jack asked.

Webb was staring at me. "You—what do you want?"

"Answer the man's question."

But the director didn't take direction. He reached up, touching his gaunt cheek. A decent-size scratch was bleeding. Webb stared at the blood on his fingers, horrified.

Jack hoisted him up by the arm, without perceivable effort. "You can get lost in the woods, Marty."

"Especially when you're in some kind of a hurry," I said.

"I was taking a walk." He yanked his arm from Jack's steadying grip. "And my name is Martin."

"Marty, I'm Jack Stephanson, FBI. You already know the lovely Raleigh Harmon."

"Touch me again and I'll file charges."

"That would help, thanks."

"What?"

"Then you can explain why you were running from us."

"And running somehow makes me guilty?" Webb smirked. "I've got news for you, this a free country."

"Free, with laws attached," Jack said, smiling easily. "One of those laws is you can't go around raping your assistants."

"What did you—"

"We know all about you, Marty."

For a second I thought Webb would cave. Mouth open, his eyes were no longer clever. He drew a long deep breath.

And screamed.

He screamed like a silly girl in a horror flick. Covering my ears, I took a step back. The shrill pitch shattered the forest. I saw Jack's lip curling in disgust as he reached for Webb's elbow again. The director released a second wave and I saw a guide come running down a trail toward us.

Young, with a thin blond beard, the guide looked panicked. I couldn't blame him. Webb's scream sounded like another animal needed to be saved.

"Oh, thank God you're here!" Webb told him, pointing at us. "These people, they chased me into the woods and knocked me to the ground." He touched his cheek again, then showed his bloody fingers. "Look!"

"Hang on," Jack said.

I yanked my credentials from the fanny pack, flashing them for the guide. "We're with the FBI, we wanted to talk to this man. He scratched his face running from us. He's fine, and you can go back to whatever you were doing."

"FBI?" The guide scrunched his nose, like he smelled cat poop. "FBI *agents*?"

"I'm bleeding," Webb sniveled. "I almost lost an eye." He pointed to someone behind me. "And you're all witnesses."

I turned around.

The tourists had followed their guide down the trail. Worse, they were looking at Martin Webb with compassion.

"You're not getting the whole story," I told the guide. "In fact, it's safe to say this man is lying." I was about to explain what happened, when a distinctive voice clanked behind me.

"And you're one to talk about lying."

I turned around again. Claire. She was pushing her way through the people.

"Here you are, hitting people again." She moved past us, standing next to Webb. "You don't need to say a word," she told him. "Raleigh hit me last night. You can have my testimony for half my usual fee."

"Fee?" Webb said.

"Okay, no charge. Just because I don't want these Nazis hurting anybody else."

"Claire, go away," I said. "This is none of your business."

She turned toward the crowd, sensing their sympathy. "Do you feel that, in the air? Feel it, coming toward us?"

People gazed at the trees, then toward the dappled sky, their faces fearful.

"A black cloud of pain and agony is coming toward us, right now."

I looked at the guide. "If you'll let me explain."

"They have guns," Claire said.

"Guns?" The guide put his hands on his hips. "This is a wildlife preserve. You can't have guns here."

"Don't say I didn't warn you," Claire said.

I brandished my credentials once more, like a priest holding a crucifix toward the devil. "This woman is a menace. She doesn't know what she's talking about."

"She's lying," Claire told him. "I work with the Seattle police, I'm a clairvoyant."

"You're a kook," Jack said.

The guide said, "I don't know what to believe right now."

"Well, you can't believe her." Claire stabbed a finger into my shoulder. "Her mom's losing her marbles and it's all her fault. She lied to her about working for the FBI." Craning her neck toward the crowd, she said, "I'll prove it to you. Nadine, where are you? Nadine? She was just here..."

"You didn't," I whispered. "Tell me you didn't."

"Would you lie to your own mother?" Claire asked the crowd. "And the poor woman's coming unglued. Did you see her? She was the woman talking to herself the whole way up in the tram."

My legs felt like stone. I watched Claire's neon-yellow sweatshirt moving away, down the path where they'd all come from, like some tropical parrot blown off course into an evergreen forest. "Nadine!" she called out. "Raleigh's here. Come see for yourself."

Jack stood at my side, watching her go. "Did she do what I think she did?"

I couldn't breathe.

"Are you okay?"

The trees blurred. Forest and faces and nausea swept over me.

"Webb—" Jack turned. "He's running again!"

My feet refused to move. I watched Jack race down the trail and thought, *She told her. She told her I'm an FBI agent.*

"Look, I don't know what's going on," the guide said. "I need some questions answered."

I kicked through the ferns, running around the crowd now moving back to the wildlife center. When I came out of the forest, I heard something like a hawk's screech. One of the leashed eagles beat its brown wings frantically. The guide struggled to calm the bird, its chain clanking against the metal wrist cuff.

Jack was tailing Webb as the director ran toward the lynx cage. A large muscular guide stood with yet another tour group, but Webb barged right in, turning to point at Jack in pursuit. Then Webb took off again.

"Hey!" the guide yelled.

When Jack raced by, the guide grabbed him. Jack threw him off and the guide threw himself like a linebacker, taking Jack to the ground. Webb stood behind the cage, watching the men wrestling on the ground, and it gave me just enough time to gain on him. By the time he saw me, the gap was closing.

Switching directions, he circled behind the lynx cage.

Jack and the guide were still tussling, neither one giving in, and I walked around the side of the lynx cage. Webb's black Nike shoes were visible, standing behind the cage.

You are going down, creep.

At first, I thought the sound was the cat. Or a wounded bird. But it was the cage. Tilting forward, I heard screws and nails ripping from the wooden timber. The frightened cat leaped inside, releasing a bloodcurdling howl as the cage plunged to the rocky ground.

The crowd was screaming. Birds screeched. Jack and the guide lay still, staring at the cage where the cat continued its agonized yowls. When I looked for Webb, he was running for the tram's wheelhouse. The silver cables glinted against the blue sky and the red car waited, its door open.

Only more disturbing: At the turnstile that led to the tram, a woman wearing pink tennis shoes pushed frantically against the metal bar blocking her path. Her black curls shook in the sunlight.

My mother.

I ran. But my feet seemed weighed down. And the harder I ran, the slower it felt. I saw my mother hand the clerk her ticket. Webb was right behind her, bouncing on his toes, and when she passed through the turnstile, he threw his ticket at the girl and banged though the gate. He leaped into the red car ahead of her.

She moved like someone afraid, like someone who feels the earth shaking under her feet.

I panted to the turnstile.

"Ticket?" the girl said.

Webb watched from the open door, his clever eyes calculating. But my mother kept her face to the window, looking out at the empty sky and distant mountains. My heart beat so fast it hurt. I stepped forward, pushing on the turnstile.

The girl said, "I need to see your ticket."

"That man." I pointed at Webb. "You need to hold him."

"Do you have a ticket or not?" she demanded.

"You don't understand—"

"No, *you* don't understand. I need proof you paid to come up here. Otherwise you're not getting in there. This isn't some free ride."

The door slid shut. Above the car, the giant iron wheel shifted. The car lurched forward on the steel cable. My mother's head was shaking, she was talking to herself, staring out the window as the shell cracked.

And I watched the tram swing off the platform and fall into thin air.

TWELVE

Running down the forest trail, I pulled out my cell phone and hit redial. The spruce trees bled into green waterfalls on either side, and when Geert answered, I didn't give him the chance to say even hello.

"I need your security team right away. Martin Webb took off."

"What does this mean, took off?"

My feet ached, sharp rocks jamming into the soles of my shoes. "I can explain later. Right now I need your help."

"You made problems," he said.

"Webb demolished one of the cages up at the wildlife center, then ran." I heard muttering, but no rebuttals. "Get your men to hold Webb at the bottom of the tram. We're coming down the trail now."

Deciding his silence was some Netherlandish version of agreement, I closed the phone and extended my stride. My mind flipped through the images. My mother's face. Webb's smirk. The door closing.

And Claire's words.

Jack thundered down the trail behind me.

"Call the Dutchman back, ask his men to help your mom get back to the ship."

I couldn't answer, because I didn't *have* an answer. If

Claire told her I was an FBI agent, the sudden appearance of Geert and his Ninjas wasn't going to soothe her paranoid mind. As I sped through the switchbacks, my heart ached for my dad. He would know what to do; he could bring her back. "Everything depends on how we love her, Raleigh," he once told me. "Everything."

"Forget Webb," Jack called out. "I'll take care of him. Tell that crazy Dutchman to help your mom."

But she would see them as people coming to take her away. Lock her up. Her greatest fear, my dad said, sitting me down one day. I was in the seventh grade. One day I came home from school and strange words were on our bathroom mirrors. Written in soap, the desperate pleas scared me. *Someone is killing me.* And *Tell them to stop.* But the worst was the word on my mirror. *Help.* "Your mother hears voices," he told me. "Not all the time. But when she was a girl, your grandmother put her in an asylum." Which explained why we never went to see her.

"Raleigh—" Jack persisted.

I shook my head and we dropped down another switchback. I could hear my own breath, on the edge of crying, and when the trail ended, I peeled out of the forest and ran downhill past the small cottages overlooking the water. I glanced at my watch, sprinting down South Franklin. Nineteen minutes had gone by since we left the summit, no way could we beat the tram.

"The Dutchman," Jack said, pointing.

Geert's bald pate gleamed outside the tram station. I searched the faces for my mother but didn't see her.

"You find Webb?" Jack asked Geert.

Geert nodded his head toward the station. "He is hiding in there. But he won't get past. My men are waiting."

"He can take the tram back up," Jack said.

"Neen." Geert calmly twirled the white handlebar. "He can't get the ticket."

"You're sure?"

"When we say no ticket, it is no ticket. These people want our passengers to come here." He turned to me. "The wildlife people are looking for you. They are not happy."

"I didn't touch the cage," I insisted. But Jack pulled me aside. I kept searching the faces, the crowd streaming around us with excited chatter.

"Go find her."

"Jack, I can't leave—"

"You can. If Claire just let the cat out of the bag, it's dangerous. Am I right?"

I nodded.

"Go on."

"Thank you."

"You're welcome. Now give me your gun."

"Excuse me?"

"You can't get it on board. The Dutchman's here with his men. And what if your mom's at the gangway?"

I turned my back to the crowd, opened the fanny pack, and waited for Jack to lift his shirt. His stomach was a tan six-pack, and he shoved the flat barrel into the waistband of his pants.

"Now run," he said.

I stood outside our cabin door, panting. My fingers shook as I slid the keycard into the electronic slot. Holding the brass handle, I closed my eyes and whispered the world's briefest prayer.

Please.

The room was full of smoke. Clouds billowing toward the open door. I rushed inside, waving my arms and gasping. But suddenly I tasted chlorine on my lips and felt my fingertips, warm and damp. Mist. Water vapor. Not smoke.

I waved my arms again, clearing the air, and saw her small dark figure. She stood with her back to the window, the blinds pulled tight against the sun, though the light refused to obey and leaked into the room. I moved closer. She was wearing her bathrobe, clutching the collar closed at her throat.

"Mom?"

I was close enough now to see her jasper eyes quivering, the green and brown colors kicking up the sands of suspicion.

"Somebody drilled holes in the beaks," she said. "The wings were broken. Twisted."

"It's a rehabilitation center." I spoke calmly. But it wasn't real. I knew where this was headed. *Oh, God.* I knew. "They're not experimenting on those animals. Nobody tortured them." I couldn't bring myself to say what she was thinking. *It's not some asylum.*

Her mouth was almost white. And hardened into a line of distrust.

"Did you see how many animals were missing eyes?"

"It's a rehabilitation center," I repeated, already tired of saying the words. Yet unable to stop. I could feel something hovering on the edge of this moment, a gate that swung back and forth, its path leading to a dark country where facts could fluctuate wildly. As I stared into her distressed eyes, my lungs seemed to tighten, struggling for air.

"Those people are helping the animals get well."

She didn't reply and I walked to the bathroom, turning off the shower. My skin was lacquered with condensation. I pulled a towel off the rack and buried my face in it, murmuring another prayer. Longer than *please*. But even more desperate.

She seemed fixed in place, like a boxed doll. I forced my smile.

"Did you know that steam from the shower can trigger the sprinkler system?" I pointed to the metal cones protruding from the ceiling. "We need to keep the bathroom door closed when we shower."

"I was cleaning the air."

I smiled harder.

"There's evil in the air and that's what made that woman hang herself."

"Pardon?"

She tightened her grip on the robe's collar, shivering. "We're too close to the North Pole, Claire says. Even the rocks are changing."

"Stay away from her. Don't listen to her. She's..." I was going to use the word *crazy*.

"Claire's been very nice, Raleigh. I was afraid to go in the helicopter with Aunt Charlotte and the rest of them, and she offered to stay with me."

"This is the same person you didn't like when we lived with Aunt Charlotte. Remember? You thought she was dangerous. And you were right. She's dangerous."

"She told me you work for the FBI."

"See what I mean?" I laughed and felt something unctuous slither down my spine, settling in my soul. "Claire probably meant my friend Jack."

"The glacier man?"

"Right. *He* works for the FBI."

God, please. Forgive me.

"Does DeMott know about him?"

I drew a deep breath, tasting the still-damp air. "I was just going to call DeMott. Would you like to say hello?"

"Somebody else is going to die. Claire told me."

"She's got it all wrong." My heart thumped. "Somebody *died*. It's over. Now we're fine."

"I was looking at those birds and a voice said somebody wanted to hurt me."

I once had a dream, years ago, but it was still vivid in my mind. In the dream, I was my mother and every time the phone rang, or there was a knock on the door, a sudden spike of fear would paralyze me. I knew people were out to hurt me, kill me, and in every word spoken, I heard veiled threats. Paranoia wasn't just suspicion; it was self-convinced knowledge, the knowing that can't be swayed. And when I woke up from that dream, clammy with sweat, I'd never felt so afraid, or so tired. Now, looking at her grayish skin, I realized how selfish I'd been. I wanted to get away, to take a vacation. But for her, this trip was a steady stream of incoming threats, a strain that accumulated more of itself daily.

"You must be so tired," I said, feeling the weight of what I'd done.

She looked at her bed. Our steward had pulled the covers to hotel-perfection, the pillows fluffed. When I pulled back the down-filled duvet, she hesitated.

"It's safe," I said.

Still wearing her robe, she climbed into bed. Around the edge of the curtains, sunlight pressed forward like some irrepressible secret begging to be told. I sat on the bed, taking her hand. Her fingers felt chilled, and I spoke to her as if she was a fevered child who insisted monsters lived under the bed waiting to grab her ankles.

"The door is locked. Nobody can come in."

"Are you sure?"

"Yes. You have my word."

My word. I felt sick saying it.

She began a trembling prayer and I closed my eyes. Still clutching her hand, I believed in what I could not see and what I could not give. When she finished, she rolled on her side, staring at the wall. I stared at her back.

"Do they spy on people?" she asked.

"Who?"

"The FBI."

"No."

I waited.

But after that, there was only silence.

THIRTEEN

She went to sleep like someone falling from a cliff—swift, sudden, gone. For several minutes, I puttered around the cabin, wanting to see if noise would wake her. It didn't and I stepped into the hallway, holding down the brass handle until the door quietly closed.

"Baby sleeping?"

I turned around.

They were a handsome middle-aged couple. The woman held a finger to her lips, then whispered, "We'll be quiet." She glanced at the man. "We remember those days. Nothing like a sleeping baby."

I gave a wan smile and waited until they had gone inside their cabin before opening my phone. I felt a sudden gratitude that we were on satellite phones that worked even if we left a port.

"Did you get Webb?" I asked Jack.

"Yes. Did you find your mom?"

"Yes. Where's Webb?"

"What did you tell her?"

"About what?"

"Harmon, knock it off. About working for the FBI."

"I told her Claire's crazy."

"So you told her the truth."

The levity made me suddenly dizzy. I put my hand on the wall, not sure if I would laugh or cry.

"You okay?" he asked.

There was no point answering. Either I'd lie again or turn to Jell-O. So I changed the subject. Again. "Where are you?"

"Coming up to the ship, then heading for the Dutchman's office."

"Where's Webb?"

"Right here in my hands," Jack said. "You want to see him?"

Boxed in on one side by Geert and Jack on the other, with Ninjas following, Martin Webb shuffled through the casino. A navy blazer three sizes too large draped over his hunched shoulders. Both the coat and his posture told me Webb was cuffed, but Geert was hiding the restraints from the other passengers.

Following the scrum, I watched Jack maneuver Webb, using the man's elbow like a rudder, navigating him to the secret hallway. Geert handed the tall Ninja a black nylon bag—our guns, I decided—which the Ninja carried down the hall to Geert's office, to the safe. We did not follow.

Geert whipped the blazer off of Webb's shoulders and pointed to the first room on the left. It was an empty office with a desk pushed to the side, the walls bare. Jack spun Webb around, then dropped him in the only chair.

"Okay, Marty. Let's talk."

Webb glared at him. "I have nothing to say to you."

"For starters we could discuss destruction of state and federal property. And that's small talk."

"I was in a hurry."

"You had time to lock yourself in the bathroom down at the base house. Then flush the toilet until it clogged."

"You guys violated my privacy," Webb said.

"It's a public restroom, Marty."

"The name's *Martin*."

Geert was twirling the handlebar mustache, his cold blue eyes frozen on Webb. But the color was darkening, like the North Sea in January.

Jack nodded at Geert. "Marty, the big guy who speaks funny English? He's the only reason you're not behind bars. But he can change his mind. And if he does, the Alaska cops would love to throw you in jail right now."

"I said I'll pay for damages."

"What did you send down the toilet?" Jack asked.

Webb smiled. "There's a lady in the room."

"Glad you noticed," Jack said. "Because if you don't answer, that lady will kick the snot out of you."

Webb scowled.

But when I stepped forward, he leaned back.

"Let's start over," I said pleasantly. "Why were you sneaking into the woods?"

"I wasn't *sneaking* anywhere. I'm scouting locations."

Jack laughed. "C'mon, Marty, give honesty a shot."

But the tall Ninja appeared, standing in the doorway. With his eyes, he gave Geert some kind of signal. Geert started to follow the Ninja back down the hallway but turned around at the last moment. He smiled at Webb. It was not a nice smile.

Webb blinked, watching Geert leave.

Just as I'd learned two days ago at the crime scene, Webb was beginning to realize this ship was not the United States. This was not ACLU America. Not only did Geert not Mirandize him, Geert didn't care about his rights. This was a place called Geertville, run by a Dutch dictator who wanted his floating village to remain peaceful.

Webb dipped his chin to his shoulder, wiping off the sweat. "Where's he going?"

"To find a noose."

"*What?*"

"Speaking of nooses," Jack continued, "let's talk about Judy Carpenter."

Much as I hated to admit it, my admiration for Jack was climbing. Judy Carpenter wasn't hung in a noose—it was a tight double knot; a noose would have tightened on her, severing her head. But the only people who knew that were us and the killer.

Webb glanced at me. Then back to Jack. "Judy? That's what this is about—Judy?" He let out a long breath, shaking his head. "Don't tell me, you two morons think somebody killed her. Is that it?"

We didn't reply.

"Everybody knows," he said. "They've known for years."

"Known what?" Jack said.

"That Milo can't keep it in his pants. Everybody knew except Judy. When she finally figured it out, she decided to check out."

"Marty, if you were playing a part in a movie, I wouldn't believe you."

"You didn't know Judy. She was having a nervous breakdown."

I said, "She seemed calm to me."

"Because she had class. Judy would never let anyone know. But inside, she was dying."

"What're you, her girlfriend?" Jack asked.

Webb raised his chin, haughty. "We were very close."

"And what about Milo?"

The director sneered. "What about him?"

"He's broken up about her death," Jack said. "Is that an act?"

"Are you kidding? Milo can't act. He never could. But the idiots in Nebraska think he's an action hero. At least they used to. These days nobody goes to his rotten films." Feeling superior, despite the fact that he was directing one of those rotten films, Webb tried to straighten his back. But the cuffs put him back in a slouch. "However, if anything is suspicious about her death, you should look at Milo. His wife being dead is the biggest career boost in year—"

The door opened. Geert filled the space. Once again he offered the director a brutally sweet smile, the white handlebars rising until they resembled fangs.

"Leave pansy boy here," he said. "My assistant's gonna babysit."

"Hey, wait—" Webb cried.

We stepped into the hall and the Ninja with the pencil mustache walked into the room, closing the door. Following Geert down the hall, I could hear Webb hollering. The sound diminished in the Dutchman's office where my Glock 22 sat next to Jack's Springfield 1911, .45 pistol. Geert headed straight to the safe and twisted the dial. It appeared stuck. "I wanted you to see why I'm taking the guns to the purser's safe. Something went wrong with mine. The guns will be safe there."

"You could always just give us back the guns," Jack suggested.

"Ach," Geert said. "What I need: you two with guns."

But I wasn't thinking about the guns. Moving to the side, I scanned the teak safe-cabinet's base. The carpet below was blue nylon and it looked faded in places. But those places weren't near the porthole, and the fading seemed unlikely, particularly on a ship obsessed with perfect appearances.

"This ship would be a whole lot safer if we carried our guns," Jack said.

"Nobody carries weapons on my ship."

"If you know what to do, a saltshaker is a weapon," Jack said.

I held up my hand, signaling a cease-fire, and asked Geert, "Could you carefully roll back your chair?"

Following my gaze, he glanced down at the carpet.

"Yes, don't touch that dust." I came around the desk. The tall Ninja was still standing by the door, and when I asked him to bring the crime kit, he looked at Geert. The Dutchman tossed his head, giving permission.

The powder-coated safe was roughly the size of a microwave. The stainless steel door was secured to a titanium baseplate, and I ran my eyes over the knob, searching for nicks in the striated surface. But there were no obvious signs of forced entry. Bending at the waist, I stared at the baseplate from below. A fine-grained gray dust rested on the safe's shelf, and more dust stuck to a tiny circle, no more than one-sixteenth of an inch, at the bottom of the faceplate. My fingers twitched, tempted to tap the ashen circle. I wanted to know if the glue or paint was still wet. Tackiness could tell time—how long since the drill bit had penetrated the baseplate directly beneath the knob, bypassing the safe's numerical code. Whoever cracked the safe had done an excellent job cleaning up. But any high-speed drill spiraling into a safe had to tunnel through several fireproof layers, flinging a dust into the air so fine it could remain suspended for hours, even days. Whenever the thief left, the dust—on the shelf and the carpet and stuck to the drill bit hole—hadn't fallen yet.

The Ninja returned with the crime kit, setting it on Geert's desk.

"Gloves, please," I said. "And if you have it, some kind of dropper. And a small sterile container."

Asking no questions, the Ninja pulled items from the case. Down the hall, I heard a sudden burst of sound. Webb, perhaps yelling about his rights. Then I heard a door close, followed by silence. I glanced at Geert.

"I sent another babysitter," he said.

"I'm free of charge," Jack said.

The handlebars twitched. "Please, tell him I said hello."

Jack left. Holding an eyedropper, I kneeled on the floor and released my squeeze on the rubber bulb, suctioning the gray dust from the blue carpet. It was the consistency of powder and I deposited it in a sterile test tube. Fortunately, the thief had missed an area under the cabinet, leaving more than gray dust. I could see pieces of vermiculite with my naked eye.

Collecting all that I could, I snapped on a new set of gloves and grabbed a sterile piece of gauze, tapping it against the painted hole. Puttied, I decided, then painted black to match the safe's powder coat. The gauze barely stuck; the paint was almost dry.

"Were you in your office today?" I asked Geert.

"Neen."

I looked over, hoping for elaboration.

"Port days are time to rest. My staff takes over."

I waited.

"I take a long sauna," he said, almost embarrassed. "I swim, get a massage."

All of which could be verified. "So when was the last time you were in your office, before we came back with Webb?"

"This morning. I gave you two your guns."

That was just before 6:00 AM. Then Geert walked us to the gangway, allowing us to bypass the security arches.

I asked the Ninja to take photographs of the drill hole before we dusted for fingerprints. Not that I was hopeful about prints; anybody this expert at safecracking wasn't likely to leave the more obvious trails. I tried not to think about the difficulties. Crime was a game of cowardice and chance. Crime fighting was a game of perseverance, of determination constantly triumphing over despair as the obstinate cat pursued the greedy mouse.

And I was right: there were no prints. Feeling we'd collected what we could, I asked for pliers, then gripped the striated knob with the tool's hinged jaw, rocking back and forth.

The insulation materials made a gritty noise as I ground them through the dial mechanism. But when enough particles had been dislodged, the dial began to turn again. Handing Geert the pliers, I stepped away and asked him to open it.

When the door popped open, he thrust his hand inside, slapping the dark space.

I knew the answer, but what was one more stupid question? "The bracelet is gone?"

"And the money."

"What money?"

"Five thousand, American."

"Your money?"

He was still running his hand around the inside of the safe, disbelieving its emptiness. In my mind, I jacked up the jewelry's price tag to six figures. Possibly seven, if the gems were extremely rare. *Blue diamonds*, I wondered, glancing around the room, searching for a camera. The ceiling held more of the starred sprinkler heads, dotting the acoustic tiles. When I looked back at him, Geert continued feeling around the safe, as if he might discover some previously unknown hidden compartment.

"Was it your money?" I asked again.

"Ship money. For emergencies."

"No video cameras in here?"

"In a security office?" He spun, facing me, about to utter judgment on my question when it suddenly didn't seem so stupid. His white mustache drooped. "The nearest camera is by the casino."

"Is there only one entrance to this office?"

He nodded, then said to the Ninja, "Check all video for today. Anybody walking through the casino."

"We're probably looking for somebody carrying a toolbox or a briefcase," I added. "Or a package that could conceal a powerful drill." I turned to Geert. "We need every drill on the ship accounted for. Can you do the same with missing or worn out bits?"

Geert grabbed the phone on his desk, pushing two digits. "Maintenance, immediately."

While he waited for someone to pick up, I asked for a list of all employees. The list he refused to give me before because everyone was "clean as whistles." His eyes were averted from me but he gave a quick nod.

"You can fax it to the FBI's Seattle office," I said, writing down Allen McLeod's name. "The violent crimes unit."

I could almost hear his teeth grinding as he ordered somebody on the phone's other end to gather all the drills in one place.

When asked, the Ninja gave me the two magnifying glasses in the crime kit, and when Geert hung up, I lifted the sterile test tube, now hazed with gray dust.

"Is there a microscope on board?" I asked.

Geert picked up the phone again. "Medical clinic. Deck Four. I will tell them you are coming."

"Thank you." And I meant it. A lesser man would've become defensive in this situation. And a man less dedicated to security would have shifted the blame.

I turned toward the door and saw Jack dragging Webb by the arm. "He's demanding to see his lawyer."

"When I tell him how my civil rights were violated—" Webb said.

Geert offered his generous and ruthless smile. "Have a seat, Mr. Webb. And let us take off those handcuffs. You must be uncomfortable."

"That's more like it." Webb sniffed.

"You want to be able to hold the pen."

"Pen? What about my lawyer?"

"When your check clears with the bank, you can call this lawyer."

"My check?"

"You want to pay for the damages to the animal people. And you want to add some donations, isn't that right?"

"Hey, that's not—"

Jack pushed him into a chair. "We tried to warn you, Marty."

Geert looked at me. "Anything else?"

"Yes, where's the laundry room?"

"Laundry?" Jack said. "You want to do laundry—now?"

I didn't reply, and Geert had his eyes pinned on Webb.

"Yah," he said. "That's a good idea. We all gonna have a little cleaning up."

FOURTEEN

A steel spine of stairs traced vertically through the ship's fore, and every one of our steps created a hollow echo through the cylindrical chamber. Coming up the stairs as we went down, the ship's food service workers moved wearily, their uniforms spattered and wrinkled from work.

When we reached Deck Three, Jack held his cell phone to his ear, keeping his voice low, while I rushed down the hallway. It was tubular and windowless, like a submarine's lowest chamber. I stopped at a set of ten-foot-wide double doors with small porthole windows that showed the laundry room on the other side. I waited for Jack to finish his phone call, listening to the rhythmic thudding on the other side, that unmistakable sound of dryers. The air smelled starched.

"Yes, the same bracelet that Raleigh found," Jack was saying into the phone. "And five K in cash. The money's always been in there, so we can assume the jewelry was the target."

On the other side of the door, somebody yelled. Not in English. Not in Spanish. It sounded Asian. Vietnamese, Cantonese?

"Now?" Jack said into the phone. "For some reason, now Raleigh wants to see the laundry room. I know I can't investigate a safe heist until my pants are washed."

The old Jack, the guy I remembered.

Jerk Jack.

"Ask her yourself." He handed me his cell phone. "McLeod."

I cleared the dry-heat tickle from my throat, then pressed my hand over my ear, blocking the sound of the dryers and Jack's muttering.

"Yes, sir?"

"I'm in no mood for games. Tell me the truth, Harmon. I won't be upset. You didn't cook up this whole thing just to get Jack up there?"

My jaw fell open.

"Pardon?"

"Neither of you has checked in since he got there. I realize technically he doesn't have to check in but—"

"Why not?"

"Because he's on vacation."

I stopped. "Could you say that again?"

"Is this connection bad? He's supposed to have a satellite phone."

I stared at Jack. Jack was leaning against the steel wall, looking smug. "Sir, this connection is *very* bad."

"I said, if Jack wants to use his vacation days to help you out, that's his choice. But our office is responsible for this case now. And I need to know what's going on." He paused. "So it's back to my first question, what's going on with you two? Is this a plutonic relationship?"

At times his malaprops struck with idiomatic accuracy. And at this moment the irony of what he'd said was the only thing holding back my fury. Nothing—but nothing—described my feelings for Jack better than Pluto, the coldest planet in the universe and a place so insignificant it had been downgraded by scientists to a nonplanet.

"Sir, it's entirely plutonic."

"Good," he said. "I wanted to check. I've seen women go crazy for that guy."

As if hearing this dubious compliment, Jack lifted and lowered his eyebrows, some flirtatious expression that worked on weaker females.

I turned my back on him.

"Tell me about this robbery," McLeod said.

"Even without the cash gone, the bracelet puts it in grand larceny territory," I said.

"And the dead woman—you're sure it was murder?"

"I'm still waiting for the official medical examiner's report but—"

"So *you* still say it's murder."

"It wasn't suicide."

With his silence, I listened to the dryers thudding. And Jack, humming something.

"When does that cruise come to end?" he asked.

"Sunday."

"Better crank up your speed, Harmon. Anything you need from me?"

"You'll be getting a fax of names. Most if not all are foreigners. I need background checks."

"You're talking Interpol?"

"Yes, sir. And we're looking for any red flags linked to safecracking, jewelry heists, robbery. And of course murder."

There was an even longer pause.

"Sir?"

"Harmon, you're calling in every last favor."

"I realize that."

"When this is over, you might even owe me a favor. Then you'll *have* to come work for me."

"Yes, sir."

I handed the phone to Jack. He was drawing a wrist across his perspiring brow. The heat made the air seem void of oxygen. Along Jack's hairline I could see traces of salt crystallized. It had been a hard day, the fast run up then down Mount

Roberts. And neither of us had time to shower. Good thing this was a plutonic relationship.

He hung up with McLeod, promising to check in more frequently.

"You ready?" I asked.

"If you'll tell me what we're doing."

"We're looking for clothing with gray dust. Check elbows and knees first. But the dust is so fine it could spread anywhere."

"Wait—we're checking *dirty* laundry?"

If I wasn't such a nice person, I would have answered the way Geert did, telling him it was a stupid question. Instead, I pushed through the double doors, ready to hunt down minerals.

In my four years at the mineralogy lab, I had two safe-cracking cases. One was sent to us from Colorado and involved an antique safe, circa 1902. The safe had contained St. Gaudens gold coins, but somebody had dynamited the thing open. The second case involved a safe manufactured in the 1980s containing valuable deeds that were suspected of being stolen and forged. That second safe was penetrated the same as Geert's: by drilling into the faceplate. But both cases hinged on the safes' insulation material and the matching dust found on the suspects' clothing.

Geology sealed their fate.

"I'm not touching any underwear," Jack said.

The laundry "room" looked more like a laundry warehouse. Riveted steel walls held up wide arches that divided the large space into separate functions, each the size of a condo. Dryers the size of small automobiles tumbled masses of beige and white. Tablecloths, sheets, napkins, I decided. In a nearby area, several Asian women scooped up white towels with wooden paddles, pushing them into machines that looked like brick pizza ovens. And in the farthest corner, a monstrous thing with metal arms took dry sheets and table-cloths, hissing like a dragon as its mechanical arms *thwhack*ed and *thwhopp*ed before suddenly dropping a precisely folded square on the conveyor belt below. The women standing by the belt inserted the squares into clear plastic bags.

Walking toward us, a bandy-legged Asian man pushed a canvas cart that brimmed with soiled tablecloths. Behind him, a ten-foot-wide steel chute guided an avalanche of sheets into an empty cart.

Jack flipped open his credentials. The man's brown eyes widened with fear.

"We're not with Immigration," Jack said.

I introduced myself, shaking the man's hand. His fingers felt calloused and dry.

"I am Nam," he said.

"Nam, where is today's laundry?"

"Clean or dirty?"

"Dirty," I said. "And we need to see clothing from both passengers and crew."

Nam moved the cart from under the chute, now full, and replaced it with an empty one before walking us to the room's farthest corner. The air smelled slippery and alkaline with the feel of soap, and along the wall white plastic bags lined the floor. Each was marked with a corresponding cabin number. I made a quick count.

So did Jack. "That's, like, three hundred bags—are you serious?"

I turned to Nam, raising my voice so he could hear me over the folding machine hissing to our left. "When did these bags come in?"

"Today," Nam said.

"I'm sorry, I meant what time."

"What time you look for?"

I calculated the hours. Geert claimed he left the office after our 6:00 AM visit. We returned with the movie director around 3:30 PM. Cracking the safe required a minimum of twenty minutes, longer if the thief didn't have a powerful drill or a diamond-tip bit. Perhaps one hour. I knew this thief was methodical, calculating a strike when Geert would be away from his office getting a sauna and massage. And he'd covered his tracks. But, I also knew, he could have struck in the middle of the night. When Geert turned the safe's dial this morning to get our guns, he apparently didn't notice any difference in the dial. But the dust was so fine, and it could take time for gravity to deposit enough insulation in the dial's turning mechanism to block it. And if that were the case, then the thief took the jewelry and the money but left our guns. Because they would set off the security arches if he tried to leave?

And then another question popped into my mind, more disturbing. Could I trust Geert? That bracelet was several years' salary. If he was close to retirement, what better ruse was there than to drill into his own safe, at night, then stay away all day, casting suspicion everywhere but himself, the head of security. I wasn't ruling out anything.

I gave Nam the time frame that included last night, and he walked to the back rows of dirty laundry bags.

"Some not done. Some we pick up this morning."

I handed Jack a pair of latex gloves taken from Geert's crime kit. "Dig in."

"Me?"

"Keep an eye out for black paint too."

He stared at the gloves. "And what're you doing?"

"I'm narrowing my search." I pulled the passenger list from my pocket. Most of the movie crew had cabins on Deck Twelve, each numbered in the 1200s. Only Milo Carpenter and the Sparks were on Deck Fourteen and there was no Deck Thirteen—sailors believing in bad luck. Only Martin Webb was staying on Deck Eleven. Alone.

With reluctance, Jack snapped on the gloves while I cross-checked cabin numbers with the plastic bags. Five bags matched the movie crew. Three belonged to men whose names I didn't recognize, possibly cameramen or extras, and one bag belonged to Milo Carpenter. The fifth bag belonged to a woman. Martha Jane. MJ. The musician.

The felon.

Squatting beside her laundry bag, I popped open the snapping top. But Nam brushed me aside.

"Nam do, Nam do!"

It seemed important to him, some kind of honor, and he followed my directions carefully, lifting each article of clothing from the bag and laying it on the steel floor. He did the same with the other four bags, moving down the line with me. Periodically he raced back to the laundry chute to replace a full cart with an empty one, then pushing the laundry to the women with the wooden shovels. As I finished examining the clothes, Nam patiently replaced them in their bags. And whenever I asked a question, he was smiling.

"Does clothing come down the chute?" Smiling, no.

"Can people wash their own clothes?" Smiling, yes.

After several minutes, his cheerful attitude made me feel uneasy. Even suspicious. Until I realized the problem.

It wasn't him; it was me. Or my country. I'd been ordering Big Macs and standing at customer service counters and waiting on the phone for technical support, seldom getting anything other than some sour, slothful attitude. After years of it, I'd come to expect low-level employees to carry chips on their shoulders, taking out their disappointment on me. While I loved my country with a heart beating with American pride, I could see why this ship hired so many internationals. Where poverty was endemic, work was a blessing, not a burden.

"Thank you, Nam."

He nodded, still smiling. "You find what you look for?"

"Not yet." I glanced over at Jack. He touched the laid-out clothing with a curled lip. I called over to him. "Jack, you have to check the underwear."

"Wha—?"

"The clothes are all bundled together and that dust can stick anywhere."

He was muttering under his breath as I kneeled to examine MJ's clothing. The dress looked like the one worn last night, a soft bohemian style with draping gothic sleeves. Only it was black, not blue.

And the sleeves were covered with dust.

I looked at Nam. "I'm going to take this one with me."

His smile faded. "You tell boss?"

"I promise, you will not get in trouble. May I please have a clean bag, never used?" I had evidence bags in my cabin, in my rock kit, for any forensic work, but that risked waking up my mother. At the thought of her, pushing away sparks of worry and guilt, I reminded myself to call Aunt Charlotte.

"Harmon, you are..." Jack continued muttering.

I checked the other bags. Trousers, boxers, damp workout clothes, stinking of perspiration. Gross, I had to agree with Jack, but all those years in the forensics lab taught me how to shift my brain into clinical detachment, so that even the most revolting deposits became simple protein-based emissions from the human body.

"See anything?" I called over to him.

"Crimes of bad hygiene."

Nam waited beside me, helpful without being servile. "Does the ship's crew wash their own clothes?"

He shook his head and motioned for me to follow. When I passed by, Jack still had dozens of bags to go. Under the laundry chute, Nam replaced another full cart with an empty one, then led me to the row of lumpy green nylon duffel bags.

Each had a plastic tag marked with a last name, a first initial, and a cabin number. The cabins all numbered in the 300s and 400s, meaning below the waterline. Crew. Officers lived way up by the captain's bridge, in the single digits, with views.

"When did these come in?" I asked.

"One, two day," Nam said. "Not such hurry."

Right. The crew needed to be kept content, but the passengers should be very happy, with laundry done promptly. Yanking open one of the drawstrings, I froze. The pants were blood-spattered.

"Butcher," Nam said. "Kitchen."

Other bags held white cotton-poly shirts greasy with cooking oil. I searched through the clothes for dust and black paint and found sets of two coveralls smeared with a black substance. It smelled like petroleum, engine grease, but I asked Nam to bundle each into separate bags, while I wrote down the corresponding crew names and cabin numbers. When Nam excused himself to rotate the carts again, I took a deep breath and leaned from side to side, trying to unknot the small of my back. My muscles felt like tight fists. Bending forward, I could feel my stomach growling for food. I straightened, taking another deep breath of the warm starchy air and saw Jack walking toward me, looking as weary as I felt. He carried a pair of faded blue jeans.

"You're the expert," he said. "But what do you make of this?"

Bleached for a high price, the jeans were faded in precise places with strategic frays. But the pale knees looked almost yellow from the dust ground into the denim weave. I moved over to a pendant light, standing directly under it to examine the particles.

"Can I ask what you're looking for, exactly, besides dust?" Jack asked.

"Vermiculite, for one thing."

"Later you can tell me what that is. First you need to thank me."

I looked up, narrowing my eyes.

"Those pants came from cabin 1410." He grinned. "Milo's cabin."

"But I checked that bag."

"And I decided to check anything that came in since we've been down here in Hades. Five minutes ago a bag came in with his cabin number."

I was struggling to get out the words *Nice work*, but got distracted by a tall lean man who stood over Nam, yelling. He wore a white officer's uniform with the gold-and-black epaulettes, and when he pushed my best helper ever into the convoy of carts, Nam looked more terrified than when he thought Jack was from Immigration.

"Put these in a fresh unused bag," I told Jack, handing back the jeans. "I'll be right back."

I could hear the officer's words as I approached. He sounded British, or high-Australian, and he wagged something at Nam. A black piece of cloth.

"You are to sort laundry! Sort!" he yelled. "You do not leave things helter-skelter!"

I stood behind the officer, watching fear deepen in Nam's brown eyes.

"Very sorry," he was saying. "Very sorry."

"You'll be even sorrier when I ship you back to Thailand."

"Pardon me." I had my credentials open, holding them ready as the man spun around. "If there's a problem it's probably my fault."

The officer glared at my creds. He had a slender face and with his planar body he reminded me of a javelin. He frowned as I explained how Geert van Broeck gave me permission to check the laundry, and that Nam was helping me.

"Geert—gave you permission? To check the laundry?"

He drew himself up, the javelin ready for throwing. "Check it for what?"

"I can't say."

"You can't say?"

"That is what I said."

"Nobody told me. Why didn't they tell me?" Worry suddenly replaced his anger. "Are you investigating us for quality control?"

"No, sir." I read his name tag. "Ozzie Stilton, Australia." I thought of Stilton cheese and my stomach growled again. "Nam's been extremely helpful. If I've disrupted his work, you have my apologies."

"His *work*," said Officer Stilton, taking the opportunity to reload the blame gun, "is to monitor these bins. He failed. And his carelessness nearly ruined an entire load of tablecloths." He whirled back to Nam and narrowed his eyes. "Do you want Danillo to come down here and see this?"

Whoever Danillo was, the mere mention of his name reinvigorated Nam's terror.

"Very sorry," he repeated. "Very, very sorry."

Officer Stilton lifted the item in his hand, shaking it. "You think I won't catch you people, but I will."

"Very sorry."

"If tablecloths turn gray, the replacement cost will come from your wages. And then I'll fire you."

Since the officer seemed ready to keep piling it on, I said, "Nam, would you please go help that man?" I pointed to Jack, checking the new bags of laundry.

"Go?" Nam asked.

"Yes," said Officer Stilton. "Go away."

When Nam had walked away, I held out my hand. "May I?"

He offered it without any hesitation, as it would prove the need for Nam's humiliation.

"Slipped in with the tablecloths. White tablecloths. Washed

in hot water. *Hot water.* He's lucky the girls found it before it went into the washing machine."

It was a black pair of pants, a cotton-poly blend. Four pockets and a one-inch cuff. Opening the fold, I suddenly stopped.

"How did these pants wind up with the tablecloths?" I asked.

"Because these are sneaky careless people."

"Could you be more specific?"

"They damage the uniforms and try to cover it up. So they don't get charged for it. Throw it down the housekeeping chute, then steal a replacement from the supply room."

I didn't dare inspect the cuffs any further. The pants had tumbled down a laundry chute, rubbed against some tablecloths, been picked up by some laundress before being shaken with fury by Stilton. In terms of evidence preservation, it didn't get much worse. My good fortune was that hoary safe insulation. Folding up the pants to keep the knees and cuffs buried, I asked Stilton what time the pants came in. Casual voice.

"When?" His brow furrowed.

"Yes, when."

"I don't see how *when* is of any importance."

I unclipped my cell phone and began hitting the numbers.

"Who are you calling?" he demanded.

"Geert. I presume you know Geert."

He glanced to his right. Jack walked toward us carrying two evidence bags.

"It's been an extraordinarily busy day," Stilton said. "I can't possibly know when they arrived."

I held my cell phone, one number from contacting Geert. "I'll let Geert know. He can interview whoever found the pants."

His eyes darted. "It was around three o'clock."

"You're sure?"

"Ye-es," he said, uncertain. "I had... I had an appointment."

Or he was somewhere he wasn't supposed to be.

"We'll need the exact time. And where, exactly, these trousers were found. If anything deviates from fact, I'll report it to the captain." For good measure, I added, "And Danillo."

Jack's blue-green eyes cut through Stilton like a paring knife. He handed me the evidence bags.

"Officer Stilton, meet Special Agent Jack Stephanson. You can tell him what happened. Everything that happened."

In the dry air of the laundry room, the officer's dripping condensation had evaporated. He asked nervously, "Where are you going?"

"I have an appointment," I said, turning his words on him.

FIFTEEN

The medical clinic's automatic doors *whoosh*ed open and a nurse looked up from the reception desk. Her starched white uniform pinched at the shoulders, boosting the abundant display of a well-endowed bust.

I introduced myself and she nodded, saying Geert had already called.

"Nurse Stephanie." She stood up, shaking my hand. Her figure had more curves than a sidewinder snake. "I'm in the FBI files."

"Really?"

"Yes. I got busted once for smuggling wine into Canada."

"Oh."

"Humanitarian mission," she said. "Back then Canadian wine tasted like grape-flavored rubbing alcohol."

I nodded, looking around the clinic. It was laid out like a wheel with wedge-shaped exam rooms spoking from the circular hub of the reception desk. From the desk, one nurse could see each patient. But the only occupant right now was an elderly man, looking frail in his hospital bed. Beside him a woman of equal age sat and stroked his wispy white hair from his forehead.

When I turned back to the wine smuggler, she was stepping from behind the circular desk. The swing of her hips probably gave men whiplash.

"You wanted a microscope?" she asked.

I followed her into a narrow space that was shoehorned between two patient rooms. It was a compact lab with a stainless steel counter, small centrifuge, microwave oven, and microscope. All the equipment was leashed to the wall for rough water.

"Gertie didn't say what you wanted the scope for."

"Gertie?"

"If you repeat that to him, you'll regret it." She smiled. "Is blood involved?"

"Pardon?"

"If blood's involved, I have to file paperwork. Regulations."

I told her this was bloodless and described what I needed. She took a small key from a pocket near her hip and unlocked the stainless cabinets, pulling out gloves, glass slides, petri dishes, and test tubes. When the phone rang, she excused herself and walked back to the desk. When she walked, I could almost hear cars crashing.

Flipping on the microscope, I tapped the dust collected from Geert's office into a petri dish, looking for telltale minerals. Until the 1930s, safe insulation was a random mixture of coal and shale, and whatever other fire-resistant materials the manufacturer had on hand from sand and gravel to ash. More recently, safes contained blends of Portland cement, gypsum, vermiculite, and/or diatomaceous earth. Like closely-held family recipes, each manufacturer used a distinct combination and the ingredients with their relative ratios allowed forensic geologists to link particular safes with specific suspects, all through the mineral trail.

"If your temperature's over 102," Nurse Stephanie was saying into the phone, "I'm locking you in here." There was a pause. "Why? Honey, have you heard of Swine Flu? SARS? Meningitis? Do those ring any bells?"

Vermiculite always jumped out first, often detectable with the naked eye. The sheets of golden silica looked like a book left out in the rain and dried by the sun, the pages rippled and curling.

"These people," Nurse Stephanie said.

I glanced up. She stood across the way, in the doorway of the elderly couple. Manicured hands planted on her fender-bender hips.

"That sneaky witch, she's contagious. And she thinks she can hide from me? Well, she called the wrong nurse. I'll find her, mark my words."

Diatomaceous earth was the most interesting addition to safe insulation. A mixture of hard-shelled algae, known as diatoms, and silica containing trace amounts of sodium, magnesium, and iron, it was porous, nonreactive, and inexpensive, making it a favorite with safe manufacturers. But it was also a favorite among forensic geologists because that hard-shelled algae worked like fingerprints. Each population of phytoplankton had a particular growth and morphology, along with pitting in the silica. But as I stared through the microscope at this dust, all I saw was a vague cloud. Unfortunately, the scope's magnification wasn't strong enough to see separate grains.

I walked over to the round desk. Nurse Stephanie was on the phone again.

"She sounded like an old bag," she told someone on the other end. "But that could be because she feels like crap. I did hear a piano in the background. Good piano. Where's Frank Holman playing tonight…in the pub? Okay, go check in there for a woman who looks like she's about to barf in her shirt."

She hung up and said, "I'll get that witch, you watch."

I nodded, with no doubt whatsoever. "Would you by chance have any hydrochloric acid?"

"What're you—crazy?"

"Just a ten percent solution."

"Honey, we *treat* people for stomach acid, we don't hand it out."

"Then could I have some plain aspirin? Noncoated."

"That we can do," she said. "How many?"

"Twenty to start."

She stared at me. Like she was going to throw me in with the fugitive fever woman. "Twenty," she repeated.

"With half a cup of distilled water."

"You want cookies with that?"

Back in the lab, I deposited ten of the aspirin tablets into the half cup of distilled water, then asked Nurse Stephanie for something to test pH levels. She unlocked a cabinet and laid strips of yellow paper on the stainless counter with a laminated card showing the colors on the paper that would correspond with various acid and alkaline levels. I dipped a pH strip in the water, then compared it to the chart. Still too alkaline. I dropped in two more aspirin, swirling the water.

"What's that for?" she asked.

"I'm making an acid solution to dissolve soft minerals."

The Portland cement was basically limestone and along with gypsum dissolved quickly in a ten percent solution of hydrochloric acid, leaving behind the durable diatoms. The fingerprints. Once again I thought of the rock kit in my cabin with its four-ounce bottle of hydrochloric acid. But I couldn't risk waking my mother, or having to explain what I was doing—or where I'd been.

For now acetylsalicylic acid—aspirin water—would have to do. But it was taking longer.

"Does the microwave work?" I asked Nurse Stephanie.

"I heat my food in there."

"I'll clean it when I'm done."

With a sterile dropper, I added the acid solution to a sample of the dust, setting the petri dish inside the microwave, hoping heat would accelerate the processes. As I was tapping in ten seconds, I heard the nurse speaking to someone by the desk.

"Honey," she said, "you *must* be in violation of something."

I glanced over my shoulder. Jack.

"Why do say that?" he asked.

"Because you've got *fine* written all over you." She winked. "Need a shot?"

"If I did, you'd be the nurse to do it." He grinned.

I suppressed an eye roll and waited for the microwave. The phone at the desk rang. And rang. When I turned around, she was walking slowly around the desk, brushing against Jack. He stared at her, immobilized by her sensuality.

I took the sample from the microwave, then carried it to the microscope.

Jack stood in the doorway, recovered. "Three twenty-three," he said.

"Excuse me?"

"The laundry girls found those pants in the bin at 3:23 PM."

"You're sure?"

"One gal was going off shift. She carried the pants into Stilton's office. He wasn't there. And he was supposed to be there. The girls think Stilton's having an affair with the woman who works the folding machine." He smiled softly. "I got all the gossip."

I checked the sample under the scope. Still no go. Walking over to the desk, I waited once again for Nurse Stephanie to finish her phone conversation. Somebody had left their medication refill at home. She asked for the name of the medicine and if they had the prescription bottle. "Bring it down," she said, hanging up. Then she leaned toward me, surreptitiously pointing at Jack. She whispered, "Who's he?"

"A colleague." I tried to smile. "White paper, sterile?"

"Help yourself." She pointed to an empty patient room and sauntered back to Jack.

I was on my own. I tore paper from the roll behind an exam table and carried it back into the lab. When I asked for a scalpel, Nurse Stephanie unlocked a drawer, continued chatting with Jack, and practically tossed the knife at me.

"Are you on the cruise with a special somebody?" she asked him.

"Yes."

"Oh. I'm sorry to hear that."

I took out MJ's dress first, then the blue jeans from Milo's cabin, then the trousers found in the laundry bin.

"If you get bored," she said, "my shift's over at ten."

I held MJ's dress over the white paper, scraping dust off the sleeves with the scalpel. I did the same with the jeans and the black trousers, placing each collection into separately marked test tubes. I also searched the trousers for any identification tags, but there were none.

After adding my acid solution to a sample of the dusts, I cooked them in petri dishes in the microwave and pretended not to notice Nurse Stephanie fanning her face.

"Warm in here, don't you think? It's cooler over by my desk."

Like a man led to slaughter, Jack followed her from the room while I wrote my notes on a prescription pad, making sure I outlined the forensics procedure for any formal documents that might come later. When I glanced at the circular desk, Nurse Stephanie was leaning forward, cleavage front and center. Jack glanced away, a sardonic smile playing on his lips.

Hoping they stayed occupied, I took out my phone and called Aunt Charlotte.

"We're just coming down from cloud nine—literally!"

My aunt's breathy voice was full of softness, but only a trace remained of her native Virginia accent. I listened to her description of the helicopter tour around Mendenhall Glacier, the sled dog run on wheels, and the salmon bake. "Raleigh, you would have loved it. And it gave me a chance to say goodbye to Judy. I released her spirit to this beautiful place, and to the universe."

Whatever, I thought sourly, before telling her about what happened at the wildlife center. I left out Martin Webb, but emphasized Claire's culpability. "After this stunt, I don't want Claire anywhere near her."

She started to protest.

"I don't have time to argue, Aunt Charlotte. I'm asking you to please check in on Mom. She was napping when I left the cabin."

"I'll do it first thing. We should be back within the hour."

"Thank you."

"I love you, Raleigh."

"Love you too."

I was closing the phone when Jack came back in the lab. "Need some help?" he asked.

I glanced past him to the desk. Nurse Stephanie was taking the elderly man's vitals. "You can help by asking Florence Nightgown for some mineral oil. But don't tell me what she says when you ask."

The cooked petri dishes now held what looked like white powder. I tapped each onto separate glass slides, and when Jack returned with a small plastic bottle, I placed one drop of the clear oil on each slide before adding the plastic coverslip. I shifted the microscope's magnification to 40X.

The limestone and gypsum had burned away and what remained looked like pitted glass Frisbees, their edges fractured.

Diatoms. Geologic fingerprints.

Beautiful.

"What do you see?" Jack asked.

"It's the dust from Geert's office." I slid the next sample under the scope. "And now I'm looking for any matches from the clothing."

The dust from MJ's dress had no diatoms. But I saw cellulose cells, wood. And lots of it. Wood hard enough to resist the acid and heat.

I grabbed the dust from the black trousers, shifting the slide right to left, up and down, until I found three diatoms. They had similar cusplike fractures. It was a start. For the match to stand in court, I would need chemical compositions, relative amounts, and the connection to the safe's manufacturer. That meant a forensics lab, either the FBI's or the state crime lab in Seattle.

"The black pants are a tentative positive match." I made notes on the prescription pad. "And now we check Milo's jeans."

There it was again.

Cellulose fibers. Wood durable enough to survive chemical and temperature assaults.

"What's wrong?" Jack asked.

"The dust on the dress matches the dust on Milo's jeans."

"Dust is dust," he said. "Isn't it?"

I shook my head. "These cellulose cells are too similar, and too specific."

"Meaning?"

"Meaning MJ and Milo were in the same place, and they both sent their clothes to the cleaners. On the same day."

"You want odds?" Jack asked.

"I want words—interviews with both." I checked my watch. "And I want Geert to trace these black trousers to their owner. Whoever wore them broke into that safe."

We were packing up the evidence when the clinic's automatic door *whoosh*ed open. An older gentleman walked in wearing a baseball cap from the Phillumenists of Philadelphia. It was a different branch than the guys burning with brotherly love. These guys were the Founding Flames.

The man looked tired. "I called you about some medicine for my wife," he said to Nurse Stephanie.

"Righty-o," she said. "The Namenda oral?"

He nodded.

"Yeah, that's what happens. You forget stuff."

She was gone when we headed out the sliding doors to the elevators, leaving the old man standing at the desk. Jack leaned down, whispering to me. "What's a phillumenist anyway?"

"Matchbook collector."

He nodded. "I should've known you'd know."

"Years of Greek and Latin," I said.

"Which is it, Greek or Latin?"

"Both, actually. *Phila* is Greek for *love*. *Lumen* means *light* in Latin. Scrunch them together and you get phillumenist, or lover of light."

Our hands were full of evidence bags, so I pressed the elevator button with my elbow.

"Hold on," he said. "You got 'matchbook collector' from all that?"

I shook my head. "From forensics. One of my cases involved the sulfur content of matches dating back to the 1930s. I got to interview a bunch of phillumenists."

The elevator opened and Jack stepped inside, holding the door for me. "You're too hard on yourself, Harmon."

"What do you mean?"

He hit the button for Deck Six. "Most people pretend they know more than they actually do. You tell the truth."

I watched the elevator doors close.

Sometimes, I thought. *Sometimes I tell the truth.*

But only sometimes.

SIXTEEN

If Claire believed a bitter cloud hung over the ship, she might've been imagining the casino. As I walked through the room, the cigarette smoke was thick enough to flavor hams. Puffing gamblers hunched over the slot machines, their eyes ratcheted to the bright flashing electronics that spun through loss after loss.

Nose itching from the smoke, I waited for the Ninja with the pencil mustache to open the padded wall-door. Though he glanced at the bags of evidence, his face revealed nothing.

In Geert's office, a maintenance worker was removing the old safe. Skin the color of cinnamon, his fingers were stained black with oil, creating topographic maps of his fingerprints. I waited as he lifted a small safe—identical to the ones in our passenger cabins—and bolted it to the shelf. He went to remove the damaged safe, placing it on a mechanical dolly, when Geert said, "Leave it here."

The Ninja escorted him back to the secret entrance, and I closed the office door.

Geert twirled the mustache. "I got a call from laundry. You took some clothes."

"Stilton?"

He shook his head. "Gossip, it is the lifeblood of ships."

I described the black trousers. "Is there a way to trace them?"

I expected a comment about stupid questions. Instead he offered a sigh that sounded like generations of Dutch fatalism. "By sizes, we can eliminate certain workers. But that will take time. Better to check the cabins."

I waited a moment, wondering if my next two questions would ruin our sudden détente. "What happened to the director?"

"Locked in his cabin. One of my men is posted outside his door. These movie people, they are spoiled children." He ran his blue eyes over the evidence bags.

"I need to lock up these materials..." I didn't finish the question.

"But you don't trust my safe," he said.

I said nothing. But he was right.

Defense attorneys got a kick out of asking forensic scientists, "Was the evidence ever out of your possession?"

And that's why I carried all the bags. If I was called to testify later, it wouldn't help the prosecution if I had to admit a grumpy Dutch security officer carried the evidence through a smoky casino, then across the midship atrium, passing thousands of passengers who were headed for dinner. At the concierge desk, where I rested my elbows on the teak counter, Geert spoke to an attendant. In the wine bar off the atrium, a delicate-looking Frenchman lectured on the merits of cabernet, his accent like clarified butter.

The concierge attendant lifted a portion of the counter, and I followed Geert back into an office where a man the color of wrought iron greeted us in a mellifluous British accent. Both his white officer's uniform and his black skin seemed to glow, the uniform so bright it stung my eyes, the skin so dark it shimmered violet.

"I am York Meriweather, first purser." He placed one hand to his chest, shaking my hand with the other. "I'm pleased to meet you, Agent Harmon. And I can assure you, *all* valuables will be secure in *my* office."

"Thank you." I placed the packages on his desk. He didn't bat an eye at the sorry state of my "valuables" in plastic laundry bags. "I don't doubt you, but may I see your safe?"

"Most certainly. I would not be offended if you doubted, after what happened today." He swept a hand toward a powder-coated column that ran floor to ceiling. It had two locks. One looked like a regular numerical combination dial, but the other involved a bizarre key that the purser held up for my inspection. Six inches long, its brass teeth flared like curling wings.

"And, as you can see"—he pointed to my left—"we have video cameras aimed directly at the safe." He pointed to my right, more cameras. The smile that spread across his face came slowly but was as blindingly bright as his uniform. "If I exit the office, an alarm system is set, backing up the two locks. Another alarm is set by the front desk."

"Very thorough."

He gave a slight bow, feigning modesty, then used the strange key to open the safe. The tumbler released with a heavy *clunk* and the door required both hands to open. Rows of safe deposit boxes were shelved above vertical dividers that held canvas money bags, the type used by banks. At the very bottom was open space.

"You should have no worries about theft," said York Meriweather. "At least, not *here*."

Geert and I made our way through the atrium, passing the little Frenchman who acknowledged Geert with a gaulic lift of the eyebrows. Geert's reply was even less friendly.

"Don't like him?" I asked.

"Gossips," he spat. "Old ladies in Zeeland do not gossip like these people. Some kind of joke. Security's safe was broken into. Ha. Ha. I am not laughing. I will crush the person who did this."

His already formidable back stiffened with defensive pride. I wasn't exactly sorry to see his humiliation; it pushed him lower on my list of suspects. For a man like this, no money was worth public shame, not even six figures of jewelry. And as we headed for the maintenance crew cabins, I felt a fraction of relief. One person, perhaps, could be eliminated from the list.

Perhaps.

Outside the upscale Italian restaurant named Pellagio, Geert opened a door marked AUTHORIZED PERSONNEL ONLY, stepping into the large kitchen. Waiters shuttled back and forth at high speed, balancing full dinner plates on both arms while dodging hollered comments from the chefs who guarded the enormous grills and ovens. The chefs wore toques and white jackets and yelled in Italian, furious Italian, where the romantic scooped lilts change into curses condemning a person to life without decent red sauce. Geert and I stood to the side like schoolkids playing double-dutch rope, waiting for an opening. Suddenly we dashed through a cacophony of clattering plates, rattling utensils, and increased yelling.

And then, just as suddenly, it went quiet. The kitchen door had closed behind us and we were crossing through the bakery, the warm scent of bread floating on the air. Plump men in white shirts and houndstooth pants pulled racks of flaky croissants and golden buns from cavernous ovens.

My stomach went into full riot.

"Hungry?" Geert asked, glancing back.

I was afraid if I opened my mouth, drool would come out. So I said nothing. But Geert either heard my stomach or saw something on my face. Speaking in a foreign language to a baker whose merry cheeks rose with his smile, he wrapped three buns in butcher paper and handed them to me. I restrained a weep of gratitude.

Possibly it was the best bread I'd ever tasted. The light golden crust melted on my tongue, followed by the bread interior that was light as a marshmallow yet as rich as butter. I wanted to hum as we walked down a long tunnel. The ship's employees rushed past us in various stages of hurry. Some carried bags of rice the size of toddlers. Others pushed steel carts stacked with folded tablecloths and napkins—fresh from the laundry room, no doubt—while men in coveralls wheeled small Dumpsters, trailing putrid odors.

"This is called the Highway," Geert said. "No public, no passengers allowed. It is our express lane from fore to aft. If I need to, I can get from one end to the other in less than four minutes." He glanced at the remaining roll in my hand. "Unless I stop to eat."

We took the same stairs Jack and I used to reach the laundry and passed a young woman wearing a two-foot-tall feathered headdress and a skimpy dance outfit. From under thick false eyelashes, she stole a sidelong glance at Geert, her tap shoes clicking on the metal stairs. There was guilt in her look, like a naughty kid passing by the school principal. How many dramas, I wondered, were taking place among the thousand-member crew?

Grand larceny might be one.

But what about murder?

On Deck Three Geert lifted the clipboard he carried from his office and ran a thick finger down the names and corresponding cabin numbers. Forty-six men worked the light-maintenance crew, wearing a uniform that included those particular black trousers. Heavy maintenance was something different, the men who took care of the engine room and the ship's hydraulics. Light maintenance, Geert had explained, were basically handymen, responsible for everything from fixing clogged toilets and broken doors to replacing broken mirrors and cracked bathroom tiles.

With relish, Geert snapped on latex gloves and rapped a knuckle on the door of cabin 301. "Orlando Diego, Raul Jorge," he called. "Open up."

The man who opened the door was short and swarthy and was rubbing his eyes. His glossy black hair twisted as though he slept in a centrifuge.

"Orlando?" Geert asked.

"Raul."

"Let me see your uniform."

The question startled him. *"Que?"*

Pushing past him, Geert slapped the light switch on the wall. Raul stumbled back, his mouth dropping open. Then closed.

It was a tiny cabin with no window. A set of bunk beds and a closet that Geert whipped open. He shoved the metal hangers across a steel pole, a sound like screeching birds.

"Where is the uniform?" he demanded.

From the bunks, somebody groaned. Geert walked over, staring at the bundled shape on the top bed.

"Get up," he ordered.

A flurry of Spanish exploded from the bundle. None of it sounded nice.

Geert glared at Raul.

"He sleep like that, mean." Raul's tone sounded like a mixture of annoyance and satisfaction. Tired of dealing with an ornery roommate; pleased that somebody finally understood his plight. Raising his voice, he spoke Spanish to the bundle of blanket. I recognized two words.

El jefe. Boss.

The sleeping man shot up, presumably Orlando. Squinting

into the overhead light, he listened as Raul gave him another dose of information in Spanish.

"Yah, that is right." Geert gave his savage smile. "I am on rampage. Now, where are your uniforms?"

Face red from embarrassment, Raul lifted a nylon duffel bag from the closet floor and pulled out four pieces. Two black shirts, two pairs of black pants. Identical to the pants in the purser's safe.

"I promise to send in the laundry," Raul pleaded. "Today. I know, it stinks. But—"

"Where is his?" Geert indicated Orlando.

Raul reached down, picking something up from the closet floor. One black shirt, one black pair of pants.

"And the other?"

Raul hesitated, glancing at his roommate before barging into the bathroom. Pulling back the plastic shower curtain, he pointed to a black puddle blocking the drain. Geert pushed him aside and picked up the soaking material. Water dripped.

"Tell him," Raul said to his roommate. "Tell him, or I will."

Orlando tried to yawn. "I do my own laundry."

Geert looked at Raul, challenging him to declare his loyalty. It did not take more than a moment.

"He was drunk," Raul said, choosing job over roommate. "He puked all over hisself last night."

"But he washed his clothes?"

"*I* wash his clothes, *I* put him to bed." Raul was stabbing himself in the chest, his tone unleashing the frustration. "I live with *un cerdo*."

Geert let go of the clothing, dropping it with a wet *thunk* on the shower floor. "If you talk about my visit, I will have you fired."

We walked out, closed the door, and continued down the hall.

"That's it?" I asked.

He was checking the clipboard again. "Silly men."

"So? Silly men commit crimes too."

"They were hired two weeks ago. They can't even figure out how to get their laundry picked up. No way would they get into my office, or my safe."

Moving methodically down the steel corridor, we went through twenty more cabins. None of the men were American, most were Hispanic, some Greek, and five uniforms were unaccounted for. Unfortunately, each belonged to a man whose waist was substantially larger than the black trousers. And with only two more cabins left on Geert's list, I was beginning to wonder whether the black trousers had been stolen from the supply room, and even worn by someone who didn't work light maintenance. A passenger, even.

Geert was rapping on the next to last cabin when I pulled out my cell phone and called Jack. When nobody answered the door, Geert unlocked it with his master key and stepped inside.

Or tried to.

"Ach," he sneered, "talk of pigs."

I stayed in the hallway, holding the phone, while Geert stretched his legs over plates of old food and dirty socks and scattered newspapers and magazines.

When Jack finally answered, his voice sounded jaunty. "How's it going?"

"Not great," I admitted. "What about you?"

"Oh, just talking to Milo." Buddies having coffee. No, whiskey.

"The *plan* was for you to ask him about the jeans."

"Oh yeah, thanks for reminding me."

I felt like closing the phone on him but watched Geert shaking his bald head as he went through the closet. Since Jack kept me waiting, I went to the cabin's bathroom, running a quick inspection. Shaving cream and razors left on the side of the sink. Soap scum. Deodorants without caps, showing dark hair. Dirty mirror. A toilet needing flushing.

I was about to turn away when I saw an eye shadow set on the filmy counter. Bright blue and copper green. Mascara tube. Lipstick, lots of lipstick. I picked up a plastic box of powder foundation, Sandstone Glow, and was still holding the phone to my ear when I carried it over to Geert.

He offered his own gift: black leather and silver chains.

"*Real* pigs," he said.

Jack's voice came back on the phone: "Raleigh, you there?"

Geert lifted another hanger. Leather whips. More chains. The bad feeling in my gut turned sour.

"Raleigh, you there?"

"I'll have to call you back."

In the small space, it was difficult not to breathe the foul odors, which were like rot and the sick sweetness of decomposition. Six feet across, ten long, the room was the same size as the others but seemed smaller, crowded with the plates of fossilized food and the clothing strewn on the floor. The bunk beds were unmade, and even though I was wearing latex gloves, the last thing I wanted to do was touch the beds. But a search meant searching and I pulled back the torqued sheets, shivering with revulsion as I combed through the bedding. Something solid cocooned in one blanket. I pulled it out.

A camcorder. I held it up for Geert, dangling it from a gloved finger.

His mustache twitched like the whiskers on a rabbit. "Only one uniform is here."

He held up a black shirt, then pointed to an area above the left chest pocket. The material was darker, with threads outlining a small rectangle.

"Name tag, gone." Geert lifted his radio, clicking the button on the side. A series of clicks came in reply. Ninja lan-

guage. Finally Geert read the names from the clipboard.
"Ahmed Ramazan and Murat Serif. Immediately."

He radioed the laundry room next, placing an all points
bulletin on any of the black light-maintenance uniforms.

I went back into the bathroom, stoppered the sink, and
dumped out the pink face powder, searching for any hidden jewelry. In the soiled shaving kits, I found a pair of cu-
ticle scissors, more razors, boxes of condoms. Then I sorted
through the trash can under the filthy counter. It was full of
used tissues and despite all those years in the forensics lab,
what I saw on those tissues triggered my gag reflex. I listened to Geert tell the laundry room to search every single
duffel bag.

At the bottom of the trash can, the black threads looked
like dried worms. And there was the rectangular patch.

I pulled it out.

"Ahmed," it said. "Republic of Turkey."

"We might have our man," I called to Geert.

While Geert printed out employee pictures of Ramazan
and his roommate, Serif, I stood at the small porthole in his
office, watching the early evening light blaze across the sea.
It looked like noon anywhere else, and when I turned toward
the noise coming down the hall, sunspots swam in front of
my eyes, blurring the image of the person that the Ninjas
dragged in.

He wore a black uniform and his swarthy face carried
several days of beard. But it was his eyes…his eyes…they
stopped me cold. Pale green but murky, they reminded me
of glacial pools contaminated with silt. Poisonous water that
suffocates all marine life.

"Serif," his name tag said on the black shirt, "Republic
of Turkey."

"Serif," Geert said cheerfully. "Welcome."

Serif lowered his chin, deepening the set of dark circles under those disturbed eyes.

"My men cannot find Ramazan. Where is he?"

Serif shrugged. "I am working." He had a thick Mediterranean accent.

"Yah, working." Geert lifted the camcorder from the desk "I have seen your 'work.'"

"What is that?" Serif said.

"You had a day off today," Geert said, ignoring the ploy. "What did you do?"

"I keyed out."

"Your friend, Ramazan, he got off the ship too?"

"You have schedule. You know. He was working."

Something felt wrong. The man was too calm, too confident. All the other employees on this ship looked at Geert the way Ugandans looked at Idi Amin. But Serif's attitude meant he was confident of something. Something we didn't know. As Geert continued to query, I could feel the thing slithering toward us, circling, about to strike. Geert must have sensed it too because he gave a quick nod to the Ninja standing behind Serif.

The Ninja struck, one viperous moment.

The Turk collapsed.

Geert stared calmly at the man on the floor. "What did you do with it?"

There was no reply. Geert nodded. The Ninja drove his foot into Serif's side and Geert repeated the question. When Serif looked up, he maintained the wicked expression.

Geert demanded, "The jewelry. From my safe. Where is it?"

"I don't know wha—"

The Ninja could've scored a field goal from the fifty-yard line. Serif's body curled into the fetal position and a queasy sensation went through me. My least favorite people were

uthless criminals, but I'd been chasing them long enough
o feel wary of my own animosity, what it could breed. I had
felt the temptation to cross the line more than once. Except it
wasn't a line. It was more like a guardrail, running alongside
some deep dark canyon where on the hottest nights it blew
with the coolest wind, washing up from the depths, whispering of revenge. But if you plunged down into that place, there
was no return. Ever.

I squatted next to Serif's curled figure. His body smelled
as rancid as his cabin.

"Serif."

After a moment, he removed his arms from around his
head. He glowered at me, the pale eyes the color of antifreeze.

"The FBI can pursue charges for pornography, perhaps
even distribution. Or sexual assault." I glanced at Geert, confirming. He nodded; he'd watched the tapes found in the
room.

Serif smiled, revealing jagged teeth. "My country does
not recognize your FBI."

This was true. Certain foreign countries built walls to repel
the FBI. Turkey was among the worst, and as its citizen, Serif
was protected from us.

But facing a power play, I played.

I looked up at Geert. "How many tourists does your cruise
line take through the Mediterranean?"

The Dutchman didn't let me down. "Hundreds of thousands every year," he said immediately. "The Turkish government would not want our ships going somewhere else."

"You see, Serif, if the ships stopped coming, it would be
your fault. Your government would know it was all because
of your pornography. What's the law like for pornographers
in a Muslim country like Turkey?"

"I did nothing." His mouth tightened. "Do you hear me?"

Another Ninja appeared at the door. The tall one. He was

flushed and out of breath, and he shook his head. Geert gazed down at Serif with naked hate in his blue eyes. "Where is he hiding?"

Serif was silent.

"This is no game," Geert said. "I can make sure you spend a long time in one of your famous Turkish prisons."

No response.

"Answer me! Where is he?"

But the power had shifted once again. Serif scratched the beard, flicking his fingers like some obscene gesture. "What day is this?" he finally said.

We waited. He enjoyed it, drawing us out.

"What day is this?" he asked again.

"It is Thursday," Geert growled.

"What number?"

"Where is he?"

Serif smiled. The teeth seemed to stretch across his face. "Now I remember. Ramazan got off in Juneau."

"He—" Geert looked stricken.

"It was his last day," Serif sat up. "He went home."

At Geert's nod the Ninjas reached down, yanking him to his feet and dragging him through the hall. Geert picked up the phone.

"Exit records, check them again. Ramazan, Ahmed Ramazan." He hit the phone's cutoff button, then punched in another four digits. "Staff records for Ahmed Ramazan. His term ends—when?"

Down the hall, I heard a door open. No voices, no yelling. The door closed. I didn't want to imagine what would happen on the other side.

"I am hearing he got off in Juneau."

Stepping into the hall, I listened to a thudding sound coming from the room down the way, the room where Webb had been detained. I opened my cell phone and called Agent Kevin Barnes.

"It's Raleigh," I said. Agents' numbers did not show up on caller ID.

"Don't worry, I already put in a good word for you," he said. "Job's yours if you want it."

"Thanks, but I need a different favor." I described the missing cruise ship employee who possibly left the ship in Juneau. "Any chance you can track him down?"

"No. I'm swamped. But there are only two ways out of Juneau. Boat or plane. Nobody can drive away. Let me make some calls."

"I'll fax you a photo."

"This guy is your killer?" he asked. "I can call in troopers if you need 'em."

"Right now, we think he stole that bracelet I told you about, the one with the blue stones? If you can get the state's help on an APB, I'd appreciate it."

"Will do," he said. "Sounds like that bracelet is worth some serious dough."

"Or it was a really nice paycheck for murder."

I glanced down the hall. Behind the closed door, the silence was eerie.

SEVENTEEN

Geert wanted to return to the cabin shared by Ramazan and Serif. The place stunk worse than before—a locker room inside a brothel surrounded by a landfill.

Crossing the room, I picked up one of the dirty T-shirts and threw it over a plate of scrambled eggs so old the yolks were orange. But Geert grabbed my wrist.

"Neen. Keep it like this."

The Dutchman seemed like a new man. No longer sullen, his eyes were sparked by a fervor that also flushed his bald pate. Though grateful for the change, I wasn't sure we were reading from the same page. Geert was focused like a laser on the busted safe and the pornography. For him, recovering the stolen bracelet meant his company would be cleared of theft, without coughing up insurance money. Meanwhile, Judy Carpenter's murder remained almost hypothetical for him. But her death was my sole focus. Grand larceny was serious, but life always took precedence over material objects. Even very expensive objects.

I kept my back against the outer wall and listened to the ocean washing against the ship's side. Geert was placing a single chair in the middle of the filth, then positioning himself opposite that, waiting for his first "guest."

Ramazan had still not been found. It was now assumed

that he did indeed leave the ship—after tossing the black trousers down the laundry chute. During those crucial hours, two women had been working the gangway exit. One was assigned to help passengers slide their room keys into the computer slot, confirming their exits and reboarding; the other woman was stationed at the X-ray machine, checking purses and bags and backpacks, and her name was Fiona O'Connell.

When the Ninja brought her to the cabin, her skin reminded me of Irish cream. Amber freckles dusted her high cheekbones. But her blue eyes seemed wary. She sat in the chair opposite Geert.

He gave the mustache a twirl. "How long you work for us?"

"Three years." Her "th" sounded like "t" in the Irish brogue. Knitting her small hands together, she placed them in her lap. "Three years, three months, and—"

"You like your job?"

Her eyes slid toward me but never made it. The dead food and stinking clothes stopped her. Finally, she nodded at Geert, but it was a tentative yes, as if saying, yes, she liked the job until that bald Dutch security officer made her sit inside this cabin.

"You worked with Letty today," he said. Not a question.

"I was on the machine. Checkin' the bags, you know."

"Letty is good to work with?" A question.

"I... I..."

"Spit it out."

"I don't want to cause trouble."

"Then you will bring trouble on yourself."

She stared down at a half-eaten hamburger, the rare meat like an open wound. "Letty doesn't work."

"Lazy?"

Fiona nodded. "And she flirts."

He shrugged, unconvinced.

A blush fired across the angular cheekbones. "She flirts

and she runs her mouth even when t'ousands of folks be wanting off the ship." Like Raul down the hall, Fiona was uncorking all the carbonated emotions that come with close quarters. Her brogue rushed like a creek. "She only t'inks about herself. Old people, they can't be standing 'round like that. Mark me words, one day while Letty runs that mouth of hers, somebody's goin' to have their stroke."

Geert said nothing, but the hook was baited. "She talks. So what?"

Fiona leaned forward over her praying hands. "She aims herself at the rich ones, she does. Follows old men 'round the ship, actin' all helpful."

"She makes tips."

"Aye."

"Does she like the money, or the attention?" he asked.

Fiona sat back, sensing her case was made. "The girl can't bear no attention."

"You can leave," Geert said.

It was an abrupt order and she froze. Still clutching her hands, she drew a deep breath, steeling herself. "I'm losing me job, is that it?"

Geert said nothing. After a moment, she gave a curt nod, stood, and walked to the door. The Ninja led her away.

It wasn't my jurisdiction and he wasn't explaining. All I could do was listen and observe, then figure out his plan.

He walked over to the Ninja standing outside the door, and I scanned the filth, longing for a window to open. Every time I turned my head, I smelled another stink coming from the floor. Geert's back was to me so I reached down and snagged a blue shirt off the floor, throwing it over the rotting hamburger. Geert didn't notice. Reaching down again, I grabbed a woman's black skirt and was about to toss it over coagulated noodles, when I saw Milo Carpenter's face.

The tabloid cover looked smudged, the garish colors cloudy

from touch, but the photograph was unmistakable. Milo held a drink in one hand, with an arm wrapped around a young brunette whose long hair obscured half her face. Below the photo, the headline identified her as "one of Milo's many mistresses." Dropping the skirt, I picked up the magazine, checking the publication date. A Special Easter Edition. Another headline trumpeted an Easter miracle: a nine-year-old boy in Arkansas cracked open an Easter egg and saw Jesus in the yolk.

Geert was stepping over filth, returning to his position opposite the inquisition chair, when I raised the tabloid. His eyes scanned the main headline, then the photograph.

"It's months old," I said.

"And the wife killed herself. Did you consider that?"

"For two seconds."

"Two?"

"She might have *wanted* to kill herself, but she didn't do it like that. Somebody killed her."

Before he could reply, the Ninja brought another girl.

Unlike Fiona's geometrical face, the girl named Letitia George, or Letty, had a face that made a series of wide slow turns. Round cheeks, round chin, an almost bulbous nose and full lips smothered with pink gloss. The only linear feature appeared when she smirked: vertical dimples slicing into the plump cheeks like hash marks on bread dough.

She plunked down in the chair.

"I'm very glad we could meet, Letty." Geert's voice was warm. "You worked the gangway today."

"Yeah."

"You keyed each person out."

"Yeah."

"Everybody, each person. You keyed out everybody?"

"Yeah and did you see how long that line was? Because the olds can't get their key in the slot because their hands shake. I have to take the card, slide it in, then explain how the stupid thing works because they always ask. Yeah, the miracle of computers."

Geert smiled, growing warmer. It was the smile he gave Martin Webb, only more frightening.

"Did you key out Ramazan?" he asked.

"Who?"

"Do not waste my time." He smiled.

"I don't know who you're talking about."

"Ramazan walked off the ship today and you did not run his card through the system."

She was a smart girl—smart enough to quit playing dumb. "That wasn't my fault."

"Do tell me."

Adjusting herself on the chair, she got comfortable for the story. "I had a long line and he pushed through everybody. He had his toolbox with him. Up high, you know, on his shoulder." She patted her shoulder, demonstrating. "He acted like Mr. Big Shot, making everybody move and yelling at them. He scared them."

"What were his words, Letty. His exact words."

"Well, first he told everybody to get out of the way. Then when they started freaking out, he said, 'Ramazan make it sure that nobody gonna break a toe.'"

Even Geert looked surprised. "Break a toe?"

"Yeah, he's a stupid Greek. I think he was trying to say, 'I'm going to fix something so that nobody breaks a leg.' But he doesn't say anything right."

"Turkish," Geert corrected. "He's Turkish. Tell me what he did next."

"He ran past so fast, I don't really know. I heard him more than I saw him, you know? That toolbox was lifted so we could all see it was some emergency. But *I* had the emergency. It was an old folks' riot, everybody crying how they were gonna break a hip."

Geert nodded. "And yet, still, you did not key him out?"

"He was just working on the gangway. It wasn't like he was getting off." She paused. Frowning. "Did he?"

"You tell me."

"I just did. He was fixing something on the gangway."

"You didn't stop and ask him questions?"

"Are you deaf? I just told you I had a thousand old people crying."

"But you stop and talk to the passengers all the time."

She stopped. "Fiona." The smirk appeared. "She tell you that, little Miss Perfect? Well, I know stuff; she's not so perfect."

Geert extended an arm, sweeping in the cabin's filth and disarray. "Does this bother you?"

She did not look around. She held his gaze. "It's disgusting."

"Yes, pigs live here. And you enjoyed the pigsty."

The round features seemed to flatten as if hit with an iron frying pan. "What?"

"They took pictures of you. The pigs. You let them."

Her brown eyes darted toward me. But I wasn't prepared for any of this. I didn't watch the videos, and if this was why Geert wanted to interview the gangway girls here, it was a real humdinger of a reason.

She turned back to Geert. "What is this?"

"How long did you know the pigs?"

"I don't know them."

"But you took your clothes off for them. I wonder. Would your mother like to see those movies?"

Again, she looked over at me, as though it was my idea to show her mother. The sheer panic I saw in her brown eyes sparked pity.

But I got over it. Real quick.

Dropping her chin, she turned toward Geert and raised her eyes, giving a lurid expression of seduction. "Did you like watching me?" she asked. "Did you watch all of it, you naughty old man?"

Geert's mustache was twitching in overdrive, but he controlled his voice, still almost tender. "Let us talk about Ramazan."

"He's insane."

"Why do you say?"

"He's killed people."

Geert glanced at me. She said it casually, like somebody describing a road with a dangerous intersection.

I leaned forward. "How do you know he's killed people?"

She shrugged a shoulder. "I don't. Not exactly. But there's a guy back in my village, in Hoonah?"

"That's here, in Alaska?" I asked.

"Yeah. There's only one Hoonah. This guy killed some people and Ram's got those same crazy eyes. They look at you like you're not even a person. Like you're just a thing."

I recalled the two acid pools in Serif's face. "Worse than Serif's eyes?"

She laughed. "Serif's the nice one."

Geert's voice was low. "You had company with these men?"

"Quit making me sound bad. I tried to get away from them. There was one time when I didn't feel like playing dress up— that's what they called it, dress up. I had the stomach flu. Throwing up, fever, everything. But Ram dragged me down here, he *made* me play. He even stuck something down my throat. I can't hardly remember anything after that."

"Letty—"

Her eyes flashed at me. "Who're you?"

"Raleigh Harmon, special agent with the FBI."

She cursed. Then she grabbed a hunk of her black hair, petting it nervously.

"Letty, do you know what he forced down your throat?"

"A pill."

"How do you know?"

"The next day I had these bruises on my throat. I got scared, because I couldn't remember anything. I went to Serif, crying, and he finally told me what happened. I wasn't playing nice dress up so they held me down and pushed a pill down my throat. Only I gagged on it. So they pushed on my neck, you know, to get it to go down."

I heard Geert mutter, "Pigs."

"And you don't recall anything else?"

"Just, like, in pieces." She continued to grip the hank of hair but stared at the floor. "I remember feeling itchy. And I remember somebody was laughing. And the next day I couldn't stop crying. I felt so sad. I wanted to kill myself. Serif said it was the pill doing that. And it would wear off."

"Ramazan," I said, "he didn't feel that sorry for you?"

She sneered. "He doesn't got feelings."

"Did they ever talk about money?"

She glanced over at Geert. He was listening intently, twirling a handlebar. "Answer her."

"They always talked in that weird language. Greek or whatever it is. I couldn't understand them."

"On this trip, after we left Seattle, did anything seem different, unusual?"

"You mean like Ram and the toolbox?"

I nodded.

She gave it some thought. "I came down here that first night we left Seattle. My shift was over at the gangway and I knocked on the door. But they wouldn't open it. I got scared, like maybe they were throwing me away for some other girl because Serif wouldn't open the door more than two inches.

I started chewing him out for it, telling him off, when Ram suddenly yanked him away." Her eyes dropped again. "He came to the door and called me a lot of names. I think it started with that whole pill thing. After that, it was like I was nothing to them."

"Did you tell anyone about that pill?"

"I went to the doctor after, because I couldn't keep my eyes open. No exaggeration. I fell asleep *in the shower*. And then all that crying, I felt so bad."

"The doctor did not report it," Geert said.

If the doctor knew, he would be required to tell the captain who would contact Geert who would toss both men off the ship.

She nodded. "I decided Ram would kill me. He said so. The guy's eyes are like a wolf."

Geert nodded. "Leave the ship in Skagway," he said. "Tomorrow."

"But—"

"You are fired."

"But—"

"You didn't report them. And you allowed Ramazan to leave the ship."

"But I just told you, I didn't have a chance, he was running. It's not fair. This wasn't *my* fault."

Geert drew a deep breath, narrowing his eyes at her. "You want to keep your job?"

"Are you kidding? I make more than anybody in Hoonah."

He sighed. "There is one way."

She looked hopeful, eager, almost natural.

"You must talk to Serif. You must ask him where Ramazan went. But if you tell him about our meeting, if you tell anyone, I will make certain Ramazan knows it was you who told us."

At Geert's command, she walked to the door, following the Ninja away.

The door closed behind her.

I said, "You trust her?"

"Neen. That is a girl without fences. But we must get the information we can get."

He was apparently done with the interrogations and was walking toward the door when I remembered Letty's description of her bruised neck.

"May I search the cabin?" I asked.

He turned, frowning. "You need more charges?"

"I would like to find whatever drug they used on her." Then the Alaska medical examiner could test for the same substance in the dead body of Judy Carpenter.

EIGHTEEN

Ask anybody about their cruise and they'll inevitably bore you talking about the food. Never-ending buffets. Four-star dinners. Glorious desserts available around the clock.

But other than a perfect steak last night and some exceptional rolls on the Highway this afternoon, my caloric intake was cruelly deficient. I was a girl who liked to eat—not nibble, but eat—and one of the biggest incentives for taking this cruise was the idea that good food would be ready twenty-four hours of every day.

Food. Mountains. Rocks.

Was that too much to ask?

Apparently, yes, I decided, carrying the unmarked prescription vials from Ramazan's cabin to the purser's safe. Hunger gnawed at my stomach, and dinner had come and gone and now my fellow passengers were enjoying nightcaps with the musicals and comedy shows in the ship's theaters. With legs that felt heavy as lead pipes, I slogged up the stairs because I didn't have the patience for elevators that opened on every floor. On a landing, I stopped to catch my breath and call Aunt Charlotte.

"We're fine," she said. "I ordered room service and we're playing cards. Your mother's winning. It's Raleigh," she added.

I heard my mother's voice, small and distant in the background.

"It's Raleigh," my aunt told her.

I asked, "Where's Claire?"

"She's getting a massage. Don't worry about us. You go finish that geology stuff and we'll see you later tonight."

What a great accomplice, I decided.

My second call was to Jack. "I've got some news. Where are you?"

"On the upper deck. They're having a memorial service, about fifty yards from where she was found hanging. In the outdoor bar. It's a celebration of her life, they say. You need to see it."

"I'll be there in a minute. Can you order me some dinner?" I gave my request: cheeseburger medium-well with everything but pickles; two orders of fries with mayo on the side; and the biggest chocolate shake they can serve.

After putting the unmarked Rx vials in the purser's safe, I hiked to Deck Fourteen. Maybe it was the climb, and the lack of food, and my mom's suffering, and the total lack of answers about Judy Carpenter's death, but when I pushed through the ship's upper doors, my mood was surly.

But the landscape refused to agree with me.

Finally dipping, the sun was placing rose-colored crowns on the snowcapped mountains, and the glaciated rock, backlit by golden rays, had the detailed splendor of finest filigree. The forests were turning midnight blue, blending with the ocean that lapped along the jagged shore. I wanted to gulp the crystal air.

The open deck was covered with chaise longues, and the people on them wore wireless headsets and snuggled under blankets to watch the movie that played on the giant white screen hanging behind the swimming pool. I glanced up to see the picture and stopped dead in my tracks.

"You've got to be kidding," I said aloud.

A young Milo Carpenter wore an undershirt that exposed his rippling muscles. His face was soot-streaked and sweating and he carried an Uzi with his index finger on the trigger. If I'd been the consultant, I would've pointed out the mistake—one twitch and the semiautomatic weapon would start firing off rounds. But Hollywood, I'd learned, felt little obligation to reality.

I gazed around the deck for the open-air bar, but it was nowhere to be seen. And the only people not watching the movie were canoodling in the hot tub, sipping umbrella drinks. Since alcohol worked like an auger for finding Milo, I walked over and asked, "Pardon me, where did you get your drinks?"

The man pointed to a set of spiral stairs that climbed up to some platform above the main deck, hidden behind the movie screen. "But that's a private party," he said. "No public allowed."

I thanked him and started up the stairs.

"Hey! I said you can't go up there!"

From above the stairs, the big guy from Milo's cabin leaned over the rail. Vinnie Pinnetta. Bouncer and batterer turned bodyguard. The mansard forehead projected like a cliff overhang.

"I tried to stop her!" the man yelled from the hot tub.

Vinnie waved at the guy, signaling absolution. I stood at the top of the stairs, waiting for him to remove the chain that blocked my path.

"Try to behave yourself," he said.

The platform was surrounded by clear plastic windbreaks, set beneath the Sky Bar with a view of the ship's wake, the white bridal train that disappeared into the dark ocean. Most of the beautiful people sat at small tables gathered around a baby grand piano that had been placed behind a wall supporting the movie screen. MJ sat on the instrument's bench, speaking into the microphone with a voice that was almost a whisper. At the far end, Jack stood at the bar with Milo and Sandy Sparks. The person missing was Larrah-rhymes-with-Harrah.

I walked the perimeter to the bar. Milo's skin had the slick appearance of damp clay and he had thrown an arm around Jack's shoulders.

"You're a good man, Jake."

Jack lifted his drink. A swaggering gesture, blurred around the edges. I took the bar stool next to him, ignoring the big goofy smile on his face. His eyes, which were set close on his face, now looked almost crossed.

I tried to keep my voice down, but I was mad. "You're drunk?"

He dropped a hand on my shoulder. It felt like ten pounds. "Harrrr-mon, lighten uuu-up."

I shrugged my shoulder away and turned to the bartender, who was serving them another round of drinks. Like every bartender on the ship, his name tag said he was from the Philippines. When he put the drinks down, Jack thanked him; Milo didn't; Sparks ignored him; and the bartender smiled at them all.

"What you have?" he asked me.

"Did you get an order for a cheeseburger?"

"Yes." He walked to the end of the bar, picking up the phone.

I swiveled to watch MJ. For a piano player, her hands were small, brushing the keys with adequate dexterity. The talent was in her voice. She sang with a voice that reminded me of rain weeping down windowpanes. And she sang about love. And pain. So much pain.

When my food arrived, I swiveled back around and said silent grace before digging into the burger. I had to restrain a moan of gratitude. The meat was tender, grilled and peppered to perfection. The melted cheddar was carmelized in places and the toasted bun was not soggy anywhere. When I opened my eyes, Milo was hunched over his drink and taking stabbing glances at MJ. Jack stared at her as well, his face looking almost grave. Only Sandy Sparks seemed oblivious to the sound, scribbling notes on cocktail napkins. When I looked over at the stairs, Vinnie the bodyguard was lifting the chain for Larrah Sparks. Her platinum hair was fluffed to perfection and she strode directly in front of the piano, heedless of the performance. When she reached the bar, midrefrain, she announced, "They told us we'd see bears. I haven't seen one."

I ate like one, relishing every carnivorous bite. Nothing could ruin it, not even overhearing Sandy Sparks tell his wife a dumb joke about bears and the woods and the pope. When he came to the punch line, there was silence. I glanced over.

"I don't get it," Larrah said.

I dipped my French fries in mayo and considered the possibility that Ramazan and Serif killed Judy Carpenter. Possible. Not probable. Their cabin showed chaos and filth. And Letty had described their erratic behavior. While Serif was cool under questioning, Judy Carpenter's murder was planned with precision. More probable: Ramazan broke into the safe. But murder?

"Oooo-waaaa-waa-waaa," Milo started singing, trampling MJ's music.

I bit another fry and considered the gossip rag in the Turks' cabin. Milo on the cover implied they could recognize him. Did that mean anything? As Geert pointed out, the ship was full of gossips. Maybe the Turks heard about the bracelet found at the scene. Maybe Ramazan decided to steal it, run away. Perhaps there was no connection to Judy or Milo.

I sipped the milkshake, still glancing around the deck and realizing that the most likely scenario was still the most disturbing: one of these beautiful people killed Judy Carpenter.

Somebody she knew.

Somebody she didn't think she needed to fight.

Somebody strong enough to lift a 172-pound woman over the deck rail.

I carried my shake over to the plastic windbreak where Vinnie Pinnetta stared out at the passing mountains, smoking a cigarette. Each time he exhaled, the gray cloud seemed to stay suspended in midair, hanging there as the ship cruised forward.

He looked over, glancing down at my milkshake. "Sure you can handle a stiff drink like that?"

I flipped open my credentials. Next to my Bureau ID, I'd placed the employee photos of Serif and Ramazan. The men looked like evil swarthy cousins, haters with bad eyes.

"You know these guys?"

He stared down at their faces, his forehead like the bill on a baseball cap. "No, but I'm guessing they're why you're not having a good time."

"I'm having a great time." I smiled. "But it's going to be better when we dock in Seattle."

He blew a cloud of smoke. "Why's that?"

"Because by then, I'll know who killed Judy Carpenter."

"You must be slow. She killed herself."

"Only she didn't."

"What kinda game are you playing?" he asked.

"No game. It's life and death."

There was a burst of applause as MJ finished her song. She leaned into the mic and announced a quick break.

Vinnie flicked his cigarette over the rail, not bothering to see if it hit water, and walked away. When he reached the bar, Milo threw a sloppy arm around him.

Away from everyone else, MJ stared out at the ship's starboard side, her black hair blowing, the color blending with the mountains across the water. When I walked up beside her, there were tears sliding down her cheeks. She looked over, then pointed to the woods along the water's edge. In the trees, a tempera of yellow light glowed from a tiny log cabin.

"That's where I want to go," she said. "Somewhere nobody can find me."

"It looks lonely." I watched her tears, wondering whether the wind made them. "Is it Judy's death that's bothering you?"

She cried without contorting her face. She cried the way actresses cry.

"It's just all so...final. She's never coming back."

I hesitated saying the next thing. It was cruel. But there was no time for sentiment. "The dress you sent down to the laundry. How did it get so dusty?"

She didn't turn to look at me. I stared at her profile and she wiped her face almost robotically before walking back to the piano and sitting on the bench. After a moment, she raised her hands. I could see her fingers trembling. She closed her eyes.

And then I heard something remarkable.

With her eyes still closed, she reached forward and let her fingertips caress the keys lightly, like someone reading Braille. The first notes that came out were minor keys. They rose so slowly I wasn't sure it was a song, but she continued to coax the bittersweet tune and the notes stretched into elongated cries of desperation and need. At the small tables, all conversation ceased and the music swam into the gloaming sky, harmonizing with its twilight hues.

Only one person ignored her: Milo. Keeping his back to the piano, he hugged his drink. I watched Jack swing himself off the bar, staggering toward me. I turned around, facing the ocean, hoping he'd stay away. But he came to the rail, hooking a boot heel on the bottom rung. A cowboy, caught in the wrong century.

"Harmon, don't look at me like that."

"How many drinks, Jack?"

"Four."

"Terrific. You'll be a big help tomorrow."

"The first two I flushed in the men's room. I spilled the third." He lifted his glass in a mock toast. "I'm nursing number four and they're all too drunk to notice."

The wind shifted, blowing hair across my face. I gave a begrudging nod, still not ready to forgive for some reason. "Did your new best friend tell you anything interesting?"

"His jeans got dirty when he fell on the floor."

"Fell where, in a dustbin?"

"In the Sky Bar. He fell because he was upset about Judy."

I looked over at Milo. He was staring at me.

No, I was wrong. He was staring at Jack.

"He's making moony faces at you," I said. "What's the deal with you two?"

"He wants an Oscar."

"For playing a drunk?"

"Harmon, do you have any idea how much I've missed you?"

I repeated my question, "What's the deal with you two, Jack?"

"All right, brace yourself. He thinks this movie will be his biggest hit. His most emotional performance ever."

"It's an emotional performance all right."

"Don't ever quit this job, Harmon. You were made for it."

"Jack, I read this script. It's not like it's *Citizen Kane*."

"Ah, but Sandy Sparks is rewriting the ending."

I waited. The movie was about an FBI agent who takes a cruise with his wife. Only she gets kidnapped and he has to rescue her. "Don't tell me."

"You got it. The wife dies. She's found hanging off the ship."

I looked at Sandy Sparks, scribbling on the cocktail napkins.

"By the way," Jack said, "Milo says you're fired."

"Do you promise?"

He laughed. "You're fired and I'm the new consultant. He asked me to come to Hollywood, work the double."

"What double?"

"A double. I stand in for Milo, when the director wants to block the shot."

"Block the shot?"

"He made a nice offer. He thinks I have a future in movies."

"Jack, that's not a compliment."

"Think about it. No more paperwork, no more perps vomiting in my car. No more days sitting at the courthouse waiting for the case that never gets called. I just might take him up on the offer."

"Go for it." Satiated with food, I didn't want to talk anymore. I wanted sleep and could feel myself fading. "Until you go Hollywood, we have work to do." I pushed myself off the rail. "See you in the morning."

"Harmon, tell the truth."

"About what?"

"If I went to Hollywood, you'd miss me."

I told myself it was fatigue. That's all. I was tired, so tired my mind was playing tricks. Because as I walked away, leaving him standing there, a certain part of me wondered if he wasn't right.

NINETEEN

The sound of the shower woke me Friday morning—woke me suddenly, woke me with a pounding heart. I bolted upright, listening to the water run, fearing this was another episode of "cleaning the air."

But the bathroom door was closed. Sighing with relief, I lay back down and stared at my watch. It was 6:23 AM and sleep would not come again. I reached for my cell phone, seizing the rare moment of privacy. There was another message from DeMott, but I bypassed voice mail and called the Alaska Medical Examiner's office, hoping to catch them before the day got busy. A woman answered, put me on hold, and three minutes later when the shower cut off, I grabbed my keycard and stepped into the hallway, figuring nobody else was up at this hour.

Wrong.

"Baby sleeping again?" whispered the nice woman from yesterday. Beside her, the man carried a camera, binoculars, and a camcorder. He stared at my pajamas. The woman pointed to the cabin next to Aunt Charlotte's. "Are they keeping you up too?"

I nodded, smiling as they passed, listening to the automated recording that gave me directions to the morgue. *Follow Northern Lights Boulevard to...* But the nice couple was just the beginning. More cabin doors were opening, and people were stepping into the hallway dressed in warm jackets and hats, all of them carrying cameras and camcorders.

Snapping my phone shut, I slid the keycard into the lock.

But I missed.

Suddenly the floor shifted and I grabbed the door handle, hanging on to keep from falling over.

People were lunging for the handrails, crying out. And then a bang went off.

On the other side of the door, my mother screamed.

I managed to get the keycard in, throwing the door open.

She squeezed the curtains, holding them open, and stared out the window. Blocks of pale blue ice floated by.

"Iceberg!" she cried. "We hit an iceberg."

The ocean water no longer looked blue. It was green—electric green—and the mountains no longer had trees. The sharp rock faces sliced the water like knives.

"We're okay," I said, feeling my pulse pound again. We had sailed into Tracy Arm, considered one of the world's most spectacular fjords. Seeing it was among my top vacation hopes—before murder and grand larceny and pornography altered my focus. "We're inside a narrow channel and there's a glacier at the other end. That's where the icebergs are coming from. We're fine. It's just going to be a little bumpy."

She did not look convinced; in fact, she looked at me like I was...a liar.

I turned away and knocked on the adjoining door. Aunt Charlotte was snapping a pink scarf like a flag. She nodded before I said a word, then called out, "Nadine, this is not the *Titanic*. Throw some warm clothes on, let's go. We're late."

I felt a surge of love for my aunt. We disagreed about so many things, yet here was family: the people who kept dancing with you, even after the music stopped.

She ran her eyes over my pajamas. "Are you coming?"

"Yes, but"—I glanced around the cabin—"where's Claire?"

"She's saving us a good spot on the top deck." Aunt Charlotte picked up her coat, lowering her voice. "I'll try to keep them apart as much as possible, but this ship's only so big." She raised her voice again. "Now g'on, get dressed!"

At the teak railing, my mother shivered and stared at ice the size of automobiles. As the ship inched forward, Aunt Charlotte stood between my mother and Claire, a human buffer. Though the morning was sunny, the air felt cold and smelled of crystallized water and silted minerals. The deck was crowded with people, but a reverential silence had fallen.

I stepped back slowly and walked toward the aft, the only person more interested in the small alcove that faced the wrong way for the view. The thin orange rope was now wrapped around the coil of thick gray mooring line, but I gazed around the area, searching for what it was that bothered me so much. Perhaps it was the location, I realized. The door back into the ship was only steps away. The sports court was right there too. And the platform where last night's socalled "memorial" took place. And beyond that, the Sky Bar perched above the wake.

And yet this alcove was almost invisible from every one of those locations.

The perfect spot.

Opening my cell phone, I hit Redial, and was placed on hold again with the ME's office. Leaning over the rail, I stared down at the water whose strange color was created by the persistent glaciers scouring the rock beneath the ice, filling the thin channel with silt and sediment. As golden sunlight shone through the blue water, the minerals made it look green.

"Need any help?"

I turned around.

Jack stood there, holding two cups of steaming coffee.

I took the cup he offered. "I'm on hold with the medical examiner, the office is in Anchorage."

The ship hit an iceberg, a light *thud*. When I glanced over the rail, the berg bobbed, sending ripples through the water.

Jack stepped into the alcove, looking it over. "I walked Milo back to his cabin last night. He wanted me to have another drink with him."

"So you did."

"Of course." He grinned. "I really should be an actor. I managed not to drink six gin-and-tonics last night. It's not as easy as it looks, even in the company of drunks."

"Did you learn anything else?"

"Yes, I asked him about the piano player, again. He went into an inebriated rant about AA and people who join it getting self-righteous and who do they think they are. It went on and on. But it made me wonder what beef he's got with her."

In the silence, his phone rang. It played a theme song from a spaghetti western. "Jack Stephanson," he answered. Then mouthed one word to me: McLeod.

I turned back to the green sea. McLeod, making sure things were still plutonic.

"Raleigh? She's right here."

I'd already lost my place in line once with the ME's office and I didn't want to start over again. But if I refused to talk to McLeod, he would get suspicious again. Handing Jack my phone, I said, "When they pick up, tell them we're calling about Judy Carpenter's autopsy. Remind them it's an expedite."

"Got it."

I took Jack's phone. "Yes, sir, this is Raleigh."

"We got him," McLeod said.

"Who?"

"Ramadan."

"Ramazan?" I said, making a rare correction. "Where?"

"Sea-Tac airport, Marvin Larsen was told we were searching for a fugitive from Juneau"—Marvin Larsen, a special agent who worked out of Seattle airport—"and when Marvin heard it was for your case, he pulled out the stops. What is it with you, Harmon?"

I connected with Marvin Larsen last fall, on my missing person's case, when he gave me a major break. My mother instilled several useful habits in me, and one was sending heartfelt thank-you notes, particularly for people with thankless jobs. Working airport security for the FBI qualified as truly thankless.

"Marvin's one of the good guys," I said. "Where's Ramazan now?"

"Larsen stuck him in an interrogation room at the airport."

"Did he find the bracelet?"

"He's fired off a search warrant for the US attorneys."

"Oh no."

McLeod sighed. "Yeah, the guy's already called in a lawyer. And with that Turkish citizenship, we've got a tough row to mow."

Jack began waving, signaling the call was coming in.

"Go ahead and take it," I told him.

"Take what?" McLeod asked.

"I was talking to Jack, he's got my phone."

There was a long silence, full of plutonic implications.

"Sir, when you called I was on hold with the Alaska ME's office. I've been waiting a long time and I didn't want to lose my connection." The defensive tone in my voice was making the truth sound like a bad excuse. "We traded phones and—"

"Raleigh, you know I never jump to conclusions. With me, everything is strictly *ipso fatso*."

I didn't even bother with substitutions. I was staring at Jack and the odd expression on his face.

"But if I didn't know better..." McLeod was saying.

If I didn't know better, I'd say something was wrong with Jack. I couldn't hear his exact words because he was over by the shuffleboard court, but I suddenly wondered if Larsen had called. Jack didn't like Larsen. Or was Jack arguing with the morgue? Either way, it was trouble and I started to walk over, vaguely hearing McLeod say something about fraternization.

"My name's Jack," he was saying into my phone. "That's right, Jack. You need me to spell it?... Raleigh? She's busy... She can't come to the phone.... Why? She doesn't want to, that's why."

Oh. No.

Oh no!

I threw Jack's phone at him, McLeod's voice going out into the air, and grabbed my phone out of Jack's hand. Closing my eyes, I put the phone to my ear and prayed.

"This is Raleigh."

"Who was that?" DeMott asked.

"Nobody." My heart was racing so fast it hurt.

"Why is he answering your phone?"

I walked across the empty shuffleboard court. My feet felt numb. "He's a colleague. Another agent."

"From Richmond?"

"No, Seattle."

"But he's on that cruise?"

"They sent him up. Tuesday. To help out."

"Help—with what?"

"DeMott, I really can't get into it."

"You're *working*?" He sounded incredulous.

I dropped my head.

"Raleigh, you said this was a vacation. You *needed* time away. You didn't say anything about working."

"It is a vacation."

"But you're working?"

I held my tongue.

"Is this why you're not returning my calls? Because of this Jack person?"

"No, DeMott, listen. I haven't had a chance to call you because something happened—"

"I'm sure it did."

I opened my mouth, but instead of speaking, I drew a long slow breath. *Slow down, back up.* In the silence I could hear the blood beating in my ears like a war drum. Staring at the mountains and the ocean, I tried to put everything else aside. My mother. Work. Jack. This was DeMott on the phone. De-Mott. My fiancé. "I'm sorry I haven't called you back. Really, I'm sorry."

He was silent.

"I'm standing on the ship's top deck and I'm looking at icebergs. Real icebergs. They're the size of your truck. It's unbelievable. You would love it."

"Maybe we can go back," he said, sounding somewhat mollified. "We can go there for our honeymoon. Pick the date and I'll book the tickets."

I closed my eyes. Wedding, honeymoon. Plans, plans. De-Mott always needed plans, and a heavy and familiar weight fell on my shoulders. When I opened my eyes, the glaciated landscape seemed merciless.

"Raleigh, do you miss me?"

"Of course."

"Do you, really?"

The ship was moving forward even more slowly now. When the hull bumped an iceberg, the sound was as soft as a distant car door closing. I watched the block of ice rolling through the water, tumbling away from us, then bobbing up and down. Each time the iceberg rose, it exposed some of the enormous blue underbelly hidden by the water. That's what made icebergs so dangerous; the greater mass was hidden beneath the surface. What we could see was a mere fraction of the thing's true size, and as I held the phone, trying to think of something to say, I realized how much my relationship resembled these blocks of pale blue ice.

"DeMott," I said, "we need to talk."

"About what?"

The line beeped. Call waiting.

"Raleigh, what do we need to talk about?"

It beeped again.

"I'll have to call you back."

"You can't do this—all this silence is killing me."

"I have to go, DeMott. I'll call you this afternoon, promise, bye." I switched lines. "Raleigh Harmon."

"This is the medical examiner's office."

I introduced myself in more detail and explained that I was checking on a body shipped from Ketchikan. She told me to wait, putting me on hold again. When I turned around, Jack was walking toward me, the sun at his back so I couldn't read the expression in his eyes.

The woman came back on the line. "Yes, we received a deceased female from Ketchikan. But we haven't processed."

I explained our circumstances, how the cruise ended on Sunday, and how difficult it would be to pursue the case when every potential witness departed to other parts of the country. "Please, if we could just get cause of death, that would be a huge help."

"I'm very sorry to tell you," she said, "but a tourist drove their RV into Cook Inlet last night. Six more vehicles were involved, and State Patrol needs immediate autopsies to find out if any of the drivers were under the influence. I'll put your request right behind that one. And I have your number."

"Thank you. If anything changes, we'd appreciate a bump up the list."

"I understand."

As I closed my phone, Jack opened his. Still holding the coffee, he tapped out the numbers with one finger.

"Yeah, it's me," he said, moments later. "Your ME's just got a body and we're waiting on the autopsy. Can you press them?" He waited. "I'm doing great. You?"

He listened. Then said, "Terrific," without conviction. "So this deceased was shipped from Ketchikan and I need cause of death, ASAP." He looked at me, lowering the phone from his mouth. "Anything else?"

"Toxicology," I said, thinking of Ramazan's unmarked vials. "Any signs of sexual assault." If Jack had a way to get this done, we might as well ask for the whole enchilada. I sipped my coffee, listening as he gave our requests, then spoke more empty small talk. "Good. That's great."

When he closed the phone, the muscles in his jaw were knotting and unknotting.

"Who was that?" I asked.

"My ex-wife."

I almost choked on my coffee.

"She works in pathology at Providence Hospital in Anchorage. She knows everybody in the morgue." He lifted his coffee, draining the cup.

I was still staring at him.

He added, "She likes to tell me how great her life is now. And she'll help us out so she can call back and tell me more good news about herself."

I nodded, still unable to say anything.

"And yeah, that's how I know Kevin Barnes," he continued, unbidden. "We spent two years together in the Anchorage field office."

"I thought you guys were at Quantico."

"We were in the same class at Quantico. His version of being nice was not bringing up my hell years in Anchorage.

But he made sure to drop the ex-wife bomb." He shrugged. "I said, *I do* and one year later she said, *I don't*."

Flight time to Ketchikan from Seattle. The location of the FBI office in Juneau. The tram. The hidden trail up Mount Roberts. That's how he knew those things.

"She was my high school sweetheart," he said.

"Jack, you don't have to explain."

"I thought marrying somebody who knew me that well would mean they would understand what this job means to me."

"Jack, really, you don't—"

"But she hated it. She hated everything about the FBI. She complained that I worked all the time. She got the idea that I cared more about my work than our marriage. And finally, she walked out."

I glanced away. I looked at the mountains, the water, the blue glowing icebergs. Anywhere. I looked anywhere but his eyes. Under my feet, I could feel the bow thrusters rumbling. The ship was pivoting, turning in slow motion so that the severe mountains moved to the other side. The crowds came streaming over the deck, trampling across the shuffleboard court, and flowing around us as we stood like two rocks in a river.

"If you marry that guy, Raleigh, make sure he knows. Make sure he understands what this work means to you."

The ship made its final pivot and Sawyer Glacier swarmed into view.

Nothing could prepare me for such monstrous beauty.

The mile-wide tongue of blue-and-white ice stretched five miles back, reaching up to a mountain peak that pointed straight to God. I heard Jack gasp, then gasp again as the front of the glacier snapped and a falling block of ice the size of an office building plunged straight down into the water, spraying a fountain of water. In the bright sun, the ocean water glistened like jewels.

And the block of ice bobbed, already hiding how much lay beneath the surface.

"I will never forget that," Jack said.

I looked over. His eyes matched the green-blue water below, and as I stared into them, the landscape seemed to fade away. I could hear the blood again, rushing in my ears.

"And I'll never forget that I saw it with you," he said.

TWENTY

I swallowed, trying to breathe. The wind was gusting in bursts of iced air and the people who crowded the deck rail looked like a wall of parkas. I stared at them because I still couldn't look at Jack.

"I need to find my family." I tried to sound calm.

Jack cleared his throat. "Yeah, and I should find Milo." He waited. "Check back in, what, an hour?"

I nodded, eyes still averted, and began walking farther back toward the aft. The ship was retracing its path down Tracy Arm, and as I walked in the opposite direction, the mountain walls appeared to stand still, as if I were treading ground. I walked faster, then broke into a run, trying to shatter that feeling of being stuck.

When I ran inside the Salt Spray restaurant, I was ahead of the crowd and took a table by the window, waiting for my mom and Aunt Charlotte with a heart that refused to quit pounding.

And it wasn't pounding from the run, that much I realized.

Minutes later they arrived—with Claire. There was no getting away from her, I realized. My mom's dark curls looked flumed from the wind.

"Where are you sitting?" she asked, staring at the three chairs.

"I have to run an errand. Go ahead and start without me."

I was holding the chair that had the best view, holding it for my mom, but Claire plopped into it.

"Hey, get a load of that view," she said. "I can do some serious channeling here."

I clenched my teeth, resisting the temptation to tip the chair over.

"You're not eating breakfast?" my mother asked. Though her cheeks were pinked by the wind, she looked drained. Almost haggard.

"I'll be right back," I said. "Eat a good breakfast and save me something good."

Claire nodded. "You've got to go hunt down whoever killed—"

"Claire!" Aunt Charlotte glared at her.

My mother was glancing among us. Her expression was like somebody receiving two different sets of directions and uncertain which to follow. My aunt suddenly softened her voice.

"Claire, I think they're making those omelets again."

"Hot diggity." Claire pushed back the chair and shot toward the buffet line.

While my mother watched her go, I mouthed a silent thank-you to my aunt, who nodded back. I held another chair out, waiting for my mom to sit. Her eyes had an almost dull expression, something remote, unreachable, and I realized another glacier was at work. This one was inside her mind, the ice smothering reality and crushing the truth, pulverizing joy and spewing forth a silt that churned in her hazel eyes. My father had once warned me of these moments. "She might not get better, Raleigh. She might get worse."

"Then what?" I had asked.

"Then we'll get better at loving her."

But now "we" didn't exist. My dad was gone. And my sister was no help. It was just me, and I was inadequate. So very inadequate. As she took her seat, she turned away from the view, gazing down at the table. I leaned over her dark hair, kissing her cheek, feeling her skin cooled by the wind. But I sensed something else. Something colder, more distant, so far away she couldn't feel my touch.

And as I uttered my next lie, I felt nauseated. "I'll be right back."

I crossed the restaurant, walking out the door and across the deck. The heated swimming pool steamed like a lake of fire. Running down to the stairs, palms sweating, I wondered if my lies contributed to her terror. No, it must be something else. Like Claire. Claire was a bigger problem than I was. Because I lied to protect her.

Didn't I?

Without a clear answer, I opened the door leading up to the Sky Bar. On this morning, it looked different. Rather than an overexposed Dalí nightmare, the space-age room was dimmed and the Plexiglas furniture seemed muted and dated. But as I came into the room, the bartender hit a switch on the wall. Suddenly the panels covering the windows and skylights slid back. Once more the place was flooded with sunlight so bright my eyes stung.

"I prefer it dark," I said.

He hit the switch again, covering up even the clear floor panels. I took a seat at the bar. Like every bartender on this ship, this guy looked Filipino. But his name tag said "Jessie, United States."

He said, "I've got a special on Mimosas this morning."

"Mimosa it is, hold the champagne."

He scooped ice cubes into a stainless steel shaker, then poured in orange juice. Watching the frothy drink fill an iced glass, I felt my salivary glands go into overdrive.

I picked up the pen on the bar, ready to sign the tab.

"It's on me," he said.

"Now that's what I call a special."

He smiled. "You're my first customer in three hours. You're helping keep me awake."

I sipped and licked the foam off my lip, gazing around the bar. The tables were wiped clean. So was the plastic flooring, including a parquet dance floor at the back of the room. There was no dust, anywhere. Milo was lying.

But to make sure, I asked, "By any chance was there some construction in here recently?"

"Yes," he said.

I spun around. "Really?"

"Yes. I think so."

"You think so?"

"Yes."

"But you don't know?"

"Yes."

I frowned, wondering what game we were playing.

"Oh, wait." He shook his head, as though clearing his mind. "I just realized what I did." He sighed. "Sorry, it's a habit I picked up on the ship."

"Playing games with people?"

"I'm sorry," he said again. "I don't know if you've noticed but all the bartenders are Filipino."

"I have noticed that. But your tag says United States."

He drew himself up. "My grandparents came over from Manila during the Marcos fiasco. I'm a proud Filipino American. But you should know that if you ask any Filipino on this ship a question, the answer is always yes."

"Always."

"Yes."

"Like that?"

"Yes. Only the 'yes' means three different things."

"I'm intrigued."

"The first type of 'yes,' means 'I agree.' Simple, right?"

I nodded.

"The second type is, 'Yes, I have no idea what you're talking about, but I'm going to agree in order to avoid conflict.' And that's what I just did with you. Sorry."

"It's okay," I told him. "I'm from the South. We have a 'yes' like that too."

"I'm glad you understand. But the third type of 'yes' gets complicated. 'Yes, I hear you, and I completely understand, but I have no intention whatsoever of complying with your request, even though I'm telling you yes.'"

"That's impressive." I sipped the orange juice. "So whatever I ask you, you're going to say yes?"

"No. I'm an American. What's your question?"

"About the construction in here."

He nodded. "Between cruises, when the boat docks at a home port, they sometimes work on the ships. For instance, we just got repositioned from Mexico. When we got to Seattle, they did some work at the dock."

"Do they ever work on the ships at sea?"

"No way. That would look bad to the passengers. And it's probably some kind of insurance risk."

I took another sip and tried to phrase my question so that it couldn't be answered yes or no. And I decided on the lawyer's trick, asking a question whose answer I already knew, courtesy of Geert. "Where were you working Monday night?"

"Right here. I've got the graveyard bartending shift. Every night."

"I heard there were some famous movie people in here that night."

He picked up a rag from behind the bar and began wiping down the plastic counter, which was already spotless. "I get it," he said. "It is about insurance. You're looking into some claim."

"Why do you say that?"

"Because that guy's wife died. The actor. Rumor is she committed suicide."

"How did you hear?"

"Everybody's talking about it." He flipped the rag over. "There's not much else to do at sea except gossip."

"The actor, Milo Carpenter, says he was in here that night."

He nodded. "He was. And he was already wasted when I came on my shift at 2:00 AM. He left at one point, then came back and ordered another Johnny Walker. Then left again."

"What time was that?"

"I'm not sure, because I try not to watch the clock. It makes the hours seem slower. But I can tell you some other stuff."

"Such as?"

"He drinks Johnny Walker Black with three cherries and ties the stems into knots with his tongue. He leaves the stems on cocktail napkins to impress women."

Knots, I thought, finishing my orange juice. "Did you see his wife that night?"

"I didn't, but the bartender working the shift before mine told me she watched her husband flirt with other women. He said it was depressing to watch."

"Do you know if she drank?"

"Funny. I asked him the same question. I wondered if she got drunk and killed herself. But he said it was Diet Coke all night. You know, we get movie types pretty often. They take cruises. And I've watched them."

"Tell me."

"They drink but they don't tip. Instead of tipping they smile, real hard, like seeing their caps is better for you than if they reached into their pockets. They pose at the bar, they hate to dance, and they laugh like they're practicing how to get a joke."

I couldn't help but smile. "There was another guy that

night." I described Vinnie the bodyguard and his forehead. "Did you see him?"

"Yes—I mean really, *yes*. But he left with some girl. Looked like a hook up, you know, one-night stand. He came back later, had a couple drinks and talked to Carpenter. It seemed like he was telling him to quit making a fool of himself."

"Why?"

"Because Carpenter got belligerent, the way most alcoholics do when you tell them to stop drinking. Carpenter stormed out, then, like I said, he came back for another drink. It might have been around three. Early part of my shift. I get off at ten. When I came off my shift, that's when I heard that somebody killed themselves. Later people said it was Milo Carpenter's wife. It seemed sad."

I reached into my credentials case and slid my business card across the bar. "Hang on to this, okay? If you see anything else that doesn't look right, call me."

"FBI, really?" He stared at the card. "For real, you're an agent?"

"Yes," I said. "Yes, for real."

Back at the Salt Spray restaurant, Claire was sipping a cappuccino and staring vapidly out the window. Aunt Charlotte was writing notes in a small book.

"Where's Mom?" I asked.

My aunt looked up and removed her reading glasses— bright pink frames with white polka dots. "Here's yet another reason why I ditched the Episcopals," she said. "Your mother said she wanted to go pray and I said, 'Nadine, look out the window. We're in the world's most spectacular cathedral. Stay here.' But no, she said she had to have a cross."

Claire closed her eyes, making a weird humming sound, like an electrical transformer.

Exasperated, I turned to my aunt. "Do you know if she ate breakfast?"

"I wasn't paying attention, I was working on my notes for the actors." Reaching across the table, she tapped Claire's arm. "Did Nadine eat anything?"

Claire opened her eyes. "Your mother is haunted by death."

"Brilliant," I said. "Of course she's haunted by death— she's a widow."

"No, it's something more," Claire said. "I tried contacting your father's spirit last night and when I told Nadine she—"

"You did *what*?"

"Raleigh, we are not connecting. It's like we're not on the same wavelength."

"We're not."

"All I wanted to do was ask your dad why she's so scared."

I turned to my aunt, prepared to unleash my fury, when several accusations turned themselves on me. Whose fault was this, really? Who left her alone with these two nuts?

And who was living a lie?

"Aunt Charlotte, do you know where she went?"

"I should have been listening."

Claire piped up. "She went to find the chapel. I told her that stuff's just superstition but—"

I was gone before she could finish the sentence.

TWENTY-ONE

The chapel was on Deck Five, a narrow room with cottony silence, sealed by a heavy wooden door.

I was panting from my sprint down nine flights and stood at the back of the room trying to catch my breath. Rows of white chairs faced a one-foot platform that was flanked by urns containing white lilies and sprays of baby's breath. The room seemed to be waiting for a wedding but there was only person in here: my mother.

She sat in the front row, with her face buried in her hands.

I walked down the middle aisle and sat beside her. She didn't seem to notice my presence. For several moments, I listened to the words she murmured into her hands. I could feel my pulse throbbing against my temples.

"That's not true," she was saying. "Stop it—*stop it.*"

I stared at the front wall where a stained glass medallion hung in place of a cross. In place of any religious symbol. The swirling blue colors seemed to follow her words, turning and twisting and tumbling like water.

"Lies, all lies. It's all lies—"

In the corner of the room a small organ waited to play a wedding march. For people who celebrated. I thought of De-Mott, and our wedding, and felt a second wave of despair.

"Please, stop saying—"

The FBI taught me many ways to stay alive. I knew how to shoot a gun and dodge incoming bullets and think like my enemy. But they also taught me something so simple it seemed laughable at the time: how to breathe. How to breathe when every instinct insisted it was time to curl up and die.

Taking a deep breath, I counted to four on the inhale. The air smelled of chemicals. Something acrylic. Epoxy or glue.

"And it can't be true," she continued. "No, she wouldn't—"

I tried another four-count breath, but the chemical odor was so strong I tasted it at the back of my throat. I stared down at my hands, automatically clasped in prayer, and saw my engagement ring sparkling with its yellow and green rays. I looked away to the Berber carpet. It was the inoffensive color of oatmeal, but a section was torn on the podium and I fixed my eyes on the spot, using it for a focal point as I tried to bring my pulse down, resisting the urge inside that demanded, *Run.*

She began speaking in tongues. "Shama-la-may, shaaaaama—"

I squeezed my hands until the bones hurt and stared at the carpet's torn nylon threads. Glued down. The epoxy was shiny and opaque like polished brown jasper, fine grains dusting the surface. When her voice rose, it sounded so desperate, my eyes climbed with it. She begged the voices to *stop stop stop* and I turned to see her fingers wound into her black curls, pulling on her hair. "Amma-shaaaama!"

I reached over, wanting to hold her, then stopped. What if I startled her?

No, worse.

Dear God. What if she's afraid of me?

Blinking against the burn in my eyes, I found another focal point, a hole in the wall. No bigger than half an inch, it held white particles that gathered along the bottom curve. I stared at them, willing her to calm down until I could see nothing but the wall, the hole, the dust inside. Wall, hole, dust.

She rocked forward, crying.

Dust.

Gray dust.

I stood, my hands feeling too warm, and walked toward the platform. At the wall, I laid my cheek against the Sheetrock. It felt cool on my skin. The dust clung to the hole's bottom curve. On the other side of the medallion a piece of stubbed metal protruded, a small bent hook that drooped toward the floor. Licking my finger, I tapped the hole, then rubbed my thumb over the grains. Drywall dust. Fine-grained gypsum.

"No no no—shamma-la-ma!" She continued to rock back and forth, nearly catatonic.

Standing at the edge of the platform, I could see how the hole was aligned with the protruding metal. Something once hung there. I kneeled on the carpet, inspecting the torn fibers. Tiny brown objects were stuck in the Berber loops and I pinched one, pulling against the snagged fibers. I held it up to the ceiling lights. The jagged edges looked like a comic rendering of lightning.

I stood on the platform, watching her. I whispered, afraid of startling her. "Mom?"

No response.

I walked to the chapel door, unable to feel my feet touching the ground. A small table by the door held a stack of Bibles, like a black stalagmite. I shimmied one from the bottom and opened its cover. The spine crackled with disuse. Turning the soft pages, I worked toward the book of Micah and placed the brown fragment at chapter six, verse eight, pushing it deep into the binding to keep it from falling out. Putting it where I wouldn't forget: alongside my father's creed to act justly, love mercy, and walk humbly.

As I walked down the aisle again, I wondered if she was speaking in tongues, or some twisted language from the dark territory that had taken her captive. Standing beside the wall,

I listened and brushed drywall dust into the Bible passage that reminded me that I was dust, and to dust I would return.

Closing it carefully, tucking it under my left arm, I could feel my pulse tapping against the Bible.

She was standing.

Her eyes were no longer dull. Polished bright, they didn't seem to see me. She lifted her hands and opened her fingers and I felt something chilling on my spine.

Her hand moved toward her face.

"No—Mom—no!"

With her nails, she clawed her cheeks. The scratches went white before blood rose like crimson ribbons. I ran toward her and she backed away, unblinking and scared.

We stared at one another, suspended in time.

Breathe. Breathe.

Looking into my eyes, she drew her nails down her face once more. I reached down for my belt, fumbling for the phone, hitting Redial.

"It's me," I said.

"What now?" Geert asked.

She was pulling her hands away, marveling at the glistening red on her nails.

"Help," I said.

Geert burst through the chapel door followed by a red-faced man wearing the white officers' uniform. He was followed by Nurse Stephanie who pushed a collapsible gurney, just like the one that carried Judy Carpenter's body off the ship.

I held my mother from behind, her arms pinned to her sides. She was writhing and I pressed my mouth to her ear, smelling shampoo and fear, and whispering words. Words about love. My love. My dad's love. God's love.

The man in the officer uniform approached us like a bomb technician, listening for the ticking sound.

"Mrs. Harmon, I'm Dr. Coleman," he said. "I'm here to help you, dear."

His voice was accented—Irish, English—and she screamed.

He turned to Nurse Stephanie, snapping his fingers. She unzipped a flat black case and extracted a hypodermic needle, using it to puncture a small glass vial. She filled the needle's plunger. I squeezed tighter, wondering that I had never held someone so close yet felt so far away.

Holding the syringe, the doctor walked closer, speaking softly and evenly, and I decided his accent was Irish. The brogue's cadence swung when he was within striking distance, telling me to hold her still, don't let her move, that's it. I buried my face in her hair, unable to watch, and felt her body stiffen. Within seconds, it went limp.

"There's a good girl," the doctor was saying. "Now you can have a rest."

She was no longer fighting. There was no resistance and I released my hold.

She spun, hand open, and slapped me before I could catch her arm.

Her black hair clung to the blood on her cheeks. When I looked into her eyes, they were no longer bright. Distant again. And now filled with hate.

My voice cracked. "They're here to help."

She swayed now, the drug taking over, and as her knees gave, the doctor caught her and lifted her to the gurney. He spoke to her in the Irish brogue.

"There's a nice girl," he said. "There's a nice, nice girl."

TWENTY-TWO

Danger to self. Danger to others.

A black line at the bottom of the document waited for my signature.

Grievously disabled. Requiring observation...

I held the pen and listened to the doctor explain the laws that insisted it was fine to lock up my mother. When the doctor paused, drawing a hand over his thinning white hair, I turned to look at her room, directly across from the circular desk where I stood holding the paperwork.

She was no longer crying out. No longer screaming.

She was silent.

I signed, giving permission for forty-eight hours' observation—all the time left on the cruise—then handed the paperwork to the doctor.

She lay on the bed, her high cheekbones raw, the blood still wet. Rubber restraints secured her arms. I couldn't tell if she recognized me. Her eyes were drugged, disoriented.

"I'm sorry." The words seemed to fracture inside my mouth. "I don't want you to hurt yourself."

Rolling her head across the pillow, she turned away, facing the wall. The room had no window. No view. And I heard no murmurs from her lips.

I had silenced even her prayers.

* * *

Two doors down, I stood in the medical clinic's small lab and called Jack, asking him to bring certain pieces of evidence from the purser's safe. Then I flicked on the microscope and sat down.

"Sucks, doesn't it?" Nurse Stephanie stood in the doorway, arms crossed. Her waist seemed impossibly small.

I set the Bible on the counter.

"My mom's crazy too," she said. "Half the reason I live on a cruise ship nine months of every year is so I don't have to see her. The other three months I stay busy avoiding her."

I looked over at her. "I need the same supplies as last time. Petri dishes, uncoated aspirin, distilled water."

She stared at me, then unhitched a hip and walked to the cabinets, keying them open and placing the supplies on the stainless steel shelf. When she turned to face me, she pointed two fingers at her eyes, then pointed them at me. "I see you," she said. "I see you *real* clearly."

A shard of irritation bristled up my spine, rising with a force that told me I needed to bat it down, now. Right now.

"Thank you for your help," I said.

She puckered her lips and sauntered away. I listened to her crepe soles squeak across the vinyl, then come back with the cup of distilled water and uncoated aspirin. She set them on the counter and left, and I snapped on latex gloves, dropping the white tablets into the water. Over at the desk, Nurse Stephanie was greeting someone.

"Welcome back, Big Guy." She sounded like Marilyn Monroe squeezed into medical whites. "Ready for your shot?"

"Where is she?" Jack asked.

When I looked up, he stood in the doorway holding the evidence bags. "Harmon, the purser told me what happened— is your mom okay?"

"Is that the right evidence?"

He looked down at the bag, as if suddenly remembering it. "Yes, I got the one you said. But what happ—"

"Thanks." I took the bag from him, removing the test tubes and the notes written on the prescription pad concerning the gray dust and the wood chips found on Milo's and MJ's clothing.

"Harmon, is she…?"

I opened the Bible to Micah 6:8 and brushed my gloved fingers into the crease, depositing the brown fragment into the clean petri dish. I did the same with the gray dust from Genesis.

Jack said, "Holy forensics, Batgirl."

I poured some salicylic acid water into the petri dishes, nuked them in the microwave, then scraped the powdered precipitates into thin sections, slipping them under the microscope. Then I compared them with the samples taken from the clothing and all the while, Jack watched from the doorway.

"You're going to have to let me in," he said.

"Okay." I pushed back from the microscope. "I found some dust in the chapel. It contains wood fragments. It looks like a very strong match to the dust found on Milo's clothing and the musician's clothing. That means—"

"Harmon, let me in."

"I'm trying to. The dust contains a specific heavy metal left behind after the acid dissolved all the softer minerals. It might be trace iron but I can't pinpoint the chemistry with this equipment. The bottom line is Milo and MJ were both in the chapel and they both—"

"Stop it."

His eyes were intense, focused. I willed myself to hold their gaze, refusing to look away. I breathed, taking in the bitter scent of the salicylic acid.

"Jack, I'm fine. Really. Can we get back to the evidence?"

At the desk, the phone rang and Nurse Stephanie answered, immediately launching into a lecture. The flu lady, again. The contagious fugitive. "Look, honey, I am not going to help you unless you get your butt in here."

I turned, bending my head over the microscope and fiddling with the focus.

"Oh really? Well, I've got news for you. I can take you by force."

The minerals scattered across the thin section like stars. Like dust. Then they blurred and my eyes stung.

"Because you're a danger to other people and the law says we can. We just did it this morning with another nut so don't think you can—"

I didn't hear the rest. Standing up, I started packing the evidence back into the bags.

"Harmon, talk to me."

I placed a hand over my eyes, shielding them from his view, telling myself that the salt and proteins from my tears could contaminate the evidence. "Jack, I'm fine—"

His arms wrapped around me. I pushed him away. He grabbed hold and I shoved him away again. He tightened his grip and the more I struggled against him, the more I felt like my mother, futilely resisting. I turned my face, his chest was there, and my mouth was buried in it. The sob that rose felt as explosive as magma, a thing held down too long, bursting at the surface. I tasted the cotton of his white shirt, smelled the clean warm scent of a man, and another sob came. I felt his hand against my back, pressing, staunching the wound inside.

"Oh, *that's* what's going on."

I turned my face to the door. Nurse Stephanie wore a knowing expression.

"Great move, honey. The tears work every time." She gave a smirk, then walked away.

Jack looked down into my eyes. "I'm holding out hope."

"Pardon?"

"I'm hoping we'll find out *she* killed Judy Carpenter."

TWENTY-THREE

The elegant Bahamian purser waited by the hospitality desk, extending his hand as I approached.

"Miss Harmon, I am so very sorry to hear about your mother. If there is anything I can do to better a bad situation, please don't hesitate to ask."

I nodded, still not able to say anything without risking tears. Jack had gone back to consulting on the movie—and watching Milo—but I followed the purser to his office behind the hospitality desk, waiting as he opened the enormous safe with the strange key, placing the evidence inside.

"May I ask how you heard about my mom?"

He locked the safe again, then offered one of the balletic bows. "Miss Harmon, cruise ships are floating cities populated with interlopers. Please forgive me for being among the busybodies, I was simply concerned."

"Forgiven," I said. "But it's safe to assume you heard about Ramazan and Serif too?"

"The pornographers," he said with distaste.

"You asked how you could better the situation. I'd like to see their work schedules, beginning with the time we left Seattle until today."

He leaned back, the dark eyes evaluating me. "And you've cleared this request with Officer van Broeck?"

Geert. "No, sir, I have not."

"I am pleased to hear you tell me the truth. I will take your request under advisement, and I will be in touch. Until then, do try to enjoy the remainder of your day."

MJ was pounding the piano keys in a lounge that resembled an English gentlemen's club. Dark walnut paneling, deep green wingback chairs, two billiard tables—and a black grand piano where the musician's hands leaped like mad cats. Unlike the music last night, she played something that sounded almost cacophonous.

I'd found her through one phone call to Geert. At any given moment, his Ninjas seemed to know where everybody was on the ship, even somebody hiding in this lounge that was closed until later in the afternoon. The piano was tucked behind a billiard table and MJ's back was to the entrance. The place was empty, not even a Filipino bartender to say yes to every question, and I waited, listening to the assaultive chords. Finally, when she stepped on the foot pedal, extending the bitterness, I walked up behind her. Cheap tricks were not my way, but time was running out. And I needed her to talk.

"That's bleak music," I said.

"Oh!" Her hands flew off the keys. The chord dropped dead. "You scared me!"

"I'm sorry." I meant it. Manipulating her made me feel like the liar my mother knew me to be. "May I talk to you for a moment?"

She had already pulled out the fall board, dropping the cover over the keys, letting it land with a felt-cushioned *thud*. "I need to go," she said. "We're filming this morning. I'm already late."

She reached for the sheet music and I touched her wrist. She recoiled as if scalded.

"You were in the chapel?" I asked.

Her eyes were darting. "What?"

"Milo was there too. And I doubt he went in there to pray." I hated this part, poking her again. "Did you meet in there before or after Judy's hanging?"

"No—!"

"So she wasn't dead yet?"

"You don't know what you're talking about."

"MJ, I have proof."

Her face fissured like an cracking eggshell, the lines of worry spreading down her face from those sad eyes, that soft mouth trembling. "He took pictures."

When I didn't respond, her hands dropped into her lap, the palms open, a gesture of devastated supplication. Under the lamp for the sheet music I could see her fingers, the tips enflamed while slivers ran like dashes down both palms.

"What happened in that chapel?"

She saw me staring at her hands and tucked them under her arms. "You saw the photos. What more do you want?"

"MJ, there are no photos."

"Then how—" She stopped. "Then you're making it up."

"No, I have proof. But not from photographs. I also know about your dope conviction."

The sheet music rested disheveled on the thin shelf above the fall board. Her eyes were scanning the lines, searching.

"Cooperation is your best option. I'm sure you learned that when you got busted."

"I never meant to hurt Judy."

I waited. She turned, her eyes now scanning my face.

"It started years ago, when I was dealing pot. I was a mess. And Milo, I believed him."

"About what?"

"He told me they had an agreement." She picked at the slivers in her left hand. "And I saw myself as damaged goods.

And here was this movie star, paying attention to me. Me, screwed up MJ."

The clock was still ticking in my head. "What does this have to do with the chapel?"

She looked up again. "If I tell you the truth, will you believe me?"

"The truth? Yes."

"I got saved."

It took me a moment and she misread my silence.

"Yeah, I know, jailhouse conversion. Go ahead, make fun of it. But I didn't do it to get out early. I did it because now I was a different me. I was a better me." She stopped picking her hands and her voice went up an octave. "And who was my biggest champion? Judy. She helped me get back on my feet. She got me to play music again."

"Did she know about you and Milo?"

She shook her head. "But I knew."

"Did she know about any of the affairs, before the tabloids broke the news?"

"I could never tell. She was crazy-blind in love with Milo, and everyone in Hollywood puts on a front. Even the nice people. But if she knew, she didn't care. And she didn't try to stop him."

"And you two took a roll in the chapel—for old times' sake?"

"No!" She came off the bench. "That is *not* what happened."

"Then tell me. The truth."

"I was playing a set in the bar—"

"What night?"

"Monday."

"The night she died."

She picked at her hand again. "I was playing in the Sky Bar. I was so tired. Really tired. I had twenty minutes of after the first set. In the old days I would've fired up a joint but I went down to the chapel. I can't explain it, there was this heaviness in my heart, like that feeling of being home-sick." She sighed. "I know now it's like grief. Nobody was in the chapel, and I just wanted to pray so I got down on my knees in front of the cross and—"

"What cross?"

She blinked.

"MJ, what cross? There's no cross in there."

Her lips trembled and as the words came I realized this confession was for two audiences. One was spoken, for me, but the other came softly, a hushed entreaty with that same sweet and devastated voice I'd heard last night—*forgive me*, she was saying—then describing the empty chapel at that late hour and how she didn't think anybody would come in—*mercy, have mercy*—and how she had knelt at the foot of a large wooden cross that hung on the wall above the platform, feeling a desperation so dark that she laid her hands on the wooden beam.

"I don't know how long I was praying. Maybe a long time. But suddenly I felt someone behind me, pulling me by my hair. I grabbed the cross, holding on and—" She lifted both hands, displaying the palms lined with slivers. Her voice was shaking. "He pulled, and I didn't want to let go of the cross. There was this horrible sound, and it must have scared him because he let go of my hair and when I turned around—*oh, God*—it was Milo."

"Alone?"

She nodded. "The cross came crashing down, just missing us. I started crying and he put his hand over my mouth. He was snarling, like an animal, telling me I'd teased him long enough."

My question cloaked the air, not needing to be spoken between two women.

She shook her head. "He was too drunk and finally he left. There I was, sprawled out with that fallen cross." She began whispering again.

"What happened after that?"

"I had to go play."

"In the bar?"

"That's part of my contract, playing at any parties. I need the money. But Sandy chewed me out for taking such a long break—like I was goofing around. Then he gave me the sniff test."

"The what?"

"Smelling me, to see if I fell off the wagon."

"You didn't tell him about Milo?"

"C'mon. Which of us would he kick off the movie? Not Milo." She opened her hands, displaying the damage. "This looks good now, but I played two sets with my hands on fire. And the next morning, when I heard Judy was dead, I decided this was the cruise from hell." She looked at me, hard. "I mean that, as a place."

I nodded. I knew what she meant.

And I wasn't about to disagree.

TWENTY-FOUR

Vinnie the bodyguard stood outside the Tiki Bar on Deck Seven, looking like something that had rolled off Easter Island.

A crowd had gathered outside the bar, primarily Asian tourists, and they held digital cameras above their heads, hoping to catch a picture of an American movie star. At six five, Vinnie towered over them. And me.

"You," Vinnie growled.

"Me." I smiled.

"Jack said to let you in." He stepped aside, reluctantly.

As I passed through the palm-treed entrance, I heard murmurs of envy coming from the crowd. I'd been granted special favor, as though the rules that applied to everyone else didn't pertain to me. Heading toward the bright lights of the movie set, the place populated by beautiful people, I could see how septic pride might seep in before it was even detectable. And I recalled Sparks's description of Milo's debauched behavior—*Guy started believing his press*. But believing propaganda wasn't the real problem. That was a symptom. Pride was the problem. Because pride created monsters.

The monster named Milo Carpenter sat in a black canvas chair sipping from a paper cup that I doubted contained water. Behind him was Jack, and to their left was a grass-skirted bar where Larrah-rhymes-with-Harrah was getting her face powdered. She pulled her lips over her teeth like somebody missing dentures and wore a teeny-tiny tank top that displayed her pneumatic chest and thin muscular arms. Beyond her, two tables had been pushed together to make the empty bar look crowded. Some scruffy-looking extras sat at the tables, playing cards. In the back corner, MJ sat at an upright piano, picking at her hands.

The director, Martin Webb, conferred with Sandy Sparks next to one of the film cameras. Since Jack and I couldn't come up with anything further on Webb, we weren't able to pursue him, at this point. He'd flushed some drugs, paid for damages to the wildlife center, and Geert was done. I watched the director pouting as he listened to Sparks and recalled our background check. Webb was nearly broke. So where did he get the money for damages?

Jack walked over to me. I stood on the edge of the set and in a low voice told him MJ's version of what happened. When I described the attack, muscles began knotting in his jaw. At the end, he walked over to Milo, still sipping from the paper cup. I followed.

"Let's go have a talk," Jack told him. "Somewhere private."

"I can't," Milo said.

"Why not?"

"My kicks, man. I can't walk anywhere. I got blisters all over my feet. Like walking on knives."

I was hoping Jack would just grab him and drag him out of the Tiki Bar.

Instead, he said, "What size do you wear?"

Milo looked down at Jack's feet. "Eleven."

"Mine are twelve. You want to try them on?"

"Hey, man, that's cool." Milo nodded. "Real FBI agent shoes. Yeah, I can get inside my character." He set the paper cup down on a copy of the script for *Northern Decompo-*

sure. Maybe this script had the new spiffy ending, where the wife dies.

Milo yanked off his right shoe. Alcohol had slowed his movements, and his toenails peeked through threadbare socks. "Someday you'll tell your kids Milo Carpenter wore your shoes."

"A real honor." Jack handed Milo his brown Clarks.

He managed to tie the shoes by himself and was standing to test the shoes when the woman primping Larrah rushed over. Her graying hair escaped from a topknot, looking like wisps of smoke. She was breathless.

"You can't wear those," she said. "They're *brown*."

"The black ones gave me blisters." Milo slurred the last word. "I've got, like, twenty pivots in this scene—and a roundhouse—and then I have to walk over and tell those dirtbags at the table what I think of them." He pointed at Jack. "And he *gave* me these shoes."

Her eyes looked tired. She stared at Jack's socks. Then his face. "Who are you?"

"He's my consultant," Milo answered. "A real FBI agent, Jack Stephens—"

"Stephanson."

"—meet Mary quite the contrary. Mary's our head of wardrobe."

"Don't remind me." Her mouth was grim. "Wardrobe, makeup, set design." She pointed at Milo's feet. Jack's russet brown Clarks were creased across the toes from heavy wear. "Are they real?"

Jack looked confused. "They seem real to me."

"What I'm asking," she said peevishly, "are these shoes what an FBI agent actually wears?"

"Hey, Mary." Milo hung on the *M* too long. "If Judy knew I had to work in those cheap shoes, she'd be taking names right now. Don't talk to me about the budget."

At the mention of Judy, she placed a hand on Milo's shoulder, the back of it covered by swaths of eye shadow and lipstick. She gave Milo a maternal squeeze, then turned to Jack with the hard look from before. "I can't pay you for those things. We don't have money in the budget."

"Mary," Milo said, "he wants to be part of movie history. The shoes are a *gift*."

I glanced at Jack. The shoes would be better if we used them for hitting Milo over the head. But Jack said nothing and pulled on the black shoes.

Mary said, "Martin throws one of his fits about continuity, I'm not taking the blame."

"We'll do retakes."

"On this budget? Think again." She hurried back to the bar and picked up her makeup kit, rushing over to the tables where the extras played cards.

Milo stared down at the brown shoes. "I'm walking in my character's heart and soul. I can feel his pain."

"Me too." Jack winced. "These shoes don't fit. I need mine back."

"You can't—I've got a fight scene."

"I've got a life." Jack yanked one of the black shoes off, holding it out to Milo.

But before Milo could reply, Martin Webb raised a compact megaphone. "We roll in one minute."

"I can't wear those again." Milo bent down to the floor, grabbing a leather satchel. He made two passes through the contents before coming up with a keycard. "There's a pair of brand-new sneakers, top-of-the-line, in my closet. They're too big for me."

Jack hesitated.

"C'mon, man, they're yours, no charge. I'll even autograph 'em."

Webb lifted the megaphone. "Let's move, people!"

With a sigh, Jack took the keycard.

Milo gave a soft bounce on his toes and lifted the paper cup, downing the amber liquid. He continued to stare up into the Tiki Bar's rafters, and when I followed his gaze, I saw fake parrots roosting over the tables. "Judy, baby," he said. "Check it out. It's just like the fat suit. Now I got this character nailed."

"Let's go!" Webb yelled.

Milo grabbed Jack's arm. "And grab me some thick socks, will ya? I got a little too much room in the toes."

He strode for the grass-skirted bar and waited while Mary buffed his face with a powder puff. Behind him Larrah Sparks closed her eyes and clutched a stone in one hand—undoubtedly something from my aunt—chanting some kind of incantation for idiots.

Quietly, Jack and I turned to leave. He walked like an old man with bunions.

"That bad?" I asked.

"Unbelievable." He smiled, slipping the keycard in his back pocket.

"That was pretty smart."

"All in a day's work, Harmon. All in a day's work."

TWENTY-FIVE

Milo Carpenter's cabin smelled of scotch and a sour stench that made me wave my hand in front of my nose. I followed Jack into the living room, and neither of us said a word.

We both knew what was about to happen.

Jack stood at the desk, running his eyes over a laptop that had been turned off, while I walked into the bedroom.

The king-size bed was made, undoubtedly by a steward, and the white pillowcases looked clean as frost. The closet's door was open and Judy Carpenter's clothes hung, the draping silks and satins waiting for her return. She favored the same sort of tunics as my aunt, paired with palazzo pants. Her sandals were high glittery things in gold and silver and brought to mind the image of her bare feet, how the dying skin had matched her blue nail polish.

In the other room, I heard a closet door sliding open, and it brought another unexpected wave of admiration for Jack. He had played Milo like a Stradivarius. There was a legal term, called "the expectation of privacy," and it was no small thing. In multiple cases, the courts had upheld the idea that if a person didn't expect privacy, he couldn't sue over the loss of it later. If a cop pulls over a driver and asks for permission to search the trunk, the driver who says yes loses any expectation of privacy. The same held true for people who left their curtains open on windows that faced public roads. When Milo gave Jack his room key, asking an FBI agent to get his shoes and socks, he also surrendered an expectation of privacy.

On the small bureau by the closet, two clean drinking glasses waited on paper doilies. Next to that was yet another copy of the script, the title page covered with notes. A woman's handwriting, curls and flourishes. I read the words. Movie talk, about scenes, where people should stand.

"Grab the socks," Jack called from the living room.

I opened the top drawer and found underwear. Women's. Expensive, lacy. And sad, given what we knew about their marriage. Searching for the socks, I pushed the lingerie aside and saw a wooden box. Rectangular, about six-by-eight inches. I stared at it, convincing myself that it wasn't inconceivable a drunk would keep socks in a box.

I lifted the lid.

The jewelry was mostly heavy, ornate necklaces, the type that anchored blousy tunics and wide satiny pants. Sets of matching earrings were equally elaborate. But the only blue piece was a turquoise combination of hammered silver, done in a southwestern style. The rest were reddish stones—pink quartz, some garnets, even a necklace with watermelon tourmaline where the pink graduated to green. Nothing like the blue bracelet.

On the inside of the lid, below the small mirror, a brass plate held an inscription.

To Judy, the real gem in my life.

—M.C.

M.C. Milo's initials. And it was dated six weeks back. Was the jewelry box some kind of truce?

Or a parting gift?

I dropped the lid.

And heard an odd *plunk*.

Opening it again, slowly, I could hear something roll. Picking up the box, I tilted it from side to side, then rapped my knuckle across the lid. The hollow sound was almost as loud as the debate inside my head, the one insisting Milo gave the FBI permission to enter his room. Permission to look for socks. And socks, they could be anywhere.

Using the small pocketknife that Geert allowed me to keep, I shimmied the thin blade between the lid's mirror and the wood. Working it carefully so I didn't crack the glass, I caught a glimpse of my face. Strands of brown hair hung over my face. My forehead rippled with worry. But that was nothing compared to the expression in my eyes. Not just tired. Not just worn out. I looked like somebody tired of listening to some story, yet afraid to hear the ending.

The mirror popped off. And a large blue stone tumbled into my palm.

"Bingo," I said.

"What?"

I whirled around.

Jack waited in the doorway, wearing the new tennis shoes. "This is not what I wanted to see."

"Then don't look." I turned my back to him.

The blue stone winked with chameleon charms, its color shifting with the fluidity of warm water. To my naked eye it looked similar to the gemstones in the gold bracelet, only this stone was much larger. Close to ten carats, it had been cut into a cabochon shape to highlight the intense internal fire. I lifted the box and peered into the secret compartment. One corner looked shiny and when I touched it with my knife blade, a black prism rolled out. It was a slender double-terminated crystal—both ends perfectly formed, closing the prism—and it seemed genuinely black. Not darkest purple, not midnight blue. Black.

Earth didn't produce many black crystals. There was onyx and some forms of hematite. Even fewer black crystals occurred naturally as prisms. Black tourmaline came to mind

Or this could be a synthetic stone, cut into form. But none of those stones were worth hiding.

Unless somebody else wanted them, badly.

Pulling several sheets of Kleenex from the dispenser on the bureau, I wrapped the stones and dropped them into my pocket. I replaced the mirror, wiped my fingerprints off the glass, then returned the box to the top drawer, once again covering it with Judy Carpenter's futile lingerie.

When I turned around, Jack was still in the doorway.

"He gave you the key," I said, my cheeks reddening. "There was no expectation of privacy and socks can be kept anywhere."

"Did you get the socks?"

My face was on fire when I turned around, opening the drawers again. "It's not breaking and entering."

"Harmon…"

"Jack, we'll never get a search warrant in time. In two days the killer walks off this ship. I just want to check out these stones, especially since I don't have that bracelet anymore."

"Check out the stones," he repeated carefully. "Then what?"

"Then back in the jewelry box."

"You don't think he's going to miss them?"

"Give me thirty minutes. He won't even know they're gone."

"And if he comes back before thirty minutes?"

"Just don't give back the key until I'm done."

"Oh, is that all?"

"C'mon, Jack. You'll think of something. McLeod always says you have a silver tongue."

"*Sliver.* He says I have a *sliver* tongue. And how did it become my responsibility to cover up for your problem?"

"He didn't give me his shoes." I looked at his feet. The shoes were pale blue, almost glacial, glowing like a really bad wedding tuxedo. No wonder Milo didn't want them. Even a drunk could see they were hideous. "How do they feel?"

"Expensive. I can sell them for food when we get fired."

"*I'll* get fired. You didn't do anything wrong." I hesitated. "Did you?"

"Harmon."

"Please, Jack. Thirty minutes." I reached over, touching my pocket. The stones felt heavier than their actual weight.

"I didn't think you had it in you," he said.

Neither did I.

While Jack tried to figure out how to evade Milo, I raced down the stairs, trying to decide who was lying.

This was Hollywood, after all. Land of make-believe, where lying wasn't just a profession, it was something you won awards for. It was possible that MJ was covering up an affair with Milo, telling an elaborate and twisted story about an attack. By the time I'd reached Deck Six, it was occurring to me that her hands might be raw from rope burns, and from helping Milo lower his wife over the rail. Since I was passing the hospitality desk, I stopped and asked if the ship had a chaplain. They did, indeed, said the nice clerk behind the counter. I was welcome to leave a message and the chaplain would get back to me. I gave my cell phone number, holding back two questions. One, did the chapel have a cross until Monday night? And two, could the chaplain please pay a visit to my mother in the infirmary?

I was turning away when the elevator next to the desk *bing*ed open. The car was empty and I jumped in, hoping to save time bypassing the crowd in the atrium. I hit the button and was taken immediately to my floor.

But when the doors opened, I wasn't on Deck Five, near my cabin.

I was on Deck Four, staring at the medical clinic. The slow doors didn't close for a long moment, leaving me to consider my subconscious error for what it was: I'd pressed the wrong button because these gems weren't the only thing I was feeling guilty about.

There was no nurse at the circular desk. My mother's door was partially open. The doctor sat on a rolling stool beside her bed, his Celtic accent like a lullaby.

"The long journey from Seattle," he said, "it can weary a soul."

From where I stood, I could only see her left hand. Her fingers scrunched the cotton blanket, balling into a fist. "The water is too loud," she said.

"Aye, bothers me too. But right now, what I need is a good listen to your lungs. What do you say?" He held the stethoscope, waiting for permission.

"You won't hurt me?"

"No, dear."

"Do you promise?"

"Like St. Patrick promises to help the poor."

His easy dialogue continued and her fingers released the blanket. The doctor asked her about her family and she mentioned my father; that he was gone. And the sister-in-law who brought her on the cruise.

The doctor waited. "And your daughter?"

Silence.

"You have a daughter?"

"I have a daughter, back in Virginia."

"And a good daughter, she is." He thought she was confused.

She wasn't. My sister Helen was back in Virginia.

Eyes prickling, I turned to leave.

I hadn't heard her approach, but Nurse Stephanie was sitting at the round desk, checking off some paperwork. As I passed by, she did not look up.

TWENTY-SIX

Himalayan flute music tooted through the open door that connected my cabin to Aunt Charlotte's. Sitting on their twin beds, she and Claire faced a purple crystal set on a chair between them like an honored guest. The rock was octahedral—pyramid-shaped at both ends—and lay on its side. Given its dusky color and its shape, I guessed it was fluorite. I wondered what great spiritual properties had been attributed to a mineral used for everything from cavity prevention to rat poison.

Eyes closed, Claire was emitting that monotonous hum of electricity. Her stout legs bent under her body like soft pretzels. But Aunt Charlotte struggled to hold the pose. Perspiration dewed her forehead and she puffed like a woman in labor. I was tempted to interrupt and tell her what happened in the chapel. But not with Claire around. Closing the door, I decided Claire's hum didn't sound electrical as much as entomological. The annoying buzz of an insect. The bug that never lands long enough to swat.

From the closet, I pulled out the titanium briefcase containing my rock kit and was setting it on the desk when my phone rang. Jack, probably, wondering what was taking so long.

"I'm hurrying," I said.

"Dr. Robert Stoller, Alaska medical examiner."

"Oh, hello."

"I have a message that there's an urgent need for information about a deceased female from Ketchikan?" He had the precise diction of an exasperated person.

"I'm sorry. Yes, sir. I called." I introduced myself. "Have you had a chance to examine the body?"

"Not thoroughly. But I was told that you needed information immediately."

"That's correct. The most crucial is cause of death. What's your verdict?"

"Juries offer verdicts, Agent Harmon. My *opinion*, based on a somewhat cursory examination, is that the woman was murdered."

I let out a sigh. Finally, somebody agreed. But that relief was swiftly kicked aside by this reality: she was murdered, by somebody on this ship. "Thank you, sir. May I ask what your first clue was?"

"Clues are for detectives. I search for *evidence*."

"I stand corrected, thank you. What evidence led you to your conclusion?"

"Granted it was culled from a rather swift examination of the body, due to our present arduous workload. But it was the thoracic area that was troubling. Chest, esophagus, mouth. And the distended tongue."

"Pardon?"

"The tongue. It was protruding."

"Yes." The tongue I saw sticking out, as though mocking somebody. "And what does that mean, Dr. Stoller?"

"What does it *mean*?"

I rephrased. "What does a protruding tongue indicate?"

"Any number of things. Quite often it indicates asphyxiation. When I examined the back of the throat, I discovered a small white feather. Eiderdown, if I was guessing, which I'm not. Those conclusions must come from the lab. But the feather was clinging to the fleshy mucous membrane on the right."

"Her cheek?"

"In a word, yes. Though the feather was small enough to swallow without interfering with breathing, she didn't swallow it. Most likely she didn't have a chance."

"Could that feather come from, say, a pillow?"

"Agent Harmon, please do not waste my time leaping to conclusions. This is Alaska. I've seen victims suffocated with down jackets, sleeping bags, even mittens."

"Yes, sir. Any signs of sexual assault?"

"None. None whatsoever. In fact, no recent sexual contact preceding death." He paused. "Would you care to hear about the facial injuries?"

"Her neck?"

"Her face."

"Please, continue." I snapped open my briefcase.

"Deep contusions spread down to the palatine bone and nasal cavity, most likely from applied pressure."

"A pillow over the face?"

"You persist in assuming. Apparently you're not acquainted with the adage?"

"Sir, I'm from the South. I've heard a lot of sayings."

"Indeed," said the doctor. "This one might sound vulgar initially, but it functions as a quite powerful mnemonic device. Would you care to hear it?"

"Please."

"The way to remember how to spell 'assume' is to recall that the word puts an 'a-s-s' in front of 'u' and 'm-e.'"

I almost laughed.

"And thus, assuming nothing, I cannot say how she was suffocated. Only that I'm fairly certain she *was* suffocated."

This conclusion would have been gold two days ago. But today was Friday, already midday, meaning it would be even more difficult to reach attorneys and judges in Seattle, particularly in summer. Then again, if I could tie her death to the drugs from Ramazan's cabin…

"Dr. Stoller, were you able to run the toxicology?"

"My assistant sent samples to the lab. When the results are available, my office will contact you. At this number?"

"Yes, sir. How long?"

"Six weeks."

I held back my startled response. Six weeks, before we knew if she had drugs in her system?

"Your silence is deafening," said the doctor. "Allow me to explain. Our toxicology samples are sent to a lab in western Massachusetts because our state legislators in their elected wisdom decided it would be less expensive than building a laboratory in Anchorage. But they failed to factor in the myriad costs that are incurred waiting for results to return from the other side of the country, a wait frequently exacerbated by weather delays both in Alaska and in Massachusetts. These delays often force law enforcement agencies, such as the FBI, to suspend cases, only to reopen them as the information becomes available. As you well know, that suspension process is not inexpensive."

"So the legislature *assumed* it could save money."

He paused. "Agent Harmon, for that interjection alone, should you have further questions you may call my cell phone directly." He rattled off the numbers and said, "It's been pleasant chatting."

My titanium rock kit was three inches deeper than a standard briefcase. The first layer held mundane objects. Things like Ziploc bags, tweezers, Sharpies, a jeweler's loupe. The second layer was more specific: two-millimeter dowels sharpened to points capable of picking up a single grain of sand; the rock hammer Geert allowed me to keep on board; an unglazed ceramic tile; a small shortwave black light. I brought the rock kit on the trip because of the fun I would have collecting and documenting Alaska specimens—pyrite, malachite, galena, bornite—but now it was all about two unknown stones taken from the dead woman's jewelry box, a move that risked my job.

Ignoring my churning emotions, I carried calipers, latex gloves, the jeweler's loupe, sunglasses, the black light, and a pocket guide to gems and crystals into the bathroom. What I didn't take was an evidence log sheet that asked questions I couldn't answer: *specimen, location, where found.* Especially not *where found.*

I locked the door and stoppered the sink and placed the stones on a white washcloth. The blue stone sparkled as if sliced from the Alaskan sky, a heavenly blue, a layered world beckoning. The black prism had a dark mysterious beauty. It didn't charm; it challenged. Like a cave in a bleak fairy tale, its reflective surface said, Enter at your own risk. I used the calipers to measure each stone, then matched its cut to a gem chart in my pocket guide. The blue stone was not cabochon after all; it was a round brilliant, coming in at twelve carats. If this thing was a sapphire, or tanzanite, or some rare blue diamond, the price tag just blasted past six-figure range.

And in some minds, worth killing for.

The black stone was more difficult to measure. Its extended prismatic shape turned my estimate into a rough guess, about eight carats. When I checked it with the jeweler's loupe, I saw no fractures, no fissures inside, and no veins of contaminating minerals, not even one varicose of quartz. But it didn't look synthetic either. Grown naturally, with the mirrored facets geologists called high schistosity, the stone was extremely rare.

And I had even less idea what it was.

I picked up the blue gem again. At twenty-times magnification, the loupe revealed several linear surface scratches along the stone's base. Marks left by a former jewelry setting, perhaps. Hefting the stone in my hand, it seemed too big for a ring, but this was Hollywood. I picked up the square tile and drew the gem's bottom across the unglazed surface. Sapphire had no "streak," since corundum was the second hardest mineral on earth, harder than ceramic tile, but when I raised the square to the bathroom light and tilted it, I could see a white line, like chalk. The stone streaked white, which took sapphire off the list of possibilities.

I tried the black prism next. It left a brown streak, the color of dried blood, which often indicated trace amounts of iron. But as the pathologist pointed out, assuming was a fool's game.

The shortwave black light was the last of my tests. Halloween haunted houses and discos used long-wave black light, which was kinder to the human eye. Shortwave could damage the retina and cause cataracts, so I slid on my sunglasses and flicked off the bathroom light. I aimed the lamp directly at the stones.

The black gem disappeared.

But the blue gem glowed so brightly that I jumped back, hitting the shower.

Under black light, a handful of minerals were known to fluoresce. Sulfur and calcium were the most common, along with fluorite—the mineral that the glowing phenomena was named after. But this fluorescence was off the scale, a neon blue so intense that when I closed my eyes, yellow orbs were swimming across my eyelids, my optical cones saturated with blue.

Blinking, I reached out for the black specimen and held it under the ultraviolet light. The prismatic shape reminded me of a dagger. Tapping my fingertip on a pointed end, I felt a shiver down my spine.

"Raleigh?"

The stone slipped out of my fingers.

"Are you in there?" my aunt asked.

I gasped and caught the thing just before it hit the counter.

"Hello?" she said.

"Yes, Aunt Charlotte." Hands shaking, I unplugged the lamp, flicking on the light. "I'm in here."

"Did you just turn on the light?"

"Yes."

"Why were you in the dark?"

This, from a woman who was just worshiping a rock, with the buzzing human insect.

"I needed to rest my eyes." My mind filled with images of the prism cracking on the floor and me putting it back broken in the jewelry box. I took off my latex gloves and dog-eared the page in my pocket guide on fluorescence, then laid a towel over the supplies.

"Did you find Nadine, was she in the chapel?"

When I opened the door, my aunt's flame-hued hair radiated from ear to ear, as if Claire's crazy current jumped through space and electrocuted my aunt.

"Mom's in the infirmary."

"She's sick?"

I started to tell her the rest but Claire trundled around the corner. She had a similar windblown appearance.

"It was the cod," Claire said. "We both ordered it last night. I've been running to the toilet ever since."

"It's not the cod." I looked at my aunt, hoping she would read my thoughts. But she was giving me a blank look. "It's not the food."

Then it hit her. Her hands flew to her face and stayed there. I nodded.

"What's wrong?" Claire demanded. "What's going on? Is Nadine dying?"

"Dying?" I said. "Who said anything about dying?"

"I can feel a spirit of death on this boat. And between you and me, Nadine looks half gone."

"You know what's half gone, Claire? Your mind." I pointed a finger at her. "And it's because of you she's suffering, opening your big mouth about my job and contacting my dad and now—"

"Raleigh," she said, "somebody's going to die on this boat."

"Somebody *did*, you moron."

"Raleigh!" cried my aunt.

Claire took her arm. "Tell her, Charlotte. Tell her how I can predict these things. Remember how I saved Beryl?"

My aunt said, "I told you how she saved Beryl—"

"Your cat."

Claire said, "I'm connected to *all* creatures."

"Don't go near my mother." I narrowed my eyes. "If I see you within fifty yards, I'll throw you overboard."

Claire stomped out of the room, then slammed the door between our cabins.

A beautiful sound.

Then I told my aunt about the chapel, my mother carving her face. How the doctor subdued her and how she wouldn't be leaving the medical clinic until we reached Seattle. By the time I finished, Aunt Charlotte was leaning against the wall, looking like she might slip down the length of it.

"Are you all right?" I asked.

She said nothing. She only sighed. And her bosom heaved with the depth of it.

TWENTY-SEVEN

I crossed the atrium with my hands in my pockets, covering the stones and feeling a heat radiating from them, searing my conscience. I climbed the spiral stairwell and vaguely heard the ship's historian down in the lobby giving a lecture on Skagway, tomorrow's port of call. Gateway to the 1890 Yukon gold rush, Skagway was a highlight on the travel itinerary.

But not mine.

I took the stones to get answers. What I got were questions.

Every cabin contained a safe, why didn't Judy Carpenter use theirs? Better yet, why did she bring these gems on a cruise, when they couldn't be worn? And why did Milo give her a jewelry box, with a loving inscription, right before filing for divorce?

By the time I reached the top of the stairs, more questions mounted and I felt the familiar sensation that I was holding a large map marked by a giant X—and no paths showing me how to get there. In some ways, every one of my cases felt like that, as if for eight years I'd been waking up to some continuing dark adventure that began: Here be monsters. That lost territory would require crossing again and again, and questions would always outnumber answers. Discouragement would claw at hope. Fear tearing at joy. And my only comfort was paradox. Deep inside, I could sense the unfathomable certainty that life did not rise randomly. By its own laws of mathematics and physics, the natural world disqualified itself from statistical accident. Planetary splendor above and atomic structure below, a world operating with breathtaking genius and design, all of this implying necessarily a designer. Chaos came in the moment, from my paltry human perspective, and most important of all, when the monsters roared, when I flailed haplessly through the swamps, forever asking outsized questions, somebody stood ready to provide comfort.

I was walking toward the movie set when the full burden of my choice struck, hitting the back of my knees like a lead pipe. I was impatient. Headstrong. Greedy. I was greedy for answers. And for control. Taking these stones could get me fired from the FBI, and that wasn't near the worst of it. My choice sent me into exile, severed from the one force capable of repelling the monsters. And walking with me.

The crowds swarmed down the promenade, shuffling between theaters and souvenir stores and bars. I moved through them, stepping over to a window. The sea had the hard look of slate, blue and gray, and when I lowered my head, offering up my surrender, I heard somebody yell, "Whales!"

I looked up.

It was like yelling "Fire!"

The hordes stampeded the promenade, rushing to my window, stepping on my toes, kicking my ankles. They smashed their faces to the Plexiglas.

"Where?!"

"Over there!"

"Where?"

"To the left—see!"

Staring over their heads, I watched the slate fracture and a slick black hill rose, climbing to a parabolic peak. A geyser blasted, spraying white mist over the water, and just as that whale descended, whipping a fantail, another rose and followed the same undulating pattern. In all, four whales came swimming alongside the ship, performing a sine-wave ballet so elegant it looked like a dream.

"Oh, look, it's a family!"

One whale. My mother wanted to see one whale on this cruise. One. Here were four. And the medical clinic had no windows.

Moving once more against the crowd, whose caps identified them as phillumenists, I walked the now-empty promenade and opened my phone. I resisted the part of my brain that wanted to call McLeod and find out the status of the blue bracelet. Maybe it was seeing that whale pod.

And maybe it was repentance.

But I didn't call McLeod. I called my sister Helen.

"Dr. Harmon," she answered on the fourth ring.

One of those annoying PhDs who grafted the letters to themselves, Helen worked as a full professor of painting at Virginia Commonwealth University.

I said, "It's me."

"What's wrong?"

Our relationship limped along beside our mother's mental health, or lack. Whenever Nadine Shaw Harmon's fragile world cracked, I informed Helen. Because Helen was busy. Helen was always very busy.

"Mom's in the medical clinic. Under sedation."

"Oh, that's just great."

"Helen, she was hearing voices—she was hurting herself."

"Didn't I tell you not to take that cruise?"

Well, yes, she did. But as usual, my sister was conveniently skirting the specifics. She told us not to take the cruise—until July. When her work schedule opened up. And Helen deciding not to come meant Claire took her place. Claire, the cross to bear. Claire, who kicked my mother over the edge.

I wanted to tell Helen it was all *her* fault. But I wanted

something else more. Taking a deep, deep, breath, I blew it out. "Do me a favor. Please."

"What?"

"Call Dr. Simpson."

"You mean there's no doctor on that ship?"

"There's a doctor. But I'd like some advice from somebody who knows her."

"Advice—about what?"

"How to get her home."

"The same way you got her out there. On an airplane."

"Let me explain the numbers, Helen. Six hours at thirty-five thousand feet with zero ability to cope."

"Don't get mad at me, you were the one insisting on that cruise," she said. "And for that matter why don't *you* call Dr. Simpson."

"I can't remember the name of his retirement home." No longer a practicing physician, my parents' doctor was the only one my mother trusted, and even that trust was tentative. But the man never locked her up.

"You're asking *me* to call every nursing home in Richmond," she said.

"Helen, they've got restraints on her arms. Her biggest fear just came true. Don't you understand?"

"Oh, I understand. I understand that you didn't take care of her. Now you wondering if I'll take over your responsibility."

Actually, I was wondering if grace was overrated. In which case I could just kill her.

But my mouth stayed closed.

Finally she said, "I'll see what I can do."

And hung up.

The crowd outside the Tiki Bar had diminished, probably because of the whale sighting, but Vinnie Pinnetta wasn't backing off his bouncer routine. As I approached, he crossed his thick arms and dropped his voice to a rough whisper.

"You think you can just come and go? This is a live set."

"I'll just stand here and yell for Jack."

He leaned forward. The brow bone came out like an awning. "I know what you're up to."

"Really?"

"Yeah. You're the type can't let nobody have any fun."

"Fun. You mean fun like murder?"

"When somebody kills themself, it ain't nobody's fault. You Fed types just wanna make points, pinning this on somebody. Make it look like you're working."

After dealing with Helen, the guy was child's play. I smiled. "Are you going to let me in, or should I start yelling?"

He stepped aside.

Hands in my pockets, I searched the Tiki Bar for Jack and found him standing behind the second cameraman, across from Martin Webb and Sandy Sparks. The director was watching Larrah Sparks act out the scene behind the grass-skirted bar. She pulled a beer tap, filling a glass, then she wiped her hand across her forehead—to show exhaustion, I guessed. Setting the glass on the bar, she pushed it toward Milo. He sat at the end, palm open. Foam dribbling down the glass counter, leaving a wet trail to his hand.

Larrah began wiping down the counter. She leaned forward, vigorously scrubbing the bar, which explained the purpose behind that teeny-tiny top.

"Lean down more," Webb whispered, directing. I'd learned that these comments could be edited from the sound later.

At the crowded tables, the extras playing cards whistled a catcall. Larrah looked up, showing surprise—her blue eyes darting around the bar, not very believably.

"Yo, Blondie," an extra called out. "Get over here."

But she moved away. Webb raised a hand, motioning to

the second camera. It was manned by a younger man with the bushy blond ponytail. At the director's signal, the cameraman drew closer to the bar.

"Lean down," Webb whispered again.

Larrah leaned down, exposing more cleavage.

I glanced at Jack. He met my eyes, then began taking slow steps backward to where I stood.

"Blondie!" hollered the same extra. "Get over here!"

He was burly. Unshaven.

She gave him a dewy expression. "What do you need?"

"*You.* Over here. Now."

She toughened up. Too quickly, if anybody wanted my opinion. But they didn't. Not anymore.

"You want a drink, come get it."

The extra stood, kicking back his chair. Unfortunately the chair was one of those heavy captain's style, weighted at the bottom, and rather than topple, it tilted. Catching the arms of the chair beside it, the chair hung, comedically suspended above the floor.

The extra waited.

"Keep rolling!" The director gritted his teeth.

The extra swept his boot into the chair's leg, crashing it to the floor. When he turned to face the bar, his neck looked wider than his head. And the brain inside that small skull convinced him to kick more chairs. None went down easily.

"Stop with the chairs!" Webb hissed. "Just get to the bar!"

The man lumbered toward Larrah. "Nobody tells me 'No.'"

She shook her platinum mane. "I just did."

"Yeah?"

"Yes. What'll you have?"

"What'll I have?"

Reaching over the bar, he grabbed her long hair. Larrah screamed and clawed at his arms, then clamped both hands on his thick wrists. Her own biceps flexed with impressive strength. The burly actor seemed to struggle holding on to her.

He delivered the line again: "What'll I have?"

They were both glancing down the bar. So were the extras. And Webb. And Sandy Sparks next to him.

Everybody looking at Milo.

The actor was draining the glass of beer.

"Milo!" Webb was seething, his face purpling. "That's your cue—*What'll I have!*"

Slamming down the empty glass, the actor jumped off the bar stool and raced toward Larrah. A ragged run, nearly sideways.

Maybe it's the shoes, I thought doubtfully.

Reaching the struggle, he punched the extra in the head. Dazed, the man released Larrah, dropping her like a block behind the bar. Staggering backward, tripping over the chairs he'd kicked, the extra clutched his right eye.

"I'm seein' stars!" he cried.

"Cut!" Martin Webb launched out of his chair. "Cut-cut! Cut!"

Milo leaned against the bar, his mouth puckering.

"What are you *doing*?" the director yelled. "You don't *hit* him."

"Yes I do. It's in the script."

"Not *then*! Not until the fight at the table!"

Milo shrugged. "I improvised."

Webb grabbed his hair.

"It's a fight scene, Martin."

"Improvised? You *improvised*? I'll tell you when to improvise." Webb was screaming again. "And quit drinking the props!"

"You told me to stay in character. My character's drowning his sorrows. Your words."

Closing his eyes, Webb massaged his temples and Sandy

Sparks walked over, placing an arm around the director's shoulders. He spoke into his ear, and after a moment Webb turned, retreating to his chair.

Sparks stood in the middle of the set and raised both arms, like a referee calling the game.

"All right, everybody. Cool down. Five-minute break."

The extras, accustomed to waiting, pulled out the playing cards. Larrah complained her makeup needed fixing. And Milo staggered back to his stool. Sparks followed him, still looking like the referee, only now he was going to explain why the foul was called.

Milo stared at his empty glass.

Jack had carefully made it back to where I stood. "Nice pebbles?" he asked.

"Very. What's going on here?"

"He's drunk. Again. They're just now figuring out that he's drinking the beer on every take."

"That seems like a no-brainer."

"I think Sparks is finally cutting him off."

Finishing his pep talk, Sparks glanced at his wristwatch. The producer, keeping the schedule.

I whispered to Jack, "Quick, hand me the key."

"If I still had it."

My head snapped. "What—?"

"Harmon, what took you so long?"

"I got...interrupted. You gave it back to him?"

"I stayed away until it seemed obvious we were gone too long. My plan was to hang in back until you got here, but Milo took one look at me and held out his hand. The guy can't remember his lines but he remembers giving me his key. Drunks, they surprise you."

Webb was gripping the megaphone. "Everyone! This is the last take." He glared at the bar. "Milo! Last take. Get it *right*."

"Jack," I whispered. "I can't keep these."

"You're just now figuring that out?"

I held my tongue. The cameras rolled and the actors went through the scene again, every word, every facial expression unfolding exactly as before. And now the burly extra's irritation seemed authentic.

"What'll you have?" Larrah asked him.

"What'll I have?" He grabbed her hair. "You!"

Milo leaped off the bar stool and ran—really ran—jumping on the extra's back. He wrapped an arm around the guy's wide neck and squeezed. The extra's face went red. His eyes bulged.

I looked at Jack. "Nice hold, huh."

Jack was watching the scene with a distant expression. But that was deceiving. When I worked with him in Seattle, I made the mistake of thinking that look was cold detachment. Only later did I realize his brain had switched on its own camera, coolly documenting every moment, committing it to memory.

The extra flung his arms around until his hands found Milo's forearm. He yanked on the arm around his throat. But he couldn't move it. Gagging, he staggered backward, crashing into the table of extras. The cards flew to the floor and the men glanced furtively at each other, then over at Webb. The director was watching intently. So was Sparks. Nobody said "cut."

Leaping up, one of the extras raised his fist and pretended to swing at Milo, who pretended to duck. He continued choking the burly man, who was now making a sound like a sick cat hacking up fur balls. And his tongue came out of his mouth. It was a burgundy color, engorged with blood.

"Hey, Milo!" Sparks came out of his chair.

Webb picked up the megaphone. "That's enough. Cut!"

Milo didn't hear. Or didn't care. He pulled tighter. The man's eyes bulged from his small head.

"Cut!" Webb said. "Milo, I said, cut!"

Two extras landed on Milo's back. The choking man staggered under the added weight. Like a rugby scrum, the man-pack shifted across the room until crashing into the bar. Suddenly the burly man shot out.

Bent, coughing, he looked up. Eyes like cups of blood.

"He was gonna kill me!" His voice sounded like rust.

Holding Milo's arms, the extras restrained the actor. He was panting, out of breath, his famous face shiny from exertion. But the most disturbing sight was his glassine eyes. They were blind. Without emotion.

Sparks walked toward him, arms open. The dad who can't believe what his son just did. "Milo—"

I turned to Jack. "That's quite an effective choke hold."

He nodded. "It gave me an idea."

"Me too. He choked her to death."

"No, the shoes."

"What about the shoes?"

"The plastic ones. The black ones. I'll tell him I want them back. Then we can get in there again."

"But those shoes don't fit."

"I'll say these sneakers are worse. I'll tell him they gave me blisters, then he can go on and on about the blisters on his feet. I'll listen while you go put those pretty pebbles back where they belong."

"You think he's going to let me into his cabin—by myself?"

"My feet hurt, remember? I can't walk."

Milo was stumbling back to his bar stool and staring into the empty glass, as though willing it to refill. Sparks was talking to the extras, explaining how his lead actor was going through "a really tough time."

Jack stepped forward, touching Sparks on the shoulder. "Sandy?"

"Yeah, Jack."

"Give me a minute with him? Maybe if I explain how an agent would handle this situation."

Sparks nodded, then looked directly at me before broadcasting his opinion. "Here's a concept. The consultant who actually helps. All right, everybody, take five."

With his back to the set, Jack leaned in so close to Milo their heads almost touched. I saw Milo glance down at the bright blue sneakers before reaching into his back pocket. Jack, like a magician concealing the more important move, began patting Milo's shoulder while his other hand took the keycard and slipped it up his sleeve. He offered Milo more pats, then waved to Sparks.

"We're good to go."

Jack stood beside me as the scene began again. When the extra kicked back his chair, it hit the floor with an impressive crash. He lumbered to the bar, growled at Larrah, and recited Milo's cue—*What'll I have?* Milo ran straight for him and Larrah jumped back in pretty disarray. The actor and the extra followed a series of choreographed punches, though Milo kept glancing down at the floor, locating the taped marks. And the extra seemed to regret every pulled punch. But they crossed the bar swinging and pivoting toward MJ, who sat at the piano, and when Jack touched the back of my hand, a sudden tingling raced up my arm. I held my breath, kept my eyes on the men, and suddenly MJ screamed.

She screamed with a pitch that could shatter glass.

I wondered how anybody could miss hearing a scream like that coming from the chapel Monday night.

I slipped the keycard into my pocket and Webb began whispering directions again. "Roundhouse on three." He leaned forward in his chair, voice rising with anticipation. "And one...and two..."

And bursting forth, "Ode to Joy."

Milo's fist was frozen in midair. The extra turned his head, trying to find the source.

I yanked my cell phone from my belt, smashing my fingers into the small keys to silence the song. Jack was backing away, his hands raised to show his innocence. When I looked up, the extra was shaking his head. Milo looked lost. And Webb needed no megaphone.

"You ruined it!" he screamed. "You killed the scene! We finally get it to work—and you killed it!"

Sparks remained nonplussed. Picking up the megaphone, he said, "Vinnie, get her out of here."

Only too happy to obey, the Forehead flashed into view.

TWENTY-EIGHT

I glanced at my phone, checking caller ID.

Area code 804.

DeMott's phone number.

With a flash of fury, I bounded up the stairs to Deck Fourteen, running down the hallway to Milo's cabin. At the other end, a steward's cleaning cart sat outside an open door. Head down, I keyed open Milo's door, went straight to the bedroom, and slid out the bureau's top drawer.

The box was gone.

I pushed the lingerie back and forth. Then opened the second drawer.

T-shirts. Shorts.

The third drawer contained pants.

No box.

Standing still, I listened for noise. The only sound was blood rushing through my head. His bed looked exactly as it did when I left. The drinking glasses were still upside down on the paper doilies.

But the closet door was closed.

Moving to the side, I took hold of the knob, turning it slowly. I threw the door open.

Nothing moved.

I waited several seconds, then came around the front and almost jumped out of my skin.

My phone was vibrating on my hip. Glancing into the closet, seeing no feet, no hands, I tore the phone off the clip, thinking, *If this is DeMott, I'm going to—*

But it was McLeod.

"Yes, sir?" My voice was pinched with fear.

"Larsen got it."

"The bracelet?"

"Yep. It'll be in the evidence vault when you get to Seattle."

"But I need it now."

"Now?"

"Yes, sir. We've got less than two days left on this cruise."

"You're serious."

I stared into the closet, searching for the jewelry box— on the floor, on the shelves—all the while knowing it wasn't here. All that remained was that draping wardrobe, those long and elegant palazzo pants, ready for a party. "Sir, when I know who wants that bracelet, I'll know who killed her."

"Wait, this guy Ramadan—"

Ramazan.

"I thought he killed her. For the bracelet."

"I wish it were that simple. Her body showed almost no signs of struggle. Her death was extremely well planned. I doubt Ramazan even knows the full value of that bracelet. I'm a geologist and I didn't realize how unusual those blue stones were until…"

"Until what?"

I felt nauseous. What could I say? *I didn't realize it until I stole some rocks from her jewelry box?*

"They're very rare, whatever they are," I continued. "And somebody on this ship knows it. Ramazan was hired to break into the safe."

"So why let him keep it, why let him run off with it?"

"I don't know. Maybe he was supposed to hold it. Or maybe he got greedy and took off. Did Larsen find out anything from him?"

"No. The guy found some crackpot attorney in Seattle who wants to sue for religious persecution. They're demanding a prayer rug for the interrogation room." McLeod paused. "And what's going on with Milo Carpenter?"

"He's at the top of my list, and one reason why I want the bracelet here. He refused to claim it." I glanced around the bedroom, then at my watch. "We're in Skagway tomorrow, ask Larsen to put the bracelet on a plane."

"Harmon, you're talking paperwork, insurance, an escort—"

"Yes, sir."

"Who do you think I am? Moses coming down from Mount Cyanide?"

I was in the living room, looking around, hoping to see the jewelry box. I didn't. In the front closet, I checked the shelves, then picked up the cheap black shoes.

"All right, all right," McLeod said, mistaking my silence. "I'll talk to Larsen. But I'm not making any promises. You might have to wait."

"I understand, sir," I told him. "Really, I do."

The black shoes protested every bend of Jack's feet as he limped down the promenade, wincing with pain.

I walked behind him. "Jack," I whispered.

"What?"

"The box is gone."

He stopped cold and turned around. His face showed a series of rapid thoughts. First shock. Then horror. Finally anger.

His blue-green eyes burned into mine. "You're kidding. Right?"

I shook my head.

He hobbled toward a chair near the window. Setting himself down gingerly, he extended his legs. The inflexible soles were propped up like water skis. "Harmon, you realize what this means?"

I nodded. "How long was I gone?"

"Which time?"

"The first time, when I went to check out the stones."

"Too long," he said. "Thirty minutes. I was on the set for fifteen of that."

He began staring down the promenade, and when I turned around, Vinnie was glowering at the passengers pausing outside the Tiki Bar.

"Did anybody leave?" I asked. "Anybody, say, like the Forehead?"

"I wasn't watching him." Jack leaned forward and pried the shoes off, wiggling his toes. "The director did call for a break."

"And?"

He thought a moment. "And it was right after I got there. Webb was frustrated with Milo. He said he needed to get some air, or he was going to kill Milo."

"He said that?"

Jack nodded. "Sparks told him to rub some rock your aunt gave him. That's when Milo walked over and asked for the key. Harmon, if you never touched that stupid box—"

"How long was the director gone?" I asked. There was nothing he could say that would make me feel worse. Or better.

His eyes seemed to brush over my face. "He was gone just about the same amount of time that it took you to run upstairs and bring me these evil shoes."

I checked Webb's balcony first.

Leaning over the railing, I could taste the sea spray cast

up by the wind and our steady progress down the Inside Passage. Milo's cabin was two decks up, four balconies forward, and one steel ladder ran vertically to the waterline, welded to the ship. But I doubted Webb could get there from here, especially within the short time he was gone from the set.

But what about Monday night, when Judy died?

I stepped back inside the cabin where Geert waited. His chin was raised so high that the white mustache looked like an elaborate letter *M*. He wasn't exactly thrilled about my request to search Webb's cabin, but the director did himself no favors with his performance in Juneau. Now, Ninjas stood around him like stockade fencing.

"I'll sue this cruise line," Webb said.

"It will cost you buckets of money." Geert walked over to the room's small refrigerator and pulled out a thermos, sniffing the contents. He set it on top of the fridge.

"Raleigh?" Jack's hands were wedged under Webb's mattress, pushing it against the cabin wall.

Geert leaned menacingly over Webb. "Hail to the queen."

On the platform that supported the mattress were three plastic bags containing a white powder. I picked them up and Jack dropped the mattress. We squeezed the bags, searching for solid objects within, then tossed them to Geert.

I walked over to the closet. While narcotics were definitely important, we already knew Webb was a cokehead. What I wanted to know was whether he was a thief, or a murderer, and if he took that jewelry box. Standing on tiptoes, I scanned the closet's upper shelves. I found more copies of the movie script and some DVDs. I flipped through the discs. They were foreign films. Indie productions.

"You wouldn't understand," Webb said, watching me. "They have subtitles. They're *art*."

Suppressing a response in French, I moved to the hangers. For such a weasel of a guy, his wardrobe was oddly thuggish. Black clothes, mostly. White T-shirts with strategically torn sleeves. A leather motorcycle jacket with chrome spikes.

"Cocaine," Geert was saying to Jack.

I looked over. Jack was still kneading the baggies, pressing the white powder in case he missed something. I felt a twinge of gratitude. He had every right to berate me. But instead of pouring salt in my wound, he offered to help.

"If you touch my clothes," Webb said, "you're paying to have everything dry-cleaned."

I patted down his clothes with both hands. I found receipts for drinks. And a woman's name and phone number. I moved to the other side of the closet, where other jackets hung with the biker getup.

"Don't touch the jackets!"

Maybe the only thing more ridiculous than the condescending remark about "art"—from a guy directing a Milo Carpenter movie—was this black leather jacket with the chrome spikes. Making sure my hands touched every surface, I felt a lump inside the left shoulder and almost let it go, mistaking it for one of the silver studs. But when I ran my hand over it again, I realized the lump was something else, covered by a two-inch patch. An embroidered logo of a green chopper. "Bikers for Earth Day," it said. Almost more ridiculous than the jacket. I pulled out my pocketknife.

"You can't—" Webb cried. "That jacket was a gift!"

The green threads snapped under my knife, but it took work. I finally got my fingers under the patch, but there was only black leather. The bump was still there. I turned the jacket inside out and poised the blade along the sleeve. Webb leaped. The Ninjas yanked him back as I sliced along the seam and ran my fingers through the polyester fill, shredding it like confetti.

"You can't tear up my clothes." Webb's skin shone as if he

were secreting tallow. "Somebody paid a lot of money for that jacket—on Melrose Avenue. Are you listening?"

My fingers were now directly under the area protected by the patch. I felt the object, pinching it to pull it out of the fill.

Its mirrored surfaces had clouded, perhaps from leather tannins, but when I lifted the black prism to the light, I saw fingerprints. Smudged, unfortunately.

I dug my fingers back into the lining. Such clever concealment, expertly done. I stared at Webb. His long jaw was working up and down like a broken puppet. When I moved to the next jacket, he whimpered.

This one was brown suede with fringed sleeves, something hippie-ish out of the 1970s. But what interested me most were the retro patches on each shoulder. I went straight to the lining, slicing until I found the small blue stone, hidden directly under the peace-sign patch. On the other shoulder, the vintage patch proclaimed "Venice, California, the Center of the Universe." And the stone beneath it was even more remarkable.

Unlike the other blue stones, this one was milky. And it formed a perfect six-sided star. A Star of David.

"You—" Webb cursed, on the verge of tears. "Marlon Brando wore both those coats on the set of *The Wild One*. You just destroyed cinema history."

"I'm more concerned with who destroyed Judy Carpenter."

"I want my lawyer. Do you people hear me?" He was yelling, at the ninjas, at Geert. "Get my lawyer."

I fingered the stones. They were just small enough to go unnoticed, tucked into the shoulder padding, covered by patches. When I looked over at Jack, lifting the Star of David, he gave a dazzling white smile.

"Way to go, Harmon," he said. "Way to go."

TWENTY-NINE

Webb was locked in his cabin, guarded by Ninjas, as I hurried down to Deck Five, carrying the stones in my pocket. Jack insisted on coming with me.

"You trust that crazy Dutchman?" he asked.

Although Geert confiscated Webb's cell phone and laptop, he wouldn't let us search them. Personal electronic devices, he said, were more complicated than the cabin. The room belonged to the ship.

"I don't know."

Keying open my cabin door, I felt the oppressive absence. My mother wasn't here—couldn't be here. Quickly, I closed the door between my aunt's cabin and mine, twisting the lock. Just to be safe, I wedged the straight-backed desk chair under the knob.

"Expecting an attack?" Jack asked.

"Yes."

I set all three stones on a clean white towel, then took out the titanium briefcase, removing my supplies. I handed the sunglasses to Jack, then walked over to the window, closing the curtains. The room went dark.

"Harmon, I've dreamed about this moment."

"Me too. But it was a different dream."

I picked up my mother's sunglasses from the bureau, slipping them over my eyes with a pang in my heart. I plugged in the ultraviolet lamp.

"What the—?" Jack said.

As I suspected, the small clear blue stone burned like a gas flame. The black prism went invisible. But the Star of David was merely six faint points, a mild fluorescence.

Jack pointed to the blue flame. "What is that?"

The cabin was pared down like a photographic negative. The shortwave light illuminated the whites and deepened the blacks. But the world seemed mostly gray as I pointed the digital camera at the stones, holding my breath to steady the open shutter. In the air Jack's scent lingered. Limes, I decided. Limes and something as clean as spring rain. The taste of his white shirt when I cried into it.

Flicking on the lights, I unplugged the lamp and took pictures of the black prism.

"You're going to make me ask again?" Jack pulled off the sunglasses.

"I'm sorry." My face flushed. I had been thinking about his scent. "This is called fluorescence. It happens when specific minerals are exposed to ultraviolet light."

"But the sun's ultraviolet light," he said. "Why pull the blinds?"

Excellent question.

"Sunlight does give off ultraviolet light, but there's too much white light with it—what's called visible light." I picked up the UV lamp. "This filters out the white light, leaving just shortwave ultraviolet."

I took the evidence log sheets from my kit, grateful that I could finally answer *where found*. As I filled in the blanks, Jack went through my rock kit. Picking up the hammer, he tapped the claw against his palm.

"That crazy Dutchman let you keep this?"

"For collecting rocks." I scribbled down the date. Friday.

Two days left. No, one and a half. Too many questions, not enough answers.

"The stones in her jewelry box, what were they like?" Jack asked.

"A blue gem and a black prism, like these only much larger. I've never seen this Star of David."

"It's not some religious symbol, is it?"

"It does look manufactured, doesn't it? But I think it's a natural occurrence. We have something in Virginia called staurolite. When it rains, the mineral can bond with the water and spontaneously form perfect white crosses. The folktales claim the rocks are the tears of angels, crying over the crucifixion." I picked up the evidence bag, taking a closer look at the star, once again wishing for an onboard mineralogy lab.

"So what is it?"

"I don't know."

"How can you not know? You're a geologist."

"Thousands of minerals, maybe tens of thousands, cover the earth. New ones get discovered all the time." I picked up the blue gem. It wasn't sapphire and it was also too soft to be a blue diamond. "Without lab equipment, all I can say is these seem exceedingly rare and valuable."

And Webb refused to talk without an attorney.

"When he left the set," I asked Jack, "where do you think Webb went?"

"To snort cocaine." Jack replaced the sunglasses in the rock kit. "That's how he gets through all those takes with Milo."

There was a knock on my cabin door. Jack's right hand instinctively moved toward his belt. Then his fingers twitched emptily. I walked over, leaning into the door but not opening it.

"Yes?"

"It is I," Geert said, sounding like some Viking invader with good grammar.

"One moment." I snapped a cap on the Sharpie, put the evidence inside the rock kit, and lowered the titanium lid. Then Jack opened the door.

Geert strode into the cabin. "I do your one favor. Now you do one favor for me."

"Favor?" Jack closed the door. "Maybe in the Netherlands it's called a favor. But in America, you did what was right. Finally."

Geert lifted his face, insulted. He turned to me. "Agent Harmon?"

I slipped into the role of good cop. "I greatly appreciate your help. What do you need?"

"The movie producer claims that without a director, they cannot make the movie."

"They don't really have an actor," Jack pointed out, "but that hasn't stopped them."

Geert lifted his face, higher. "These people do interviews. Movie people. Television sends their words around the world. My sisters in Zeeland know of this actor and already his wife's suicide—"

"Murder," I said.

"—is being talked about. If the movie is shut down because of us, it will cost my company millions in bad news."

"You want to release the director," Jack said.

"The man is swine. He belongs with the pornographers. But famous people talking bad gives me a very big problem."

"Your men could guard him, on the set?" I asked.

"I would insist."

"Hold on, Harmon." Jack narrowed his eyes, evaluating the Dutchman. "What's in it for us?"

"You just told me." Geert gave the ruthless smile. "Americans do what is right."

"And fair," Jack added. "This helps *you*, but we lose any leverage for getting that guy to talk."

I held up my hand, signaling a truce. "Would you let us tell the producer it was our idea to release the director?"

Geert considered it for a moment. "Because you are feeling responsible for shutting down his movie? For costing him money?"

"Right."

"Yah." Geert looked over at Jack. "Half to half."

"You mean half-and-half?" Jack asked.

The smile played under the white handlebars. "It's what you Americans call 'going Dutch.'"

We carried the evidence to the purser's safe, adding it to our holdings, which now included the two gems from Judy Carpenter's jewelry box because no way was I risking loss or theft—of my own theft. As an extra precaution, I wrapped the large gems in layers of paper towels and labeled the plastic evidence bag BODY FLUIDS.

From the purser's office, Jack and I climbed the stairs in silence to Deck Fourteen. Somewhere around Deck Nine, I felt a companionable silence, similar to what I'd had with DeMott before we got engaged. Once the ring was on my finger, he suddenly felt a need to know my thoughts. Every single thought. It was exhausting, and annoying, and I suddenly remembered that I hadn't called him back.

Worse: I didn't want to.

Jack knocked twice on the penthouse door. When Larrah Sparks finally opened it, she wore a fluffy white robe and a sour expression.

"You better have good news for him," she said.

In the hot tub on the patio, Sandy Sparks looked even less happy to see us.

"What do you want?" he growled.

The hot tub jets were on high and ribbons of heat rose from the bubbling water, climbing over the balcony until the wind swept them away. The producer's hair was a damp black cap over his reddening face.

"Mr. Sparks," I said, "we're sorry for the financial hardship placed on you by detaining Mr. Webb. We're willing to release him for work purposes, provided he's monitored by the ship's security."

Sparks flinched. Then scratched his ear. He was clearly surprised, but he said nothing and gazed past us to the patio door. Larrah stepped out. She was barefoot and dropped her white robe to the deck, offering a delicious shiver before slowly making her way to the water. Her bikini appeared to be three cocktail napkins strung together with fishing line. I glanced at Jack. Studiously, he watched the rocky shoreline across the water.

"Honey," Larrah said to her husband, "your dad called."

Sparks groaned.

Standing on the platform, Larrah swirled her toes in the frothy surface and showed off an anklet decorated with black pearls. In her hand, she carried an iPod, and though she gave another shiver, she seemed in no hurry to get into the warm water. "He wanted to tell you not to forget you're helping him set up tonight."

"Why would I forget?" Sparks cursed. "I'm not the one with Alzheimer's."

She gave a barely perceptible shrug, then continued her slow descent. Twice she glanced over, making sure Jack was watching. He wasn't. And neither was Sparks, who was rolling his head side to side, loosening some kinks in his neck.

Jack asked, "What's happening tonight?"

"My dad's part of this convention." Sparks threw his hands up, scratching his head. He splashed water on his wife. She squeaked. He didn't seem to notice. Or care. "They meet every other year, get together and talk about their collections. This year was a cruise to Alaska."

"Your father's a phillumenist?" I said.

He turned toward me, suspicious.

Since Larrah told me, and I didn't want to get into a battle, I said, "Just a guess. I've seen the caps. It's hard to miss them."

"Yeah, 227 of those guys came on this trip." He scratched his shoulder. "You know what they do?"

"Collect matchbooks."

"Huh." He evaluated me. "Nobody ever knows that."

Jack smiled. "Smart girl."

"But her idea for filming is stupid. And I already promised to help my dad tonight."

"You always do this," said Larrah, finally settled in the water. "You cram too many things into one thing. Your dad has to take the cruise, so you decide we should film a movie on it too. You've always got too much going on."

"No, I don't."

"Remember Sherman's wedding in Brentwood? You scheduled a conference call during the reception because you said it was all just small talk anyway. Then Sherman asks you to give a toast and where are you? On the phone."

"That was an accident." He tugged at his earlobe.

"And our Oscar party, when you combined it with—"

"Are you done?"

"I'm just *saying*." She grabbed the iPod resting on the edge of the tub and stuck in the earbuds.

He watched her for a long moment. Jack cleared his throat. Sparks was still fuming when he turned to us.

"Martin Webb can't direct. Not like that. On a good day he's a nervous Nellie. I'm not about to waste time and money putting him behind a camera with *security* breathing down his neck. And the whole shoot's already been ruined because for some reason you guys"—the hands shot up again, pointing at us—"want to believe somebody killed Judy Carpenter."

"It wasn't a suicide," I said.

"So you keep saying. But what makes you an expert—because you know what a phillumenist is?"

"No, because the medical examiner in Anchorage says it's not a suicide."

"Oh, okay. Some yahoo from the Arctic Circle. Probably not even a real coroner. Like that dumb woman they had up here as governor."

Jack gave a cold, cold chuckle. It sounded like a sheet of ice when it begins to crack. Reaching into his sportcoat, he pulled out Ramazan's photo, the cruise ship employee ID.

"Have you seen this man?" Jack asked.

Sparks wiggled his sausage fingers, refusing to come closer. Jack leaned forward, placing the laser-printed photo in his wet fingers. The ink began to run.

"Should I know him?" Sparks asked.

"Have you ever seen him?" Jack asked.

Shaking his head, Sparks handed the photo to Jack and pushed himself back into the roaring jets. "Let me guess," he said, speaking more loudly over the noise, "you think he killed Judy."

"What gave you that idea?"

"Because you two need to blame somebody, and that guy looks foreign. That's a bonus. You Feebs can make it look like you're fighting terrorism instead of hassling people."

Behind us, the sliding glass door opened. An elderly man took one tentative step out, wearing a baseball cap for the Phillumenists of Philadelphia. I suddenly recognized his face. He was the man we saw in the medical clinic, the one who picked up some missing medicine from Nurse Stephanie. His face had the same worried expression, but his clothing had changed quite a bit. He wore a quilted red vest decorated with matchbooks that flashed like metallic Boy Scout badges.

The man nodded at us politely, then turned to Sparks.

"Lysander," he said, "you're coming to help me tonight?"

"Yeah, Dad. I'll be there."

"Chinese Palace, Deck Six." His father glanced at Larrah. She was singing softly, eyes closed, tunelessly crooning to herself. He looked back at his son. "You really think she can watch your mother?"

"Dad, room service and television. What could go wrong?" Sparks tipped his head toward us. "But if you're worried, maybe these nice folks from the FBI will babysit for you."

"FBI?" Mr. Sparks looked even more worried. "My wife doesn't know what she's doing. She's got Alzheimer's, she didn't mean to take those—"

"Dad." His son held up a hand. "No, Dad, no. It's not about that. It's okay. I'm sorry. I'm kidding. Everything's fine. I'll see you tonight."

His father's face had filled with an unspeakable sadness. For his wife, and perhaps for the fact that he didn't understand what just happened and why we were here. Giving an obedient nod, he slid the glass door closed. My heart pinched. His worry reminded me of my mom. As he walked across the living room, I could see the matchbook covers flapping as if waving good-bye.

"What?" Sparks asked.

I turned around. He and Jack were looking at each other.

"Oh *that*." Sparks shrugged his hairy shoulders. "It wasn't federal. My mom stole some stuff from a store in Ketchikan. And Juneau. It's this stupid thing with her memory. Sweetest woman in the world turned into Mrs. Sticky Fingers."

Jack nodded, suddenly sympathetic. "My uncle started hot-wiring cars."

"Yeah?" Sparks actually looked interested.

"He was a mechanic," Jack said. "A total gearhead. Back in the seventies he built his own electric car, way ahead of his time. But two years ago he took a hit on the head and the next thing we know he can't remember our names and he's stealing all the cars around the neighborhood and taking them for joyrides. Takes them, then gets lost. The cops kept bringing him home."

"That sucks," Sparks said. "My mom didn't get hit on the head, she just got weird. Like, she stuck all the silverware in her purse the first night on the ship."

Larrah yanked out her earbuds. "Is this about your mother? What did I tell you? I told you she'd be trouble."

"Are you done?"

She stuck the buds back in.

Looking somewhat mollified by Jack's sympathy, Sparks said, "Hey, look, I appreciate the offer about Martin directing. But I already promised tonight to my dad."

For all his obvious flaws, Sandy Sparks seemed like a devoted son. Even Larrah admitted that. If I'd reached up right then, I could've touched the plank in my own eye.

"And besides," Sparks said, "I already found a new director."

"Really?" Jack said. "That was fast."

"The kid who runs the second camera. He graduated from my alma mater, San Jose State. When you guys hauled Martin off the set, he rushed over to say he's always wanted to direct, yada, yada. And he doesn't even want more money." He shrugged. "So there you go. I don't need Martin. Are we done?"

"One more question," Jack said.

"One, then I gotta go."

"'Lysander'?"

Sparks grinned, then stood and worked his way to the stairs. His back hair was flattened to his skin like a pelt. Taking a towel on the rack next to us, he rubbed himself down.

"My dad's a classical kinda guy. Back in Philly, he taught

Greek and Latin. He named me Lysander. My sister got sad-
dled with Persephone. We call her Percy."

"Philos, adelph," I said. "Seems like an ideal place for
teaching Greek."

Jack said, "What?"

"Philadelphia," I said. "The name's got Greek roots."

Sparks gave me that look again, part fascinated, part disgusted by nerd knowledge. "Right, city of brotherly love," he
said. "How about Lysander, can you peg that one?"

"The Spartan general who defeated the Athenians."

"Right." He wrapped the towel around his girth. "And
Persephone?"

"Daughter of Zeus and Demeter. Kidnapped and forced
to live in Hades."

"You got it. And my sister spends every minute staying out
of hell." His next words were sneered. "She's a *Christian*."

"Heaven forbid," Jack said.

Sparks laughed, thinking the joke was for him.

But Jack winked. The joke was for me.

"Hey," Jack said. "You mind if we stop by tonight?"

Sparks turned. One hand held the towel, the other was
reaching for the door. "That's cool. Sure. Come on down."

"Great," Jack said. "I mean, how many times does a person get to meet real live phillumenists?"

THIRTY

I was standing in the buffet line, trying to decide between chocolate cake with raspberry filling or carrot with cream cheese frosting.

Both, I decided, putting them next to the plate of salad. I looked over at Jack. "You want to explain why we're going to the phillumenists' convention?"

His tray only held salad. "I didn't like the way Sparks looked at Ramazan's picture."

I added a plate of broiled halibut with butter, lemon, and cracked black pepper. "How did he look at it?"

"I'm not exactly sure." Jack shook his head at the server who offered the fish, then slid his tray toward the roast beef carving station. He took two thick slices with au jus. "I asked if we could come tonight to see his reaction."

Nodding at the next server, I accepted chicken cordon bleu. Melted Swiss cheese and ham peeked from the glistening golden meat. "You think he recognized Ramazan?"

"I don't know if it was recognition," Jack said, staring at my tray. "But he stared at the face for a while. It wasn't his usual brush-off."

I thought back to that fateful morning, when I showed Sparks that blue bracelet. His face was blank, I remembered. Unlike the actor. "And what about Milo?" I asked.

"I'll see him later tonight. I still think he's just a sloppy drunk who is—"

"Who is giving the best performance of his life."

Jack shrugged. "I won't rule that out. But consider this. The director hates Milo and the feeling's mutual. So why does Marty have stones hidden in his jacket that match the ones in that jewelry box?"

That jewelry box.

At the thought, my wolflike hunger vanished. For three seconds. Regaining fortitude, I pressed forward to the pasta section and selected a generous serving of cheesy lasagna and a plate of spaghetti Alfredo. Jack declined the pasta and followed me to the bread section where four dinner rolls and twice as many pats of butter joined my tray. When I lifted the thing, my shoulders almost locked.

"Harmon, you're going to eat all that?"

"Actually," I said, "I'm hoping for some help."

At the elevators outside the Salt Spray, I pushed my elbow into the Down button, then glanced back into the restaurant. Jack was sitting alone at a table for two, gazing out the window. The early evening light had a happy childlike quality, that golden feeling of sun and cold water and mountains so unspoiled and untouched by man, that we seemed the first to see them. As he stared out at the passing beauty, Jack kicked off the mean black shoes that made him limp and wiggled his toes. There was no pouting. No taking up his right to blame me for the mess we were in, and before I could stop it the thought licked across my mind: *DeMott wouldn't be this nice, especially if he had to eat alone.*

I stared down at the heavy tray. Plates were wedged beneath more plates, like some visual demonstration of tectonics. Subducted lasagna, metamorphic Alfredo, dinner rolls rimming the tray like a chain of volcanic islands, complete with butter-pat lava. When the elevator *ding*ed open, four women stepped out, each wearing an Alaska-themed sweatshirt. The best was "Moose me yet?"

Inside the elevator I propped the tray against the handrail and pushed the button for Deck Four. The infirmary. The ten-floor descent took seven stops. Everybody was heading to dinner, nobody got on alone, and each offered my caloric allotment expressions that ranged from curiosity to pity. The last couple exited at Deck Six, the level with the Italian trattoria, and when the door closed and the elevator dropped again, my mind drifted back to the Greek myth of Persephone, descending into the underworld.

It was a story that captivated my imagination from an early age. Both impossibly scary and perfectly plausible, the myth involved a lovely maiden who was kidnapped by the ruler of the dark underworld. After Persephone is taken, her mother grieves, walking the earth, waiting for her return. Persephone is finally allowed to leave, but only for a short while. The pattern repeats annually, and the Ancient Greeks used the myth to explain the seasons. Spring life when Persephone leaves Hades, autumn death as she returns. But as I carried the food-laden tray into the clinic, I felt something uncomfortable, that sensation that precedes sudden and unpleasant realizations. I suddenly knew why that myth captured my imagination.

My mother's worst episodes plunged her into some dark and cavernous territory. And while she was gone, her family waited for her return.

But another element, even more disturbing, hit me as the automatic doors to the clinic *whoosh*ed open. *Persephone was the daughter.* But our roles reversed in these dim hours and here I came bringing food, nurturing the lost child, trying to lure her back into the light. And I was trying everything. When my mother felt good, she ate nothing but health food. Which explained my choosing salad and broiled fish.

But when the chasm opened, she craved comfort food. Cake. Lasagna. Bread and butter. Like ballast anchoring her to the world above.

I rested the heavy tray on the circular reception desk. My shoulders burned from the weight. Nurse Stephanie was on the phone.

When she hung up, she looked at the tray and said, "Did you ask Dr. Coleman if she can eat that?"

"No."

"He just upped her medication. She could be nauseated."

"Can I see her?"

"No. Somebody's already in there."

I stood at the edge of the door and saw Aunt Charlotte sitting on the edge of the bed. Her bright silk clothes looked even more colorful against the room's white sterility. When she looked over, I waved. She gave no response and turned back to my mother. Squeezing her hand, promising she would come back, my aunt walked from the room, pushing me out of the way and pulling the door closed.

"She doesn't want to see you," she whispered.

Behind me, Nurse Stephanie clucked her tongue.

I looked over at her. She picked up a file from the desk, feigning interest in the medical forms. Aunt Charlotte grabbed my hand, leading me into the next room. It looked identical to my mom's. White. Disinfected. Lonely.

"She's afraid," my aunt said.

"I know, that's why she's here. So she can feel safe again."

"No, she's afraid of *you*."

"Me?"

"You've committed her to an asylum."

"This is an infirmary."

"She says you're after her money."

"What money?"

"I had the same thought." My aunt gave a slow shake of

her head. The amber hair was dry, brittle. "David was a great man, but he never cared much about money. Or the FFVs."

First Families of Virginia, the Colonial settlers who became British burgesses, then Revolutionaries, and later Confederates whose precious bloodlines were tracked by Richmond's ruling oligarchy. David and Charlotte Harmon's blood ran straight back to Jamestown. Mine didn't. Not unless adoption counted. And in that cloistered circle of status, it didn't.

"If it weren't for you, your mother would be in the poorhouse," Aunt Charlotte said. "Where she got this idea about money, I don't know. But she said you kicked the boarder out of her house. Wally? Was that his name?"

I sat down on the empty bed. The crisp white linens were stretched over the mattress tight as straightjackets. Closing my eyes, I leaned forward and tried to breathe. Wally Marsh had lived with us for several years in the big house on Monument Avenue. He was like family. Unlikely family—a rail-thin photographer with a chip on both black shoulders. But Wally was among the loyal few who waited for my mother's return from the dark underworld. Last December he died, and in the aftermath, I chose to tell my mother that he decided to move out, find his own place. Another lie. Another deception. Another attempt at protecting her. And now something cinched around my lungs like a lariat. *I lied to protect myself.* My heart accelerated with the thought, running to escape.

"Raleigh? Are you all right?"

I nodded.

"You want to hear the rest?"

There's more?

Lying again, I nodded.

"The FBI bugged our cabins with listening devices. And her food's poisoned."

I placed my hands on my head, repeating three words. *Do not cry. Do not cry.*

"And she thinks there's a madman loose on the ship, trying to kill everyone. But then, Claire says the same thing."

"Because Claire's crazy too." I looked up.

"You're wrong. Claire is spiritually tapped in."

"To what—a sewer line?"

"You're so hard on her, Raleigh."

"No, you're too soft. All this stuff about crystals and vibrations, all this earth-worship nonsense, it's dangerous. Especially for her."

She waved her plump hand, dismissing me. "Not this lecture again."

"Listen to me, Aunt Charlotte. How do you know all this hocus pocus *didn't* cause her breakdown?"

"Because I know." She crossed her arms stubbornly. "I know how when I tore that Episcopal brace off my neck, I felt free. Finally. I could live *my* life the way *I* wanted. And I've never been happier."

Her defensive tone silenced me.

I knew my aunt's life. We lived with her for several months. Her life was one long chasing after wind. She followed the currents as though each shift meant there was a new intentional path. But somewhere deep within her heart, the void persisted. It was real. And I could see it, a hunger in her soul that yearned for peace and tranquility and truth. That was what drove her, that was what spurred the search for harmony. But like a traveler whose journey never ended, because it had no authentic destination, her quixotic path filled me with sadness.

"I don't want to argue, Aunt Charlotte."

"Neither do I. The real issue is Nadine. What do we do? Somebody needs to stay with her but it can't be you. She doesn't trust you. That leaves me. Or Claire."

"No Claire. No way."

"But—"

"Don't make me say it again."

She sighed. "Raleigh, you've got some kind of...vendetta against Claire."

"It's not a vendetta. It's about keeping Mom safe. I'm sorry, I realize that puts more pressure on you, and that it's totally unfair, especially since you were the one who got us these cruise tickets but—"

"Don't you dare." She pointed her finger. "Don't you dare insult me. We are *family*."

In her bright eyes, across her intelligent broad forehead, I saw my dad. There was a piece of him here, and *not* here. The fragile presence made my bond with his sister feel both tangible and too delicate to touch. A wafer-thin connection, capable of shattering with one careless flick of the wrist. We disagreed, she and I. We saw the world from distinctly different plateaus. It mattered. And it didn't.

When she opened her arms, there was no hesitation.

Her hug was warm, sheltering, and my throat tightened against tears. I held them back, feeling that cocoon, that nest, the kin who call you their own.

They are the people who stand up in this hard, hard world, holding out that soft landing.

THIRTY-ONE

The phillumenists, it turned out, weren't meeting in the Chinese Palace. They were in the conference room next door.

It was a plain space—remarkable on the ship for simply being ordinary—but smelled of sesame oil and peppered beef and I was suddenly wishing for the food I left at the medical clinic. I left it all, hoping to lure Persephone from the dark.

But my stomach was growling as Jack and I made our way past the many tables that displayed different matchbook collections. Some silver-foiled, shiny as magpie lures; others made of bark and balsa wood and cut into shapes resembling medallions and coins and wheels. There were even antique matchboxes with Revolutionary War emblems, faded down from the Ben Franklin era.

"Striking, aren't they?" Jack asked.

I groaned.

"It's safe to say these guys have a burning desire for matchbooks."

"Jack, enough." But I couldn't help smiling.

"One more?"

"No."

"I'm fired up about this case."

"Stop." I felt almost dizzy, still clutching that despair from the medical clinic, now catching Jack's buoyancy and laughter.

"You do realize," he said, "the last name is Sparks?"

The elder Sparks stood in the far back wearing his phillumenist club cap and the quilted red vest with the flapping covers. To his left an overhead projector beamed a bright square on the back wall, waiting for a presentation. Beneath that, Sandy Sparks was digging through some boxes as his father looked on. Sandy also wore a cap but it wasn't for the phillumenists. It was the blue-and-gold spartan cap, the one he wore to my aunt's seminar.

And standing with the Sparkses was a young guy with a fulsome blond ponytail. It was the second cameraman. The guy who wanted to direct.

Sparks opened another box, looked through it. "We'll work something out," he told the cameraman. "Maybe a percentage of the profits."

The guy's face lit up. "Yeah?"

Jack whispered to me, "Like that movie's going to make a profit."

I nodded, trying not to think about how good he smelled.

"Keep the dad busy," Jack continued. "I'll go talk to our pal Lysander."

All three men froze as Jack approached, but the elder Mr. Sparks showed the most fear. When I came up on his other side, I pointed to the matchbooks on the table.

"Is that Zazu Pitts?" I asked.

Startled, he turned. Then gazed down at the table. "Yes. Yes, it is."

"And that one looks like Gloria Stuart."

He leaned back. "You're correct."

I named the other faces lined up in a row on the table. Katherine Hepburn. Slim Summerville. George Raft.

Mr. Sparks gave the vest a firm tug, bouncing the matchbook covers. "You seem much too young to know."

"My dad and I watched the old classic films. They were his favorites."

"Mine as well," he said. "This particular collection is known as The Silver Screen Test set. It's quite rare. I had to travel all the way to Australia to find Richard Arden. Frances Dee? She made me go to Newfoundland."

"You've been collecting awhile?"

"Thirty-seven years."

"Really?"

"Started the day I quit smoking."

"That's an interesting connection."

"Yes, it seems odd to people, until I explain that a matchbook's value plummets if the cover is struck. You can't collect them and use them."

Over by the boxes, Jack was taking Sandy aside, speaking to him confidentially.

"And you probably appreciated the term *phillumenist*," I said. "Your son told us you taught Greek and Latin."

"He did?" The father looked pleased.

"Yes." I smiled. "*Lysander* mentioned it."

His skin buckled back, thick but pliable. There was a forensic term for that skin. Ichthydermis. Literally, fish-skin. The Greeks once again showing their precision for naming.

But his smile faded as he looked over at his son. "He never cared for his name. Now I understand. But when he was born, my passion for ancient Greece consumed every thought. Lysander seemed like a strong, noble name. It wasn't until years later that he told me how the children teased him, called him 'Lice,' all sorts of horrible monikers." He sighed. "Fortunately he doesn't hold it against me, and he kept me in his last name, but everyone calls him Sandy now. Except me. It was my wife who—" He turned, suddenly remembering me. "He explained her problem? She doesn't mean to take things."

"Yes." I nodded. "Her Alzheimer's must be difficult for you."

"Doris." His old gray eyes misted. "I called her Dorics. My classical column, holding up the whole structure. She really understood the children much better than I. When Lysander left for college, I pressured him to study the classics. But Dorics insisted he should find his own path, way out in California. She always said he was more Athenian than Spartan. And she was right." Gazing once again at his progeny, the father seemed a little awed. "My son has done quite well for himself. And do you know he still calls us every single day?"

The crowds were filling the meeting room, working their way around the tables. The elder Sparks seemed anxious to get his collection fully displayed. He looked nervously at his son. But Lysander didn't seem in any hurry to unpack.

"May I ask you a question?" I smiled again.

"Certainly."

"Did you know Judy Carpenter?"

The sadness swept back over his face, the skin sagging at his mouth. "Judy was always extremely nice. Friendly, disciplined. I truly admired her discipline, especially given the way her husband carries on. Her suicide is difficult to comprehend. But it reminds me of what Plato said."

I waited, but he didn't continue. "Plato said so many things."

He leaned back again, lengthening his throat and tugging at the vest. I suddenly saw the classics high school teacher, a man whose passion for ancient Greece was completely unappreciated by randy teenage minds. "Among the great adages of Plato was this: 'Must not all things at the last be swallowed up in death?'"

I wanted to respectfully disagree, since I knew of someone who was not swallowed up in death. But a man was staring intently at the Silver Screen set. The bill of his cap said "Twin City Phillumenists—We Know Matches."

Lifting his cane, the man pointed and said, "Where did you get Irene Dunne?"

"Ft. Lauderdale," said Mr. Sparks. "Guess what I paid for it?"

"Don't even tell me."

"A dollar. They had no idea what it was."

Jack was stepping away from Sandy, so I offered my good-bye to the elder Sparks, who barely noticed now that he was talking with a fellow phillumenist. Jack and I walked toward the exit, gazing at the collections from old five-and-dimes, and every restaurant along Route 66—in order from east to west—and a series that commemorated great torch singers. Military matches. Matches from presidential campaigns.

"Here's the deal," Jack said, keeping his voice down. "They'll shoot tomorrow if I can keep Milo sober. While they're shooting, you and crazy Dutchman can search the cabins for that jewelry box."

"You cleared it with Geert?"

He had stopped at one of the tables, checking out another collection. "No, I didn't talk to him."

"Then forget it," I whispered, glancing around at the crowd. "He's not letting us search without a good reason. And I can't exactly tell him about that box."

Jack pointed to one of the matchbooks on the table. The collection was advertisements for self-help programs. "I could have written that," he said.

On the cover: "Light Up Your Life."

"Jack—"

"Not here."

Taking my elbow, he led me through the crowd. I didn't resist his hold, and on the wide promenade we passed groups

of giddy passengers, everybody laughing as they headed to
the nightly shows or for drinks in the bar.

"Harmon, don't look so down. You're forgetting the carrot."

"What carrot?"

"The Dutchman wants that bracelet back. And we have it.
If he wants it back, he has to let you search the cabins. And
you don't need to tell him why. But those stones have to go
back in that box."

I nodded, too ashamed, too tired to say anything.

Jack stopped at the stairs. "I'm off to see Milo."

"What for?"

"I'm going to get him drunk."

"Way to aim high."

He laughed. "My plan is to get him so drunk, he only needs
maintenance booze tomorrow."

"Good luck." I smiled.

"You don't believe in luck," he said.

"Exactly." I was still smiling, but felt sad inside. "I'll go
find Geert."

"No, you won't."

"Pardon?"

"Harmon, you look exhausted." He reached up, brushing
hair off my face. "Beautiful, but exhausted."

I turned my head away, cheeks on fire. "I'm fine."

"I've heard that a million times from you. Tomorrow's a
big day and you need sleep. That's an order." He gave my
arm a soft chuck. "And if you argue, I'll make you stay up
and drink with Milo."

THIRTY-TWO

A bride was posing for pictures on the atrium's winding staircase, her white satin dress spilling down the stairs like a champagne fountain. At her feet, a woman wearing a mother-of-the-bride blue suit arranged the train, setting it just so. The photographer lifted his camera and my cell phone vibrated. God, I decided. He wanted DeMott to call at the exact moment I saw this.

Closing my eyes, not bothering with caller ID, I said, "Raleigh Harmon."

"Pilot's on his way."

"Marvin?"

"At your service." Marvin Larsen, our FBI agent at Sea-Tac airport.

I breathed out. "Thank you. When does he land?"

"I have no idea."

"Pardon?"

"Raleigh, all I can tell you is, the minute that ship docks in Skagway, run for the airport. Alaska's got weather that shifts on a blade. If the wind keeps blowing like it's been, I can't guarantee this pilot will wait around. He'll take off again. With the bracelet."

"But he's coming?"

"Let me put it this way. He's flying in that direction. But I'm not promising he can land in Skagway."

We had a brief talk about Ramazan, who was under arrest for stealing the bracelet but still not talking.

"Thanks for trying, Marvin. I appreciate what you've done. Really. Even if that bracelet doesn't get to Skagway, you're still my hero."

"Oh, gee whiz." He was one of those tough old FBI veterans, easy to embarrass.

I promised my first priority tomorrow was the airport, and we hung up.

The bride was still standing in the same spot on the staircase. She clutched her bouquet of lilies so tightly the blossoms shook. But the woman who was presumably her mother now fussed over the brown curls that dangled beside pearl-drop earrings. The bride's smile was as icy as Sawyer Glacier.

Standing outside my cabin, fishing for my keycard, I heard Jimmy Buffett's voice ambling down our hallway. It was followed by a young man wearing a floppy straw hat, wasting away again in the wrong time zone. His merry face was flushed, a bottle of beer in one hand.

"The music too loud for you?" he yelled.

I shook my head.

"Good," he yelled. "That fat egg next door keeps complaining."

I hoped he meant Claire, not my aunt, and pushed open my door. My first step landed on a white envelope. It lay on the crimson carpet with my name written on the front. Inside, I found a brief note from York Meriweather and three pages that detailed the work schedules for Ramazan and Serif. I scanned their calls. Fix leaking toilet. Remove broken chair. Repair broken shelf. Adjust sticking door. I ran down the passenger names that called; none matched with the movie crew.

And on the night that Judy Carpenter died, Ramazan was

working way down on the Highway, helping repair a busted freezer. Serif was off duty. Which meant Serif could've been anywhere, at any time.

"Raleigh, is that you?"

My aunt knocked on the locked door between our cabins. When I opened it, she was standing at the bureau mirror, removing her makeup. Her eyes had the lashless appearance of a white rabbit, making her look even more tired.

Claire came trundling out of the bathroom carrying a glass of water. She walked to the windowsill and began talking to the plants she'd brought on board. Some feng shui thing. But I decided that maybe she was talking to the crystals. They were lined up there too.

"Even when I'm not here, I'm thinking of you," she told the vegetable or mineral. "And I know that noise next door bothers you."

I glanced at my aunt.

She gave a soft shake of her head. "Really, who can say it's wrong?"

"You want a list?" I asked.

"Raleigh…"

"How's Mom?"

"Heavily sedated," she said grimly. "She wakes up scared, the doctor gives her more drugs."

I looked away. Jimmy Buffett sang through the walls, telling me about changes in attitudes, changes in latitudes, and Claire began humming that odd vibration. Then suddenly she stopped.

"Charlotte." She lifted a rock. "Something's wrong. This aquamarine. The vibration is not working anymore. Did you call the steward?"

"Twice."

I was incredulous. "You asked the *steward* to fix the mineral vibration?"

"Of course not." Aunt Charlotte leaned into the mirror, rubbing night cream on her face. "I called him about the noise next door. Claire hasn't been able to sleep."

Claire lifted another stone, a lighter blue. Perhaps tourmaline. "And it's not helping that we're this close to the Arctic Circle."

"We're one thousand miles from the Arctic Circle," I pointed out.

"That's still closer than in Seattle." She set down the rock like it was an uncooked egg. "These are very delicate vibrations, Raleigh. If you paid attention, you would understand."

Once more I looked at my aunt, but held my tongue. With her makeup gone, I could see the tension lining her forehead, her brows gathered with concern. A close acquaintance was dead; her sister-in-law had lost her mind; and if she hoped to work in movies, it wasn't going well.

And she had to share a room with Claire, listening to her whine about the noise.

I decided Jimmy Buffett was right.

"Claire," I said, changing my attitude, "why don't you take my room?"

She turned from the windowsill, surprised. "Really?"

"It's quieter. I haven't heard the music." I looked at Aunt Charlotte. "If that's okay with you?"

Her eyes seemed moist. "I think it's a wonderful idea."

Bundling up the plants like babies, Claire hurried them over to my cabin. "Don't touch the crystals," she called out. "I'm coming back for them."

Once she was in the other room, I whispered to my aunt, "Please tell me the steward changed the sheets today."

Her eyes were still moist, but my aunt's plump face dimpled with a smile. "Raleigh Ann Harmon, under all that toughness you really are a *very* sweet girl."

* * *

Sleep refused to come.

It wasn't because of the Parrotheads next door, who did indeed party all night. And it wasn't because of Claire, whose snoring drilled through the wall like a jackhammer. I couldn't even blame my aunt, who talked in her sleep. She talked nonsense but said it all with great urgency so it was impossible not to listen.

I tossed and turned, then finally pulled back the curtains on the window above the bed. The sky was liquid amethyst, washing over the narrow channel, heavenly hues over the snowcapped mountains.

Sitting up, I pulled on my sweats and stepped into the hall. My watch read 12:16 AM.

I walked down to the atrium where a grand piano lingered on the marble floor, its ebony beauty awaiting tomorrow's new song. The elevator was also empty and carried me directly down to Deck Four, and when the medical clinic's automatic doors *whoosh*ed open, the nurse who glanced up from the round desk had wide-set blue eyes and corn-silk blond hair. Apparently Nurse Stephanie had returned to her coven for the night.

I introduced myself, then said, "My mom's in here, Nadine Harmon." I nodded at the darkened room across from the desk.

"I'm Shannon." She extended her hand. "And I'm sorry to tell you this, but the doctor said you're not...we're not..." She was too nice to finish the statement.

I nodded. "I was just wondering if I could stay in the next room, if it's empty?"

Her frown notched the skin between her wide eyes. "The rooms are only for patients."

I imagined Claire, snoring in my bed. "I feel sick," I told her.

"Fever?"

"Could be. But definitely nausea."

She snapped some paper into a clipboard. "Follow me."

In the room next to my mom's I lay down on the bed, feeling the vinyl mattress cover under the sheets. The nurse placed two fingers on the inside of my wrist, then stared at her watch.

"Your pulse is remarkably slow," she said.

"I might pass out."

"That's just what I was thinking." She smiled and wrote something on the form. "We can't be too careful. There's a bad flu going around."

She finished quickly, then left me alone. Except for the night-light over the emergency call button, the room was dark. The clinic's antiseptic odors began to fade, but I could hear faint intermittent beeps coming from the room across the way, where the elderly man lay with his wife by his side. Closer, I listened as the nurse's shoes squeaked into my mom's room.

No words were spoken. None. The drugs kept her dreaming, or maybe she had nightmares. Nightmares about me. I held my wrist to the emergency light. Twenty minutes to 1:00 AM. In five hours the ship would dock in Skagway. A long day was ahead, as Jack pointed out. I turned on my side, drawing several deep breaths. I willed myself to sleep.

But those thoughts kept coming. And behind them, they dragged condemnation.

I lied.

I cheated and broke my code of ethics.

I broke the Bureau's rules.

I was a bad fiancée. Maybe the worst.

In the night while everyone slept, my flaws rose up glaring and raw, refusing to leave me alone. Defeating me. At times like this, I almost understood why my aunt worshiped the earth. Human beings were filthy creatures. Filled with weaknesses and ugly imperfections, committing stupid and selfish and evil mistakes. But those polished crystals stood shining, their pristine beauty unchanging and solid. Something visibly greater. The rocks and the mountains, this ocean with its wind; I had felt the pull of their gravity.

But as I tugged the blanket to my chin, I could hear my dad's advice, whispering in my ears.

Get to the source, Raleigh.

My passion for geology started young, with the first rock found in the backyard garden. I spent hours gazing at picture books and reading about the great catastrophic forces that created the monumental landscapes. Earthquakes and floods and meteors. Minerals and rocks. By college I'd fallen in deep with crystal axes and atomic attractions and all that stunning order and symmetry. Intoxicating to think about it. So intoxicating that one day my dad felt compelled to remind me that it would all disappear. Every rock, every hill, each stitch of order. One day the oceans would rise and the mountains bow down, and every last speck of this cherished earth would be forced to recognize true power and true majesty.

My dad didn't want me fooled.

Get to the source, Raleigh.

Pulling the blanket over my head, I realized the most stunning part of it all. The same God who created these breathtaking landscapes listened to me now. My confession of fear. My surrender of pride, all pretense of holiness gone.

My dad was my adoptive father, and the greatest man I've ever known. But he was gone. And he was never coming back. That was fact.

But another father adopted me and sent his own to pay my ransom. Here under the covers, I called out his name.

I called out his name. And he heard me.

And he caught every tear.

THIRTY-THREE

When I opened my eyes, Nurse Stephanie's face hovered inches from my nose.

"You don't look sick to me," she said.

I pushed myself up in bed.

"What do you think this is, a hotel? You're going to get charged for taking this room."

Swinging my legs off the bed, I stared at my socks. My shoes were nowhere in sight.

"These beds are for *sick* people."

As soon as my feet hit the floor, she yanked the blanket off the bed. I shuffled out of the room.

Standing by the empty desk, I stared into my mom's room. Nurse Stephanie continued to gripe and strip away my presence as I walked over to her bed. Her slack mouth drooled on the pillow and disheveled black curls covered half her face. The other half was exposed, displaying scratches like enflamed war paint.

Dear God. What have I done?

"Raleigh?"

I spun around.

Aunt Charlotte, her chartreuse caftan crowned with a green turban. Her face was wrinkled from sleep, and baffled. "What are you doing here?"

I looked down at the bed. My mother didn't even stir at the sound of our voices.

"I stayed down here." I nodded to the room next door, where Hurricane Stephanie continued to storm. "I couldn't sleep."

"Last night? But I didn't hear you leave."

I nodded again, glancing at my watch: 5:07 AM. "Isn't this a little early for you?"

"I wanted to check on her before the day got away from me. Sandy needs all new crystals." The caftan shuddered with her sigh.

I didn't want to ask. Really, I didn't. But she was my mother's only available visitor. "He needs all new crystals because...?"

"Because he found a new director and now the chemistry among the cast is completely different. Larrah's in a dither over it."

"Does that take long, changing the stones?"

"With these people? It could take all day."

Before I could point out the obvious—there was only one day left on the cruise—Nurse Stephanie swarmed into the room. Her eyes bugged.

"Get out." She pointed at the door.

"I was just leaving."

"Good, sign your release."

I scrawled my name across the document's bottom line. First name chosen by my mother for the city in North Carolina. Last name bestowed by my adopted father. But the signature looked foreign, as if it belonged to somebody else.

Somebody who, unlike me, was worthy of both.

My hair still wet from the shower, I met Geert at the gangway. It was ten minutes before 6:00 AM and passengers were already lined up at the exit. Geert waved me around the computer, staffed this morning by Fiona, the Irish girl interviewed in Ramazan and Serif's cabin. She glanced at me, then quickly looked away. Letty was nowhere to be seen.

At the bottom of the ramp, Geert reached into the black canvas bag and returned the Glock 22 to its delighted rightful owner.

I slid the gun into my fanny pack. "Did Letty tell you anything more?"

"Yah. Serif doesn't know what happened, she said. Now Letty is gone for good. But we are still watching him. And he'll be gone for good when we reach Seattle." His eyes moved toward my small pack. "Do not cause more trouble in Skagway."

"I hardly ever shoot people," I said.

"Ach." He turned to watch a police cruiser pulling into the dock's parking area. Two Alaska State patrol officers got out.

"What's this about?" I asked.

"I need my men back." His mustache twitched. "The director wants his lawyer. Let him call from the Skagway jail. I called the troopers about the drugs."

I didn't want to lose Webb this way, but Jack and I couldn't guard him and pursue the rest of the case. As for Geert, the FBI had no jurisdiction over him, and I understood his concern. While his men guarded Webb, they weren't providing security for the rest of the ship. When Geert turned to speak to the officers, I raced for the airport.

A time-traveler's dream, Skagway seemed lifted straight from the 1890s gold rush. The painted wood facades lined up along boardwalks whose planks creaked under my feet. There was even a marker pinpointing the exact spot where the scoundrel Soapy Smith was shot dead, killed for stealing other people's pokes of gold. As if continuing the Wild West theme, Skagway's geography reminded me of a broken arrow pointing north from the channel. Two steep mountains funneled wind off the water, and this morning gray clouds were being pushed into the valley. The sun was a faint halo trying to burn through, and when I reached the airport on the edge of town, the orange wind socks blew parallel to the ground.

The landing strip was empty.

A mile of tarmac stretched along the base of one mountain. In the middle was a small building, no bigger than a nursery school. The terminal, if you could call it that. But the door was locked. No air traffic tower. No radio transmitters. The airport was a dozen or so empty Cubs and Cessnas and prop planes, resting on a gravel shoulder, their guy-wires anchoring the wings against the fierce wind. I glanced at my watch, 6:13 AM.

Marvin Larsen's groggy voice confirmed my second worry: I woke up the guy who had helped.

"I'm really sorry to wake you, Marvin," I said feebly into my cell phone.

"Oh, hey." He perked up. "Did you find Chad?"

"Who?"

"The pilot. Chad."

"I'm standing at the Skagway airport, Marvin. Nobody's here. What time did he leave Seattle?"

"Yesterday. He took off from Paine Field. You don't see a dark-blue four-seater with SKI TO HEAVEN painted on the door?"

"Is that a joke?"

"No. He flies people to the glaciers, when he's not working as an air marshal."

I gazed down the long tarmac. The wind in my face made my eyes water. No blue planes. "There's not even a control tower."

"That's what I was trying to telling you. Skagway is officially the busiest uncontrolled airport in North America." He said it as though this was a lifelong destination of mine.

"It's not looking particularly busy this morning. In fact, it looks dead."

"How's the wind?"

I stared at the shaking guy-wires. "Blowing, hard."

"That's why he's not there. Wait for the wind to drop."

"Marvin, how well do you know this guy?"

"Don't go there, Raleigh. He's one of our best air marshals."

I didn't care if he was the director of the CIA; he wasn't here and neither was the bracelet. And if that piece of jewelry was worth what I thought it was, this pilot might decide to turn south and live like a king in Paraguay. And without the bracelet, I lost all my leverage with Geert to search the cabins. To find that stupid jewelry box. "The ship pulls out of here in eight hours. Is there a way to contact this guy?"

"He'll be there," Marvin said. "But this is the thing about flying in Alaska. It's more like combat duty. With that weather, your number can come up any day. Only the very best pilots live to old age."

"How old is this guy?"

"Sixty-two. Stick to the airport."

Unlike the cliff-hanging houses in Juneau and Ketchikan, Skagway's buildings were spread across a flat-bottomed basket, with the streets as level as Kansas. At the Sweet Tooth Cafe, I ate a hearty omelet and drank enough coffee to inflict a heart attack while staring out the window at the sky above the airport.

By 7:20, the tourists were streaming in through the bell-ringing door and the waitress was giving me the eye. I left a big tip, then wandered down Broadway. The pedestrians walking down the boardwalks created a sound like horses crossing a covered bridge—wooden and hollow. The shopping bags swiped against my legs and backpacks landed punches every time another tourist whirled around to exclaim, "Hey, lookit that!" Although the stores sold many of the same things as stores in Ketchikan and Juneau—Ulu knives, mukluks, gold nuggets, and T-shirts for "High School Moose-icals"— the jewelry stores made a point of reminding shoppers that Skagway was the "last chance" to buy "real Alaska jade and gold." And alexandrite—a semiprecious gem that changed color depending on the light. Much like the stones in that missing bracelet.

I glanced at the sky again. No messianic plane appeared. It was only that blustering wind, pushing clouds as if they were late for a good storm.

I spent the next hour walking from one end of Skagway to the other. From the white-capped water and cruise ships, to the railroad tracks leading into Canada, the historic train route that took miners into the Yukon for a gold rush that died almost as soon as it began.

And still no plane. I stood outside the hardware store, staring at the display in the picture window and deciding that if I got fired for taking those gems from the jewelry box, I could go work in a hardware store. Shopping for clothes was my idea of purgatory, but places like this were heavenly. I could see fishing nets cloaking the ceiling next to suspended kayaks and life rafts and a dusty floor with rows of smart knives and odd gadgets and the doohickeys only found in hardware stores, like the window display of salmon bait made from sex pheromones and fear pheromones—fish smells to excite predators—a stink "taken naturally from injured fish."

Hardware store heaven.

I turned and scanned the sky. What if I went inside for just one minute...but something caught my eye.

And it wasn't a plane.

Vinnie Pinnetta pushed through the tourists on the boardwalk. His urgency matched the wind, but he stopped beside a blond girl standing outside a jewelry store. The girl wore an 1890s costume, the ruffled skirt short to look like extravagant panties and a leather halter around her neck. The halter helped her hold up a large tray that displayed gold jewelry.

Vinnie stepped into the store.

I crossed the street. People streamed past the store's open door and I could see only bits of Vinnie's looming frame. He seemed to lean over a glass counter, speaking to someone. But he turned suddenly, staring out the door. I darted to the right.

The girl at the door gave me a smile. "You know what would look great on you? This." She picked up a gold necklace from her tray. "If you go in, they have one you can try on."

I didn't even look at the thing. "Great. Thanks."

She beamed like twenty-four karats, waving me inside. But when I stepped over the threshold, an electronic eye beeped. I froze.

Vinnie didn't turn around. Neither did the man behind the counter. He was small, compact, and held a jeweler's loupe to his right eye.

Leaping toward me, a salesman called out, "How can I help you?"

I turned my head, shielding my face, but once again Vinnie was fixed on whatever the small man held in his hands. The salesman continued to prance toward me, looking like a blade of grass in a thin green suit that bagged at the knees. Keeping my voice down, I told him the girl outside showed me a necklace.

"Wonderful, wonderful!" He stuck out his hand, the grip soft as a child's. "I'm Marcus and we have many *delightful* accompanying pieces." Marcus hopped behind the counter opposite Vinnie and the jeweler. "Some really *spectacular* sets. And imagine when you tell people that you got it in Alaska!"

He unlocked the counter's back and slid open the door. I

glanced once over my shoulder. Both men continued to lean over the object.

"And where are *you* from?" Marcus asked.

I didn't answer, hoping he would shut up. But he asked again.

"Virginia," I whispered.

"Virginia!" Marcus started naming every city he could think of. "Vienna? Norfolk?"

I shook my head.

"Chesapeake?"

When I turned around, Vinnie was bent low, speaking into the ear of the small man. When he straightened, the jeweler's face rose with him. He looked surprised. And I saw the object in his tiny hands.

A bright blue stone.

"We have same-as-cash twelve-month financing," Marcus said. "You can be wearing this in Virginia as soon as you get home."

Vinnie turned toward Marcus's prattle. I pivoted, dropping my chin so my hair would cover my face. After a moment, I picked up a hand mirror on the counter and held it to one side. In the reflection, the mansard brow shadowed his eyes. But his head was moving furtively, checking the front door and the jeweler.

"Hell-*lo*?" Marcus was holding up a gold necklace, waiting for me.

Since Vinnie's back was toward us, I pivoted again and lifted my hair. Marcus clasped the necklace and I watched the jeweler shift the blue stone back and forth, the facets sparkling under the display lights.

"There you go!" Marcus said, giddy.

I dropped my hair, turned, and lifted the mirror.

"Oh!" Marcus gave a clap. "It looks *amazing* on you."

In the mirror, I watched the jeweler saying something to

Vinnie. I reached up, touching the necklace, pretending to be interested. But the gold felt smooth and warm, and I could sense the peripheral glow, pulling my eyes like a magnet. I shifted my eyes. Gold lapidary leaves circled in a twenty-four-karat halo, with each leaf holding a dewdrop emerald. Marcus was beside himself.

"Stunning!"

Something my mother would wear. Elegant, and she would pair it with some flamboyant outfits she favored in good mental health. Gazing into the mirror, I stared over my shoulder again. I was doing some quick math when the jeweler lifted a short index finger, signaling Vinnie to wait. The man walked to the back of the store, disappearing around a corner. Vinnie wiped his forehead, looking anxious.

"I'll take it," I said.

"Really?"

"Yes."

"Do you want to know how much it is?"

"No, I want it gift wrapped."

"Oh certainly—*certainly*! We gift wrap." Marcus paused, feigning graciousness. "And how, um, would you like to pay for it?"

In the mirror Vinnie stared directly at my back. I saw him squint, like his brain hurt, and as he began walking toward me, I knew time was up.

I turned around. "Find something you like? Or maybe you're selling."

Vinnie opened his mouth as the jeweler stepped from the back of the store. Marcus waved. Marcus waved like he was hailing a cab, afraid it wouldn't stop.

"Mr. Lister, Mr. Lister!" His voice was speeding up. "She wants to purchase the *leaf* necklace! With the *emeralds*! Gift wrapped!"

Mr. Lister gave me a warm nod, so warm I started recal-culating the necklace's price tag.

"*Very* nice choice." His voice sounded like three packs a day with a lot of yelling. And he proved me right on the second part. He yelled, "Cheyenne!"

The pretty blonde poked her head inside, making sure the jewelry tray still faced the boardwalk.

"I need you in here! Gift wrap! Now!"

She ducked her head under the halter's leather straps, try-ing to maneuver the tray without spilling the valuables, when she suddenly fell to the boardwalk and the jeweler started yelling again.

"Get him!" he cried. "Get him!"

Confused, I looked at Marcus. But he was tickling the air with his soft fingers, uselessly.

"Catch that thief!" The jeweler was bug-eyed. "Get him!"

Cheyenne whimpered on the boardwalk, and a crowd was gathering. But Vinnie didn't move one gigantic muscle. He stared at the blue stone in the jeweler's hand.

"I'll call the police," Marcus said, leaping for the phone.

I ran out of the store and collided with a woman carrying a large bag. I tried to follow the string of exclamations burst-ing down the boardwalk, tracking the thief's progress, but the path was clogged with rubberneckers. Jumping to the street, I raced to the corner and caught a glimpse of the runner's back. A kid, no more than twelve, thirteen years old. And both hands clutched long strands of gold. When he turned the corner, I realized his flight had sparked the red-blooded American males on the boardwalk. They were in hot pursuit.

Or warm pursuit.

The first guy wore orthopedic shoes and whipped his fists through the air, yelling like he'd been personally robbed. Two men in Sansabelt slacks chugged like coal trains, cursing at the kid. As I ran past I heard the loose change jiggling in their pockets. One guy was ahead of me. He was tall and his arms pumped like a sprinter, closing the twenty yards between himself and the thief. The pebbly concrete was empty, the road wide and lined with picket fences and long front yards that set the houses far back from the cracked sidewalk.

At the next corner, a dirt bike leaned against the stop sign. The sprinter was only fifteen yards behind, but the kid grabbed the motorcycle and kicked down the start. Gold fell from his hands as a blue cloud billowed from the tailpipe. And just beyond him was the forest. No houses, no roads. No way to catch him.

"Get down!" I yelled.

The sprinter turned, took one look at my stance, and dove for the ground.

The kid's hands clutched so much gold that he was struggling to steer the dirt bike as I unzipped my fanny pack. He spun out a U-turn, spewing loose stones across the intersection. I aimed the Glock for the back tire. My first round clipped asphalt. The second *ping*ed the mud-splattered rear fender and went into the woods. The third round exploded rubber.

The bike slid out from under him, but he still held the throttle. The engine whined and the blown back tire lopped torn rubber. The bike was racing in a circle, rushing toward his body when the sprinter leaped up and ran over, yanking the kid away. His fingers sprung open, gold spilling on the ground.

The bike coughed and died.

His other hand was still threaded with gold, tennis bracelets wrapped around his fingers like gilded worms. When I stood over him, staring into his young face, I thought at first his skin had road rash. It was his eyes that changed my mind. Deep brown, almost black, they had the vitreous blank expression of a hard-core addict. All shine, no light behind it. On his face the pox oozed.

Automatically I patted my belt. No handcuffs. And in his eyes, the crazed impulses rattled around his damaged brain. In broad daylight, in the middle of town, with thousands of would-be vigilantes around him, he decided on grand larceny.

"Roll over," I said. "On your stomach."

The kid didn't move. The sprinter picked him up like a twig, flipped him over, and placed his hand on the back of his head. "Hold still, son. Y'all got some explaining to do."

"Y'all?" I said.

He started to answer but was interrupted by Marcus.

"There she is!" he cried. "That's her!"

In his shiny green suit, he was skipping down the street. The three guys in warm pursuit were coming too. And zipping around them all was a police officer, gunning a four-wheel ATV. He pulled to a stop near us.

"She was part of it!" Marcus told the cop. "See that necklace? She stole it!"

Slowly I raised both hands. The Glock was still in my right hand and the cop looked young, and scared. "I'm an FBI agent."

"Oh, puh-leaz!" Marcus stood behind the officer. "She was supposed to divert our attention. She wasn't even listening to me, she kept looking over her shoulder, using the mirror to watch the entrance. I guess when I went to gift wrap she was going to pull out that gun and clean us out."

The police officer's eyes snapped between me and the boy. The gold on the ground. The necklace. The sprinter, who also had his hands in the air and his knee in the boy's back.

"My ID is inside my jean jacket," I told the officer. "In the left pocket."

The officer didn't move.

The sprinter said, "Son, I'm a retired state trooper. I saw

the whole thing. She blew out his tire. Otherwise y'all'd be lookin' for this fella in them woods."

The officer told me to put my firearm on the ground and take out my ID. I pulled it out slowly, flipping open the case.

"You must be kidding me," Marcus said.

The trooper apologized.

I put the creds back in my pocket. "You're being careful."

"We're a little jumpy," he said. "Two days ago one of them pulled a knife. Sliced the man's face. They're crackheads."

The boy's bloodshot eyes darted like pinballs as the officer peeled the jewelry from his fingers, then handcuffed his wrists behind his back and radioed for a cruiser. Our audience began drifting back to Broadway, back to families and shopping and the best story to tell at dinner tonight. Marcus stammered, picking up the gold from the ground.

I extended my hand to the retired trooper. "Raleigh Harmon, thanks for your help."

"Bob Barner. Powhatan, Virginia."

"We're neighbors," I said. "Richmond."

"That right? Well, I'll be." He grinned. "Nothing like a takedown to add some zip to a vacation, huh?"

I didn't agree, but then, I was on a cruise from hell.

"I'd love to talk to y'all," he said, "but I better get on back. My wife's gonna have a conniption."

The Skagway officer asked for a quick statement, and as they talked, I cupped a hand to my eyes. There was a distinctive buzz in the air.

The dark blue plane swooped above town like a stellar jay. As it dropped, I could see white lettering on the door. I reached into my creds case and pulled out a business card, handing it to the Alaska trooper.

"I've got to meet that plane."

"Wait!" Marcus said, still picking up the jewelry. "You've still got our necklace!"

Fiddling with the clasp, I handed it out to him but now he was reluctant to take it.

"For what you did," he said, "I'll bet Mr. Lister would take ten percent off."

"Thanks anyway." I dropped the necklace into his hand and ran for the airport.

THIRTY-FOUR

Skagway's hearty souls lived along the western side of town. I ran past weather-beaten houses painted bright colors, defying winter with pink and turquoise and yellow, and small yards that sprouted fishing lines and crab pots and rubber rain boots turned into flower planters.

When I reached the airport, the dark blue plane was taxiing to a stop. Behind the controls, the pilot wore a straw cowboy hat that looked as if somebody regularly sat on it. I flashed my credentials at the window and he leaned over to his right, keying open a small compartment beside the instrument panel.

He opened the cab door and handed me the package sealed with FBI evidence tape. "Drugs?" he asked.

I shook my head. His blue eyes were bleached from years spent staring at sea and sky and snow. "Can I buy you a cup of coffee, breakfast?"

"Thanks for the offer." He craned his weathered neck, peering up at the sky. "I gotta get out before the weather changes again. You can't take any chances up here. That's how people get killed."

"It's one way," I said.

The bracelet was stuffed deep in my pocket as I walked down Broadway. When I turned into the jewelry store, it was like royalty calling.

Mr. Lister ran toward me, both arms extended for an embrace.

"Thank you, oh, thank you. Last week they robbed the pharmacy. Two days ago they tried to kill the bank clerk." He must have seen the look on my face and went on, compelled to apologize for his town. "This is a nice place, Skagway. We're nice people. Our biggest problem used to be potheads. And what problem were they? None. Too lethargic to bother anyone. But these people, they're like animals."

Crack. Meth. Ice, Ecstasy. All the hard-core drugs were seeping into even the smallest communities, and the seep always turned septic. I was a little surprised the epidemic had reached this remote area, but as the Ketchikan mortician pointed out, the Internet was even offering tutorials on the sexual thrills of choking.

"And *you* caught him!" He opened his arms again, still ready for that hug. "For you, anything in the store, twenty percent off."

I glanced around, not for jewelry. For Vinnie. The girl, Cheyenne, sat in a chair behind the counter, holding an ice bag to her right elbow. She looked impossibly sad. Marcus was wiping down the stolen goods, polishing them with a chamois cloth—and ignoring me.

"May I speak to you in private?" I asked.

"Then thirty percent." He closed his arms; with that discount, no hug.

"Thank you. Really. But I need to speak with you."

He led me down the counter, then around the corner where he disappeared earlier. It was a small space, a compact workshop with the tangy smoke scent of soldering metals. The planks on the floor were old and a foot wide, probably logged from the forest just beyond the back door.

"The man in here earlier, when I left—?" I pointed to my forehead.

"Yes, yes." He nodded. "Here when the thief struck."

"Right. He gave you something to look at."

He immediately stiffened. I smiled, trying to keep him open.

"A blue stone, it looked beautiful."

The merchant quickened. "You're interested in it?"

"It was such a lovely stone. Do you have it?"

He struggled to size me up. "I might be able to get it back."

"It's gone?"

He waved his small hand, disgusted. "He wanted an astronomical sum, then refused to let me research its background. That large? It could be synthetic. Though I must say, I didn't see any manufacturing tags."

"Do you know what it was?"

"Benitoite." He waved the hand again. "Or so he claimed. But that's another reason I wondered if it was fake."

"Why?"

"Benitoite, that large…" He paused, calculating again. "But if you're interested in something like that, I have a marvelous specimen of alexandrite and with your thirty percent discount, we could possibly work something out. Why don't you come with me, Marcus can show you…"

"Where've you been?" Jack stood at the edge of the film set, arms crossed, feet planted. The posture of a security guard.

"I was playing cops and robbers."

That morning's shoot was in the atrium, which was empty because most passengers had taken the Whitehorse Yukon steam train over the pass. The train ride took most of the day; I knew because my mother and I were supposed to be on it, marveling at the wooden trestles and mountains and scenery we might never see again.

"Did you get the bracelet?" he asked.

I nodded and told him it was in the purser's safe. I wasn't taking chances. "How's Milo—sober?"

"'Functioning' would be more accurate."

Sitting in a wingback chair in the middle of the atrium, Milo stared at nothing in particular. Behind him Vinnie guarded the elevator doors and walked around the table where my aunt and Claire had set up their crystals. When he picked up the small white cards, explaining each stone's powers, the mansard brow made Vinnie look like a remedial reader.

"Mr. Bodyguard has a blue stone that looks like the one from the jewelry box." I told Jack about the morning adventure in law enforcement. "Vinnie told the jeweler the gem was something called benitoite."

"Hold on," Jack said. "You took out the back tire? *Nice shot.*"

My eyes stayed on Vinnie. With his bloated sense of menace he was scowling at a passenger coming out of the elevator—in a wheelchair. Vinnie eyed the old guy as a potential terrorist.

"He didn't want the jeweler looking into the purchasing background either."

"What about our stolen gems records?" Jack asked.

"I just called." On my way back to the ship, I left a message with the mineralogy lab in DC. Due to the time change, it was Saturday afternoon back East, but I left a message for the forensic geologist, Nettie Labelle. "We might hear back, but I can't count on it."

"All right, go find the Dutchman," Jack said. "I'll keep an eye on Vinnie. If your cell phone rings, don't even answer. Just start running."

A block of Dutch ice escorted me down the hallway of Deck Fourteen, past the steward who lifted stacks of white towels from his housekeeping cart. When Geert paused, pre-

tending to read from the papers in his hand, the steward went
inside the open cabin two doors down. Quickly the head of
security inserted his master key, opening the cabin at the
top of our list.

As a second thought, I reached back, grabbing trash bags
from the cart.

But the cabin was spotless. "Has the steward been in here?"

"Stupid question." Geert pointed to a dollar bill, pinned
to the desk by a drinking glass. A tip.

But the bill told me other things. Vinnie Pinnetta was a
compulsive neat freak. Under the dollar, he'd left a note requesting a clean blanket, clean duvet, and a new pillow. "Not
pillowcase," he wrote. "Pillow." Underlining the word.

"Will he get all new bedding?"

Geert looked offended, the white eyebrows shooting up.

"I'm saying, a new pillow seems extravagant." I checked
the closet and the trash can in both the living area and bathroom. I ran my hands under the mattress and looked beneath
the desk. No jewelry box. No jewels.

"What happens to the pillow?" I asked.

"It goes to laundry. Customer says it is dirty, it is dirty."

I took both pillows off the twin bed and stuffed them into
the plastic bags from the steward's cart.

"You said search," Geert said. "Not take. I have enough
worries without you taking our property."

They were nice pillows. Airy and fluffy, full of down
feathers. Maybe small eiderdown feathers, the kind the coroner found inside Judy Carpenter's cheek. "If you want to
worry, worry about somebody else dying on this ship."

He twirled the mustache. "Help yourself."

Standing on the bed, I ran my hands over the curtains. The
sun continued its valiant battle with the clouds, and the water
was a pewter stage with bright spotlights flashing, awaiting the performer. The curtain rod had carved wood finials,

flourishing classical motifs. When I grabbed the finial, the rod came with it.

Geert looked shocked.

"I take it that's not supposed to happen?"

"They are bolted to the wall, for safety."

Lifting the rod, I slid the curtains down to the right and unscrewed the finial. It was a metal rod and hollow, another safety consideration, and when I forced my fingers inside the tube, I felt something like pages in a book. I pulled out what I could. It was a wad of bills. The outer hundred tore but there were more of them. Plenty more. When I held up the money, Geert shook his bald head.

"Now you feel vindicated."

But I didn't. And I couldn't tell him why.

The jewelry box was still missing.

As Geert slipped his master key into the penthouse door, I glanced over my shoulder, checking on the steward. He was five cabins down the hall. When I heard the handle turn, I stepped forward and walked straight into Geert's back.

He didn't budge. I was a fly hitting a bull.

"So good to see you both," he said, speaking to somebody at the door.

My heart thumped. I pressed myself into the wall.

"Were you looking for my son?" the man asked.

"Yaa-aah…" Geert was big, not fast.

"He's not here at the moment." The elder Sparks, the dad.

"No, no, I wasn't looking for him."

I wanted to break into a run. *"Yah"* then *"no"?* Geert plundered on.

"You, I was looking for you. Yah. You are expected at the wine tasting."

"Wine tasting?" Mr. Sparks asked, echoing my own incredulity. "We didn't sign up for a wine tasting."

"No need to sign up," Geert said. "And it is free."

"Free?" The classics teacher applied the Socratic reasoning. "How could it be free?"

"It is only for our best guests. Our loyal passengers. Who stay on board. Who don't take the tours. Yes, they are waiting for you downstairs."

I began inching away, sensing this whole scheme was about to blow wide-open. The search would be over, forever.

"My wife and I are not inclined to drink these days," he said. "Alcohol interferes with her medications. But that was quite thoughtful. Thank you."

He closed the door. Geert turned, looking for me. I was already heading for the exit and checking my watch: 10:22. We would dock in Seattle in less than twenty-four hours. And then a killer would walk free.

"I've got to get inside that cabin," I told him.

"Neen." He shook his head. "What do you Americans say? 'It is how the cookie crumbles.'"

"No," I said, "The American saying is, 'It ain't over 'til it's over.' You've got to get me into that cabin, one way or another."

THIRTY-FIVE

On Deck Three, where I could hear the laundry room's massive folding machines *thwhack*ing away, a woman named Viola stood in the maid's changing room and tried to teach me how to knot an apron.

"No bow." She untied my second attempt. Her brown fingers were dry and chapped from cleaning. Whipping the white tails, she magically produced a Windsor knot.

I offered her the white cap, the last item for the uniform.

"No necesario," she said.

"Sí necesario." I handed her bobby pins. "Por favor."

With a baffled shrug, she placed the cap on my head, then tried to get me to pull back my hair. It hung around my shoulders, draping my face, but I insisted on leaving it. Very necesario. When she had the hat secured, Viola gazed at my appearance and stifled a giggle.

"Gracias," I said, picking up the vacuum cleaner.

In the hallway, Geert leaned against the riveted steel wall. A granite boulder of hostility, he led me to the service elevator where I slid my mom's reading glasses on my nose. The world rippled like a waterfall.

I let the glasses drift down, peering over the rims. "Does housekeeping get trained in tying knots?"

The mustache twitched, perhaps from the temptation to

say it was a stupid question. But he didn't say it, because he was probably thinking the same thing. Judy Carpenter's death required inside help. It was difficult to imagine one passenger, even two, pulling off such a complicated killing, leaving almost no trace behind.

But the head of security said nothing as we rode the staff-only elevator up to Deck Six and walked twenty feet down the Highway to another staff-only elevator. Geert keyed it into service—there were no buttons—and we rode up to Deck Fourteen, nonstop. The elevator smelled faintly of refuse, that sweet soupy scent, and opened at the midway between fore and aft. Geert did not get out.

"Walk to the right," he ordered, holding the door for my vacuum. "Cross to the passenger elevators. Find the steward. His name is Manuel. He keeps his mouth shut. He tells no one nothing. On this ship he is a lonely man, but he gets the best tips."

"How much does Manuel know?"

"He knows you are a worthless waitress. We are moving you out of the restaurant." He ran his blue eyes over my hat. "And you look rejected. Other girls refuse to wear such a ridiculous hat."

The elevator closed and I pushed the glasses to midbridge, squinting. For once I was grateful my mother was paranoid. She thought half-frame reading glasses were a diabolical conspiracy to keep the world out of focus. Her own reading glasses were enormous, the heavy black frames covering nearly a third of my face. My eyes were watering and a headache was already forming between my brows.

Two doors from the penthouse, the stocky steward was unwrapping bars of soap and stacking them in a column on his cart. The air was floral and alkaline.

I blinked away tears in my eyes. "Manuel?"

"Sí." He pointed the naked soap bar at an open cabin door. "Vamanos."

My mother's glasses made the navy-blue carpet look like a furling flag. I pushed the vacuum like a blind man's cane into the cabin, which didn't belong to any of the movie people. Following directions, I started cleaning. Manuel came in twice, told me what I was doing wrong, and as I was shutting off the vacuum, I heard him in the hallway.

He was calling out, "Stew-ward."

I adjusted my silly cap for the dozenth time, stabbing my scalp again with bobby pins, and rubbed the spot between my brows where the headache pounded.

"Stew-ward," Manuel repeated, in his broken English.

I stepped into the hallway. The penthouse door swung open. Dropping my head, I stared down at the vacuum, feeling the white hat slide forward.

"Our mirrors are streaked," Larrah Sparks said. "Are you cleaning them?"

"Sí," Manuel said. "Sí, I clean."

"Then clean them better. It looks like I'm standing in the fog."

Leaving the door open, she sauntered across the large cabin. My head was still down but I stole a glance at Manuel. His deep brown eyes looked at me. We had a common enemy now: Slave Driver Barbie.

I lifted the spray bottle that was hooked to the pocket of my apron. "I'll clean the mirrors."

He took several fresh white rags from the cart, handing them to me, and I pushed the vacuum into the penthouse. My chin nearly touched my chest, sending my hair forward to cover my face. I followed the vacuum into the bedroom. Sheets and blankets hung off the king-size mattress, spilling onto the floor. Larrah Sparks faced the closet, her back to me as she grabbed the bottom of her tight shirt and lifted it over her head.

I made it into the bathroom before the shirt was off.

Twice as large as our bathroom down on humble Deck Five, its mirror was five-foot-square above double sinks. It didn't look streaked. But it was covered with opaque flecks of dried toothpaste, probably from the electric brushes standing in their chargers on the tile counter. I lifted the reading glasses, pushing them up against the cap, and blinked at the impressive collection of cosmetics, creams, and hair tools. Her eyelash curler was plugged into the wall. When I touched the thing, it was warm. Glancing at the door, listening, I picked up the prescription bottles that lined the back of the counter. Ambien, for her. Viagra, for him. Prozac, for both.

"Clean that mirror right or no tip, comprendie?" she called from the bedroom.

I could hear her coming closer. Dropping the glasses to my nose, I rushed to the toilet, spraying it down.

"Did you hear me?" She stood in the bathroom.

I nodded but kept my back to her, meekly wiping down the commode with one of Manuel's rags. After several moments, the shower came on. I took a furtive glance over my shoulder.

She was stark raving naked, flapping a hand in and out of the spray, testing the temperature. I continued wiping down the commode. The air grew moist, hot, and pungent with the ammonia from my spray bottle. I coughed and she started dancing back and forth, kicking up her leg to show off another cute anklet, when I suddenly realized the actress's motivation.

They were in the business of envy. Here was an actress of superficial talent, taking every opportunity for performance, any chance to parade her ripe physique among those less fortunate. In an industry dependent on covetousness and jealousy, maybe I didn't need to worry about being recognized. In Larrah Sparks's mind, the maid wasn't worth an effort of perception. The maid was a faceless worker bee, existing only to shuttle honey to Slave Driver Barbie.

Perfect.

When she climbed into the shower, pulling the curtain and starting to sing, I walked out of the room. My mother's glasses were fogged and I let them slip down my nose. Plugging in the vacuum, I peeked into the living area. Manuel squatted in the kitchenette, wiping down the cabinets. Sparks's parents were gone.

I turned on the vacuum and pushed it over to the bureau. I slid out each drawer, looking through the clothes. Itty-bitty shirts, short-shorts. Two sweaters. His clothes were utilitarian. T-shirts, white socks, khaki shorts. Jeans. His boxer shorts had that Spartan mascot on them, the one on his baseball cap. When the shower cut off, I closed the last drawer and ran the vacuum across the sandstone-colored carpet, lifting the disheveled bedding. A platform bed, nothing could be hidden underneath.

She was still naked when she came out of the bathroom and said, "Finish cleaning in there."

She never looked at me.

Despite choking on shampoo-scented fog, I closed the door to within an inch of the jamb and shoved the glasses up to my forehead. At the commode, I lifted the back cover, checking the underside. A stretch, but time was short. Nothing was hidden there. Or behind the toilet. I glanced around the room. Wet towels lay on the blue tile floor. I leaned down to pick them up and checked the counter's underside.

Nada. No box.

Hearing her footsteps again, I dropped the towels and grabbed the spray bottle, pointing it at the misty mirror. But I didn't spray.

The mirror was shiny in places, clear of fog.

Then I realized it was lettering. Something had been writ-

ten on the mirror with…soap? Shaving cream? But the residue
had changed the mirror's surface cohesion. The simplest sort
of physics: The tiny water droplets that make fog stick to glass.
But residual "grease" kept the water from beading up. It was
the same principle behind waxing a car so that rain slides off.

I leaned forward, trying to read the letters. Two words, it
looked like. The first letter curved. Like a *C*. The next letter had vertical and horizontal bars. *T*, maybe *I*. The rest was
even less legible and the second word had two clear letters
at the end: *KS*.

"You know this for a fact?" Larrah said, just outside the door.

I pushed the glasses down.

"Yah."

Geert?

I took a clean rag and wiped around the light switch on
the wall, peeking out the door into the bedroom. She wore
a little yellow bikini now, like butter pats over her privates,
and Geert followed her, gazing around the room. Our eyes
met, and one white handlebar twitched. In his hands he carried the black nylon bag used for toting my gun.

She stopped at the closet door, shoving clothes to one side.
I heard a series of electronic beeps and then the unmistakable *pop* of a lock. Larrah stepped back.

I ducked my head back.

"See?" she said. "Ours still works."

"Yah, good, good," Geert replied. "Please confirm everything is there."

I stole another look, wiping down the door frame. She
stood with her back to Geert, taking items from the safe. But
my side angle offered a clear view. She took out her anklets.
A wad of bills.

And blue stones.

"All there," she said.

I ducked back into the bathroom, heart pounding.

"Such relief," Geert replied. "But I have brought fresh batteries, just to be careful."

"You really should do a better job," she said. "This isn't the first time we've had trouble with these things."

"Yah. I understand. I am sorry."

"If something gets stolen because of some screwed up safes, my husband's not going to book another boat ride with you people."

"That is why I am here. I will make the problems go away, even before they happen."

"How about them not happening at all?"

Their voices faded as they moved out of the room. I turned to the counter and dug through the leather shaving kit. Minoxidil hair regrowth, extra bottle of Viagra, spare contact lenses, night-bite guard—Sandy ground his teeth—and with the toothpaste, a plastic bag. The surface was wrinkled and filmed with gunk.

But inside, the moonstone glowed like a white orb. Opening the bag, I held the purple crystal to the light. The edges showed a distinctive red tinge, amethyst, most likely. There were also several translucent white stones—quartz, calcite, perhaps—and some blue crystals that looked like glass. At the very bottom, I found three black stones polished to high shine.

Cut into prisms.

"And I want *all* new towels, even the ones we didn't use," she called from the bedroom.

I shoved the plastic bag into the shaving kit, yanked down my glasses, and picked up the spray bottle.

"And that mirror better be—"

She came around the corner. My hair draped like curtains over my face and she watched as I lacquered the mirror with the ammonia and rubbed the surface clean.

"That's more like it." She turned her back to me, walking away.

I wiped the mirror, watching the ghost lettering disappear.

THIRTY-SIX

In the maids' changing room, I pulled on my jeans and re-clipped the phone to my belt. It was buzzing with unanswered messages.

Three calls from DeMott, all within the last hour. The fourth call was from Jack—a text message warning me that Larrah left the set early.

Yes, thanks.

And a fifth call was area code 703. Quantico, Virginia.

The FBI had moved its mineralogy lab from the downtown DC headquarters to Quantico, adding the geologists to the other forensic technicians already there. The smallest portion of the lab, mineralogy was usually the last in line for everything, from new equipment to new spaces. But we did get a new geologist, a soil scientist named Nettie Labelle. I worked with her in December, when she helped pinpoint some obscure chemical compounds. I found her resolute, precise, adamant—and without one worry about being right. She only cared if her facts were right. That was crucial in a scientist. I pulled on the rest of my clothes and returned her call. It was near noon in Alaska, so almost 4:00 PM in Virginia.

"Labelle, mineralogy."

"It's Raleigh."

"Hey, how's it going?" She didn't wait for a reply, as usual. "We don't keep records for private gems that get stolen."

"I know that."

"I know you know," Nettie said. "But your message wasn't clear and I had to conclude that you wanted me to check the NCIC records."

"I'm sorry, that's what I meant. It's been a chaotic morning." The federal database for crime information, The National Crime Information Center, linked to state records. "See if anything pops up for California. In particular Hollywood or LA."

"Will do. And if you go online, you'll find the records for stolen gems are linked to the mineral descriptions. Dipyramidal Wulfenite, there's the picture."

"When did this happen?"

"Just something I've been working on."

I closed the locker. "How many minerals did you link up?"

"About six thousand. Why are you laughing?"

Because I remembered those days, when the microscope, some geology, and a crime to solve meant a perfect day. Back in my early twenties, back before death hunkered down to teach me about life. "Do you happen to know anything about benitoite?"

"That's why you're asking about California?"

"Why do you say that?"

"Benitoite is California's state gem."

I waited a moment. I'd never even heard of benitoite. "How do you know that?"

"Don't feel bad," she said, sounding superior. "It is *sort of* obscure."

"Nettie?"

"Okay, I memorized all the state gems. In alphabetical order. Alaska is jade. Arizona is turquoise, Arkansas is diamond, California is benitoite. You want me to go on?"

I opened the door. A group of women came in, all speaking Spanish, but they fell silent when they saw me. The hallway was crowded with more employees coming on and going off, some noon shift change. "Hang on," I told Nettie, walking down to the elevators. Standing in a quiet alcove, I described the powerful florescence and the black prism.

"Blue could be benitoite," she said. "Black? No."

"How do you know?"

"It's bugging you, isn't it? Me knowing and you not?"

"Nettie, just tell me."

"Nope. You're a geologist, find out for yourself. Can you get to a computer?"

"Not a secure one." The ship had Internet access, but I had avoided it for security reasons.

"Doesn't need to be secure. Check the UCal records for benitoite. You won't regret it."

I sighed. There was no arguing with the woman. "But you're checking the NCIC for stolen benitoite, right?"

"If you'd let me get off the phone," she said, hanging up.

I was still holding my cell phone when the elevators opened to the medical clinic. I was trying to decide why DeMott would call three times in an hour. Maybe something happened. Maybe Madame, my mom's dog, was hurt.

The phone rang at Weyanoke. And rang. Then rang some more. As I listened, growing more concerned, I also got more annoyed with DeMott. He refused to carry a cell phone and his antiquated attitude was another reminder of how life played out on that plantation, the days and nights scarcely changed since Robert E. Lee danced the Virginia reel in the ballroom. By the twelfth ring, when I was feeling that old Weyanoke suffocation—*they didn't even want an answering machine*—his sister MacKenna picked up.

"Hi, Mac. I'm returning DeMott's calls. Is anything wrong?"

I wasn't exactly MacKenna's favorite person. Not that I

blamed her. I'd already managed to delay her wedding, get her father investigated for tax evasion, and put her fiancé on the FBI's domestic terrorism watch list. And we weren't even related yet.

There was a loud *thunk*, followed by silence, leaving me to guess that she had either gone to get DeMott or was literally going to leave me hanging. Waiting to find out which, I leaned against the wall outside the medical clinic and listened to the background noise in the phone. Music was playing. Voices. A girl laughed.

When DeMott answered, he was out of breath.

"Raleigh, is that you? Hey. How's it going?"

"You sound winded."

"Oh. Yeah. Well. Mac… Mac's throwing a party." He cleared his throat, mumbled something.

"Pardon?"

"It's just for some old friends, back in town."

It was something in his voice. Something tentative. False. I'd known DeMott Fielding since grade school and one of the things I most admired was that he was a terrible liar. "Who's back in town?" I asked casually.

"Oh, just old friends."

"So you said. Anyone in particular?"

He rattled off some names, Flynn Wellington among them. She lived on a neighboring plantation. But Flynn, like the other names he offered, was local. DeMott saw them often. And it was only as he continued down the list that he tucked one name in among the regulars. "And John Coker and Tinsley Teeger and—"

Tinsley. Beautiful scheming Tinsley. My classmate at St. Catherine's school, she was a bright blond bombshell who blew out of Richmond right after graduation, headed for Manhattan. She sold high-market real estate and from eighth grade on, she'd carried a torch for DeMott.

"Tinsley," I said, feeling something acidic at the back of my throat. "Didn't she get married?"

"How's vacation?"

I turned, staring into the glass doors of the medical clinic. Nurse Stephanie had found her broom and ridden back to work. "It's great," I said. "Everything's great. I thought Tinsley married that guy from Dartmouth?"

"Mmm. They got divorced. And your mom's having a good time?"

"Oh, super. Just super." Tinsley comes back in town, a free girl. Mac throws a party. Conveniently, I was gone. That knife named jealousy nicked my heart. I could hear the music playing in the background. The words were muddy but there was no missing the slow beat, the crooning in a love song. I stared through the clinic's glass doors. The elderly woman staying with her sick husband came out of their room and spoke with Nurse Stephanie, her tired face full of tender worries. "DeMott, is something wrong?"

"Wrong? No. Nothing's wrong. I just…"

"What?"

"I just wanted to hear your voice. I feel like…"

I waited. "Like what?"

"I feel like you're a million miles away and never coming back."

The woman inside the clinic nodded, thanking the nurse and walking back to her husband's room. My heart ached. I didn't like his structured life, his stringent family of snobs, but were those good enough reasons to throw away love? Wasn't it when circumstances got difficult that love showed its true colors? Like the couple in the clinic. Like my parents. True love was never easy.

"I'm sorry." The words struggled out, strangled in my throat. "I've been so busy—"

"Busy? Raleigh, you're on vacation."

"DeMott, listen—"

"Or maybe you mean you're busy with that guy who answers your phone."

"Please listen. I'm working. On a case."

"You can't stop. All you do is work. You can't even take a vacation—without your fiancé."

"Right now is not a good time, DeMott."

"It's never a good time. When were you planning on telling me?"

"Telling you what?"

"About that guy. Is he why you didn't want me on that cruise?"

"DeMott, don't do this—"

"Oh, here we go again. Don't pry. Don't bother Raleigh. She needs her privacy. Everything's all bundled up inside." He gave a dry sort of laugh. "You must take me for an idiot."

Every bit of tenderness had evaporated. I felt a bitter resentment climbing up my back and crystallizing around my heart. The words left my mouth before I could stop them. "You want me to open up? Fine. Here it is, DeMott. I work. I work while y'all are lazing around Weyanoke dreaming about the past and throwing parties. I work because I have to make a living. So go on, have a good time, because I'm sure Tinsley is *very* happy to see you. And I'm sure the feeling's mutual."

"I'm going to pretend you didn't say that."

"Of course you are."

"Excuse me?" he asked.

"Life at Weyanoke. One long game of Let's Pretend."

Snapping the phone shut, I stormed into the medical clinic and prayed Nurse Stephanie would pick a fight so I could rip her head off. But as if to annoy me further, she politely dabbed at her mouth with a paper napkin. A bowl of chicken soup waited on the desk. She used the napkin to point at my mother's room. "The doctor's with her," she said. "Don't g[e] anywhere."

Behind the door, his Irish brogue was lilting through [a] series of casual statements that disguised probing questions The same tactic FBI agents used with reluctant witnesses.

"Hard to believe tomorrow we'll be back on land," he ven— tured.

No reply.

"They say it's been raining in Seattle. I don't care muc[h] for the rain. It's why I left my family back in Ireland."

He kept on. But there was only silence. When finally h[e] stepped from the room and saw me, he gestured silently an[d] I followed him to the room where I spent last night.

He closed the door. "What're your plans?" he asked.

"After tomorrow? We go back to Virginia."

He wore a somber expression, that distillation of Irish mel— ancholy, the face that says, *It will be a struggle until the en[d] of days.*

"Why do you ask?" I asked.

"There's a doctor, he works with the Washington stat[e] facility."

"Facility?"

"Lassie, I've given your mother enough tranquilizers t[o] drop the draught horse in green sod."

"Then take her off them."

He opened his arms, looking almost helpless. "She need[s] help."

"Yes, but not from some *facility* run by the state."

He drew his hands over the cumulus of white hair. "Sh[e] can't get on an airplane."

"I've thought of that. We can stay in Seattle for a few days My aunt lives there. Soon as she's better, we'll go home t[o] Virginia."

"And who'll watch over her night and day, you? Rising with both the roosters and the owls?" He shook his head. "They'll bring the vehicle right to the dock."

"Thank you for your concern. I appreciate it. But we don't need the *facility*."

His hands went into the pockets of his white officer's uniform. "That stubbornness of yours, 'tis done you some good in your life, I'm certain. But now it's not. Your mother's had a psychotic break. She's as sick as I've seen in twenty-four years practicing medicine."

"It's the ship." I could feel the headache from her reading glasses, pounding with new force. "As soon as we're off this ship, she's going to feel better."

He shook his head. "I wish it were so. But we walk beside walls, all of us. You're getting a good look at yours. It's your mother. And that wall 'tis made of stone."

The headache moved down to my neck, my shoulders. I was suddenly very tired and sat down on the bed. "How long?" I asked. "How long do you think she needs?"

"Walls are odd things," he said. "Nobody knows how far they go. But you're not close to the end."

"How long?" I repeated.

"It's not days. And not weeks."

"Months?"

He gave a noncommittal nod.

"Then I'll find her help in Virginia."

"Can you?"

"Of course."

"She's afraid of you. You want her breaking down on the plane?"

"I've already considered that and I'm looking for another way to get home. I can rent a nurse, buy her a plane ticket, whatever it takes."

"Lassie, you might get your mother home," he said, "but I've seen people not come back."

His words hovered in the air between us, gathering their full meaning.

On the upper deck, Jack stood with his back to the rail. The steady wind that blew into Skagway ran its fingers through his hair, tousling it like a boy's. Above him the sun continued to burn through the clouds, illuminating a lush green valley between the mountains.

"You look like somebody died," Jack said.

The movie crew had set up tarps for windbreaks across the deck. The plastic sheets rippled in the wind, sounding like distant thunder, and the extras were scattered as if directed by that same wind. Vinnie stood scowling at a lone passenger who was getting some exercise by walking laps around the deck; he forced her to turn around. I didn't see Aunt Charlotte anywhere. Or Claire. But to the port side Sandy Sparks conferred with his new director whose blond ponytail filled with the wind, looking like a dandelion blossom.

"Sparks is keeping some interesting stones in his safe," I told Jack. "And in his shaving kit."

"His what?"

"His safe, in his room."

"No, the other thing."

"Shaving kit."

"Harmon, what did you—?"

"I didn't take anything. Geert sent me in, dressed as a maid. They've got blue stones in the safe. And some others are in his shaving kit."

"Some other what?"

"Amethyst, I think. Moonstone. Maybe jet and cut glass."

"Hey, scientist, bring it down to my level."

"The amethyst might be worth some money. Not a lot but

not chump change either. And definitely not something you keep with toiletries."

Sandy Sparks was pointing toward his wife. In her butter-pat bikini, Larrah stood shivering, though the cold wind wasn't enough to keep her from another opportunity to display her figure. She was a striking sight, and only one person wasn't watching her: Milo. He leaned against the ship's smokestack wall, his skin as green as pool water. In his hand, he held a silver flask.

"What scene is this?" I asked. "She's supposed to be the bartender."

"Beats me. I'm guessing it's something the new director dreamed up."

"And how's Milo?"

Jack sighed. I couldn't remember ever hearing him sigh. "I quit trying to keep Milo sober. Like teaching an octopus to run." His blue-green eyes stared at me, evaluating. "I expect the full answer to this question. How did you get into his safe?"

"Geert showed up." I explained the Dutchman's story and how he told Larrah that some safes had been compromised due to failing batteries. "Apparently, it happens. When the batteries fail, the safe suddenly pops open automatically."

"The crazy Dutchman's on our side?"

"I wouldn't say that. He wants the bracelet to save his job. But he's starting to realize something's not right with these people." I described the money hidden in Vinnie's room. "Vinnie's also got a big blue stone, just like the Sparks have in their safe, and Martin Webb had in his jackets, and your buddy Milo—"

"Milo is not my buddy."

"All of them, Jack. They're all hiding these stones."

He watched them for several minutes. Milo was swigging from the flask. Larrah looked cold as a popsicle. And Sparks had taken a seat behind the windbreak, pulling on a jacket that had that same Spartan mascot on it.

Jack said, "I don't suppose you found the jewelry box."

I shook my head.

"Too much to hope for." He sighed again. "Short black dress, white apron?"

"Pardon?"

"Your maid's outfit. Was it a short black dress with a white apron? C'mon, Harmon, I need some cheering up."

I grabbed my phone, flipping it open.

"You're reporting me for harassment?" he asked.

"No, I'm calling Kevin Barnes. I just thought of something." I kept my eyes on Vinnie, still scowling at the wind. "The forehead might've tried to unload stones in Juneau. Maybe even some black prisms."

Kevin Barnes's voice mail said he was often away for days and usually somewhere so remote he was unable to return phone calls. Must be nice, I decided, leaving him a message anyway, asking him to call immediately.

"Now what?" Jack asked.

"Now you can call the jewelry stores in Ketchikan and see if Vinnie tried to sell them anything."

"Me? I'm busy." He placed a hand on his chest. "I've got a movie star to babysit. Why can't you call the stores?"

"Because tonight's our last chance."

"Harmon, I've waited a long time to hear you say that."

"Keep waiting. Tonight's our last chance to catch these people."

Hardcover books lined the library walls, but since they were locked behind stabilizing doors, the computers seemed like the most important part of the room. At a desk by the window, a woman was typing on a keyboard. She looked up as I came into the room, then acknowledged me with a sad smile. The elderly woman from the medical center. I nodded and she returned to typing, using only her index fingers.

I sat down across the room from her and searched public domain information only, quickly realizing why benitoite escaped my radar. Not only was the mineral rare, but in terms of geologic time, it was discovered last week.

In 1907 some California prospectors were searching the Diablo Mountain Range for gold when they stumbled across some blue rocks, randomly distributed around the headwaters of the San Benito River. The stones looked like sapphires and the prospectors carried them quietly into town, to a geology professor at the University of California. The geologist found the gemstone was a silicate mineral containing traces of barium and titanium. Beautiful, stunning, and there was nothing else like it on earth. The geologist named it benitoite, for the location where it was found in San Benito County, near the San Benito River.

Although some later geochemical matches were found in places such as Japan and Australia, gem-quality benitoite still came from only one tiny region in the California mountains. And even there, benitoite played hard to get.

Only a few thousand carats had been mined, cut, and polished. By the 1970s the mines were basically abandoned because so few gemstones came out, making benitoite rarer than rubies and emeralds—by several orders of magnitude. It was even rarer than Tanzanite, the bright blue gem found only in Tanzania. When an earthquake struck the Coalinga fault line in the 1980s, hitting 6.7 on the Richter scale, prospectors poured into the Diablo mountains, hoping the hills had shaken loose their benitoite. But the mountains refused to cooperate and these days rock hounds had resorted to night searches, clamping on ultraviolet headlamps to expose the gem's singular quality: powerful fluorescence.

Mineralogically, benitoite was what was called a dichroic

mineral, meaning the color shifted depending on the type and angle of light. It was also birefringent, with a "fire" more powerful than diamonds. Colorless varieties had been found, along with some pink and orange specimens, but those were considered even rarer than the blue specimens. Geologists attributed benitoite's changing color to small inclusions of yet another rare mineral, Neptunite.

Neptunite was pitch black.

Under ideal conditions, it grew into perfect prisms.

Leaning back in my chair, considering all the information, I watched the woman from the medical center stand up. She gathered a sweater off the back of the chair, then looked around as if forgetting something. The back of my mind seemed to tingle, as if an idea was forming yet still out of reach.

I watched the woman walk across the library, into the empty atrium. Standing alone at the elevators, she waited for the descent back to the medical clinic, back to her ailing spouse, a trip where they had not been able to venture beyond the ship. As she watched the numbers above the elevator door, her back was straight, her chin raised. And in her defiant posture, I took all the hope it offered.

"The magistrate already called me about it," Kevin Barnes was saying. "Something about a blue rock?"

I shifted the phone to my other ear, leaving the library and heading for the purser's office. "Why did the magistrate call you?"

"Because his wife runs a jewelry store in town. Some guy walked in, asked her to buy a blue rock, and she told her husband the guy gave her the creeps. He called me but I haven't had a chance to call him back."

"That didn't seem urgent to you?"

"Raleigh, we get ten thousand people walking off those

cruise ships every single day from May to September. You're lucky she even saw the rock."

"I don't believe in luck."

"Why should you?" he said. "You're working with Jack."

"Did the magistrate say anything else about the guy who came in?"

"Heavy."

"He was fat?"

"No. Heavy, as in, heavyweight. A guy who breaks knee-caps. That's all I got."

"That's more than you know," I said, stopping near the concierge desk. A man and woman were talking to the clerk. I turned my back, speaking low into the phone. "Anything from your LA contacts?"

"No. And now it's the weekend."

"If by some miracle you talk to them, see if they have any local information on a guy named Sandy Sparks, aka Ly-sander Sparks. And the 'heavy' is named Vinnie Pinnetta."

Kevin asked me to spell the names, stumbling over "Ly-sander." Then he asked, "When do you need this by?"

"Yesterday," I said.

Pink tights. Red sweatshirt. Fuchsia fleece. The yellow raincoat. It was all flung across the twin beds in my cabin while Andes flute music tooted, every note poking my brain like a sharp stick, reigniting the headache. But the pain was nothing compared to the agony of seeing Claire's attempt at dancing. She was humming that weird sound, trying to har-monize with the puffing whistles.

"Do you feel it?" she asked.

"I feel something."

"Darkness, death. But I'm getting some answers from be-yond."

I didn't have the time—or interest—to deal with her. I

opened the closet, grabbed my clothes and suitcase, including the titanium case.

"I was wondering what that was for," she said, staring at the rock kit. "It looks top secret."

"How could you even see it? It was inside my suitcase."

"Well, I..."

"You were snooping."

She shook her head, the asbestos spikes of hair not moving. "I'm a clairvoyant, I saw it in my mind's eye."

"In a pig's eye." I lowered my voice, threatening. "If you touch anything that belongs to me or my mom, I'll turn you in for those parking tickets."

She gasped. "You know?"

"I know a lot of things, Claire. And I don't make idle threats." Carrying my things into my aunt's cabin, I slammed the door and twisted the lock. I set the rock kit on the desk, closed the curtains, slipped on sunglasses and latex gloves, and took out the bracelet retrieved from the purser's safe. Turning off the lights, I flicked on the shortwave lamp.

I pulled the bracelet closer.

Then I shook it.

Then I brought it so close the blue stones touched the lamp's bulb.

No glow. No fluorescence. And I stood in the eerie dark, trying to wrap my brain around the new order of things.

This wasn't the bracelet.

This was fake.

Who switched them, the pilot? But the FBI's evidence tape was intact on the package. And where would the pilot get a fake that fast? Larsen, our airport liaison?

No way.

In Claire's room little birds had started tweeting on the CD player, making me wish I had my gun. Flicking on the lights, I unplugged the lamp and took off the sunglasses. Picking up the jeweler's loupe, I examined every millimeter of the bracelet under twenty-times magnification.

Definitely not the same stones.

If these even were stones. More likely, dyed glass. Plain old silica. As I turned the bracelet back and forth, the bracelet looked attractive, not cheap. But nobody in their right mind would kill for this thing.

And that ruined my whole plan.

THIRTY-SEVEN

"All right, all right," said the man opening the chapel's heavy door. "I'm here. I'm here."

The wedding was over and the white chairs were folded and put away, leaving the room with a dim and dusty odor, a tired scent, like stuffed animals left on high shelves their entire lives.

"What did you need to talk about?" he asked, walking down the aisle toward me. "What was it again?"

Lanky except for a potbelly that made him look like he'd stuffed a volleyball under his black shirt, the chaplain was trying to smile. Bloated jowls hung over the Nehru collar.

"Reverend Dennis?" I asked, making sure.

"Please, call me Den." He sat on the carpeted platform, crossing his legs, directly under the stained glass medallion.

I sat down beside him and he smiled. A reflexive gesture. Like my official FBI smile.

"So. What did you want to talk about?" he asked.

"My mother," I said. "The ship's doctor, Dr. Coleman? He believes she suffered a psychotic break. She's in the medical clinic, sedated. And I can't talk to her." I paused. "She *won't* talk to me, but I thought she might talk to you, since you're a chaplain."

"Okay, okay." He nodded, graying hair brushing the black collar. "Is this the woman who broke down in here?"

I nodded. "She was praying and then—"

He tossed his thumb over his shoulder, pointing at the medallion. "The cross got knocked down. That one?"

So it did happen. MJ wasn't lying. "You heard about that?"

"Oh yeah. The ship thought I'd be upset. The cross was pretty broken up. But I said, hey, it's just a religious symbol." He nodded again, agreeing with his own wisdom. "And your mom's the one yanked it off the wall? She must be strong for her age."

"No, sir. Different incident."

"*Man.*"

"Pardon?"

"Man, oh, man." His hand rubbed the round stomach, circling its contours. "Two really bad happenings. What's up with that?"

His brown eyes, almost circular in shape, went perfectly with the jowls and belly. With the shaggy hair, he reminded me of a strange teddy bear. Youthful yet graying. Enthusiastic and still lethargic. Well-fed, still malnourished.

"Perhaps you could reassure her," I ventured.

"Right, reassure her."

"She's a strong believer. If you could let her know she's going to be okay. Remind her that God's in control."

"And hey, look around. This is God's country."

"Yes, except she can't look around. The medical clinic has no windows."

"Oh. Got it. Okay, got it."

"Her strongest foundation is her faith but—"

"But you want me to build on that. Build it up. Make something of it."

I wasn't sure what to say and in the silence he stole a glance at his wristwatch.

"Sir, I don't mean to offend, but…" I struggled for the correct words.

"Hey, no offense taken. That's what this room is for, non-judgmental release. Like when I heard about the cross getting knocked down. I thought, We're probably better off. Crosses tend to really bum people out."

A second silence followed. He gave the watch another glance.

Dinner, I decided.

That was the hurry. His next cream-sauced meal and nice bottle of red, followed by coffee and cognac and conversation with people from Arkansas. What a great gig, what a cozy way to shepherd a flock. A parish that revolves weekly, requiring only one sermon, endlessly recycled every Sunday through the Inside Passage or the Mexican Riviera, the Bahamas, Australia. At worst, two sermons, for when the cruise lasted fourteen days. A riff on Jonah, the whale. And something about Noah, because we're on an ark. Ha-ha holiness, pass the potatoes, please.

He stood up, shaking out his legs as if he'd been sitting a long time. "Right after dinner, I'll go see her. Right after dinner."

Maybe that was why he said everything twice, the recycled pabulum a habit now.

I stood up with him. "On second thought, before you go to any trouble, let me check with her doctor. I want to make sure your visit is okay with him."

His muddy brown eyes showed their first hint of depth. Relief poured into them. Pure relief. Visiting a wounded sheep like my mother could cause all-night indigestion. Shaking my hand, the reverend told me good-bye twice and left the room, letting the heavy wooden door close behind him.

I felt too tired to walk.

Sitting down again, elbows on my knees, the fatigue weighted my shoulders and rolled down my spine. My mind filled with hard thoughts, uncharitable thoughts. Cold notions about sterile seminaries and simplistic sermons and Christian clichés. Angry, disgusted, betrayed by the over-fatted calf who had waltzed in here, refusing the sacrifice that might taint his next meal.

Dropping my head, I tried to evict him from my mind. Plucking the bitter seeds from my heart, I thought about a veil torn in two, a vacant tomb offering me the right to speak directly to God. No minister was needed to sieve my petition, though all I had to give right now was sadness and humiliation.

And that was enough.

Even in this dark moment, I knew there was light, somewhere.

Somewhere, light was shining.

I opened my eyes, suddenly, gasping at the idea.

Light.

Of course. That was it.

The lights.

With nineteen minutes left before the ship pulled out of Skagway, I ran down the gangway and sprinted across the dock. Wind at my back, I raced around the Whitehorse Yukon train station, then turned down Broadway. The streets were deserted, the boardwalks waiting for some shootout to begin. Hanging a fast right, I whipped open the door to the hardware store.

The man behind the cash register stared, slowly chewing his gum.

"Hi," he said.

"Hi," I panted. "Black lights, you carry them?"

He nodded and ambled from the cash register. I danced on my toes behind his dusty denim overalls, wanting him to shuffle faster down the wide-planked floor. I checked my watch. *Fourteen minutes. And they would leave without me.*

The man had no hurry in him. Staring at a small lighting display near the spools of chain and fishing lines, he pointed to one shelf, then another. "I know we got some somewhere."

"Yes, where?"

"Ah." He pointed to the lowest shelf. "There."

I saw rows and stacks of white boxes with small UPC labels. "I don't see any black lights."

"In there, somewhere. You want flood or reg'lar?"

"Both."

He nodded, chewing. "I figured. How many?"

"All you've got."

He stopped chewing. "I knew it. You're the new health inspector?"

"Pardon?"

"Don't worry. I won't say anything. You can go incognito."

Most crime kits contained a small black light. It was used for investigating body fluids. The proteins within would glow like neon under UV light. A health inspector could use the lights for documenting rat urine.

"You think we got another rodent problem?" he asked.

"Sir, I'm not the health inspector."

He stepped back, curious. "But you still want all the lights?"

"Yes, sir." I took out my wallet. "It's a different kind of rodent problem."

The Ninjas had emptied the Sky Bar, and now the one with the pencil mustache stood on a wooden ladder, screwing purple floodlights into the ceiling above the dance floor. I was standing beside the ladder, still sweating from my run back to the ship.

"You should wait," Geert said. His eyes looked as sharp as blades on ice skates.

I gazed out the window, pretending not to hear him. Sailing

south out of Skagway beneath a sun that had ripped through the clouds with no intention of setting, I finally shook my head.

"Sparks says the party is in the pub," Geert continued. "Put the lights there."

"No."

Tonight at seven, the movie crew would have its wrap party, despite not finishing the movie. It was scheduled for the English Pub, but I wanted it moved to the Sky Bar.

The last place anybody saw Judy Carpenter alive.

"Technical difficulties," I said. "Lack of adequate services. You can think of something."

"I already told him. He is still insisting."

"I'm insisting too." I handed the Ninja another lightbulb. Four floodlights, one 60-watt lightbulb. I bought them all, uncertain which would work for my plan. *If* they worked. "I want those people back in here, just like they were that night." And now they would be standing under black lights that exposed any and all benitoite.

I glanced over at the bar where a second Ninja waited.

"Cover the skylights, please. And windows."

A vibration thrummed across the bright space and the room began to darken. Steel shutters rumbled over the Plexiglas skylights, the picture windows, the clear floor, sealing everything as if a bad storm was battering us at sea. The place was a cave.

"Perfect," I said. "Hit the lights, please."

The Ninja on the ladder, wearing all-black clothing, seemed to disappear. All except his epaulettes. The glowing white shoulders seemed to float in thin air. On the dance floor Geert's white uniform beamed below the handlebar mustache, now shining like the enigmatic smile of the Cheshire Cat.

"And I'd like that same bartender here. Jessie. The one

who worked the night she died. But he'll have to start earlier and stay all night."

"And if Sparks does not go along with this?" Geert asked

"The man loves money. Make him a deal."

"Ach. You think we have unlimited funds?"

"No, but it's cheaper than replacing that bracelet."

The mustache twitched. "You don't even have the right one."

"No, I don't." I smiled, sensing the white glow coming from my teeth. "But tonight I'm going to find out who does."

The nurse on duty in the medical clinic was the nice one. Nurse Shannon. She was writing notes at the desk and checking off names on a list. When she saw me, she picked up the phone and told somebody I was here. When she hung up, I felt something cold at the back of my neck.

"Is she any better?" I asked.

"The doctor wants to speak with you."

I guessed that was who she called. I tried to smile. "May I have some petroleum jelly?"

She looked startled, her large blue eyes growing even larger. "Vaseline?"

"It doesn't matter which brand, but I need about half a cup."

"Half a—what in the world for?"

Again, I smiled. "I need to take it with me."

She hesitated, then closed the folder that she was working on. In the small lab, she opened a locked drawer and squeezed a tube of petroleum jelly into a small plastic bag. When the phone rang at the desk, she handed me the bag. "Don't leave just yet."

She left the room and I took the fake bracelet from my pocket. Depositing it in the petroleum jelly, I kneaded it for several seconds, then put it in my pocket. As I was leaving, the nurse cupped the phone.

"Dr. Coleman wants to speak with you."

"It'll have to wait," I said.

Around 6:30 PM, I walked up the enclosed ramp from the ship's top deck to the modern marvel known as the Sky Bar.

The Bird Girl who'd written the press release about Judy's death waited at the top of the ramp, clutching her ever-present clipboard. The Sky Bar's neon and Plexiglas atmosphere stretched like a space-age landscape behind her, but above that the real sky was cloudless, abraded by the wind, so blue t looked as fine as tourmaline.

"Where do you think you're going?" said the Bird Girl in her flat tone of voice.

But she didn't wait for an answer. Extending a talon, she snatched the white jacket of a passing food service employee. He wore heavy-duty oven mitts and carried a stainless steel bin covered with foil. As she hooked his sleeve, he reeled back, trying to keep the hot container from spilling.

Bird Girl peeled back the foil. "I smell broccoli." She fanned the clipboard over what appeared to be fried rice. In the rising steam, her nose wrinkled. "Broccoli, it's in there. I said no broccoli."

The guy didn't seem to speak English. Glancing over his shoulder, he searched for reinforcements. Nobody was behind him.

"Take it back," she ordered, pointing with the clipboard. "Tell them no broccoli. You hear me?"

He turned automatically and rushed across the room where another peon came, carrying white plates. As the men passed the neon-lit Plexiglas counter, the bartender named Jessie glanced up as if uninterested. I felt a small relief. Not only was he observant, he could be depended on to cover the windows and skylights, darkening the room for the big surprise: black lights over the dance floor. Benitoite black lights. Because these people would recognize the gem. The same way somebody recognized Judy Carpenter's blue bracelet and wanted it so badly, they had a fake made, ready for the switch.

The fake I now had in my pocket to be used like a human fishing lure.

Bird Girl was another problem.

"This is a private party," she said, quirking her head at me. "And you're not invited."

"I'm helping the psychic."

"What?"

I pointed. Claire was wheezing up the ramp, the tails of her bright-yellow sari flapping about her ankles. Once again the third eye peered from her forehead.

"She's reading auras and palms tonight. I'm her assistant." Lifting my arm, I displayed the swath of folded black velvet and a small banker's lamp in my hand. The lamp borrowed from Geert's desk. I called over to the bartender. "Where are we supposed to set up?"

Jessie looked up from slicing the lemons, as if he just noticed me. With the paring knife, he pointed to a card table by the dance floor. As if I didn't know.

Bird Girl still didn't like it. Her brown hair was pulled back in a severe style, revealing dendritic blue veins under pale skin at her temples. She squinted. "Did this get cleared with Sandy?"

"Sandy *asked* her to do the readings. His wife wants her aura read."

The same food service guy was trying to sneak behind her. He was almost tiptoeing, carrying another bin of hot food. But she was uncanny. Without turning her head, she reached out and snatched his arm. As she pulled him toward

her, I grabbed Claire almost the same way and shuttled her
to the card table.

"Raleigh, thanks for helping me out," she said.

I draped the black velvet over the Plexiglas table. When I
went to plug in the lamp, I wondered if God would slay me
on the spot, some deadly electrical shock that I deserved.

"I'll read your aura for free," Claire said.

I glanced out the picture windows. Not yet dusk, the sun
burned deep gold, gilding the rocky peaks. The mountains
stood elegant and cold and looking at them, I felt a heart-
ache similar to what I felt standing beside my father's grave
in Richmond. Those times when I understood the smallness
of my life, the insignificance, and the absolute need to keep
going. No matter what.

I plugged in the light. No deadly shock.

"Claire, I've been rude to you."

It seemed appropriate that she wasn't listening. When I
finally got to the point of making things right, Claire was
on another plane. She stared over my shoulder and I turned
to see Jessie offering me a white plate with two foil packets.

"Some guy ordered this for you," he said.

The first packet contained a cheeseburger with everything
but pickles. The other packet, fries.

"And extra mayo." Jessie set down a ramekin between the
packets. "He said you'd drink a Coke, no crushed ice." He
turned to Claire. "What can I get you? Drinks are free for
anybody with the movie."

"I'm an alcoholic," she said, honestly. Then pointed to her
third eye. "I got sober after I realized I had this special gift."

"Yes," said Jessie, sounding Filipino.

"Large iced tea. Lots and lots of sugar."

I said grace and dove into my burger. Claire stared at my
fries; I pushed them toward her, showing her how to dip them
in mayonnaise. All the while, I shoved back the treasonous

thoughts wandering through my mind. DeMott hated this food. Especially fries with mayo. White trash wonders, he called them. But that wasn't the most treasonous thought.

It was this: *Jack had known exactly what I wanted.*

Somewhere right now, he was with Milo, trying to surreptitiously search the cabin one more time for that jewelry box.

Babysitting a drunk, and he still managed to order me dinner.

Claire had polished off the fries and had closed her eyes, making that weird humming noise. The skin on her forehead wrinkled around the pink stone. I wondered how long I could stand it. Claire's real assistant, my aunt, was coming later. First she was trying to get my mother to eat something.

Claire's eyes opened halfway. "I almost had a heart attack walking up here."

"Sorry."

She pointed with her arm. "How come they get an elevator?"

I swiveled to see what she was talking about. More kitchen employees. They toted the racks of desserts while others pushed large trash cans on wheels. Bird Girl was inspecting the buffet table and coming up the ramp was the Forehead. He walked over to her and I balled up the foil packets, pretending to go throw them away. But as quickly as possible, I headed in the other direction, following the kitchen employees who walked around a back wall. I didn't think Vinnie would throw me out, once the party got started. But before anyone arrived?

On the other side of the wall, inside a tiny alcove, an elevator waited, keyed open. The stainless-steel walls were dented, the embossed metal floor worn from heavy use. And inside a large plastic trash can rested on wheels. I lifted the lid to deposit my trash. The can was perfectly empty, ready for the party, lined with a heavy-duty black plastic bag.

"Get out."

I looked up. Vinnie filled the door.

"Get out," he repeated. "You're not with the movie."

"I'm with the psychic."

"And she's what—working in the elevator?"

I smiled. "She tends to go up and down."

"Get out."

He followed me back to the table. Bird Girl stood with her clipboard talking to Claire, who now had all three eyes open.

"When does Charlotte get here?" asked Bird Girl in her flat tone.

"I'm not sure, want me to read your aura?"

"Do I look like I want you to?"

"No. But that means you really need it."

Narrowing her beady eyes, Bird Girl turned to me. "Sandy says he never invited you."

"What did I tell you?" Vinnie said, smug.

"But I need her help. After a couple readings, my mind starts to fry."

"Yes. But when is Charlotte coming?"

Claire nodded.

Exasperated, Bird Girl looked at me. "The minute Charlotte shows up, you're gone. Understand?"

Claire said, "I think your aura might be black. That's not good."

She turned, walking back to the ramp to stand with Vinnie. He had now positioned himself at the entrance, but kept looking over at me. I glanced at my watch, wondering how long before Aunt Charlotte showed. Not long. Not when my mom thought her food was poisoned.

"Do you think we could ever be friends?" Claire asked abruptly. "I know, I'm not really a normal person. My family always told me that. But I can't help it. All this stuff goes on inside my head. People don't understand how crowded it is up there, nobody gets it. I really wanted to help your mom. I think she's got kind of the same problem." She pointed to her third eye. "Dead people keep talking to me."

Her eyebrows were slanted up, like a snapped teeter-totter, and the crazy asbestos hair looked like it was trying to leap from her troubled mind. And in that moment, I felt pity for her, a woman whose spiritual quest was destined to circle back to hopelessness and despair. She searched without listening. She wanted truth, only if it was convenient. But something bothered me even more. Who was more despicable, Claire the lost soul or the one manipulating her?

"Claire, one day maybe we can be friends."

"Can I read your aura?"

"No." I took a seat at the table and pulled the chain on Geert's lamp. It held the 60-watt black-light bulb. Glancing at Vinnie and Bird Girl, I reached into my pocket. Inside the plastic bag, the bracelet continued its petroleum jelly bath.

"I need a favor, Claire." Keeping my hands under the table, I wiped down the bracelet with a napkin, then held it under the lamp. The glass glowed, almost as good as the real thing. Among its other ingredients, petroleum jelly contained various rare earth phosphors that absorbed ultraviolet radiation and produced blue and green light. I'd just made cheap glow-in-the-dark gems.

"Whoa," Claire said.

"Hold out your wrist." The clasp felt slippery from the jelly. And the bracelet was large. It even slipped over Claire's hand. I tried to recall Judy Carpenter's arms and wrists. She was a big woman...

"Are you giving this to me?" Claire slid her wrist under the lamp, transfixed.

"For the night. I want you to wear it all night."

She was leaning down close, inspecting the glass. "It must have special powers."

But the bracelet wasn't what caught my interest. The pink stone was glowing on her forehead. Glowing just like blue benitoite.

"Claire, where did you get that stone on your forehead?"

She sat up, touching the third eye. "From Charlotte."

"My aunt had that?"

"In her collection. And pink is good. Pink auras mean love." She smiled sheepishly. "And now that we're friends, I can tell you a secret. I picked it mostly because the back is flat. Sticks better."

I tried to smile. "Did Aunt Charlotte say what it was?"

"Sure. Rose quartz. Increases my self-esteem." Claire leaned back, once again examining the long bracelet. The pink stone lost its fluorescence.

Rare pink benitoite. I'd read about it on the website. Rarest of all benitoite were the pink, orange, and colorless varieties.

"What's on this, grease?" Claire took the velvet, about to wipe down the bracelet.

"No—!"

She looked startled.

"It's a protective coating. Please be careful."

"That valuable, huh?" She turned her wrist back and forth, gazing at it curiously.

Across the room, Bird Girl was greeting arrivals and my aunt stood, waiting to get past her. I shifted the lamp to the middle of the table, where the black light would glow on both her forehead and wrist. "If anybody asks, Claire, the bracelet is mine."

"What makes you think they'll ask?"

"Consider it my version of being clairvoyant."

"Now you're talking," she said.

My aunt had reached the front of the line, and Vinnie was escorting her toward us, no doubt so he could take me away. His mansard brow was lowering like a boom. I stood up and made my way toward the exit, moving past the clear tables and space-age chairs, giving Jessie the silent signal to cover the windows.

THIRTY-EIGHT

For this last night on board, Jack had the gym to himself. I imagined the restaurants and buffet lines and bars were packed with people making the most of the final hours. But Jack pumped his arms through a set of curls, his biceps glistening with sweat. The sleeves of his gray T-shirt were torn off and I couldn't say I was sorry about that.

"We've got a problem," he panted.

"Just one?" I asked.

He faced the windows looking out over the empty sport court. Down below I could almost see the small alcove where it all began.

"Sparks kicked me out of the boys' club." He hefted the thirty-pound weights, then rested them on his sweating deltoids. Great shoulders, I had to admit.

"Why'd he kick you out?"

"Because Vinnie caught me searching Milo's bedroom."

"That's a good reason. Where was Milo? I didn't see him up at the wrap party."

"Unfortunately he passed out on the bed. I asked permission to search his cabin right before he went out. He said yes."

"Glad it was legal, but I take it you didn't find the box."

He shook his head and started a set of shoulder presses. The veins popped on his forearms, engorged with blood.

I told him Claire was wearing the fake bracelet and the pink third eye that was benitoite. "I don't know how that gemstone wound up in my aunt's crystals, but I'd be surprised if they know what it is."

"Interesting." Jack pumped harder, his mouth tensing. "Ready for the rest?"

"No."

"McLeod called." He panted. "That guy we picked up at Sea-Tac?"

"Ramazan."

"He's not. Ramazan."

I felt my heart stop. When it restarted, I felt that same strange feeling that crept over me when I realized the bracelet was fake. Somebody was double dealing, switching things up. Playing us for rubes.

"How is that possible, Jack? We have his photo."

"Larsen ran his prints through Interpol. Ready?"

"No."

"His name's Serif."

"The roommate?"

Jack nodded.

"That means…"

He dropped the weight. The iron pounds hit the steel caddy with a loud metallic smack.

"You got it," he said. "Ramazan is still on board."

I held the phone to my ear, waiting for Geert to locate "Serif."

Jack held his phone, talking to Barnes.

We both walked along the top deck.

"He's in the theatre," Geert said. "Something wrong with the lights. Why?"

"Thank you," I said, hanging up.

"Understood," Jack was saying into his phone. "But I'm giving you a courtesy call. Before I make direct contact."

His golden-brown hair was damp from his speed-shower, and while he listened to Kevin Barnes, I glanced out at the water. Stretching out the hours, the sun began mixing afternoon gold with gloaming dusk and it suddenly seemed impossible that this much tragedy was taking place amid this much beauty.

"No, you can't," Jack said.

When I looked over, his blue-green eyes were roaming over my face and when the wind burst, blowing hair in my eyes, Jack reached up, absently brushing it away. I turned my face away, my heart skipping beats again.

"Fine, she's right here." Jack handed me his phone. "He wants to talk to you."

Kevin Barnes said, "Have your SSA in Seattle light a fire." Supervisory Special Agent, McLeod. "My LAPD contact isn't calling me back and Romeo says you're in a big hurry."

"Right."

"And don't waste the connection," Kevin said.

"Pardon?"

"Make sure management knows you want the job in Juneau."

The Italians were yelling again. Only this time they yelled at me and Jack as we barged through the door marked Au-THORIZED PERSONNEL ONLY. The tall lanky chef swung a long ladle, flinging tomato sauce and Mediterranean curses. But Jack yelled back.

"FBI!" He flipped open his credentials.

The Italians fell silent.

And we hurried through the suddenly quiet kitchen. Down the Highway, the food scents seemed even more distinct, as though settling throughout the day. The salt-and-iodine of shrimp, the acute acid of sliced pineapple and oranges. But as we passed the produce, I grabbed Jack's shirt, stopping him.

The first elevator, the one Geert used to take me to the penthouse, was on my left, and I suddenly saw Vinnie's face looming, telling me to get out.

"Staff only," I said. "Maids and stewards. It goes straight up to Deck Fourteen."

"Thanks for letting me know, Harmon."

"No, seriously. I just had an idea. Vinnie, he didn't want me at that party. But he *really* didn't want me in that elevator. I thought he was just being a tough guy but…" The look on his face. Anger. And concern in those predatory eyes. "There's another elevator."

Jack looked at his watch. "All right, show me. It's not like Ramazan can leave."

We followed some crew who wore coveralls. They pushed a procession of garbage cans, wheeling them toward the back end of the Highway. It looked more like industrial storage, leaving behind the bakery and the fresh food. Mostly Hispanic, the men had been talking but stopped as we walked behind them. The air they trailed smelled slippery and sickeningly sweet, that scent of decomposing waste.

At the end of the Highway, an embossed steel wall held signs in English, Spanish, and French. Warnings about electricity, fire, automatic doors that were cutting off the stick leg of the stick figure, radiating black lines indicating the stick man's extreme pain and suffering. The men folded back the plastic lids on a set of large green Dumpsters and I turned a slow circle. Jack watched as they hoisted bulging trash bags, flinging them like slingshots into the steel containers. I stared at the elevator. The dented doors were closed and a key stuck out of the wall panel. Jack reached over, turning it. The door slid back. The garbage guys stood still, staring at us.

"This runs to the Sky Bar?" he asked them.

When nobody answered, he repeated the question in Spanish. One of them replied. "Sí."

Silent again, they waited for another question. But there wasn't one and they pushed the now-empty can back up the steel tunnel, taking quick glances over their shoulders to watch us.

"The bartender saw her leave," I said, once they were out of earshot. "She walked out of the bar. Nobody disputes that."

"So no elevator?" Jack asked.

"Somebody *else* could have used the elevator. Then nobody would have seen them walk into the bar." Geert had told us there was a camera at the bar's entrance. On the deck, pointed at the door. "The Dutchman even says she walked out."

Jack turned the key again and the doors slid shut. "Who do you think used the elevator?"

"Let's go ask Ramazan."

At the other end of the Highway, we headed up the set of steel stairs Jack and I used to get to the laundry, the ones Geert used to search the crew cabins. Once again a showgirl rushed past us. She wore a 1920s flapper costume and her patent leather tap shoes *click-click-click*ed down the steps.

On Deck Six we found the dressing room for the stage. Naturally I took the women's, Jack took the men's, and I opened the door to find five girls leaning into bright mirrors, fixing their makeup, wearing only bras and panties. They looked over as I opened the door. "I'm with security," I said.

They went back to the mirrors, with the unselfconscious nakedness of dancers. I heard a garish sort of music and it seemed to pulsate through thin walls. Across the room, another door was marked STAGE. I was heading toward it when a green light flashed. The girls squeaked and rushed past me, grabbing dresses from a metal rack. Tenting elbows to protect their makeup, they slid into sequined and fringed tank dresses. The back door flew open. The flapper from the stairs raced in.

"You're cutting it close!" scolded one of the girls.

"I had to go!" the flapper cried.

"You can't use this bathroom?"

"The door's locked."

"If you laid off all that Diet Coke—"

"I'm trying to stay awake—"

The green light flashed again and though still bickering, the girls *click*ed out of the room in their tap shoes.

I followed and came out stage left. Heavy black curtains dropped from a cable, puddling on the stage. I could see another set of young women can-canning, swishing ruffled skirts before the cheering audience. When cymbals crashed over the sound system, the Charleston suddenly cranked up and the flapper girls shimmied on stage.

The can-canners went off stage right, washing past Jack who stood in the wings looking lost. And like he wanted to laugh. Catching my eye, he tipped his head toward the back-stage and I stepped through the side curtains. The dance hall girls zipped across the truncated space, their quick steps timed to avoid electrical cords that snaked like vipers.

"You see him anywhere?" Jack asked.

I stared into the dark and cavernous space above us. Rows of canister lights beamed pastel columns to the stage. Nothing looked broken.

Jack grabbed a young man passing by. He was dressed in black, looking like a stagehand. "We heard you're having problems with the lighting."

"Check with Kez." He was American and pointed stage right. "Kez is in charge."

Deep in the wings with a battery headset clamped over copious brown curls, a woman watched the Roaring '20s number. Her mouth twisted critically to the side. When she saw us, her expression didn't change.

"Kez?" Jack asked.

"Yeah." It came out cockneyed. *Yea-eh.*

"We heard you needed some lights fixed," Jack said.

"Is that a joke?" She flexed the word. "G'on, climb up. Right now, get some applause."

"We heard—"

"Nothing's wrong with me lights. And if you fool with them again, I'll punch yours out."

"Right." Jack smiled.

I took out my credentials, which still carried photos of Ramazan and Serif. "Have you seen the one on the right?"

She looked down, genuinely interested. "You mean there's two of them? I thought it was one weirdo."

"They do look alike," I agreed. "The one on the right, has he been here tonight?"

"Yea-eh. Came and doodled with me lights. Check bickstage." She flicked her wrist, meaning backstage, then turned away because the flappers were stampeding toward us. The music shifted to rumba, and on the other side, more dancers rushed forward, dressed like torch singers.

Backstage, I watched as the same flapper we saw on the stairs ran on tiptoes, her bare shoulders hunched like someone trying to be quiet.

"Liza, you can't possibly—again?" whispered another girl.

"Shhh," hissed the others.

"She's making us late!"

"Her bladder's *infected*, let it *go*!"

The flapper jiggled the knob on a door with an OUT OF SERVICE sign. Crossing her long legs, she laid an ear on the wood, listening. Then, with the desperate frustration of someone trapped, she yanked the knob with all her might, almost whimpering. The other dancers had disappeared into the dressing room, and when she raced after them, she was on tiptoes again, tap heels up, not disturbing the rumba on stage.

Jack walked to the door, testing the knob. It was a simple lock, no dead bolt. When I pulled out my pocketknife, offering it to him, he slipped the blade into the lock, rocking the knob. After several tries, I pushed my keycard against the frame, pressing down as another flurry of dancers raced past us. Sock-hoppers, ready to rock around the clock.

The lock popped. The small bathroom was dark and seemed empty. Two stalls and a double sink. No doors on the stalls. Toilet in one, urinal in the other. But over the urinal, a metal tripod stood as though using the facilities. And a framed poster was propped on the floor, demanding employees wash their hands. Where it was supposed to hang, on the wall over the white ceramic appliance, light was leaking through a two-inch hole.

I stepped into the women's stall. Same poster, but still hanging on the wall. I lifted it and found another hole, the same size as the other. When I leaned into it, I saw a rush of bright color. And I heard their voices now. Dancers, young women changing costumes. Running past in bras and panties. Jack was already at the sink. The mirror above was bolted to the wall, just as the posters should have been, for seaworthiness. Squatting down, I opened the doors on the double vanity. The cleaning supplies were scattered. I poked my head in. The back panel was gone. I felt cool air blowing up. Crawling in farther, sticking my head into the opening, I saw short two-by-fours running down into a small open area. A ladder of some kind.

I backed out of the vanity.

"Call the Dutchman," Jack said.

THIRTY-NINE

The Highway had shifted into an after-dinner frenzy. The long tunnel's traffic was as backed up as rush hour, with more garbage cans and stacked carts of soiled napkins and table-cloths. Jack wasn't helping. He stopped each one, pawing through, searching. For a video camera. Or even Ramazan.

I hit Redial on my cell phone.

Geert answered, "What now?"

I turned my head away from the crew passing by and quickly described the tripod in the bathroom. "They're filming the dressing rooms. And they made an escape route through an air vent."

Jack turned, rolling his hands at me, signaling *hurry up.*

"We're on the Highway, in pursuit."

"I'm coming down—"

"Good, but where's the best hideout down here?"

There was a pause. "Cold storage. The freezers. They will be shutting down for the night."

At its middle, the Highway opened like a cross, splitting into two refrigerated wings. Jack ran left, I turned right. My feet splashed through warm water that smelled of bleach.

In one corner, a man wearing rubber boots blasted a high-powered hose at the welded steel floor.

"See anybody run through?" I asked.

He smiled. "What I see?"

As he reached down, twisting the brass nozzle to increase water volume, I felt a twinge in my gut. He kept smiling pleasantly and spraying the area. The air filled with bleached steam.

I held up a hand, signaling him to stop. But he kept spraying.

"Thanks!" I yelled, stepping around him. "I'll try somewhere else!"

I moved to the door he seemed to be guarding. My right hand automatically patted for my gun. *Rats.* I glanced back at the guy. His smile was gone. He laid the hose gently on the floor and raised his hands in surrender as Jack approached with a finger to his lips, telling the man to keep quiet.

"No see nothing." The guy backed away even farther. "See nothing!"

Jack pointed down the Highway. The guy splashed across the wet floor.

We stood on either side of the door, staring at each other. I waited for his signal, then he pivoted, ducking inside. I followed.

It was the butchery. The long steel counters glistened with water. A shelf above held industrial-size rolls of white butcher paper and twine. Below that, magnetized strips displayed dozens of knives. On our right, three freezer doors were labeled for pork, beef, and chicken.

Jack pointed to the knives. There was a gap. Judging from what hung on either side, a bone slicing cleaver was missing. Reaching up, Jack yanked two knives from the magnetic strip. He gave me the six-inch utility blade; he kept a ten-inch thing shaped like a machete.

We stood on opposite sides of the first freezer door. A small square window was covered with condensation and I wondered how long Ramazan could survive in there. The cleanup guy was probably supposed to open the freezer after the threat passed.

In exchange for—what?

Porn?

Jack signaled, reached out, and yanked the long chrome handle. The heavy door swung open. Cold air rushed out, smelling of heavy metals, the iron of beef blood. Jack jabbed his head—in, out, in—then gave the all clear. I stood up. Icy shelves stocked with brilliant red cuts, veined with fat.

Quietly Jack closed the door and I crouched, scurrying under the window in the next door. But I never made it. The door suddenly burst open, striking the top of my head like a sledgehammer. White lights flashed in front of my eyes. I fell to the floor and heard my knife drop. Clamping both hands on top of my head, I tried to stand but lurched instead, blind with pain. Jack was yelling but the room was blurred. I saw two dark shapes, running, escaping through the pocket door.

I staggered forward, bumping into the counter before I tripped over the threshold, splashing through the puddle outside. The world spun and the smell of bleach made me want to vomit. The hose was slithering like a snake across the wet steel, trying to release its hot water. Jack was calling my name. I placed one hand on the wall, moving toward the next room.

Eyes watering, I pivoted toward his voice. I smelled apples. Fruit. Produce storage room. I blinked and saw Ramazan standing with his back to the shelves. The meat cleaver was raised, daring us to approach, and the lights played on the flat of the blade. In his eyes, in his cold pale eyes, I saw the predator's sense of play. A shiver shot down my spine.

"Raleigh?" Jack kept his eyes on Ramazan, not turning toward me.

"Right here." I stepped over the door's threshold. The room

seemed to shimmer. And I realized my knife was back in the other room.

"Ramazan, we know about you and Serif," Jack said. "He's in custody. Put down the knife. There's nowhere to run."

The moment was short. Ramazan lowered the blade in his right hand. His left came up, as if to surrender, but his fingers grabbed the edge of a box. It was above his head and he thrust it, slashing down with the blade.

Jack jumped back from the knife. The box flew forward and apples came pitched like baseballs. Jack and I both kept our arms up, guarding our faces, but Ramazan was flinging more boxes, oranges and limes firing through the air. Crouched to the side to avoid being hit, I saw Ramazan making a run for the door. I swung out my left leg, trying to tackle him. He swung the cleaver down, aiming for my knee.

"Raleigh, let him go!"

He jumped over the last of the rolling fruit and was leaping through the door when he reached back. His open palm slapped a bright red button beside the door frame. A siren screamed, ear-piercing, as Ramazan yanked his arm though the opening. The pneumatic door slammed shut like a guillotine.

I had both hands over my ears, pressing hard. But my eyes hadn't quite figured out the sight at the door.

The fingers splayed, twitching. It looked as disembodied as a glove. Then it turned red and blood poured down the door seam.

Despite the siren, despite a four-inch steel door between us, I could hear the bloodcurdling scream of the predator.

FORTY

Hands placed on curvy hips, Nurse Stephanie guarded the operating room. For once, she wasn't buying Jack's charm.

"One question," he was saying. "I just need to ask him one question."

Behind the white door, Nurse Shannon was working alongside Dr. Coleman, trying to save Ramazan's hand.

"The man's in *shock*," said Nurse Stephanie. "He can't speak."

"He can nod."

"He might lose that hand."

"That's what happens to thieves."

She narrowed her eyes. "What?"

"He's from Turkey, they might just as easily cut off his hand. So this isn't really a tragedy. It's a consquence." He smiled. "See my point?"

"No."

"Just one question."

"This is a medical facility—he's our patient."

"Ten seconds," Jack said. "C'mon, Stephanie. Please?"

She swiveled a hip, trying to dig in. But her towers crumbled under his smile.

Jack said, "How long does the operation take?"

She batted her big beautiful eyes. "Do I look like a doctor?"

"You wanted to give me a shot."

"And the offer stands, despite your bad attitude."

I took a step back. Neither of them noticed. When I turned around, walking away, they remained locked in some flirting argument about amputation.

The ship had two medical clinics. One served passengers, but the other one didn't have sliding glass doors or a fancy circular desk. It looked like a standard physician's office, where the doctor treated the staff. Kitchen burns, stomach flus. Sprained ankles and bladder infections. It's where Letty would have gone after the pill was pushed down her throat.

The small operating room anchored the two halves. It was equipped with state of the art technology, Geert said. Mandatory by law, since the ship was sometimes days from civilization. Dr. Coleman was a former army surgeon, Geert said. "He might even save the pig's hand," he added, with a disgusted twitch of the mustache.

The circular desk sat empty now. Across from my mom's room, the elderly woman lay on her husband's bed, their hands clasped. He slept. She stared at the ceiling.

I walked into my mom's room. Her mouth was slightly gaped and almost looked relaxed. The scratches didn't seem as enflamed. But her blanket and sheet were torqued from fitful sleep, leaving her teal-blue hospital socks exposed. I gently covered her feet, then leaned down to kiss the top of her head. The powdery scent in her hair mingled with something acrid, talc mixed with vinegar, and as I smelled it, all my worries rushed forward.

I could not make her well.

I stood, staring down at her, feeling the top of my head throbbing from the freezer-door punch. My thoughts felt cloudy, uncertain. As I reached out to touch her hand, Beethoven burst from my phone.

"David?" She turned, mumbling in half sleep. "David, is that you?"

My father.

I flipped open the phone, cutting off the tune that David Harmon used to hum around our house. Just as quickly, she was gone again. Her mind retreated to its anesthetized land and I carried the phone out of the room.

"Raleigh Harmon." I leaned against the empty nurse's desk.

"Harmon, it's me." McLeod. "I just got off the phone with LAPD. I tried. It's not much, but here you go."

I took a pen from the cup on the desk and tore a sheet of paper from a pharmaceutical company pad that recommended Nicoderm. As he spoke, I kept having to ask him to repeat his words. My head was thick with pain, my hearing distant from the siren that had screamed until Geert arrived and shut it off. He had rushed Ramazan to the medical clinic before we could find out if he was a contract killer or safecracker, or just another cheap pornographer. In the aftermath, Jack called McLeod twice, begging for information on these movie people.

"I'll start with the worst and move down the list," McLeod said. "First, Vinnie Pinnetta. LAPD's vice has him on a watch list. They think he's moving stolen goods."

"What kind of goods?"

"Name it. Italian suits, perfume from Brazil. Hijacked shipments at the Long Beach port. PD thinks Vinnie's the front."

"Jewelry, gems, anything like that?"

"I told them you're holding a bracelet worth a small fortune. They checked the files. All that came back was a rock collector."

"Judy Carpenter."

"No, nothing on her. But you gave me another name. Sandy Sparks? He collects rocks."

The pen seemed to bobble in my fingers. "What kind of rocks?"

"Don't ask me, you're the geologist. But somebody broke into his Beverly Hills mansion and cleaned him out. Home theater system, computers, his wife's jewelry. And the weirdest thing was a bunch of rocks. LA says the rocks are worth over a million bucks."

"Benitoite."

"Say again."

I repeated it.

"Never heard of it. Could it be worth that much?"

"Depends. Any suspects for the robbery?"

"None. No fingerprints, no sightings. It's a dead trail. It was six months back and they're getting ready to put it in the cold case file. Nobody's even tried to unload the jewelry."

The stones.

The stones were on the ship. "Was there anything else, sir?"

"Traffic violations. Drug possession. Drunk and disorderly. You want those?"

"Not right now."

"Sorry, Harmon." He paused. "Probably seemed glamorous at first, working with those Hollywood types."

"A little." I replaced the pen in the cup, folding the note.

"We think they're something special, movie stars. But they're no different from anybody else. The problem is, they have so much affluence on the population."

"Yes, sir."

"Oh, I almost forgot. You probably already have this. But LAPD says that's not his real name."

"Who?"

"Sparks. He filed an insurance claim for the rocks under his legal name."

"Lysander."

"Can you believe it? If that was my name, I'd change it too. Lysander Butz."

"Pardon?"

"Butz." McLeod spelled it. "Butz, Lysander Butz. Not exactly made for the movies."

Adrenaline tingled down my arm.

"Okay, that's it," he said. "Call me when you get to Seattle. And, Harmon?"

"Yes, sir."

"Don't give up. You'll cross this huddle, just like you always do."

I closed the phone and considered the hurdles. Sparks filed insurance on the missing benitoite. Nobody tried to sell any of the gems. Until now. Until Vinnie walked into the jewelry store in Juneau and Skagway.

I walked around the desk, searching for the forms. When I picked up the clinic log listing patients and visitors, I searched back through the days, through names of people who came in for Band-Aids and sore throats and diarrhea and prescription drugs that were left at home. I searched until I found the man who came in wearing the phillumenist's cap from Philadelphia. The old man we had passed, carrying away our evidence of the safe heist.

Sandy Sparks's dad. The man who needed Alzheimer's medicine for his wife.

And there it was.

His name was Hermann Butz.

My heart pounded at my ribs as I walked back to the employee side of the clinic.

Jack leaned against the wall by the operating room door.

A Ninja had arrived. The tall one, taking sentry for Nurse Stephanie who was nowhere in sight.

"Where is she?" I asked.

Jack gestured to the operating room. "The doc called her in. Touch and go. Apparently Ramazan lost a lot of blood."

Expressionless, the Ninja pretended not to watch. I pulled Jack out of earshot, over to some waiting room chairs.

"Sparks's dad, do you remember how he looked that day on the patio," I asked, "when he heard we were with the FBI?"

"Scared," Jack said. "But his wife's a kleptomaniac."

I told him about the last name, Butz.

"Is that a joke?"

I shook my head and told him about the stolen collection of benitoite, and how Vinnie was on the LAPD watch list. "You think he stole the stones?" he asked.

"I don't know. But I know Claire's wearing a lure, and I need to check on her." I looked at my watch. Close to 10:00 PM. "The dad's probably not at the party. Can you find him, see what he knows?"

"You got it," Jack said. "Where do you want to meet up?"

"My cabin."

"Harmon, I've waited—"

"Keep waiting. The purser gave me a list of places Ramazan and Serif were working. I checked for the name Sparks, not Butz."

Having woken from his drunken sleep, Milo struggled to focus on the glass in front of him. Arms braced against the Sky Bar's neon rail, he stared down as the neon glow washed over his famous face, a blue color resembling the skin on his dead wife.

From where I stood by the staff elevator, I could see the new director too. He was wagging his head eagerly, listening to Sandy Sparks. The producer, however, kept his sharp eyes trained on his young wife. Even from across the room, it was difficult to miss Larrah Sparks.

Blond hair piled high on her head, she spun on the dance floor under the black lights, boogie-oogy-oogying until she just couldn't boogie no more. Bare arms lifted—the better for admiration—she shook her backside against a partner who moved in the shadows behind her. What I could see of him stepped back and forth, side to side, like somebody kicking his own ankles. The muscle-bound attempt to stay on the beat. It was too dark to see his forehead, but I could guess: Vinnie.

I walked from the service elevator to the palm reading table. The music sounded muffled in my ears, and the room looked like a cave warmed by neon and black-light fires. Jessie the bartender had covered the windows with the storm shutters, and at the black velvet table, Aunt Charlotte sat with MJ, the piano player. I ducked my head, trying to avoid being seen as I pulled up a chair.

"How's the party?" I asked.

My aunt shook her head. "I'm too old for this crowd."

"And I have the spirit of Marilyn Monroe," MJ said. "That's why I'm an addict. And I'm going to die young."

I repressed a groan. "Claire?"

MJ nodded.

Suppressing an eye-roll, I looked around. "Where is she?"

My aunt sat up, gazing around the dark bar. "She was just here." Her voice dropped confidentially. "She might be in the bathroom, she had a bit too much to drink."

"I thought she was an alcoholic," I said. "She told the bartender she can't drink and give readings."

"She can't. She was just drinking iced tea but she got loopy. Then woozy." Pushing back her chair, my aunt stood up. Her silk tunic was creased across the lap, telling me she'd sat for most of the party. "I'll go check the restroom."

She left and MJ looked down, studying her hands. The

black velvet washed over the table and seemed to blend with her flowing dress, the bohemian waves of dark hair.

"MJ, who ran the pot operation in San Jose?"

She lifted her eyes. They were such soft intuitive eyes. And they were so full of fear. "I told you, I don't smoke anymore. Claire was just telling me why I *was* an addict. I'm clean, honest."

"I believe you. But you went to prison for distribution."

She began picking at her palm.

"You're not the business type."

"I set that whole thing up."

"You're an artist," I said calmly. "You probably can't even balance a checkbook, if you even keep a checkbook. Somebody had to be the bank on that operation. Somebody took care of the books. Who was it?"

She turned. The boogie song had ended, the dancers were wandering off the floor, leaving the purple orb of the black lights. Larrah Sparks was fanning her face and following her—like an oversize puppy—was the man Milo tried to choke. The burly extra.

"Tell me, MJ." I tried to control my voice, but time was running out.

"I need this job." She fumbled with the plastic chair, trying to push it back. "It's all I've got."

"It was Sparks, wasn't it?" I grabbed her wrist before she could run away. "He ran it?"

She yanked her arm away, fleeing. Her gossamer black dress floated behind her as she ran to a keyboard, set up along the wall by the dance floor. She sat down awkwardly. She even tried to smile.

Bird Girl suddenly saw me. She was flapping across the room, right behind Aunt Charlotte, whose distance was shorter.

"I can't find Claire," she said.

"Charlotte, this is a private party," Bird Girl said. "Mr. Sparks has been more than generous with you. He's given you and your family very comfortable—"

"Comfortable?" My aunt guffawed.

Bird Girl blinked.

"After this week, I'm going to need months of therapy," my aunt said.

Bird Girl opened her mouth.

But I stood up, cutting her off.

"Don't worry," I said. "I was just leaving."

FORTY-ONE

The Parrotheads next door sang along with Jimmy Buffett, insisting that when Monday comes everything will be all right. I wanted to believe them, fishing in my pocket for my keycard, but I could also hear Claire on the other side of the door. Playing that bizarro music. Even in my cottony ears her loud voice grated. She was talking to the crystals. Or maybe the plants.

"Do you love me?" she asked. "Because I *looooove* you."

Keycard poised, I felt an urge to run the other way. But Claire had the bracelet and the pink stone. And I needed to know if anybody had asked about them.

I slid the card into the slot, taking a deep breath.

Then I heard a crash, followed by the sound of Claire grunting. Holding the door handle, bracing myself, I prayed the woman was dressed. But just to be safe, I knocked on the door and waited, giving her time.

But before I could open it, the door swung. I fell into the room. The door slammed shut. A hand clamped over my mouth. An arm wrapped around my neck.

I punched, whipping my elbows back. It felt like I was hitting granite.

He breathed into my ear. "One word and I'll kill you both."

Claire was picking herself off the floor. She staggered toward me, the yellow sari torn down the front. Her glazed eyes seemed aqueous, like shining opals.

"Raleigh…" She bumped into the desk and bounced off it like a Nerf ball. "My friend. You're my friend."

Drunk. Blind blotto drunk. On her forehead the pink stone hung like a scab, the skin bleeding from where he'd tried to tear it off. I glanced at her right wrist. Thin sharp lines traced her pale skin. No bracelet remained.

His arm pulled tighter. And I knew what I'd done: I'd made her a target.

Vinnie's target.

"Where are the stones?" he whispered.

His hand over my mouth tasted bitter, like rust.

When I didn't respond, he pulled tighter. My eyes bulged as I picked up my right foot and came down with full force, grinding my heel into his foot. He faltered with pain and I spun, twisting my body away. But his grip tightened. I grabbed his forearm, scratching, pulling at the muscles that rippled under my fingers, flexing like a boa constrictor.

"I know you took them from the box," he said. "What did you do with them?"

I was choking. His fingers were blocking my nose too.

Claire tipped forward. "Whaatt?"

I tried kicking again but he lifted his arm, dangling me like a rag doll.

"What are you two doing?" Claire asked.

I twisted my waist, aiming a knee for his crotch.

"Hey, my turn!" Claire cried.

He shifted side to side as I kicked. Laughter in my ear. "It won't work," he whispered. "You're mine now."

"I get a turn!" Claire, sounding petulant, the spoiled child.

I was squinting, trying to press back the force pushing at my eyes. My head was going to explode. When he leaned back, lifting me higher, my feet came off the floor, treading thin air.

"I want to swing!" Claire said. "Let me swing! Swing, swing—"

Swing.

Taking his forearm like a branch, I swung my legs back and forward. Again and again, swinging until my right foot connected with Claire. I kicked her, hard. She stumbled back, hit the bed, and gazed down at her leg, where my foot struck. I started swinging again, ready for another kick, when Vinnie started backing up. Still holding me off the ground, he kept me from braking his path through the adjoining door. At the last second, I kicked out both of my feet, hooking my toes on the door frame. He tugged. My neck cracked and popped. Legs trembling, my shins burned. I closed my eyes, trying to breathe.

"You kicked me!"

The yellow sari appeared at my feet.

"Why'd you kick me?" she demanded.

I closed my eyes and kicked her again. I felt my shoe connecting right before Vinnie yanked, pulling me off the frame.

He dragged me into my aunt's cabin and moved the hand until it covered my nose.

"Tell me where you put them. Or I swear I'll kill you."

Far away I heard Claire, crying. "You hurt meeeee!" And the Parrotheads next door sang about getting drunk. My fingers tingled, losing circulation. They slipped off his arm, unable to hold on. I closed my eyes again. Praying. One gulp of air. *Please.* One breath.

The slap on my face opened my eyes.

Claire didn't disappoint. In a rage, she hit wildly, striking at my face but connecting with Vinnie's arm too. I felt the ground under my feet. Took a breath. Took another punch from Claire's windmilling arms. I leaned forward, taking

Vinnie down with me. Close enough now that Claire could strike his face. The crazy slaps flew, fast and unpredictable. He couldn't control us both. Forced to the choice, he kept the arm around my neck. But his hand left my mouth completely. I gasped, opening wide. Claire kept erupting. Numbed by alcohol and anger, she propelled herself into us. When he lunged for her, I twisted sideways.

I spun out from under his arm.

They tumbled to the floor. Claire was snarling like a wild dog.

Turning away, I slapped my hands on the bureau, searching. My fingers didn't feel the drawer as I pulled it out. And my thumbs felt just as detached sliding over the latches on the titanium case. Sliding again, until the lid popped up. Shoving everything away, I grabbed the rock hammer.

The steel claw pointed forward as I whirled around. Claire was pinned to the floor but still fighting, a drunken dervish. Sensing me, Vinnie turned his head. He saw the raised hammer. Under that brow the eyes grew large and I swung, so certain of connecting that I thought it was the force of my blow that toppled me.

I lay on the floor, stunned. The hammer was still in my right hand. But my left leg, it ached.

His thick fingers clamped down around my wrist, squeezing until my hand shook. I couldn't move my leg and in horror, I watched my fingers spasm open. The hammer clunked to the floor. A heavy leaden sound. Somewhere in the back of my mind I wondered if anybody could hear it.

Anybody.

Please.

Claire whimpered on the floor, crying and holding her arms to her body. Vinnie picked me up and flung me like a toy, throwing me on my aunt's bed facedown. He pressed on the back of my head, pushing my face into the pillow.

ried to breathe, and heard Jimmy Buffett describing a dying little town, and when Vinnie's full weight fell on me, covering my entire back, my lungs suddenly compressed, pushing out all the air. My mind begged. One breath. One breath. But the pillowcase had filled my mouth and fireworks exploded across my eyelids. I sent up another one-word prayer, desperate. Panicked. Fading with the Parrothead music until it was only the blood in my ears, washing like the sound of the sea. His enormous frame pressed down, making sure, making sure no air ever came back. I felt his mouth beside my ear. He was breathing as if to say good-bye. My body floated off the bed, rising weightless as the fireworks faded and my lungs no longer strained, and the last thought I had was this: *Take care of her.*

It felt like falling asleep. I released all my fear, letting go, breathing again.

"I just wanted to swing."

I held still. Then opened my eyes.

"If you'd just let me swing."

The lead weight on my back was motionless. He was no longer pressing. But he still breathed in my ear.

No, not breathing.

He was snoring.

I lifted my head, turned. Vinnie's head slid across my back. His heavy arm dangled on my shoulder. The thick fingers were bloody. Bitten.

"I like to swing." Claire sounded like a girl. A sad child. "That's all I wanted. To swing. But you didn't let me be part of the game."

I pushed with my arms, and he slid farther off. I glanced over my shoulder.

She stood over the bed. In her right hand the rock hammer faced the wrong way. The claw pointed toward her.

Torquing the rest of my body, I shrugged Vinnie off. He slid to the right, slamming into the wall.

The Parrotheads banged back. "You shut up!" somebody yelled.

I heard laughter over the music.

Pulling my legs out from under him, my arms felt strange. The way they do when they've fallen asleep but are coming back. My face was hot with fever. Slowly, with both hands extended, I reached out. Her vapid eyes were still bright. Still drunk. Blind drunk. Blackout drunk.

"I like swinging," she said.

"So do I, Claire." I took the hammer from her hands. "So do I."

FORTY-TWO

Vinnie was damaged.

But not dead.

As Vinnie had pressed my face into the pillow, Claire came up behind him and slammed my rock hammer toward his head, connecting with the top of his spine, just below the cerebellum. One inch higher and Vinnie would've dropped dead. But the woman with broken-clock accuracy hit a hole-in-one. The perfect strike, immediately shutting down Vinnie's deranged motor.

As Jack said, drunks will surprise you.

Holding her hands like she was a misbehaving child, I maneuvered her back into my cabin, setting her down on my bed. She was still babbling about swinging, and some thin strands of dried Superglue dangled from her forehead. As she prattled on, I yanked the pink benitoite. She didn't even feel it.

Backing away, smiling, I leaped into my aunt's cabin, locking the door.

Vinnie snored on the bed. In profile, the forehead looked like a continental shelf.

I took the nylon evidence tape from my rock kit and wrapped his wrists behind his back. I taped his ankles together, moving quickly because he was stirring, grunting toward consciousness. Once he was tied, I went into the bathroom and grabbed a washcloth.

When he grunted again, I stuffed the cloth into his mouth and sat on the twin bed opposite him. From the cabin phone, I called the concierge and reported a drunken woman in cabin 513. She was behaving erratically and needed immediate help.

Vinnie's eyelids were fluttering as I hung up. When they opened, he stared at the bedside table for several long moments. But somebody was already knocking on Claire's door and I got up. In the hall, I saw Jack standing at her door, holding a plastic bag.

"Wrong one," I said.

"Why is your face so red?"

"Hurry!" I motioned for him to come inside, and as he passed through the door, he handed me the plastic bag. It advertised a Ketchikan gift shop.

"Open it," he said.

The jewelry box was inside.

When I looked up, Jack was already standing beside the bed, staring down at Vinnie. "You want to ask me how I found it, but I want to know how you hog-tied this guy."

I set the plastic bag on the bureau, relief spilling out of my heart, welling in my eyes. I could only nod.

"Okay, I'll go first," he said. "Dad was keeping the box." He looked down at Vinnie. "You rotten creep. Dragging those old people into it, like they don't have enough problems. I should throw you overboard right now, with your hands tied."

"Jack."

He didn't hear me. Or couldn't. Locked on Vinnie, his eyes had that cold camera-lens expression. I reached out, touching his arm.

He pointed at Vinnie like he was Exhibit A. "He took the box. That day Milo sent us to get his shoes. Vinnie realized that if Milo noticed the box was gone, he could blame the FBI. And the bodyguard had a key to the cabin."

Vinnie tried to turn his head, gagging on the washcloth. The forehead dripped with sweat.

"After he grabbed it, he had to get back to the set. He was on a supposed bathroom break, and the girl with the clipboard was watching the door. Whose cabin is three doors from Milo? Sandy's parents, Mr. and Mrs. Butz." He looked down at Vinnie again. "You miserable thug. You killed her, didn't you? You killed Judy Carpenter."

The forehead rippled, the eyes darted.

Jack sat down beside him, leaning down close. "That bracelet and those stones in her jewelry box, that's what this is about—she died for some pretty rocks?"

Vinnie shook his head, then moaned in pain.

I rifled through my rock kit, searching through the mess I'd made. When I found the list from the purser, I checked the names again. I didn't get far. Third name from the top: *Herman Butz.* I stared at the sheet, dumbfounded. According to the schedule, it was on Sunday. Ramazan worked for more than ninety minutes. *Safety concerns for handicapped passenger.*

"Jack, did his father say anything about a handyman?"

"No. Why?"

I walked over, pointing to the schedule. Suddenly I remembered something Larrah Sparks told me. "His mother was causing problems before the ship left Seattle. She locked her husband's wallet in the safe, then forgot the code."

"The safe, huh?"

"Ninety minutes seems like a long time."

The name! I kicked myself. That might have been my biggest mistake. When I spoke to the father at the phillumenist convention, he was grateful that Lysander-turned-Sandy had "at least kept me in his last name." Sparks. I thought that was

their name. But Sparks was a stage name. The son was hon-
oring his father's passion for collecting matchbooks.

Lysander Butz of Philadelphia became Hollywood's Sandy
Sparks.

I had assumed—and it did exactly what the medical examiner said it would.

Jack slapped Vinnie on the back, hard.

The bodyguard winced, moaning again into the washcloth.

"I'm sure you know what happened, and why. You knew
enough to give the old man the jewelry box. And if Raleigh's
got you bound up like this, she's got plenty of *rope*. Get it,
Vinnie, rope? You're going to a place where they'll call you
Vickie. If you're lucky, it's Vickie." He paused, letting the
image sink in. "But I'm a nice guy, not like that Dutchman.
Did Martin Webb tell you about him? The big guy just does
not care at all about your rights. And when he hears what you
did on his ship…" Jack shook his head, feigning compassion.
"You'll wish somebody was calling you Vickie."

Vinnie started talking into the washcloth.

Jack pinched the edge but didn't pull it out. "But here's the
deal. You can tell us the truth—and I mean the whole truth—
and it will buy you some really good favor with us later. Or
you can not tell us and we'll hand you over to the Dutchman
who will be happy to take care of it. Which one?"

Vinnie gave his answer to the washcloth. Jack still didn't
pull it out.

"And make it fast," he said. "We don't have a lot of time."

FORTY-THREE

It was 2:47 when I rode the service elevator up to the Sky Bar. Two Ninjas rode with me.

The buffet tables were gone, the shutters lifted, the black lights turned off. The wrap party was over and the public had been allowed inside. On the dance floor, a bleary couple swayed together although no music played. At the large windows, where coral-colored clouds streaked a sky that was neither dusk nor dawn, a valiant middle-aged couple pulled all-nighters, sipping coffee drinks. I stared at the mountains across the silver sea. The rock looked black, but the crowns were backlit by a sun ready to rise again.

I nodded, the way Geert would. The Ninjas moved silently. Bar closing, they told the passengers on the dance floor and at the windows. Move along, folks, nothing to see here.

I watched from a spot protected from sight by a half wall near the elevator. The remaining movie people sat at the bar, ducks in a guilty row. Sandy, Larrah, Milo. Next to Milo, a pretty brunette half his age gazed at him with a star-struck expression. When the Ninja approached, Milo started to argue about having to leave.

I walked over as the Ninja led the brunette away.

"Too late," Sparks said, rising from the bar stool to leave. "They just said the bar's closing."

I picked up a stool and placed it beside him and his wife. At this hour, the blond actress looked strange. Ravaged and skeletal, her pale hand clutched the drink in front of her. A short skirt displayed her long bare legs and a gold starfish anklet.

"I have a surprise for you." Reaching into my pocket, I dangled the fake blue jewelry. It wasn't a bracelet. That's why it seemed large even on Claire's wrist. "Is this yours?"

She glanced at her husband before answering. "No."

I laid it on the bar. Jessie stood across from me, behind the counter. If he was tired from the long shift, it didn't show. His alert brown eyes followed the Ninjas when they returned to the bar. They would ask him to leave next.

"Coke, please?" I asked, before he left. "No crushed ice."

"Yes," he said.

Yes.

Jessie said yes tonight each time Vinnie ordered a Long Island Iced Tea, extra sweet. The highball combined sour mix, triple sec, vodka, gin, tequila, and rum—with cola, so it resembled real tea. "Extra sweet" meant extra cola, enough to cover the taste of alcohol. Claire sipped one while she peered into Vinnie's palm and discovered several odd intersections on his lifeline. She drank a second "iced tea" while reading his aura—gray, she informed him. And when he leaned over the table, whispering in her ear, Claire was ready. Claire wanted love; Vinnie wanted that pink stone. And now the bracelet. His lucky night. Claire had already complained to him about the noise next door to her cabin. My cabin was now her cabin. Which meant Vinnie could search for the stones from Judy Carpenter's jewelry box.

Benitoite and Neptunite. Each stone worth tens of thousands of dollars.

Finders keepers.

On the bar Larrah's pale hand inched toward the jewelry. And a strange expression came over her face. Some idea was rying to cinch down on her brain. But her forehead muscles only quivered, paralyzed by botulism toxins. All that Botox now made her look like an inebriated puppet.

"You're sure," I said. "That's not yours?"

She nodded.

"Absolutely sure?"

"Leave her alone," Sparks said. "She's drunk."

"So's Milo. But he can tell me about breaking into your mansion."

Jack was right. Drunks, they surprise you.

Milo gave a slow turn of his head. With his shoulders hunched, he reminded me of a turtle. The green eyes glanced first at Sparks. Catching the producer's expression, the movie star let a smile blaze across his face.

Then he laughed.

"Milo," I said, "don't even bother." I was too tired for this many games. "Vinnie already told us how it worked."

Vinnie told us three times. Start to finish. Twice in my cabin, a third time in Geert's office. It all began more than a year ago, when Judy started begging Sandy Sparks to make a sequel to Milo's most successful movie. She insisted work would save their marriage. But Sparks didn't want to make the movie. He told me as much, sitting in the hot tub that Tuesday morning after we found her body. Milo, he said, wasn't exactly box office gold.

But Sparks had another reason: he was broke.

I picked up my Coke, sipping. Ninjas had taken Jessie and now they stood as sentries. One blocked the exit ramp to the upper deck. The other guarded the elevator. I took another sip. Sugar, bubbles, caffeine. I could get through this.

I could.

"So Milo and Vinnie broke into your house," I said, turning to Sparks. "They took the usual. Electronics, computers, your wife's best jewelry. But all that was a cover. They came to steal your benitoite. That irreplaceable collection of benitoite. What's it worth now, a million six?"

For once, Sandy Sparks made no nervous gestures. "I heard your mom went crazy," he said. "Must run in the family."

I smiled, officially. "The way collecting runs in your family?"

In Geert's office, as Vinnie told us the facts again, Jack started an Internet search. As a producer, Sandy Sparks didn't have much press in the entertainment magazines. But four years ago he loaned his benitoite collection for an exhibit at San Jose State. His alma mater. Home of the Spartans. The mascot on his baseball cap and boxer shorts, the campus that sat just north of the San Benito mountains, with those singular mines. His obsession with the mineral began in college, when he first heard about how rare and unusual it was. His collection grew with his income, and when he loaned it to the school, its estimated value was $1.4 million. But benitoite was very special. With each passing year, it increased in value: nobody could make more.

"You filed an insurance claim on the benitoite," I said. "LAPD told us. But like your dad, you're a true collector. And collectors don't like to sell, like your dad won't sell any of his matchbooks. It's hard letting go."

Reaching into my pocket again, I set the pink stone on the bar.

Claire's supposed third eye.

Sparks couldn't take his eyes off it.

"In exchange for making the robbery look real, Vinnie got money. Milo got his sequel. And Judy came on as co-producer. But Judy was more clever than you."

In the quiet bar, these people hung on my words. So silent, that I heard the service elevator brush open. When I looked over, Geert was coming around the half wall, pushing a large trash can on wheels.

I took a deep breath. Fresh horses. And I was tired.

"All that stolen benitoite was supposed to come back to you. File the claim, keep the stones. What a deal. But Judy knew you. And she knew you didn't want to make the movie. If you decided to back out, her marriage was really over. So she kept some collateral. And with it, she kept you over a barrel. Now you had to make the movie. Or she could report you for insurance fraud."

Geert stood behind us, the trash can at his side.

"Smart woman," he said. *Woman* no longer sounded so derogatory, though the same could not be said for her home state. "Smart, even from Caw-lee-for-nee-ya."

In no hurry to explain the trash can, he probably would have liked me to continue. String it out. Leave the lid on. But even with a clean bag inside, the trash can must have stunk. I reached over, plucking off the lid.

Sparks jumped. "What the—"

Jack stood up, grinning. "How you doing?"

He wore the black jacket from Martin Webb's closet. The motorcycle jacket supposedly worn by Brando. But I doubted that; I doubted everything about these people.

"Milo," Jack said. "Help me out of here, would ya?"

But the action star was as wooden as when he was on-screen. "Where…" He struggled for words. "Where did you get that?"

"This?" Jack looked down at the studded leather. "You like it?" Since Milo wasn't helping, Jack reached over and placed his hands on the actor's wide shoulders, pulling his leg behind him. "I hate to tell you this, man. I like you. But your buddies killed your wife."

"Now hang on," Sparks said. "You think her suicide looks weird, and you might have a point. Something does seem a little off. But if anybody killed her it was Milo."

Milo was breathing through his mouth. The green eyes

had their usual marbled-glass quality, but beneath the vitreous surface something was cracking.

Sparks continued, "You saw what he did, choking that guy on the set?"

"It was very convincing," I agreed.

Jack patted Milo's shoulder. "But you can't improvise, not when you're that drunk. If I recall, Sandy pulled you aside right before that scene. Choking that guy was for our benefit."

Milo stared at the producer. "You said Martin wanted me to. You said he would calm down if—"

"Do you want to hear the rest?" Jack asked.

"I want to know where you got that jacket." Milo looked confused, angry. Scared. The way he looked after she died and he saw the anklet. "My wife, my wife—"

He couldn't finish.

"Webb?" Jack asked.

"That was a gift." Milo's face crumpled. "My wife, she was a giver. She was a giver!"

Jack squeezed his shoulder. Milo turned his face away. But his sobs were loud. Drunk and lost. His wife, the expert seamstress, had sewn some of Sandy's stones into the vintage lining, covering the slight bulges with patches. Then she gave the jackets to Webb, a gift from the co-producer to the director. Welcome aboard.

I watched Larrah. Her large eyes drifted to the anklet.

"Go ahead, take it," I said. "It's fake. Your husband has the real one, somewhere."

Geert leaned forward, his bald head shining at Sparks like an interrogation lamp. "Where is the real one?"

"I don't know what you're talking about."

"Yah." Geert straightened, turning to me. "The wife doesn't know about it. What did I tell you? The husband. He is always guilty."

Larrah picked up the anklet. She rubbed her thumb over the greasy petroleum residue.

"That night," Jack began, putting his arm around Milo, "your wife watched you flirt with the women in here. Then she went back to her cabin. Depressed and lonely. She took her Ambien, climbed into bed, and Vinnie came out of the living room closet."

Placing a pillow over her face, the bodyguard held it there until she died. Vinnie's original plan was to hang her body over the balcony. But Sandy Sparks had come up with a better idea. He thought. Something to throw everybody off, he insisted. And later it would bring in money. He could get his benitoite back and build a new income stream.

I turned to Larrah. She wiped her fingers on a cocktail napkin.

"I want to thank you," I said.

"What...for?"

"You told me your husband always tried to do too many things at once. And you told me about your mother-in-law, that she was a pain even before the ship left Seattle. I should have been listening more closely." When I looked at her husband, his skin was slick with sweat. "The dutiful son. You called the concierge when your mom locked your dad's wallet in the safe. But they couldn't tell you when the handyman would get there. You asked them to come to Milo Carpenter's cabin first, then you would walk them down to the problem. You were having drinks in the Carpenters' cabin. You, Milo, Vinnie. And Judy." I looked back at Larrah. "You weren't there."

"I was getting a massage." She said it desperately.

"The handyman knocked on the Carpenters' cabin."

Ramazan.

A shallow and cruel man devoted to gossip rags, Ramazan immediately recognized the movie star. He gushed, got an autograph, then Sparks walked him three doors down to his parents' cabin. Ramazan opened the safe—easy, he insisted, he knew safes—and Sparks offered him a tip. But the Turk refused. It was an honor, he insisted. He wanted to help a man like Sandy Sparks. Hollywood producer. Friends with Milo Carpenter. And Ramazan confessed he, too, was a filmmaker.

"At first, I thought Vinnie was lying," I said. "It seemed like a big risk, bringing on a stranger. And crew. But you made sure Vinnie asked Ramazan for help. Vinnie's not the sharpest knife in the drawer and he's awfully greedy. But he did finally figure out you were setting him up. And it was only a matter of time before you got rid of him too."

After suffocating Judy, the bodyguard had wrapped her body in a blanket. When he heard a single knock at the door, he found the trash can, with a fresh liner, waiting in the hall. Placing her body inside, he tied the trash bag into a knot so nobody could see her and left. Minutes later Ramazan rolled it down the Highway, over to the Dumpsters. At that hour, the Highway was almost empty. And if anyone saw him, he was doing janitorial work.

He rode the elevator up to the Sky Bar.

Jack gave Milo's shoulder another squeeze. "Vinnie was sitting at the bar, telling you to go talk to your wife. Go make things right. What a concerned friend. And you left, ruining your alibi. And she was here, in the bar. Dead."

Ramazan wheeled the trash can through the Sky Bar and out to the deck. On that cold wet night, he wore a cap, pulled down low, and left the trash can by the rail. After Milo walked out of the bar, Vinnie took care of business.

"Yah, loyal cruisers," Geert said.

"What's that supposed to mean?" Sparks said, offended.

"You know where things are. Things like mooring lines."

Milo didn't look like an actor anymore. His face contorted, like a man. "Sandy?"

"Give me a break, Milo," he said, laughing. "This is like a bad movie."

"Almost as bad as *Northern Decomposure*," Jack said agreeably.

When I looked at Larrah, she was draining her drink. I picked up the anklet from the bar. "Are you done with this?"

She set down the drink. It clunked on the bar. "If that's fake, then—"

"Judy wore the real one. But Vinnie didn't see the anklet until he was dropping her over the rail." Those long palazzo pants, which she favored even in pajamas, rose up on her legs, the same way they did when hours later, Geert pulled her back over the rail. "Vinnie got the clasp open, then dropped it. He didn't have time to search." I pointed to the windows, to the sky that was neither morning nor night. "The light wasn't great. He planned to come back the next day."

But I found it.

I looked over at Milo. "I owe you an apology, Milo."

For once his eyes held a genuine light. I felt a pang of sadness. That feeling of seeing someone who suddenly realizes what they threw away. Judy never told him she kept some benitoite. She didn't want to humiliate her beloved husband, letting him know she needed that much collateral because of him.

Jack was right: Milo mourned for her.

"When I showed you the real one of this"—I held up the anklet—"you recognized it. Not from your wife wearing it. She kept it hidden from you, and it wasn't hard. Separate beds. You barely looked at her. And she wore those long trousers. But you saw benitoite. Did you run to Sandy? Tell him the FBI knew about the robbery, the insurance scheme?"

His head dropped. He nodded like a man with an evil hangover.

"And I showed it to Sandy too, while he bubbled away in the hot tub. The handyman must have seemed like a brilliant inspiration. The safecracker. Ramazan could steal it from Geert's safe—"

"Ach."

"—and bring it to you."

Larrah pointed at the anklet, forehead quivering. "But you said that's fake."

"Right." I handed it to her. "And it belongs to you."

"The *fake*?"

"Yes. He had it made for you, years ago. Apparently he doesn't like sharing his benitoite with anyone. Your fake was with the stolen jewelry. The real one was with the benitoite. And I'm guessing all your jewelry has come back after the robbery?"

She looked around the bar. She seemed to want another drink.

Sparks laughed again. "This is incredible."

Jack agreed. "But if you wrote movies this good, you wouldn't be broke."

"You're broke?" Larrah asked.

"Vinnie," Sparks said. "That's your problem, right there. Vinnie told you this? The guy's a Neanderthal. He killed her and he belongs in jail."

"He's going," Jack said. "But the Neanderthal was smart enough to cut a plea deal."

I wanted to believe the tears hanging in Milo's eyes. Just like I wanted to believe that inscription inside the jewelry box. He called Judy his "real gem." But he was a philanderer, they were divorcing, and only now did I understand the point. Gratitude. It was a thank-you note. Judy got him the movie, staging the robbery.

I finished my Coke, slurping down to the bottom because it had been a very long day. When I climbed off the bar stool, the Ninjas stepped forward. Jack performed the honors, taking evident pleasure in uttering the names.

"Sandy Sparks, also known as Lysander Sparks, also known as Lysander Butz, and as a kid probably known as Sandy Butz, you are under arrest for the contract killing of Judy Carpenter."

"You're kidding." The smile was razor thin.

"You are also under arrest for grand larceny, insurance fraud, lying to federal and state law enforcement, transporting stolen goods across state lines—"

"I didn't—" He stopped.

"Right." I nodded. "Judy transported the benitoite."

As Jack continued, I watched Larrah. Her bleary brain was pumping against reality, and square pegs were jabbing round holes, nothing fitting together.

Not to her liking, at least.

"Oh, Sandy!" she cried. "How *could* you?"

He ignored her.

She reached up, grabbing her flumey hair. "What—have—you—done?"

"You're a bad actress." I smiled. "But shrewd." I remembered her onstage in Pharaoh's Tomb, telling my aunt that none of the crystals were working. And I recalled those ghost words on the bathroom mirror. Finally, I'd figured out what was spelled. Two words. Beginning with C and ending in KS.

Charlotte's rocks.

Larrah drew back, sucking in air. Her clavicle looked like a clothes hanger. "I was trying to get my role right."

"Keep trying," I said.

Geert offered handcuffs, Jack clamped them on Sandy's wrists. The producer hunched over his paunch, his head bowed. Not from shame. Shame wasn't in this man's repertoire.

"Was there even film in the camera?" Jack wanted to know.

But he didn't get answer.

Lysander Butz had taken the Fifth.

FORTY-FOUR

On the top deck, where I stood five days ago as the ship pulled into and out of Ketchikan, I ran my fingers over the teak rail. Beads of morning dew slipped off the varnish like liquid pearls, splashing into the ocean below, disappearing without a trace.

Seattle's dock was choked with yellow cabs that formed a golden horseshoe. Climbing out of the taxis, toting suitcases, people hurried for the US customs building; and moments later passengers rushed off the cruise ship, dropping into the cabs with that post-vacation weariness, tired but satisfied.

I forced myself to scan the other vehicles.

The unmarked van made my eyes burn.

It was white and was parked beside an EMT vehicle. The emergency wagon was there last week, when we boarded the ship. The standard precaution, in case someone got hurt. But this van was for a special case.

My mother.

I finally agreed with the doctor: there was no other choice, not if I loved her.

Reaching down to my belt, I unclipped my cell phone and dialed a local number, waiting for Allen McLeod to pick up. It was 8:43 AM Sunday morning.

"Good morning, sir. Sorry to bother."

"You're not bothering, Harmon. I'm stuck in my car waiting for a tow." He described his drive to church this morning, which ended when another car ran a red light and smashed into McLeod's front end. "The guy totally blind-sighted me."

Malaprop as oxymoron. It was impressive. "Was anyone hurt?"

"No, but I can't move the car, front wheel's destroyed." He offered a prodigious sigh. "Was something wrong with the LAPD information?"

"No, sir. That helped quite a bit. Thank you." I told him we were working with Washington State Patrol and taking several people into custody later this morning.

"Good," he said. "But my wife's here, wondering. So I have to ask. The actor?"

"Milo Carpenter didn't kill his wife. But he did some really stupid things."

"Well, he's a movie star, what do you expect?"

I stared down at the dock. The white van pulled forward, then backed up to the gangway.

"Sir, did you say there's a position open in the Seattle unit?"

"I was just kidding, Harmon."

"Oh."

"You don't owe me a favor. I like helping you out. Really."

There was a significant pause. I watched the man climb out of the white van. He wore a white uniform—white van, white uniform, probably white walls where she was going. He walked to the back of the vehicle and opened the barn doors, waiting.

"Actually, sir, I'd be interested in hearing about it."

"Really? You're sure?"

"No, sir."

"Good, that's what I want to hear. This assignment isn't for just anybody, Harmon." He began mumbling something, then said, "Okay, look, I have to go. Tow truck's here. Call me first thing tomorrow."

I closed the phone. Passengers came down the gangway in waves, the cruise ship making sure two thousand people didn't try to disembark all at once. Even from this distance, her long black hair was striking, blowing behind her as she strolled down to the dock in her bohemian dress. MJ. A free woman, carrying a burden. The pot house in San Jose was owned by a company named Spartan Enterprises. The local police brushed over it. The landlord lived out of town, and Spartan was not a remarkable name in San Jose, what with the state college's mascot. But that was the name of the production company belonging to Lysander Butz.

MJ took the fall for Sandy Sparks. She went to jail; he promised her work when she got out. Judy took her under her wing. Last night, when she learned Sparks was going to jail, MJ's confession came like a dam breaking.

"You doing all right?"

I looked over.

Jack's tan skin looked sallow, his eyes bloodshot. Neither of us had slept last night. I suddenly wondered how bad I looked.

"You okay?" he asked again.

"McLeod wants me to come into the office tomorrow," I said, avoiding his question. "We can write up the paperwork then. Unless you think we should get it done today."

"Today I want sleep." His voice was hoarse. "Then I'm flying to Ketchikan to get my plane. Your first priority is your mom. I'll take care of the paperwork when I get back."

"Thank you."

He nodded. "Think we'll ever get anything from Ramazan or Serif?"

"That would be nice, wouldn't it?"

Right now, we could only speculate why Ramazan didn't

take the anklet and run. My guess was that he really did consider himself a filmmaker. And Sparks probably encouraged the idea. Porn, a new income stream. And now Sparks thought he could control Ramazan the way he controlled MJ. Providing that trash can, Ramazan made himself an accessory to murder, and there was no statute of limitations. Serif, meanwhile, had traded his identity for the five thousand dollars from Geert's safe and some fake jewelry. Letty, I imagined, saw who stayed on board but was too terrified to tell us.

"Maybe Serif will talk." Jack scratched the dark whiskers on his face. They made him look even more rugged. "But one way or another, Sparks and Vinnie are going down. The way I see it, our biggest problem is working with the crackpot."

Claire.

Claire was part of a real case. A witness, her dream come true. And with her broken-clock accuracy, she had pegged another part of the scheme. The crystals were changing; Judy was exchanging my aunt's best crystals of fluorite and aquamarine and jet for Sandy's benitoite and neptunite. My aunt was none the wiser but Larrah and Sandy figured it out. In my mind's eye I could still see those ghost letters on the bathroom mirror. Two words. Beginning with C, ending with KS.

Charlotte's rocks.

"Maybe we can get rid of Claire on a plea deal," Jack said. "You know, all those parking tickets?"

I smiled. The smell of brine and creosote rose from the wooden pylons covered with white barnacles. It was odd to me, how time seemed so different on the ship. Days had felt more like weeks; it could have been a month ago that we found Judy's body. Even longer since I hung up on DeMott. But it was only yesterday, and he had not called back. I would call. Once I got things settled with my mom, I would call.

"Do you know what assignment McLeod is talking about?" I didn't want to meet Jack's eyes and stared down at some driftwood floating past the ship's hull. Then a blue cushion bobbing at the surface. Its vinyl cover was torn, taking in water. It would go under soon.

When Jack didn't reply, I looked over. He was gazing at the Seattle sky. Gray clouds marched over the Cascade Mountains, heading for the city where the Space Needle stood like a child's toy dropped in a corporate boardroom.

"Be prepared," he said.

"For what?"

"Hard work, for one." His blue-green eyes studied my face. "You won't have a life outside of work."

"I don't have one now."

"But you won't have contact with the Bureau either," he added. "That gets lonely. And it's dangerous, Raleigh."

For some reason, when I heard him say my first name, my heart felt like breaking.

"Think you can handle it?" he asked.

"The assignment?"

"Yes."

I looked down at the man standing beside the white van. He checked his watch. Impatient to get moving.

"I don't know," I told Jack honestly. "But we'll find out."

* * * * *

ACKNOWLEDGMENTS

In 1885, a family of fierce Orthodox Jews carved their way to Juneau, Alaska, from Russia. That same year the Goldsteins opened a mercantile at the town's muddy docks and welcomed their youngest of eight children, Belle. That daughter would live one hundred years, watching Alaska change from a distant US District into a US Territory into its 49th state.

In 1934, amid the Great Depression, a young actress and widow named Frances Kennan Connor sailed to Juneau by steamship. Classically educated, from an affluent mid-West family, Frances was completely ill-suited for the rugged atmosphere of a gold-mining town. And she stayed.

Perhaps more than anyone, Belle and Frances are responsible for this book in your hands. They were my grandmothers, and they poured stories into me. Belle talked about her life, which was epic and included a kidnapping by Tlingit Indians when she was five years old, and a thirty-years-long feud with her eldest brother, Charles, who rescued her from that kidnapping. (In Juneau the buildings that Belle and Charlie erected continue to glare at each other across Seward Street.) Meanwhile, Frances—ever private about her own personal tragedies—fed me books. A city librarian, she designated a shelf behind the front counter and left adventures there. Lloyd

Alexander, Joan Aiken, C. S. Lewis, Madeleine L'Engle. Better still, she was eager to discuss them.

Whether writers are born or made, I can't say, but it certainly helps if their tribe cherishes stories. As a reader, you've surely had similar family experiences, and I pray that you continue that love of words with your kin. And I hope you see Alaska some day. That's the other great gift bestowed by my family, in particular by my parents, Roger Connor and AnnaBelle Simpson Connor, who loved and served the Last Frontier.

But with any book, other people deserve thanks too; please bear with me.

First, the strangers who become friends offering their knowledge and talent. Two gentlemen with the esteemed Holland America Cruise Line provided invaluable help with security issues: Charlie Mandigo, head of fleet security, and Johan Onnink, manager of nautical operations. From the Princess Line, cruise director Lee Childers went the extra nautical mile, meeting at midnight in the cigar bar to answer still more questions. And the entire crew of the Princess Sapphire who traveled with us to Alaska: well done.

For crime and geology, thanks go to Bruce Hall, retired FBI agent, walking textbook in forensic mineralogy; Martha Holman, much too beautiful to be an FBI agent; cheerful George Johnston of the Washington State Crime lab; lovely Kimberly Garretson, funeral director of the Ketchikan mortuary; Special Agents Kevin Ellsworth and Steven D. Larson in Juneau; and Kemp Woods, owner of the Whimsy Mine in California, who cherishes benitoite. Though not directly related to my research, Victoria Finlay's superb book *Jewels* provided much inspiration.

Safe harbors arrived with editors Traci DePree, a novelist of tremendous gifts, and Amanda Bostic, an in-house editor most writers can only dream about. Thanks also to the rest of the crew at Thomas Nelson Publishing. And always, a hearty ahoy to my agent Brian Peterson, a rock of Gibraltar.

After funding, a writer's biggest challenge is time. My husband and I are fortunate to homeschool our children, but we have several gifted teachers guiding that endeavor. Sara Loudon of Covenant Christian Middle School, and Christine Proctor of Akoloutheo Academy. And Diana McAllister, making sure we don't fall into rabbit holes. Thank you for living out Iraneus's wisdom: "The glory of God is man fully alive."

To the people who touch my life in large and small ways, particularly the stellar mothers at Heritage Homeschool Co-op. For brainstorming ideas: Stephanie Harrison, Debbi Goddeau, Monica Lange, Catherine Madeira, CJ Darlington. To Pastor Mark Driscoll of Mars Hill Church: thanks for your courage. And to the Colllums and Woodburns—instant friends met while standing outside the governor's mansion in Juneau. And to Governor Sarah Palin, thank you for your gracious attitude.

My love for family knows no bounds. Laughter and goading as needed: the Labellos of Ohio, Raineys of Redway, Quinns of Florida, and the spoking Simpson clan that includes Robbs. Thank you, particularly nieces Maria, Teresa, and Serena. My sons, Daniel and Nico, who make every minute precious: may God bless you for your good humor on deadline, your steady persistence at school, and for not rolling your eyes when your mother forgets everything from keys to shoes. (And when I do forget my shoes, thanks for lending me yours so I can still go into the grocery store.)

The best for last: my husband, Joe. Hunk of Italy. The leader brimming with love and unswerving support—and the fastest wit in the West. With each book, you deserve more thanks. But on this one, thank you for saying, "Some day we should really take a cruise to Alaska…"

Soli Deo Gloria.

About the Author

Sibella Giorello began writing as a features reporter for newspapers and magazines. Her stories won numerous awards, including two nominations for the Pulitzer Prize. Her novel *The Stones Cry Out* won a Christy award. She lives in Washington State with her husband and family.